International Perspectives on Research in Music Education

Music Education

*Proceedings of the 26ᵗʰ International Seminar of the
ISME Commission on Research, London 18-22 July 2016*

International Perspectives on Research in
Music Education

*Proceedings of the 26th International Seminar of the
ISME Commission on Research, London 18–22 July 2016*

*hosted by the **Paul Hamlyn Foundation**,
11 Leeke St, London WC1X 9HY*

EDITED BY

Graça Boal-Palheiros

International Perspectives on Research in Music Education

Proceedings of the 26ᵗʰ International Seminar of the ISME Commission on Research, London 18-22 July 2016

edited by Graça Boal-Palheiros

ISBN: 978-1-905351-34-3

© 2016 The contributing authors

Published in Great Britain in 2016
on on behalf of the International Society for Music Education (ISME), and the Society for Education, Music and Psychology Research (SEMPRE)
by the International Music Education Research Centre (iMerc)
Department of Culture, Communication and Media
UCL Institute of Education
University College London
20, Bedford Way
London WC1H 0AL

design, typesetting, production and printing: Sonustech digital solutions

copy requests
http://copyrequests.imerc.org

British Library Cataloguing-in-Publication Data

A CIP record is available from the British Library

Table of contents

Acknowledgements

The ISME Commission on Research expresses its appreciation to several colleagues and organizations for their support for, and sponsorship of, the 26th International Research Seminar of the ISME Commission on Research, which was held in London, from 18th to 22nd July 2016, prior to the main ISME World Conference in Glasgow. Our thanks to the Paul Hamlyn Foundation and Katherine Zeserson; SEMPRE – the Society for Education, Music and Psychology Research; Prof. Graham F. Welch, University College London, ISME Former President; ISME – International Society for Music Education; and iMerc – International Music Education Research Centre (iMerc) Press.

This book includes the selected papers that were presented at the Seminar of the ISME Commission on Research in alphabetical order (first author's surname). All papers were fully blind refereed by five research commissoners. I am very grateful to Evelyn Orman and Bo Wah Leung for their second editing of the papers and to Patricia Gonzalez and Rosa Omolo-Ongati for their work in the selection of papers.

I would like to acknowledge the generous assistance of Dr Pedro Santos Boia in revising and editing the texts. I would also like to express my gratitude to Prof. Graham Welch for his proposal and encouragement to develop the format of the Seminar Proceedings into a publication that is available to a wider audience, and the International Music Education Research Centre (iMerc) Press for offering to typeset and publish this book in hard-copy.

Finally, I wish to thank the valuable contributions from all the authors, without whom this book would not have been possible.

Graça Boal-Palheiros, July 2016

ISME Research Commissioners 2014-2016
- o   Graça Boal-Palheiros, Portugal (Co-Chair and European Representative)

- o   Bo Wah Leung, Hong Kong (Co-Chair and Asian Representative)

- o   Evelyn Orman, USA (USA Representative)

- o Susan O'Neill, Canada (Australia, Canada and New Zealand Representative)

- o Patricia Gonzalez, Mexico (Latin American Representative)

- o Rose Omolo-Ongati, Kenya (UK and African Representative)

- o Secretary of the Commission

- o Sérgio Figueiredo (Past Co-Chair 2012-14)

Honorary Life Members
- o James Carlsen

- o Clifford Madsen

Vision and Mission of the ISME Commission on Research

The ISME Research Commission was established in 1967 and the first Seminar was held in Reading, England in 1968. It holds as a central value that the theory and practice of music education be underpinned by a strong research evidential base. It promotes the development of an inquiry-based approach to the theory and practice of music education that draws on a range of research methods and techniques.

The mission of the ISME Commission on Research is to:

- o examine, through research, important issues facing music education worldwide;

- o develop, refine and demonstrate a range of research approaches, methods and techniques to critically examine issues in music education;

- o provide a forum for the communication, critical analysis, and dissemination of research innovations in music education; and

- o deepen and develop the research knowledge base for practitioners, policy makers, and researchers in music education.

The Commission on Research accomplishes its mission by providing workshops, lectures, seminars, and demonstrations in different locations in order to build research capacity and to promote research expertise in all regions of the ISME membership.

The Commission seminars bring together early career and experienced researchers from a broad geographic representation and from the various branches of music including music pedagogy, psychology, performance, theory, composition, sociology, and musicology. A common interest in the pursuit of inquiry and scholarship contributes to a learning environment for early career and experienced researchers alike that is characterised by hard work, strong scholarship, and collegiality.

inspire-music welcomes the ISME Commission on Research Seminar

Katherine Zeserson
Paul Hamlyn Foundation, London, UK

katherine@zeserson.com

Graham F. Welch
University College London, Institute of Education, London, UK

graham.welch@ucl.ac.uk

inspire-music is a professional learning initiative designed to help make musical learning more consistent, higher quality, more diverse and more sustainable for children and young people in England. It was established by the Paul Hamlyn Foundation (PHF) in Spring 2015, based on key recommendations from the earlier research-based national report that the Foundation had commissioned from Katherine Zeserson and Professor Graham Welch. This was published in Spring 2014 as *'Inspiring Music For All: The next steps in innovation, improvement and integration'.*

The headline findings in the 2014 report were that:

o   The place and status of music in English schools continued to vary widely across the country;

o   The best music in schools was significantly more inclusive, more musically diverse and better quality than it was a decade ago; yet

o   The quality and reach of schools-based music education was still unacceptably variable and inconsistent at all levels.

The key underlying issues were identified as:

o   Low teacher confidence stemming from insufficient depth of ITE and lack of engagement with post-qualification CPD and professional networks;

o   Widespread weaknesses in curriculum and pedagogy;

o   Inconsistency of pupil retention and progression in music;

o   Insufficient support for music from school Senior Leadership teams;

- o Insufficient local and national support structures for practitioners; and

- o Negative impact of wider education policy changes since 2010.

inspire-music was established in 2015 to address these issues and is an experiment in connecting policy, research and practice. The **inspire-music** Working Group[1], chaired by Professor Graham Welch, is made up of 20 experienced and knowledgeable practitioners, researchers and educators drawn from across contexts and locations in England, supported by a National Reference Group of leading national music education organisations and headteachers. At the core of the programme is a mission to connect practitioners and policy makers with the principles that underpin effective music education – recognising and accounting for diversity of goals, context, musical language, pedagogical strategies – through case-based evidence and analysis.

inspire-music and Paul Hamlyn Foundation take a stand against a deficit-driven model of practitioner development and towards an affirmative, asset-based approach to collective reflection and professional learning; making key assumptions about professional practice:

- o **Outcomes matter** – teachers and music learning professionals want to do their best to support students to flourish and make progress;

- o **Reflection matters** – the better we understand what is going on in our learning environments, the easier it becomes to make new or different choices;

- o **Information matters** – the more we know about what other people have tried and what they've learned, the more knowledge we have to draw on in making our own choices;

- o **Context matters** – one person's 'excellent' practice might not be viable in another situation;

- o **Support matters** – feeling understood, valued and respected encourages us to take appropriate risks, try new things and share our experiences honestly.

Early in the life of the initiative, the Working Group took the decision not to talk about good, bad or even excellent practice; but rather to explore the idea of effective practice. What works in what situations and against what criteria? What ingredients produce positive music outcomes for children

---

[1] www.inspire-music.org

and young people? How are those positive outcomes being generated? What conditions are in place? How can those be learned from and/or replicated? Thus our approach is for **inspire-music** to showcase a diversity of practices and philosophies, and to make explicit, using an agreed set of principles, those elements that make such varied activities and approaches effective. Practitioners can then access these cases of music education effectiveness and make their own informed choices about how to learn from and use that information.

inspire-music has articulated a principled framework for effective practice. This is being using during 2015/16 to capture a wide variety of case studies, linked to research and evidence, to be presented through an interactive web portal, launching in October 2016. This resource will enable teachers and other music practitioners to consider new approaches, access research and evidence to help support their thinking, and share their own effective music learning practice and strategies. **inspire-music** intends to advance consistency, positive partnership working and high quality standards. These will help schools to plan and organise better music learning opportunities; and to inspire teachers and practitioners to investigate a range of approaches of effective, established, emerging and innovative practice.

On behalf of the **inspire-music** team and the Paul Hamlyn Foundation, Katherine Zeserson and Graham Welch welcome you to London and look forward to learning more from our research colleagues across the world.

Music Early Learning and Development in Childcare: An Australian case study of provision and support

Margaret S. Barrett

m.barrett@uq.edu.au

Libby M. Flynn
The University of Queensland, Brisbane, Australia

l.gleadhill@uq.edu.au

Graham F. Welch
University College London, Institute of Education, London, UK

graham.welch@ucl.ac.uk

Abstract

There is a growing body of evidence that early engagement in active music-making impacts beneficially on children's development. Recent research indicates that individual and shared music-making in family contributes to positive parenting practices and identity development in young children. Children who participate in shared music-making at age 3 are better prepared for School experiences at age 5. These findings suggest music should be a compulsory requirement in any early childhood program. This paper reports the findings of a case study investigation of the provision of music in an Australian Childcare Centre. Findings suggest that music provision is best supported when there is a high value for music amongst staff, there are a range of value-added as well as integrated uses of music, and, there is sustained music professional development for all staff.

Introduction

There is a growing body of evidence that early engagement in active music making impacts beneficially on children's development, including: aural perception and language skills (Putkinen et al., 2013; Williams et al., 2015); reading (Long, 2014); verbal memory (Roden et al, 2014); spatial reasoning (Hetland, 2000); self-regulation (Winsler et al., 2011); pro-social skills (Williams et al., 2015); and general school attainment (Wetter et al., 2009). These advantages have been documented in studies that have controlled for socio-economic status. A key factor in such studies is music-

making that is active (singing and playing instruments), involving genera-
tive opportunities (composing and improvising), undertaken in
groups/individually, and a 'fun' positive experience for the children (cf
Barrett, 2012; Hallam, 2015).

Recent research indicates that individual and shared music-making in
family contributes to positive parenting practices (Barrett, 2009) and identity development in young children (Barrett, 2011, 2015). Children who
participate in shared music-making at age 3 are better prepared for School
experiences at age 5 (Williams, Barrett, Welch, Abad & Broughton,
2015).

Given the evidence, music should be an essential element in any early
childhood (0 – 5) program. This paper provides an overview of recent developments in early childhood policy and practice in Australia to contextu-
alize a case study analysis of music provision within one childcare centre,
including those factors that facilitate and constrain provision.

Theoretical Framework

The Australian Early Childhood sector is experiencing significant policy
and practice change, embracing a *National Quality Agenda for Early Childhood Education and Care* (NQAECE; 2012)[2] and including the first national framework for early childhood education, *Belonging, Being and Becoming; The Early Years Learning Framework* (EYLF, 2009). Providing
structure and observable targets for educators, the EYLF places children's
play-based learning at its core through the use of play that is sensory, creative, physical, symbolic, projective, role, and dramatic and games with
rules. However, music is virtually absent from the document with no specific guidance on the inclusion of music in children's early learning experiences.

The outcomes of such absence are highlighted in a study of one teacher's
music-making in an Australian childcare centre (deVries, 2005, 2006).
Despite participation in researcher-led PD, the teacher was unable to implement a comprehensive developmental music program. Such findings
point to persistent problems in Australian music education, including inadequate music provision in Early Childhood and Primary (ECP) teacher

---

[2] In 2009, the Council of Australian Governments (COAG) agreed to a National Early Childhood Development strategy leading to the signing of a National Partnership Agreement (ACECQA Annual Report, 2013-2014; DEEWR, 2014). As a result, the Child Care Act
of 2002 was abolished and in 2012, the National Quality Framework (NQF) was instated
to facilitate all parties working collectively towards a National Quality Agenda for Early
Childhood Education and Care (NQAECE).

education (an average of 17 hours of music education across their degree, Letts, 2015) and little acknowledgement in professional policy and practice for childcare workers (Department of Education, Employment and Workplace Relations, 2009; Suthers, 2008). Research indicates that, as teachers' education during training informs their practice and personal philosophies of childhood education (Garvis, 2012), such poor preparation leads to limited confidence in presenting music experiences and fears of losing control (Bainger, 2010; Kim & Kempel, 2011).

The HLE (Home Learning Environment) offers another opportunity for young children to experience music. However, parents do not use music in the HLE on a daily basis, the majority once a week or less (DeVries, 2009). This low rate was attributed to lack of time, devolution of responsibility for music development to others, and the availability of musical materials (DVD's/CD's) not requiring parental input or engagement. All but one parent (63 in total) held the belief that ECEC provides a complete musical education for their children (ibid).

In the absence of national guidance or curriculum for the 0-5 ECE sector, the provision of music education is at the discretion of individual Centre (Suthers, 2004, 2007). The National Quality Framework Snapshot for Quarter 2, 2015 (ACECQA, 2015) identified 14,910 child-care services across Australia (13,944 centre-based childcare, 966 family day-care). The quality rating of these services is in progress, with some 9,347 assessed thus far against a five-level benchmark[3]. Of these 33% are yet to meet the Standards requirements (ratings 1 and 2). Non-compliance ranges from 79% in the Northern Territory to 21% in Victoria. Significantly, only n=36 of registered providers across the country were rated excellent (rating 5), with 28% rated as exceeding the National Quality Standards (rating 4). Those Standards in which childcare provision was least adequate related to the Educational Program and Practice.

Given these figures, it is likely that music provision in childcare is also limited and of variable quality. This paper investigates those factors that facilitate and constrain the provision of music experiences in childcare through a case study analysis of an Australian Childcare Centre.

---

[3] The following ratings are used: 1. Significant improvement required; 2. Working towards National Quality Standard; 3. Meeting National Quality Standard; 4. Exceeding National Quality Standard; 5. Excellent

Methodology

This investigation sits as one strand within a national study of music early learning and development in Australian families (Barrett & Welch 2013 – 2016)[4]. The strand focuses on music education provision in Australian childcare and entails a collective case study of eight childcare centres in diverse settings, and a subsequent national survey. This paper reports one case, identified as "Meeting National Quality Standard". The case-study approach is instrumental in purpose as it seeks to understand a phenomenon, "music education provision", within a specific case, an Australian childcare centre (*cf* Stake, 2008). Data generation methods and techniques included: two full days of observation in the Centre, and interviews conducted with the Director (1), Lead Educators (4), and Parents (3).

Case Description

The Centre is located in a suburb of Brisbane (Queensland), population 16,830, with a median age of 34 years. 46.7% were born in Australia, 49% speak English only, and 23% are employed as "Professionals" (QPZM, 2015). The largest immigrant population in the community is ethnic Chinese and is represented in the Centre enrolment. Unemployment is 7.8% (against a national average in 2015 of 6.2% (Australian Bureau of Statistics, 2015). The Centre is one of a group of family-owned centres providing childcare since 2003 and located across Brisbane to reflect the "character of the local communities" (Centre website, anonymised).

The Centre has an enrolment of 134 children aged 15 months to 5 years and is licensed to enrol 75 children per day. This figure is less than the national average and the Director describes the centre as "Boutique". The Centre hosts four rooms[5] and conforms to the national standards concerning student: educator ratios (ACCQA, n.d.–a). A Lead Educator and Assistant are allocated per room and additional staff incorporated during intense activity (lunch, settling to sleep time, staff breaks), or as relief for planning and documentation responsibilities.

The Director's responsibilities include overseeing the daily operations and administration; management, leadership and guidance of staff; developing relationships with families and communities; and ensuring compliance with legislation and policy.

---

[4] Barrett, M.S. & Welch, G.F. (2013- 2015). Being and becoming musical: Toward a cultural ecological model of early musical development. Australian Research Council Discovery project DP130102488

[5] Emu Room = 10 children aged 15-24 months; Kangaroo Room = 16 x 24-36 months; Echidna Room = 24 x 36-48 months; and Crocodile Room = 25 x 48-60 months

Lead Educators are identified as being in charge of the room with responsibilities to: ensure the development of a curriculum that has clear goals and expectations for teaching and learning within their program; provide mentorship and guidance to assistant staff; complete all documentation relevant to activities and events in the room including child reports; and, build positive relationships with families and communities (ACECQA, n.d.-b).

Methods and techniques

Extended observations were undertaken across all areas of the Centre (four rooms and outdoor play areas). These documented human and physical resources, the nature of musical provision within the Centre, and children's incidental use of music. Interviews with the Director and Lead Educators probed: work history, training and qualifications; the participant's musical background; beliefs about the role of music in children's lives; policy and music use in their programs; and music within the Centre culture. Parent interviews explored music and its use in the HLE, beliefs about the role of music in their child's life, and perceptions and understanding of music and its use within their child's childcare.

Observation and interview data were analysed to identify emerging themes. The analysis moved back and forth between observation, field notes and interview data to identify corroborating and/or anomalous data.

Findings

Music as value adding opportunity

The Centre dedicates considerable human resources to the provision of music in several ways. The Centre engages external contractors to provide *value adding opportunities* through specialist extra curricular activities. For no additional fee, all children receive weekly 30 minute Kodaly music classes and fortnightly, the upper age-groups (Echidna and Crocodile) receive 60 minute Tiny Art classes. For an additional fee, children may participate in piano, dance, movement, exercise, sport and chess programs (see Table 1).

Table 1: Centre extra-curricula program (core and options)

Activity	Frequency	Cost	Total of female's attending	Total of male's attending	TOTAL CHILDREN PARTICIPATING	TOTAL CENTRE PARTICIPATION[6]
Kodaly	Weekly	Free	35	40	75	100%
Piano	Weekly	$37 individual; $17 group	7	0	7	9.33%
Happy Feet	Twice a week	$10.50	n/a	n/a	40	53.33%
Dance Pointe	Weekly	$11.00	9	0	9	12%
Dance Along	Weekly	$11.00	3	0	3	4%
Tiny Art	Fortnightly	Free	27	22	59	100%
Tennis	Weekly	$11.00	3	4	7	9.33%
Ginger Sport	Weekly	$11.00	0	5	5	6.67%
Chess	Weekly	$11.00	0	3	3	4%

High value for music

All educators value music and hold strong beliefs concerning its importance in young children's learning and life. They provided numerous examples of how they had observed music assist children in the wider development, including literacy, numeracy, mood regulation, motor coordination, self-esteem and identity and social skills. Lead Educator 1 explains:

Yeah, I would say for children it's [music] definitely more educational, because they're learning so much through it. Like, through a lot of the songs that we sing to them, they're learning colours, they're learning to count, they're learning body parts, you know, lots. And especially for these guys, they're learning English as well, because it's not their first language, and when we sing to them we show a lot of gestures, so they can associate the words with the movements that we're doing as well. So for these guys it's really educational, I think it's an awesome way to learn.

Whilst all the educators valued music in children's learning and development, few were experienced in music education, or alert to policy and re-

---

[6] Based on daily enrolment rate of 75 children per day

sources that might guide their music practice. Most (see Table 2) had received minimal or no music instruction during their training. All interviewees emphasised the importance of the weekly Kodaly music classes (which they attended) as a form of weekly informal professional development:

Look, I don't know much about policies in music and childcare, but what I really enjoy, we've got Kodaly music once a week here and …the music teacher always brings more resources than we've got, especially the musical instruments. And that half an hour, it's a pleasure to watch, because she's specially trained music teacher so she can do more than we do here. And children looking forward to spending that half an hour on Monday morning. It's nice.

Q: Does it give you ideas as well? Like do you get to see the classes?

A: Yes, I'm always staying here so I can actually learn if there is something. I love to learn. And then we can extend on it. When I saw her dancing with the special scarfs, I just make streamers and the following time we just dance with streamers. You can learn from whatever she does with the children. I can always extend on what we already know. (Educator 2)

Table 2

Position	Music/Arts included in training qualifications	Music experience and engagement
Director	No	n/a
Lead Educator 1	No	Piano and dance
Lead Educator 2	No	Piano, flute, accordion and voice
Lead Educator 3	Yes – minimal	Voice?
Lead Educator 4	Yes	Dance and recorder

Staff professional development

The Centre provides non-compulsory formal music-based continuing professional development opportunities for all staff. These consist of a Kodaly Training Course and an annual conference featuring music presentations for all Centres affiliated with the ownership group. The value of these is highlighted below:

> …so we are getting lots of training and it's up to us to attend or not to, but it's always helpful to attend something because you're learning. It doesn't matter how old we are, we are still learning always something new. You always

> learn from people who know more about those things and
> it's up to you how much you absorb from them. (Lead Ed-
> ucator 1)

The benefits of providing music-based professional development opportunities were two-fold: first, educators confirmed the experience to be an
empowering one,

That pretty much clarified that most of our day is singing. It was really
good. It gave them lots of ideas to walk away with. It was really empowering. Made you feel like, I can do this. (Director).

Second, Lead Educator 4 who is completing the Kodaly Training Course,
notes that PD has created a significant shift in her understanding of the
role of music in childhood development:

> I think initially [I viewed music as] just music for the sake
> of music. But now doing that training it breaks it down a
> little bit more for me and it points out that it all does inte-
> grate into development areas and I think that's--I like mu-
> sic and I like singing and so that's why I do it, but then I
> also realise that I am teaching the children something
> while singing to them. I am building that bond with them.
> Even singing the Bee Bee Bumblebee song, and building
> the children's confidence in singing back.

These findings suggest that practice-based, sequential and sustained PD
provides early childhood educators with opportunity to overcome deficits
that may arise from training.

Integrated music practices

Music use was a deeply embedded practice across all rooms. All educators
used songs to signal transitions into new activities, or routines such as
packing away, washing hands and moving to the mat. Children knew that,
when Pharrel William's "Happy" started playing, they needed to pack
away, understanding that the quicker they packed away the more time they
would have for dancing to the song. All educators used music to teach
elements of the curriculum. In the younger rooms, this largely focused on
language acquisition, with both educators dedicating time for singing children's songs (*Wheels on the Bus, Baa Baa Black Sheep*) prompting children
to complete or alternate phrases, sing naming songs (*Bee Bee Bumble Bee*)
and songs with simple directions (*Heads and Shoulders*). In the older rooms
these concepts continued, alongside a focus on numeracy through the in-

clusion of counting songs (*Ten in the Bed*) and increasingly complicated direction sequences (*Bluebird Through My Window*). During these more formalized learning/activity times, whilst music was largely educator-led, time was provided for child-led opportunities, either asking children to contribute suggestions of 'favourite songs', or spontaneously responding to child input.

Children were observed initiating and incorporating music into their free play. When this occurred prior to the day's 'formal learning time', the educator would incorporate their singing into the learning program for the day. Songs that were introduced during 'formal learning' were often taken up by children in subsequent free play. For example, the Echidna room used *Old MacDonald* to explore animal sounds. Afterwards, whilst children were playing with animal figurines, they sang the song spontaneously. The educator built on this by singing what animals should be included in a farm under construction. More formal music making was observed as children practiced their end-of-year graduation songs. Children practised songs with accompanying actions in groups of four, whilst the educator coached the children throughout in matters of projection, pronunciation and posture.

Instances of receptive music experience were evident in all rooms as the Centre has a sleep policy that states "relaxing music will be played to help the children relax and fall asleep". Whilst no specific music is outlined in this protocol, the music tends to be instrumental, often classical or world-music in genre. The use of receptive music outside of sleep time has limitations due to governmental regulations. The Director explained that CD's/background music can only be used if it is "linked to our program...and an extension of a particular experience you are building on".

Physical Resources

Each room was equipped with CD players and CD collections largely compiled by the Lead Educator. These included: children's music (Wiggles, Playschool and Hi-5); adult easy listening (Enya, Andrea Rieu); instrumental/world music (traditional Celtic); and classically arranged lullaby compilations and rainforest sounds. The Crocodile Room contained a listening station for the children to directly interact with during free-play time. Within the older age-group rooms, there is a marked increase in the use of digital technology, ranging from interactive whiteboards with sound speakers to digital learning programs such as Letterland. The Centre owns a modest collection of musical instruments (primarily un-tuned percussion instruments, such as maracas, tambourines, claves, and drums. However the Emu and Kangaroo room also have access to a number of toy xylophones that are shared between the rooms and are used by educators during planned activities, or if a child requests musical instrument play. In addition to the age-group rooms, the Centre also contains a piano teaching studio and a dance teaching studio.

Discussion

Music is valued in this Centre. First, provision is available to every child through specialized weekly music lessons. Significantly, this instruction provides informal PD opportunities for the Educators. Second, the Centre adds to its curriculum through providing additional music services for a fee. That parents value this is evidenced by 53% of children participating in the "Happy Feet Fitness" music and dance-based program. Third, the Centre supports staff in music PD opportunities that extend their capacity to use music in the program. And fourth, the Centre fosters integrated music practices into the daily program. These values and opportunities are supported by the provision of physical resources to implement music learning opportunities. The implication of these findings are that quality music education can be provided for young children when music is valued, well resourced, and supported through on-going PD opportunities for Educators.

These case findings should be considered against the larger context of ECEC in Australia. Australia has one of the lowest participation rates in early learning, with just 18% of 3-year-olds enrolled in childcare pre-primary education, compared with 70% on average across OECD (OECD 2014a, 2014b). Given that this Centre sits in the 25% of the 14,910 registered providers that are identified as "Exceeding National Quality Standards" for Quality Area 1 (Educational Program and Practice), we hypothesise that – despite official policy providing little specific guidance on early years music – high quality Centres are likely to evidence a variety of effective music opportunities interwoven into their daily activities to support learning *in* music and *through* music. Nevertheless, a second hypothesis is that, if significant numbers of providers are not meeting the Quality Standards, then many pre-primary-aged Australian children have much less opportunity for effective and enriching music learning and engagement. These hypotheses continue to be explored in the larger project.

References

ACECQA (Australian Children's Education and Care Quality Authority) (2015). *NQF Snapshot Q2 2015*. Sydney, NSW: ACECQA.

Australian Bureau of Statistics. (2015). 6202.0 – Labour Force, Australia, Sep 2015. Retrieved from http://www.abs.gov.au/ausstats/abs@.nsf/mf/6202.0

Australian Children's Education and Care Quality and Authority. (n.d.-a). New educator to child ratios for education and care services 1 January 2016. Retrieved from http://acecqa.gov.au/Article.aspx?pid=806&preview=True

Australian Children's Education and Care Quality and Authority. (n.d.-b). The role of the educational leader – information sheet. Retrieved from http://files.acecqa.gov.au/files/Information%20sheets/Portal%20-%20The%20role%20of%20the%20educational%20leader%20-%20information%20sheet%20PDF%20version.pdf

Bainger, L. (2010). A music collaboration with early childhood teachers. *Australian Journal of Music Education, 2*, 17-27.

Barrett, M.S. (2015 in press). Attending to "culture in the small": a narrative analysis of the role of play, thought, and music in young children's world-making. *Research Studies in Music Education.*

Barrett, M. S. (2012). Music learning and education in early childhood: An overview. In G. E. McPherson & G. F. Welch (Eds.), *Oxford handbook of music education* (pp. 227-228). Oxford, UK: Oxford University Press.

Barrett, M. S. (2011). Musical narratives: A study of a young child's identity work in and through music-making. *Psychology of Music, 39* (4), 403-423.

De l'Etoile, S. K. (2001). An in-service training program in music for child-care Personnel working with infants and toddlers. *Journal of Research in Music Education, 49* (1), 6-20.

De Vries, P. (2005). Music-making in a childcare Centre: A case study. Australian Association for Research in Music Education: *Proceedings of the XXVIIth Annual Conference; Reviewing the Future*. Melbourne: Australian Association for Research in Music Education, 53-60. (http://search.informit.com.au/documentSummary:dn=245911675688754:res=IEHLHSS>ISBN0958608687 (accessed 29 October, 2015).

De Vries, P. (2006). Being there: Creating music-making opportunities in a childcare centre. *International Journal of Music Education, 24* (3), 255 – 270.

De Vries, P. (2009). Music at home with the under fives: What is happening? *Early Childhood Development and Care*, 179 (4), 395-405.

Garvis, S. (2012). Exploring current arts practice in kindergartens and Preparatory classrooms. *Australasian Journal of Early Childhood, 37* (4), 86-93.

Gillespie, C. W. & Glider, K. R. (2010). Preschool teachers' use of music to scaffold children's learning and behaviour. *Early Childhood Development and Care, 180* (6), 799-808. Doi: 10.1080/03004430802396530

Hallam, S. (2015). *The power of music: A research synthesis of the impact of actively making music on the intellectual, social and personal development of children and young people.* Department of Culture, Communication and Media, UCL Institute of Education, University College, London: Music Education Council and International Music Education Research Centre (iMERC).

Hetland, L. (2000). Learning to make music enhances spatial reasoning. *Journal of Aesthetic Education, Special Issue,* The Arts and Academic Achievement: What the evidence shows (Autumn-Winter, 2000), 34 (3/4), 179 – 238.

Kim, H. K. & Kemple, K. M. (2011). Is music an active developmental tool or simply a supplement? Early childhood preservice teachers' beliefs about Music. *Journal of Early Childhood Teacher Education, 32*, 135-147.

Long, M (2014). 'I can read further and there's more meaning while I read': An exploratory study investigating the impact of a rhythm-based music intervention on children's reading. *Research Studies in Music Education, 36* (1), 107 – 124.

OECD (2014a). *Education at a Glance (EAG) interim report.* Accessed October 17, 2015 at: file:///Users/uqmbarre/Desktop/Country%20profiles%20-%20Education%20GPS%20-%20OECD.webarchive.

OECD (2014b OECD). *OECD Family database.* Accessed October 17, 2015 at: www.oecd.org/social/family/database

OECD Education GPS http://gpseducation.oecd.org/CountryProfile?primaryCountry=AUS&treshold=10&topic=EO

Putkinen, V., Tervaniemi, M. & Huotilainnen, M. (2013). Informal musical activities are linked to auditory discrimination and attention in 2-3 year old children: an event-related potential study. *European Journal of Neuroscience, 37* (4), 654-661.

QPZM. (2015). *Sunnybank Hills Demographics (QLD) Local Stats*. Retrieved from http://sunnybankhills.localstats.com.au/demographics/qld/brisbane/southern-suburbs/sunnybank-hills.

Roden, I. Grube, D. Bongard, S. & Kreutz, G. (2014). Does music training enhance working memory performance? Findings from a quasi-experimental longitudinal study. *Psychology of Music, 42*, 284-298.

Stake, R. E. (2008). Qualitative case studies. In N.K. Denzin & Y.S. Lincoln (Eds.), *Strategies of qualitative inquiry* (3rd edition, pp. 119-150). Thousand Oaks, CA: Sage.

Suthers, L. (2008). Early childhood music education in Australia: A snapshot. *Arts Education Policy Review, 109* (3), 55-61.

Suthers, L. (2004). Music experience for toddlers in day-care centres. *Australian Journal of Early Childhood, 29* (4), 45-49.

United Nations Human Development Index (2014). Retrieved 6 November 2015 from http://hdr.undp.org/en/content/table-1-human-development-index-and-its-components

Wetter, O.E., Koerner, F. & Schwaninger, A. (2009). Does musical training improve school performance? *Instructional Science, 37*, 365-374.

Winsler, A., Ducenne, L., & Koury, A. (2011). Singing one's way to self-regulation: The role of early music and movement curricula and private speech. *Early Education and Development, 22*, 274-304.

Williams, K.E., Barrett, M.S., Welch, G.F., Abad, V., & Broughton, M. (2015). Associations between early shared music activities in the home and later child outcomes: Findings from the Longitudinal Study of Australian Children. *Early Childhood Research Quarterly, 31*, 113-124**.

** Awarded the Inaugural Music Trust Award for Research into the Benefits of Music Education. September 2015.

Making music in *Orquestra Geração*: From discipline to empowerment?

Pedro Santos Boia

psboia@ese.igp.pt

Graça Boal-Palheiros

gbpalheiros@ese.ipp.pt

CIPEM – Centro de Investigação em Psicologia da Música e Educação Musical / INET-md

School of Education, Porto Polytechnic, Portugal

Abstract

This paper presents results from a larger research study that investigates how social inclusion through music may be promoted in *Orquestra Geração* [OG], the Portuguese version of Venezuela's *El Sistema*. A case study of OG is examined in order to gain a better understanding of the actual mechanisms through which music making may eventually be "transformative" and produce changes in the lives of the young participants through the acquisition of dispositions and skills. Selected videos of rehearsals combined with semi-structured interviews with OG young players were gathered and analysed. Results of the interviews indicate that orchestral socialization in OG is consequential upon the participants' sets of dispositions and skills. As such, OG may successfully empower participants, fostering inclusion and eventually social mobility. Rehearsal practices and processes through which these dispositions are generated and internalized by participants were examined using a video recording of a rehearsal. The findings show that the interactions between conductor and players, the production of order and discipline, and music making (sonic materials, instrumental playing) constitute an active part in these internalization processes. A critical reflection about discipline and its wider implications for education is presented. Rather than providing definitive answers, the data here should serve as a catalyst to stimulate discussion.

Keywords: El Sistema, discipline, dispositions, skills, social inclusion

Introduction

Orquestra Geração [OG] is the Portuguese incarnation or appropriation of *El Sistema*, primarily aimed at children and adolescents that are more vulnerable or at risk socially or educationally. Participation in these types of programmes may foster the acquisition of dispositions and skills through music learning and making. By approaching OG as a case study, our aim is to increase our understanding of the actual processes through which music and musical practices may have "transformative power" (Tunstall, 2013) in the lives of young participants. This study is part of a larger investigation of how social inclusion may be promoted through music making in OG[7].

We approached the socialization process within the orchestra by investigating how dispositions (Bourdieu, 1977[1972], 1990[1980]; Lahire, 2003, 2011) are generated and internalized in real-time during orchestra rehearsals. Defined as socially produced predispositions for acting, thinking and judging in certain ways rather than others, these dispositions may potentially configure themselves as skills and these skills may then empower young people by promoting their social inclusion and eventually social mobility.

'Musicking' (Small, 1998), understood both as collective and organized activity and a means of socialization, generates dispositions and ways of acting that are potentially transferable to other realms of life (e.g. academic performance, future professional trajectory). Furthermore, being "active ingredients" of social life (DeNora, 2000, 2003), sonic and music materials, musical instruments and instrumental playing are constituents of both 'musicking' and socialization, which become resources for the production of social order, cognition, embodied action and identities (ibid).

This paper addresses the musical practices and the interactions between participants that occur as part of the work carried out collectively to achieve a common goal: effective and productive rehearsals followed by good public performances. Particular attention is given to how order is produced in rehearsals and to how the participants' practices are organized and disciplined.

[7] This research is supported by FEDER Funds through the Competitiveness Operational Programme - COMPETE and National Funds via the FCT – Foundation for Science and Technology within the project PTDC/CPE-CED/120596/2010.

Method

This study investigated selected rehearsals of the annual OG summer camp in July 2013. Summer camps are special events in which OG nuclei from various locations gather in one school to play together under guest conductors, some of whom from Venezuela's *El Sistema*. During these events, children spend a few days away from home, daily schedules are fully devoted to section and tutti rehearsals, and there are several concert performances. Summer camps are intended to be a response, even if temporary, to the quest for "intensity" (in terms of work, number of participants and sonic outcome) which in OG is not as high as in *El Sistema*, but is nevertheless an explicit concern of the project implementers and leaders[8]. Even though more intense, the activities carried out at summer camps have features in common with the everyday routines that take place during the rest of the school year. Participating in summer camp activities and working with guest conductors represent specific moments of OG's life, which have their own contingencies. However, to a certain extent, they also reflect aspects of the orchestral training that takes place during the academic year.

During the OG summer camp, a video camera was positioned strategically in the rehearsal room. Placement of the camera was as unobtrusive as possible while maintaining an angle that captured as much of the action as possible (see Heath, Hindmarsh & Luff, 2010). All rehearsals were recorded and recordings were subsequently viewed, in full, multiple times. Relevant excerpts were categorized and systematically analysed both quantitatively and qualitatively. The analysis focused on what conductors, teachers and students say and do and how they interact, considering bodily actions, gestures and embodiment, as well as aspects of musical interactions and performance.

In addition to the video recordings, semi-structured interviews were conducted with OG participants. This paper reports the results of seven semi-structured qualitative interviews with children and adolescents from the Apelação OG nucleus. Interview questions addressed their socialization and trajectories before participation in OG, as well as their experiences as members of OG and the subsequent impact of those experiences in other realms of their lives. The aim was to understand to what extent orchestral socialization within OG may be consequential upon the participants' internalized sets of dispositions and skills.

---

[8] Interview data

Results and discussion

Semi-structured interviews: Dispositions and skills as resources for inclusion and empowerment

Dispositions, as defined in sociological theory, are "principles which generate and organize practices and representations" of social subjects (Bourdieu, 1990[1980]:53). They are produced and structured by the conditions of existence specific to their positions in social space (ibid; see 1977[1972]:72). The dispositions are internalized – or 'incorporated' – by subjects through the socialization that occurs within family, at school, at work, etc., and they are "durable" and "transposable" (ibid). The purpose of this study was to detect dispositions that are produced by music making and learning, and are potentially transferred to and active in other realms of life (Lahire, 2003, 2011) such as school, family, and peer groups.

The accounts of OG young participants from the Apelação nucleus collected through interviews indicated that new dispositions were developed or old ones changed as a consequence of being part of OG[9]. Broad categories of these dispositions include:

o Group work, including collaborative peer teaching and learning and mutual help

o Relational skills (e.g. "I learned to interact with people")

o Heightened sense of responsibility

o Better concentration (at school)

o Discipline, attention and mutual respect

o Time management and self-regulation skills

o Widened musical tastes and cultural practices – starting to enjoy 'classical' music and going to concerts

In addition to learning how to play an instrument or read a musical score, musical practices in OG are consequential in shaping participants' socialization by generating ways of thinking and acting (and 'behaving') that may configure themselves as skills and abilities potentially transferable to extra-musical settings (on transferrable skills see Bridges, 1993; Pellegrino and Hilton, 2012). "Concentrating better" is a cognitive skill, while "discipline,

---

[9] The preliminary analysis of a total of 35 interviews with young participants from four OG nuclei (Amarante, Apelação, Vialonga and Miguel Torga) has shown similar results. The accounts of school class directors and teachers also suggest an improvement in school performance of students who participate in OG.

attention and mutual respect", an increased ability to interact and work with others and to manage one's time, and a "heightened sense of responsibility" refer to ethos and ethics, attitudes, and postures. These are by no means less important as skills often seen as 'personal qualities' that are valued by society (including the school and job market). Objectively, by facilitating access to certain positions in the social space and thus widening up the range of possibilities, these dispositions and skills are resources that may empower individuals and foster their social inclusion and social mobility.

Musical socialization in OG may be consequential in these aspects. However, what are the actual practices, processes and mechanisms that lead to those changes? A careful analysis of the video-recorded rehearsals served as a means to investigate this issue. Below we present the results of a portion of a video-recorded rehearsal.

Video recording analysis: aspects of orchestral socialization in real-time

The first half of a rehearsal with a guest conductor from Venezuela's *El Sistema* was analysed. This part of the rehearsal was exclusively devoted to the practising of "scale techniques". The categorization and frequencies are shown in Table 1.

Table 1: Categorization of selected rehearsal events

Categories	Subcategories		Events
1. Conductor's leadership and mutual tuning-in of participants	1.1-pitch		[numerous]
	1.2-rhythm		
	1.3-dynamics		
	1.4-articulation		
	1.5-playing in sequence/'canon'		
2. Manifestation of authority and motivation	2.1-negative reinforcement		[twice]
3. Conductor's verbal orientation & feedback	3.1-general verbal feedback	i) stimulating self-assessment	[1]
		ii) highlighting importance of being focused	
		iii) expressing trust/ but no condescendence	

Conductor's leadership and mutual tuning-in of participants

Through body gestures, moving his arms, but also clapping the beat and counting loud "one, two, three, and...", the conductor leads the OG ensemble socially and aesthetically through an ongoing relational process between conductor and musicians, "showing them the sound" (Koivunen,

2011). Sometimes, he also gives instructions related to instrumental technique.

In the development of the orchestra, discipline has been crucial. "Because orchestral music requires many instrumentalists to play the same thing at the same time, orchestras demand a high degree of musical discipline" (Spitzer and Zaslaw, n.d.). The aesthetical aim of achieving similar intonation, attack, articulation, dynamics, phrasing, bowings (in the case of string instruments) and even fingerings explains the emergence and the institutionalization of the role of the conductor, particularly from the 19th century onwards (see Spitzer et al, n.d.). Having developed from the earlier "time beaters", the conductor stands on the top of the orchestra hierarchy. With his conventionalized conducting gestures, he plays a crucial role in helping the musicians "play the same thing at the same time".

As they rehearse the scales, the players progressively begin to play more in tune and more precisely together. The maestro 'orchestrates' their cognitive and embodied actions. Not only do they adjust to the conductor, but there is also a mutual 'tuning-in' to each other (Schutz, 1951). Playing scales is above anything else about playing 'in tune' and together – therefore, in such performance, it is particularly observable how 'tuning-in' is simultaneously a social and a musical process. Embodied interaction and visual and aural awareness are crucial in the production of intersubjectivity (Schutz, 1951). These "scale techniques" consist of playing scales in the same keys as those of the musical pieces from their concert programme, with variations of rhythm, dynamics (f, p, crescendo, diminuendo) and articulation (legato, staccato).

Since the orchestral tutti plays the same thing most of the time, togetherness in bodily-instrumental action is practiced and learned. In terms of pitch, the goal is to achieve similar intonation while rhythmically they aim at synchronized togetherness. They also play the scale in canon (each section playing in sequence), which enacts orderly, disciplined action and may favour the internalization of representations of hierarchy and order. Repetition during individual practice, lessons, and rehearsals is crucial to acquire the skills needed for musical performance. Simultaneously, such repetition potentiates the internalization of dispositions for self-control, social interaction and group work. This may be seen as an embodied, experiential way of learning discipline and orderly conduct.

Sonic materials (scale notes, intervals, rhythms), instruments and playing techniques (learned psycho-motoric actions on/with instruments) work here as 'technologies of self' (see DeNora, 2000, on music as a technology of self from the perspective of 'users'; Foucault, 1988) in the sense that they discipline participants' bodily and cognitive actions. This happens through 'entrainment' – "the alignment or integration of bodily features with some recurrent features in the environment" (DeNora, 2000:77-78). In this case, the sonic properties of the scales and the musical instruments' own sonic and material properties serve as the environmental features. These situated ways of music making do not happen randomly. They are framed by historically rooted and institutionalized forms of organization such as the orchestra, as well as by roles, practices, repertoire, goals and aesthetic values.

Manifestation of authority and motivation

The conductor often counts and claps loudly to give the beat, saying "[we're tired and it is hot but] come on!", "wake up" "we must play", sometimes walking around with a very prominent posture. This is a strategy to discipline, motivate and energize the players. The rehearsal and concert routine is very intense during summer camps and the players, who had given a concert the previous evening, are visibly tired. Later in the rehearsal there is a clearer and explicit manifestation of the conductor's authority through the use of negative reinforcement (see Skinner, 2014[1953]:174-178). He threatens to delay the break until participants play the scale accurately. He then urges them to "put a smile in your face (...) and play C major, because if you don't do it..." He then claps to re-energize and motivate them.

What happens here? The conductor threatens twice to remove or postpone a previously scheduled pleasant stimulus (the break). The threat of an aversive stimulus (postponing the break until players play the scales accurately) is a strategy that intends to increase a desirable behaviour in participants (concentrating and playing well). The expected behaviour is that players will do their best to 'get it right' as soon as possible in order to avoid the negative stimulus.

The aim is to improve their musical performance. The conductor's level of authority in this rehearsal is partially a consequence of his own style and personality, since we observed variations among different conductors: some are more authoritarian while others interact with participants in a more relaxed way despite a similarly intense rehearsal environment. This reinforcement strategy is nevertheless related to intense repetition, which has been pointed out as a feature of *El Sistema* music pedagogical practices. This is intentionally used as a resource for learning and teaching with the aim of increasing the players' ability. They played eight scales for more than one hour. As a "labor-intensive organization" (Baker, 2014:133; e.g.

see Tunstall, 2013:28-29), discipline and authority have been also referred to as strong features of *El Sistema* orchestras (see Baker, 2014:190-198). Again, situated musical practices are framed by institutionalized practices, routines and pedagogies.

Conductor's verbal orientation and feedback

Throughout the rehearsal, the conductor often gives specific feedback, telling or reminding the participants about the structure of scales. Shortly before the break, he stimulates their self-critical awareness and self-assessment by asking "Do you think it was ok?" In silence and completely focused, they reply assertively "No". "But... do you know what happened?" [silence] "Can anyone tell me why we did it well when we played it in sections and now that we played the whole scale it didn't work?". Spontaneously, some say "lack of concentration". "Exactly!" the maestro replies, stressing this was the reason why some things during the previous night's concert did not go well. "When students lose their focus, all the work we have done is worthless: the cellos run, [etc.]". "So one must focus towards the great aim [the concert]".

Highlighting the importance of being focused in order to perform well, the conductor expresses trust in the participants: "well, I trust you and what you have learned". However, waving "no" with his finger, he shows no concession for them being tired or unfocused. It sounds as if he is 'lecturing' them, to make them realize the whole point of the *tour de force* of playing scales during the entire half of the rehearsal: practicing stamina, persistence and concentration. The internalization of such dispositions may be useful for performing both musical and extra-musical activities. Before they restart playing he tells them for the second time that they will not get the break until they play the scale correctly.

Conclusions

Music may have "transformative power" (Tunstall, 2013), at least upon some of OG's young participants. This study sought to increase our knowledge of those changes and the actual processes through which they occur, through empirical observation and semi-structured interviews. The generation or reshaping of participants' dispositions through music learning and orchestral socialization is a key element of that change.

As shown in the analysis of the OG rehearsal, the transformative capacity attributed to music does not simply emerge from its aesthetic ('transcendent') 'powers', but very much from mundane practices and socio-musical interactions[10]: the production of order and discipline, verbal, embodied and gestural communication and leadership, sensorial 'tuning-in', music materials, instruments, and embodied performance, all play a role. Music materials, instruments and music making practices are "active ingredients" of social life and identities (DeNora, 2000, 2003) by becoming *constituents* of the internalization processes. Acting as "technologies of self", music and instruments do not achieve that in themselves. Combined with words, gestures, ways of rehearsing, performing and teaching music, as well as with social, ethic and aesthetic values, music and instruments co-discipline the practices and postures of participants. Those practices are framed by Sistema pedagogies and modes of organization and by the conductor and the orchestra as historically rooted institutions with underlying structure, roles and hierarchies.

In his recent book, Baker stresses the need for a rational rather than emotional approach to *El Sistema* (Baker, 2014 - Introduction), deconstructing the tendency to idealize it. Dispassionate studies and debates on whether and how Sistema projects produce change are needed, but one must also reflect about the positive versus negative aspects of discipline in social and educational projects, as well as about which kind of discipline. However, both *a priori* idealism and over-criticism should be avoided.

The orchestra as a hierarchical and authoritarian model of society as well as the over-use of repetition in Sistema pedagogies have been the objects of criticism (see Baker, 2014, chapter 6). It is indeed important not to reify them but rather to explore the possibilities of alternative, more democratic models of the orchestra as well as opening up to a plurality of pathways for becoming a musician, while continuously assessing and, if necessary, redesigning music pedagogies. An authoritarian approach is certainly not desirable, but a moderate degree of discipline may be empowering, particularly for children and adolescents with less structured trajectories.

In the *tour de force* and final 'lecture' given by the conductor to OG participants in the rehearsal analysed here, he expressed trust in their work but also pushed their limits, highlighting the importance of concentration, effort and persistence in order to get the scales 'right' and play 'well' in concerts. As a performing artist a musician is given one attempt only in a given performance. There was a degree of authoritarianism (e.g. negative reinforcement) and one wonders whether more efficient and pleasurable approaches might have been used as an alternative to repetition of scales.

---

[10] We observed that some participants acquired dispositions of attachment to music and their instruments as a consequence of participating in OG. Therefore, we must acknowledge the importance of aesthetic experience in that "transformative power" as well.

Sometimes participants looked tired and perhaps bored. More than an hour of collective practice of scales could have been demotivating. But one also wonders if that *tour de force* of insistence and persistence – where discipline played a major role – besides training the participants' ability to focus and work hard, was perceived by them as a 'life lesson', in terms of attitude towards effort and work. "Raising expectations and challenging comfort zones" (Tunstall, 2015) through collective hard work may be empowering through the internalization of certain dispositions and skills.

What kind of discipline and how it is woven into educational practices, as well as the distinction between positive (gentle) authority and authoritarianism are aspects worth discussing. We should neither neglect the importance of pleasure in learning and making music nor undervalue positive forms of discipline and effort. Rather than providing clear-cut answers, the data presented here will hopefully stimulate this discussion.

References

Baker, G. (2014). *El Sistema: Orchestrating Venezuela's youth*. Oxford: Oxford University Press.

Bourdieu, P. (1977) [1972]. *Outline of a theory of practice*. Cambridge: Cambridge University Press.

Bourdieu, P. (1990) [1980]. *The logic of practice*. Cambridge: Polity Press.

Bridges, D. (1993). Transferable skills: A philosophical perspective. *Studies in Higher Education, 18*(1), 43-51.

DeNora, T. (2000). *Music in everyday life*. Cambridge: Cambridge University Press.

DeNora, T. (2003). *After Adorno: Rethinking music sociology*. Cambridge: Cambridge University Press.

Foucault, M. (1988). Technologies of the self. In L. Martin, H. Gutman & P. Hutton (Eds.), *Technologies of the self*. London: Tavistock.

Heath, C., Hindmarsh, J. & Luff, P. (2010). *Video in qualitative research: Analysing social interaction in everyday life*. London: Sage.

Koivunen, N. (2011). Show us the sound! Aesthetic leadership of symphony orchestra conductors. *Leadership, 7* (1), 51-71.

Lahire, B. (2003). From the habitus to an individual heritage of dispositions: Towards a sociology at the level of the individual. *Poetics, 31* (5-6), 329-355.

Lahire, B. (2011) [2001]. *The plural actor*. Cambridge: Polity Press.

Schutz, A. (1951). Making music together: A study in social relationship. *Social Research*, 18 (1), 76-97.

Pellegrino, J.W. and Hilton, M.L. (Eds.) (2012). *Education for life and work: Developing transferable knowledge and skills in the 21st century.* Washington: National Academy of Sciences.

Skinner, B. (2014) [1953]. *Science and human behavior.* The B. F. Skinner Foundation. [Ebook available at http://bfskinner.org/store/]

Small, C. (1998). *Musicking: The meanings of performing and listening.* Hanover, NH: Wesleyan University Press, University Press of New England.

Spitzer, J. and Zaslaw, N., (n.d.). Orchestra. *Grove Music Online. Oxford Music Online.* Oxford University Press. Retrieved from http://www.oxfordmusiconline.com/subscriber/article/grove/music/20402

Spitzer, J., Zaslaw, N. and Kennedy, M., (n.d.). The conductor. *The New Grove Dictionary of Opera* (Ed. Stanley Sadie). *Grove Music Online. Oxford Music Online.* Oxford University Press. Retrieved from http://www.oxfordmusiconline.com/subscriber/article/grove/music/O901114

Tunstall, T. (2013). *Changing lives: Gustavo Dudamel, El Sistema, and the transformative power of music.* New York: Norton.

Tunstall, T. (2015). "Do we have to rehearse *again*?". *The Ensemble – A Newsletter for the U.S. & Canadian El Sistema Movement,* September 2015. Retrieved from http://ericbooth.net/the-ensemble/

Exploring Teaching Approaches to *Brundibar,* A Children's Opera

Ruth Brittin

Department of Music Education, University of the Pacific, Stockton, CA, USA

rbrittin@pacific.edu

Abstract

This study examines 5th-grade students' responses to an instructional unit on the opera *Brundibar* preparing them for attending a live performance. The opera *Brundibar,* written and originally performed during the Holocaust, has been presented numerous times world-wide over the last dozen years. Over 1500 5th-8th grade students attended a local performance of *Brundibar,* which concluded with remarks by Ela Weissberger, Holocaust survivor and member of the original cast. To examine the effects of specific preparatory activities, two 5th grade classes were presented with a series of age-appropriate lessons: a short introduction to opera, a lesson on the opera's history within the Holocaust, a lesson exploring how artists/writers communicate their messages, an art project making remembrance butterflies, and attending the opera. One class heard the "history lesson" before the "art lesson"; the other class heard those lessons in reverse order. Pre-post unit surveys showed a significant increase in enthusiasm for opera, similar to previous studies, with both classes. There was a significant order effect of the two lessons; the class that heard the "art lesson" first were far more engaged in the "history lesson" that followed, and the class that heard the "history lesson" first reported significantly lower learning in the subsequent "art lesson". Students' wrote about their impressions (facts learned and emotions felt) after each activity. Most 5th graders knew very little about the Holocaust or World War II prior to the unit, and they wrote down a number of facts learned and impressions gained over the lessons. There were many comments regarding the importance of standing up to bullies, both in the context of the opera's plot and in regards to what happened in the Holocaust. Many students were strongly affected by seeing "Ela the Cat" and hearing her comments. Many students reported a range of emotions throughout the unit. Responses indicated *Brundibar,* with substantive preview activities, may serve as a meaningful vehicle for developing and reinforcing empathy and thus may be a good pedagogical choice for building anti-bullying values with pre-adolescents.

Keywords: affective response, pedagogy, social studies, Holocaust, bullying, emotion

Music educators use music to prompt learning that crosses boundaries. For over 20 years in the USA, the national standards have stipulated that educators help students in "understanding relationships between music, the other arts, and disciplines outside the arts" and "understanding music in relation to history and culture" (National Standards in the Arts, 1994). In the most recent "common core" documents (National Core Arts Standards, 2014), music educators are asked to guide students in understanding, "How do the other arts, other disciplines, context, and daily life inform responding?" Music does not exist in a vacuum. Teachers are interested in making connections across subjects, and to life in general, in both cognitive and affective domains.

Studies have assessed effectiveness of large performances and educational previews for children (Brittin, 2010; Clarke, 1970; Myers, 2005; Sims, 1992; Suthers, 2008; Winterson, 1996). In general, live performances provide exposure and inspiration to students, and substantive preview projects prompt more learning. Moving beyond "support" and "partnership" to "collaboration" between partners is of most value (DeNardo, 1997).

The opera *Brundibar* has been performed increasingly across the world the past decade. Interest has been spurred by renowned author Maurice Sendak and playwright Tony Kushner bringing forward an English version and an illustrated children's book of the same name (2003). The original *Brundibar* opera was written and performed by Jews persecuted during the Holocaust. The opera itself depicts a "fairy tale" where the child protagonists prevail over the bully, the antagonist Brundibar. The opera and book may be enjoyed by various ages.

The opera and illustrated book have become vehicles for teaching about the Holocaust. They may be used to reinforce anti-bullying in general, or understanding elements of the Holocaust; it should be noted that the history of the Holocaust is usually taught to older students (7th or 8th grades) in the USA.

Understanding the meaning of music during and after the Holocaust (Cunningham, 2014) and finding ways to present this music (Chetel, 2014; Dobbs, 2013; Freeman, 2007) and the book *Brundibar* (Larsen, 2012) is of interest to scholars and teachers. This study focuses on a *Brundibar* teaching unit, targeting the effects of presenting particular preview lessons to 5th grade students. The study focuses on an order effect of presenting particular lessons on *Brundibar* and the Holocaust.

Method

Over 1,500 students (grades 5-8, in the Western United States) attended *Brundibar* at the local university, with a special guest appearance by Holocaust survivor Ela Weissberger. All attendees' teachers were provided teaching materials prepared by the researcher on *Brundibar* and its history, including materials/lesson plans gleaned from websites of Holocaust museums (Washington D.C., Houston, Los Angeles, Terezin, and Israel), and opera companies. Every class was given copies of the books *Brundibar* (2003), *The Cat with the Yellow Star* (2006), and *I Never Saw Another Butterfly* (1993).

Two particular classes were targeted for in-depth analysis of their two-week unit of instruction. Lesson plans were developed, four lessons in the classroom were videotaped, and students completed learning packets by writing down impressions after each lesson, plus a pre- and post-survey of attitudes. The unit included: a 15-minute introduction to opera in general and *Brundibar*; a 30 minute lesson on the opera *Brundibar*'s history in relation to the Holocaust; a 30 minute lesson on the book *Brundibar*, reading aloud the story and highlighting artistic elements of Sendak's illustrations (relating them to the opera); a 30 minute art project where students made remembrance butterflies to bring to the opera; attending the opera at the university, with comments from Ela Weissberger at the conclusion.

Lessons were designed by the researcher and four graduate students, incorporating advice of students' classroom teachers. The introductory lesson was taught by the researcher. The history lesson was taught by one pair of the graduate students, and the art lesson taught by the other pair. One class received the art lesson before the history lesson, and the other class received the history lesson before the art lesson. All lessons were taught on the same days, in the regular classroom. Classroom teachers led the butterfly art project.

Pre-and post- unit surveys (modeled on Sims, 1992; Brittin, 2010) were given by the regular teachers. Writing prompts elicited student impressions after each lesson. Before the introductory lesson, each class made a "word bank" of emotions in class discussion (sad, happy, excited, bored, angry, etc), to be prepared with possible answers when asked to describe their current emotional states.

After the "history lesson", students wrote down points remembered (i.e., who did you learn about, what happened, where/when did it happen, why did it happen?). After the "art lesson", students were asked to write a brief synopsis of the story's plot and to address similarities/differences in Sendak's illustrations in *Brundibar* and in *Where the Wild Things Are*, to point out symbolism, and to hypothesize why writers/artists choose certain techniques.

Students signed assent and their parents signed consent forms. Those who did not return forms and a packet with at least one lesson's writing responses and the post-test were not included. Twenty-six of the 30 students in Class One, and 16 of the 29 in Class Two, returned forms and responses. Surveys were analyzed by comparing means. Free response items were classified/ counted for patterns of response (reliability check between the researcher and an experienced general music teacher, $r = .89$ [agreements divided by agreements plus disagreements]).

Results

Fifth grade students ($n = 42$) participated in a unit on *Brundibar* and the Holocaust, completing pre-and post-test surveys and writing prompts following lessons. There was a significant positive change in responses pre- to post- survey (F = 16.8, $df = 1, 82, p < .0001$). For responses to "is seeing an opera fun", "is seeing an opera interesting", "is opera singing beautiful", "are opera singers talented", "would you like to see an(other) opera", mean responses rose. The mean score for the pre-test was 3.8 and for the post-test was 4.4. The two classes were similar in their mean responses (Class One's pre-test = 3.8, Class Two's = 3.7, Class One's post-test = 4.5, Class Two's = 4.3).

The first class's respondents ($n = 26$) received the "art lesson" first, followed by the "history lesson", while the second class's respondents ($n = 16$) received these in the opposite order. On the post-test, students were queried whether they had learned "a lot", "some", "not much", or "not at all" regarding 1) the history of *Brundibar* and 2) how writers, composers, and artists convey their ideas through their art. Overall, responses were similar to the two questions (mean of 3.6 for the history and 3.4 for conveying ideas through art). An interesting pattern emerged. Both classes gave similar scores to the lesson they had heard first (Class One's mean for art = 3.5 and Class Two's mean for history = 3.56). However, there were differences between the two classes regarding their perceived learning for the second lesson heard. Class One's mean for learning in the second lesson (history) was 3.62, while Class Two's mean for their second lesson (communication through art) was 3.13. A repeated measures 2-way ANOVA revealed this interaction was significant, F = 5.81, $df = 1, p = .02$. Thus the order of the lessons had a significant effect. Those who heard about art first, followed by history, had a significantly more positive response to their learning on the second lesson.

Students wrote down facts and inferences following the lessons. At the beginning, very few indicated any familiarity with World War II, the Holocaust, or the meaning of democracy. After the history lesson, virtually all wrote down information pertaining to the Holocaust, most often referring to treatment of the Jews, the concentration camps, conditions for children at Terezin, and the fact that they would meet a survivor at the opera who was a member of the original cast. Responses to the communication through art lesson were less consistent, but all students wrote down elements of the opera's plot correctly, and most commented on either the symbolism or illustrative techniques that Sendak used, when comparing illustrations in *Brundibar* and *Where the Wild Things Are* (Sendak, 1963).

The students' emotional reactions to the project were surveyed with each activity. Students were asked to share how they were "feeling about the *Brundibar* project today" and "why do you feel this way", after completing other writing prompts. Being "excited" was the most oft-reported emotion (100% of students used this term, and some reported it every single time they wrote). They were excited, primarily, at going to see the opera, though some also reported excitement at learning more about the history of the opera. Many mentioned that they had never seen an opera or were curious or interested to see what the opera would be like. Many reported excitement at the chance to meet Ela, and these responses increased with each lesson. Some students reported multiple emotions (such as, "happy and sad... happy because I get to see an opera but sad for all the people that died").

Most students expressed what would generally be considered a positive emotion at the conclusion of the project; the emotions "I feel awesome", "amazed", "good", "happy", "fun", "enjoyful", "loving it", "funny", "glad", and "great" were predominant. Reasons for being "happy" included responses such as "they did a good job", "saw original performer", "learned lots", "it was interesting", "met Ela", "Ela and learned her history", "saw fun show", "play had a lot of meaning", and "beautiful singing". One student reported feeling "bad" (for the children who went through this), one felt "sad" (for what Ela went through) and one felt sadness at "greediness". Four students reported feeling "happy and sad" (liked story, but people died; opera was great, but felt sad for Ela; it was beautiful, but sad for WWII), one felt "mad" (at Brundibar being so mean). One child reported feeling "better" because "Brundibar learned his lesson". One reported feeling "shocked, scared, OK, sad" because "over 1,000,000 people were murdered". Four of the 26 in Class One reported a sad/mad/bad affect in their last writing prompt, while three of the 16 in Class Two felt this way; half of these reported a mix of positive and negative emotions.

A few emotions were reported infrequently at various points in the unit, such as "bored" (because the opera will be long) or "tired" or "sleepy" (because the singing will be loud or the music will not be "jumpy"). A few students expressed being "mad" (because Brundibar stole the money or was mean or was bad); these feelings generally occurred after the art lesson that focused on the plot of the story. Some mentioned feeling "weird" or "confused" after some of the earlier lessons, although none used those terms at the conclusion of the project.

Because *Brundibar* can be a catalyst for promoting anti-bullying values, students' responses to the following questions were examined: "Does the storyline of Brundibar teach us any lessons for the future, or for our own lives? Please explain" (following the art communication lesson) and "Are there any lessons to be learned for the future from the history discussed today?" (following the history lesson). Most students addressed bullying in at least one of those answers.

Emotional responses to bullying were explored, too. The art lesson had an explicit message regarding bullying, in regards to the plot. The history lesson made specific reference to Hitler's annexation of countries, the world's initial appeasement policies, and asked the question, "If someone is bullying others, will he realize what he's doing and stop, or do other people have to say something to stop it?" These questions were developed in regard to suggestions on emphasizing roles of perpetrators, victims, bystanders, and resistors (United States Holocaust Memorial Museum, 2015). When students explained their emotional response, there were nine comments after the art lesson regarding bullying or the need to stand up for others or protect them, and four more comments specifically addressing bullying/need to stand up after the history lesson. Five more comments were made regarding a bully being put in his place, or bravery, after the butterfly-making project. Others may have had bullying in mind when they referred to "the story" or "the history" as an explanation for their emotional response; for example, one student mentioned the "story teaches kids lessons" after the art lesson. Altogether, a quarter of the students specifically used the words "bully", "stand up to", or "protect" in explaining why they felt a particular emotion after one of the lessons.

Discussion

This study was designed to explore the learning of two fifth-grade classes that participated in a two-week unit previewing the opera *Brundibar*, an opera with history in the Holocaust. The unit culminating in visiting the local university to see the opera and hear Ela Weissberger, Holocaust survivor and member of the original cast, speak. There were three main points studied: the overall change in enthusiasm for opera, the effect of targeted lessons, and the emotional states reported at different points in the unit.

Overall, students' pre- and post-project surveys showed an increase in enthusiasm for opera. The mean increases seen here were larger than the increases seen with a previous *Brundibar* project done several years earlier (Brittin, 2010). In that study, 526 students completed the pre- and post-opera survey; the mean pre-survey response was 3.3 and the post-survey response was 3.7; here, with a much smaller number of respondents, the mean rose significantly from 3.8 to 4.4. In both studies, probability was less than .0001. In both studies, students expressed higher levels of feeling that the opera was fun, interesting, and featured beautiful singing by talented singers, and students expressed greater interest in attending operas in the future. In the previous study, the preview units were taught by many classroom teachers in three different schools; thus, there was a wide range of time and activities devoted to instruction. This raised the need for a more in-depth, empirical look at how a particular unit of study might affect students' knowledge and attitudes.

The current unit included a lesson on the opera's plot and how artists, musicians, and writers convey their messages, and one on the history of the opera in relation to the Holocaust. One class received the art lesson first; the other class received the history lesson first. Additionally, a shorter orientation to opera in general, and *Brundibar* in particular, preceded these more in-depth lessons, and an art project creating remembrance butterflies followed the two targeted lessons. Finally, students attended the opera (along with almost 1,500 other students) at the local university and heard the Holocaust survivor and original member of the Brundibar cast, Ela (Stein) Weissberger, speak.

Because the subject matter of the Holocaust is not typically included in US history/social studies until middle school (World History and reading 'The Diary of Anne Frank"), it was important to track these 5th graders' reactions. While the two classes had very similar mean responses to their first lesson, regarding how much they felt they had learned, there was a significant interaction from the first to the second lesson. Specifically, those who heard the "art lesson" first remained relatively consistent in their responses to their learning in the subsequent "history lesson". However, those who heard the "history lesson" first had notably lower mean scores on the second lesson (the "art lesson"). While these were intact classes and other uncontrolled variables may have contributed to this interaction, it seems likely the order of the lessons contributed. The same teachers conducted the lessons, both sets of teachers felt more comfortable on the second lesson taught, both second lessons went "smoother" than the first (discerned by watching videotapes), and students had their second lesson at the same time of day as their first lesson. Thus the most likely reason is that the order of the lessons matters.

Possibly the history lesson seemed more substantive or riveting than the art lesson, and thus the art lesson paled in comparison when it followed the history lesson. Or perhaps the students who heard the art lesson first had a chance to become oriented to the plot of the story, which then prepared them to be more intellectually and emotionally ready for the history lesson on the Holocaust. Or perhaps it was a combination of these two issues. It was noticeable that the class receiving the history lesson second asked far more questions after that lesson (virtually all 29 students asked questions, with over 35 questions asked), compared to all other sessions. In all other lessons, two or three students asked a question at the end of the presentation. It appears the order may have increased both the students' interest and comfort in asking difficult questions concerning the opera's history and the Holocaust. Overall, it appears the art lesson preceding the history lesson prompts perceptions of greater learning.

Finally, the students' emotional responses were of interest. "Excitement" at seeing the opera and meeting Ela Weissberger was predominant. Many students expressed sadness towards events of the Holocaust, and a number seemed to find some level of catharsis in having the butterfly art project as an activity. About half referenced something specific in how they made their butterflies, including being "inspired", wanting to symbolize "hope" or "joy/God" in their butterfly, representing a realistic butterfly, depicting sadness, referencing art/symbolism in the book, or using the butterfly to symbolize standing up to bullies. There were many responses throughout the lessons regarding the importance of standing up to bullies or empathy for those who have been victimized/bullied (either in the opera's plot or in the Holocaust). Although these lessons did not explore specific actions to deter bullying, it did appear to lay groundwork for reinforcing empathy, and empathy has been found to be a significant factor in deterring bullying (Sahin, 2012). One quarter of students mentioned bullying in their emotional responses. Establishing anti-bullying values with pre-adolescents may have positive effects as those students move into the social stresses of their teenage years. Perhaps future educators may use such lessons on *Brundibar* to build a foundation on which more specific anti-bullying information can follow.

References

Brittin, R. (2010). *Brundibar:* a catalyst for engaging 4th-8th grade students and teachers in opera. Presented at *Music Educators National Conference*, Biennial National Conference on Research in Music Education and Music Teacher Education, Anaheim, April.

Chetel, D. W. (2014). Reconciling *Brundibar:* Practical considerations for producing Hans Krasa's children's opera. Unpublished dissertation, University of Kentucky. Retrieved at http://uknowledge.uky.edu/music_etds/22/

Clarke, P. (1970). Children's information seeking about the symphony. *Bulletin of the Council for Research in Music Education, 19,* 1-15.

Cunningham, D. A. (2014). Musical meaning in the lives of those affected by the Holocaust: Implications for music education. *Update: Applications of Research in Music Education, 33,* 65-72.

DeNardo, G. F. (1997). Authentic assessment of student learning in a community arts education partnership. *Bulletin of the Council for Research in Music Education, 134,* 1-8.

Dobbs, T. L. (2013). Remembering the singing of silenced voices: *Brundibar* and problems of pedagogy. *Philosophy of Music Education Review, 21,* 156-177.

Freeman, T. R. (2007). *Using Holocaust music to encourage racial respect.* Unpublished dissertation, Rutgers University. Retrieved at https://rucore.libraries.rutgers.edu/rutgers-lib/40070/

Larsen, K. M. (2012). Navigating worlds of "Trouble and Woe and Worse" in children's literature: An exploration into the double text of Tony Kushner and Maurice Sendak's *Brundibar. Children's Literature in Education, 43,* 27-47.

Myers, D. (2005). Preparing performers and composers for effective educational work with children. *Art Education Policy Review, 106 (*6), 31-38.

National Core Arts Standards (2014). *Introduction and list of standards.* Retrieved at http://www.nationalartsstandards.org/, Oct. 30, 2015.

National Standards for Arts Education: what every young American should know and be able to do in the arts. (1994). *Content and achievement standards for dance, music, theatre, and visual arts; grades k-12.* Reston, VA: Music Educators National Conference.

Rubin, S. G. & Weissberger, E. (2006). *The cat with the yellow star: coming of age in Terezin,* NY: Holiday House.

Sahin, M. (2012). An investigation into the efficiency of empathy training program on preventing bullying in primary schools. *Children and Youth Services Review, 34* (7), 1325-1330.

Sendak, M. (1963). *Where the wild things are.* NY: Harper & Rowe.

Sendak, M. & Kushner, T. (2003). *Brundibar.* NY: Michael Di Capua Books/Hyperion Books for Children.

Sims, W.L. (1992). Effects of attending an in-school opera performance on attitudes for fourth-, fifth-, and sixth-grade students. *Bulletin of the Council for Research in Music Education, 114,* 47-58.

Suthers, L. (2008). Concerts for young children. *Australian Journal of Early Childhood, 33,* 50-54.

United States Holocaust Memorial Museum (2015). *Guidelines for teaching about the Holocaust.* Retrieved at http://www.ushmm.org/educators/teaching-about-the-holocaust/general-teaching-guidelines

Volavka, H., ed. (1993). *I never saw another butterfly* (2nd ed.). NY: Schocken Books.

Winterson, J. (1996). So what's new? A survey of the education policies of orchestras and opera companies. *British Journal of Music Education, 13,* 259-270.

Note: Great thanks go to graduate students Celia Boutiette, Rebecca Fitch, Lauren Gibson, and Scott McColl, who participated extensively in preparing and presenting these lessons to study participants.

What Do You Do With a Music Degree? Examining the Musical and Non-Music Roles Held by Alumni of Undergraduate Music Programs

Julia Brook
School of Drama and Music

julia.brook@queensu.ca

Sue Fostaty-Young
Centre for Teaching and Learning, Queen's University, Kingston, ON, Canada

Abstract

The purpose of this research was to explore the types of work in which alumni of music programs are currently engaged, and how they use the skills and knowledge gained through their undergraduate music programs in both music and non-music contexts. The contemporary Canadian music industry has undergone many changes over the past century that include the expansion of musical genres as well as the ways that music is performed, recorded, and shared. The extent to which alumni are able to engage in this dynamic environment requires further investigation. Using survey research method, alumni who had graduated from a music program at a medium-sized university between 2007 and 2014, inclusive, were invited to participate. Survey questions related to alumni's undergraduate experiences and current work contexts. Findings indicated the undergraduate program provided sufficient opportunity to develop specific western Classical musical skills as well as more generic critical and creative thinking skills, but lacked opportunities to explore a variety of musical genres or to improvise. In terms of the participants' work context, many had portfolio-based careers that often included the roles of performer and teacher. Others balanced music with non-music roles while still others reported no longer having a connection to the field. A great majority felt that they were able to transfer the musical and thinking skills learned in their undergraduate program to their current work context. Others felt that they lacked the requisite knowledge to successfully navigate the world of music. These findings illuminate that while Western Classical music skills continue to be pertinent to the music field they also underscore the need for undergraduate music programs to introduce students to a wider range of knowledge and skill development so that they may become better prepared to engage in a broader spectrum of the field.

Keywords: Higher education, transfer of learning, music field, undergraduate, music majors

Aim and Related Literature

The contemporary Canadian music industry, like other Western contexts, has undergone many changes over the past century (Bennet, 2007; Campbell at el, 2014). These changes not only include the expansion of musical genres, but also ways that music is performed, recorded, and shared (Campbell at el, 2014). The American College Music Society's Report of the Task Force on the Undergraduate Music Major observed that "contemporary tertiary-level music study – with interpretive performance and analysis of European classical repertory as its center – remains lodged in a cultural, aesthetic, and pedagogical paradigm that is notably out of step with its broader reality" (Campbell at el, 2014, p. 11).

While tertiary music education programs consider curriculum changes to align with the current world of music, graduates of music programs, armed with their post-secondary knowledge and experience, must find employment. Some research studies have found that graduates have been adequately prepared for their new musical contexts (e.g. Latorre & Lorenzo, 2013; Renshaw, 2015). Others argue that post-secondary music training graduates do not develop complementary skills that would enable them to pursue and secure work in the field (Bennett, 2007; 2009; Bennet & Bridgstock, 2015).

Research has also illuminated that musicians typically do not hold single salaried positions, but rather hold several positions that form a portfolio-based career (Bennet, 2007, 2009; Bennet & Bridgstock, 2015). Bennet (2007) introduced a broader definition of 'musician' as referring "to an individual directly or indirectly involved in the performance of music. This included performers, instructors, directors, composers and those whose supporting role is integral to the performance itself" (p.182). Bennet surveyed 207 musicians working in the UK and Australia and addressed questions around participants' demographics, working patterns, and education and training. She found that "far from making a living by making music, the majority of musicians finance music-making by making a living" (p.185). Musicians were wholly or partly self-employed and worked in a variety of inter-dependent roles throughout their lives and often relied on income earned from work outside of the music field. Bennett concluded that "performance-based education and training in classical music does not provide graduates with the requisite skills to achieve a sustainable career" (p. 187). She advocated for post-secondary music programs to encourage students to see the intrinsic and extrinsic benefits of pursuing a composite career incorporating a variety of roles and interests.

Transfer of Learning

Being able to apply skills learned in one context into another is referred to as transfer of learning. "Transfer of learning is understood to be that process whereby prior learning affects new learning or performance in an activity where that activity differs in some significant way from the original learning, task or context" (Marini & Genereau, 2013, p. 2). Most often, transfer of learning is considered to be a deliberate and purposeful process of abstracting skill or knowledge from one context for use in another (Perkins & Solomon, 1988) and is almost "universally accepted as the ultimate aim of teaching" (McKeough, Lupart & Marini, 2013). In addition to transferring musical skills from one context to another, research examining the transfer of learning also explores how one can transfer skills, such as creative thinking, across disciplines. A music degree, with its opportunity for students to be immersed in musical creative thinking, may prove to be valuable for skill development regardless of the field the graduate eventually enters (Webster, 2014).

Florida (2002, 2014) defined a 'creative class' referring to 'knowledge-intensive jobs that involve the production of new ideas and products, or that engage in creative problem solving' (2014, p. 197) and lists fields such as design, computer and mathematical sciences, law, medicine, finance, musicians, actors, and university professor as examples (Florida, 2014). Similarly, Higgs, Cunningham, and Pagan (2007) identified what they referred to as a Creative Trident – a structure that sees creative work embedded in creative and other sectors and that includes support occupations that are part of the creative industry. The breadth of fields represented in this list underscores the importance of creative thinking skills across a wide range of disciplines. Webster (2014) surveyed architects, chefs and industrial designers who also had a music background and found that these participants linked their previous musical experiences in part, with the creative thinking that was required their present jobs.

The transfer of skills from one setting to another may not be an automatic process for learners. Therefore, the extent to which alumni are able to apply the wide variety of skills learned in their undergraduate music program to their various musical and non-musical roles requires more investigation. To gain better understanding of the ways in which graduates use the skills and knowledge gained through their undergraduate programs we used the following questions to frame our research: (a) What types of music and non-musical roles do undergraduate alumni currently hold? (b) To what degree do music program graduates perceive their learned skills and knowledge to transfer to their current role(s)?

Method

Survey questions aimed to ascertain the types of music courses students took during their programs, any additional education attained since graduation, and inquire into their current work situation. Survey questions built on existing music education literature as well as a survey developed by Webster (2014) that examined the extent to which professionals various creative industries correlated their creative skills to their prior musical experiences. The survey used in this study also examined students' perceptions of the musical and extra-musical skills they gained through their music degrees and the extent to which they used these skills in their current work or study context. Six recent graduates of music programs piloted the study to validate the questions for clarity and readability. Their responses and feedback informed the final version of the questionnaire. An email invitation of participation was sent to all graduates who completed music programs (e.g. B.Mus; B.A) between 2007 and 2014 at one medium-sized Canadian university (n=242). Surveying this demographic enabled us to examine those who were early in their career and thus gain a richer understanding of the issues associated with establishing a career. One hundred twenty-one alumni completed a survey resulting in a 50% response rate. Descriptive statistics were used to gain insight into career paths undertaken by these graduates, the skills that they gained through their undergraduate experiences and the ways in which they are using knowledge and skills gained through those experiences. Participants who volunteered to do so were recruited to participate in semi-structured interviews designed to elaborate upon areas of inquiry initiated through the questionnaire.

Findings

Alumni from across the selected graduation years completed the survey. Specifically, 22.4% of the respondents had graduated in 2007 or 2008, 17.2% had graduated in 2009 or 2010; 25.9% in 2011or 2012, and 34.5% graduated in 2013 or 2014. As one would expect with recent alumni of undergraduate programs, 28.1% of the respondents were under 25 years of age, 53.8 % were between the ages of 25 – 29; 15.7% were between 30-34 years of age, and 2.4% were 35 years old or older. Most of the respondents identified as female (77.7% female; 21.5% male, 0.8% preferred not to answer).

Education

Credentials: The majority of respondents had completed a Bachelor of Music (80%) degree, while the remaining 20% had completed a Bachelor of Arts degree with a Major, Minor, or Medial in Music. Both the Bachelor of Music (B.Mus) and Bachelor of Arts (B.A.) program did not contain any streamed or specialization within the program. Rather, each degree plan (e.g. B.Mus, B.A.) had a set of core courses. For example, all students were required to complete courses in music theory, musicology, music education and applied study. There were a variety of courses in music theory, musicology/ethnomusicology, music education and applied students can take within the undergraduate music programs. Within each of these areas, a variety of knowledge and skills can be developed through a range of genres or traditions. Using a 5 point Likert scale, we asked respondents what motivated them to take music courses or enroll in a music program. 70.7% strongly agreed that they wanted to keep music in their lives while 57.4% strongly agreed that they chose their program/courses because they wanted to pursue work in music. Only 32.2% strongly agreed that they chose music courses because it was fun; and hardly anyone chose music courses or enrolled in a music program to boost their GPA (0.9%).

Using the same scale, respondents were asked about the opportunities presented through programming for various music-making activities within their undergraduate program. Respondents could indicate if their opportunities weren't available or whether they did not take advantage of opportunities that were offered. In terms of playing their own instrument or learning new instruments, many respondents agreed or strongly agreed with the statement that they had sufficient opportunity to become more proficient on their instrument (88.6%), to participate in large or small ensembles (75.5%), or to learn new instruments (65.5%).

Musical Skills and Knowledge: Opportunities to compose also seemed to be available as approximately one third of respondents (34.2%) indicated that they agreed or strongly agree with the statement that they had sufficient experience to compose; only 13.1% disagreed or strongly disagreed with this statement. However, 30.4% indicated that they did not take advantage of the opportunity presented to them through programming. Conversely, there seemed to be fewer opportunities to learn more about composition or improvisation as only14.3% of respondents indicated that they had opportunity to compose while 45.6% of respondents either disagreed or strongly disagreed with this statement and 17.9% of respondents admitted that they did not take the opportunity to improvise. The limited number of students who engaged in composition and/or improvisation activities suggests that universities may be offering some courses where students are asked to create music; however these opportunities may be limited, and further, some students may also not be interested in learning to compose or to improvise. The lack of opportunity to improvise may be symptomatic of undergraduate programs that privilege notated music and/or attract students who are primarily interested in learning through notation.

Overall, most respondents indicated that the music courses they took did introduce them to new ideas and to repertoire they would otherwise not have known; however, only half (49.1%) the respondents indicated that they were able to develop the skills necessary to play a wide variety of music. Interestingly only about two thirds (65.7 %) of respondents felt the courses in their undergraduate program prepared them as a proficient musician and 57.0 % felt that as a result they were now able to navigate the world of music. The extent to which their musical skills and knowledge are pertinent to their present situation is explored later in this paper.

Other Types of Skills and Knowledge: Many indicated that their undergraduate music courses helped them think creatively (79.5%) and think critically (72.3%); however fewer students agreed or strongly agreed with statements about the ways that programming helped them challenge their assumptions (49.6%) or developed their skills to build an argument (51.8%).

In general, respondents indicated that their communication skills were enhanced through programming. Specifically, 63.7% indicated that their writing skills improved, while 50.4% felt their oral communication skills improved and that they became better able to collaborate with others (75.0%). Similarly, 61.9% indicated that their undergraduate music experiences helped them develop problem-solving skills and 59.8% felt that these undergraduate experiences contributed to their development of time management skills.

Additional Credentials Earned: Since completing their music degrees the majority (89.4%) of respondents had pursued additional education. More than half (54.5 %) of respondents completed a Bachelor of Education degree, one quarter (25.3%) continued their music studies through a college or university program. 21.4 % pursued other non-music program (aside from a bachelor of education) at the college level (6.5%), and undergraduate level (e.g. second Bachelor's degree) (3.3%). Fewer than 10% of respondents indicated pursuit of a graduate degree outside of music and just 2.4% reported undertaking a professional program (e.g. law, medicine, or business) after finishing their music degree.

Employment Status & Positions Held

Respondents reported a variety of employment conditions working as employees or entrepreneurs or a combination of both. Many (43.9%) were full-time employees and 4.1% indicated that they were entirely self-employed. Others balanced employee and self-employed work with 13.0% indicating that they were both a part-time employee and self-employed. 6.9% were full-time employees and well as being self-employed. Nine percent maintained their status as full-time students and 4.1% indicated that they were not currently employed in any capacity.

The respondents were almost evenly split in terms of their primary role with 52.2% working primarily in the field of music and 47.8% working primary in other fields, although three-quarters of respondents (72.4%) felt that the skills and knowledge gained from their music courses were pertinent to their work, and 76.6% of respondents felt that they could readily transfer the skills and attitudes learned in their undergraduate program into other aspects of their lives.

Many of those who worked outside of music held non-music positions in education, retail/sales or administration for public, private or non-profit organization. In addition to the types of positions alumni held we also asked participants to indicate all the music-based work (paid or unpaid) in which they engaged; most indicated that they were music teachers in school and/or community settings. Specifically, 36.6% were independent studio teachers; 32.6% were K-12 music teachers, 8.1% taught community-based group music lessons, and 4.9% were post-secondary music teachers. Many respondents were also performers with 22.0% performing in a large ensemble such as a choir, orchestra or band; 22.8% performed in a small ensemble such as a chamber group or rock/pop band; 24.4% performed as soloists and 14.9% were accompanists while 10.6% reported being composers or singer-songwriters. Few respondents (5.7%) indicated that they worked as arts administrators/grants officers; fewer still, music librarians (4.9%). Other positions respondents held included roles in the academy such music theorist, musicologist/ ethnomusicologist, examiner or adjudicator for festivals, competitions or conservatory exams. Fewer reported roles in broadcasting or music production including DJ, radio host, or sound engineer.

Many of the respondents reported working outside the field of music. This was evidenced by the fact that one-fifth of respondents (19.5%) indicated that they did not engage in any music activities (paid or unpaid), and only 27.7% indicated that they did not work outside the field of music. Some respondents also indicated that they integrated music into their roles in other fields such as care providers or classroom teachers. We asked why respondents chose to work outside the field of music. For almost half this choice was made because they could not find sufficient work in music (52.2%) or to make more money (43.9%). Fewer worked outside of the world of music because they liked the work better (15.7%). When asked whether or not they still aspire to work in the field of music, 51.9% of respondents agreed or strongly agreed with this statement while 18.9% disagreed or strongly disagreed with this notion.

Conclusions and Implications for Music Education

In summary, our research study found that many alumni of these undergraduate programs had sufficient opportunity to play their instrument and/or learn new instruments. Similarly, many respondents felt that they had gained skills to help them think critically and creatively, and many felt that the skills gained were pertinent to their work and that they could transfer skills and attitudes learned in their undergraduate program to other aspects of their life. Nevertheless, while many respondents indicated that they were exposed to new repertoire, they felt that they lacked opportunity to learn a variety of music and to improvise. These findings echo other research (e.g. Campbell, et al., 2014; Renshaw, 2015) that call for a broadening of musical genres and associated skills within undergraduate music programs.

The findings also align with conclusions from Bennet (2007; 2009) and Bennet and Bridgstock (2015) that many musicians have a portfolio-based career where they balance a variety of roles that often include roles as performer and teacher. Fewer of the respondents held administration or other positions within the world of music. Many respondents, who were not employed in music, left the field in search of additional employment. Further, approximately half of the respondents felt that they had knowledge significant and requisite to navigate the world of music. This finding also underscores the need to support multi-faceted musicians in undergraduate programs by exposing students to a broader range of career possibilities within the world of music and providing opportunities to develop salient knowledge to support entry into this world of work.

More research is needed to provide an in-depth examination of the transition from post-secondary to the world of work and how graduates apply the skills and knowledge gained through their undergraduate program into their present work situation. Findings can also inform curricular changes to further support graduates' ability to thrive in the multi-faceted world of music.

References

Bennett, D. (2007). Utopia for music performance graduates. Is it achievable, and how should it be defined. *British Journal of Music Education, 24*(2), 179 – 189. doi: 10.1017/S0265051707007383.

Bennett, D. (2009). Academy and the real world: Developing realistic notions of career in the performing arts. *Arts and Humanities in Higher Education, 8*(3), 309 – 327. doi: 10.1177/1474022209339953.

Bennet, D., & Bridgstock, R. (2015). The urgent need for career preview: Student expectations and graduate realities in music and dance. *International Journal of Music Education, 33*(3), 263 – 277. doi: 10.1177/0255761414558653.

Campbell, P., Myers, D., Sarath, E., Chattah, J., Higgins, L., Levine, V., Rudge, D., & Rice, R. (2014). *Transforming music study from its foundation: A manifesto for progressive change in the undergraduate preparation of music majors.* Missoula, MT, USA: The College Music Society.

Creswell, R. (2013). *Qualitative inquiry and research design.* Thousand Oaks, CA: Sage Publications.

Florida, R. (2002). *The rise of the creative class.* New York: Basic Books.

Florida, R. (2014). The creative class and economic development. *Economic Development Quarterly, 28*(3), 196-205. Doi: 10.1177/0891242414541693.

Higgs, P., Cunningham, S., & Pagan, J. (2007). *Australia's creative economy: Definitions of the segments and sectors.* ARC Centre of Excellence for Creative Industries & Innovation (CCI): Brisbane http://eprints.qut.edu.au/archive/0008242/

Latorre, I., & Lorenzo, O. (2013). Relations between study and employment: Music graduates in Puerto Rico. *Arts and Humanities in Higher Education, 12* (2-3), 161-168. Doi: 10.1177/1474022212473524.

Marini, A., & Genereaux, R. (1995). The challenge of teaching for transfer. In A. McKeough, J. Lupart & A. Marini (Eds). *Teaching for transfer: Fostering generalization in learning* (pp. 1-20). New York, NY: Routledge.

McKeough, A., Lupart, J., & Marini, A. (Eds). (1995) *Teaching for transfer: Fostering generalization in learning.* Routledge, NY: NY.

Latorre, I., & Lorenzo, O. (2013). Relations between study and employment: Music graduates in Puerto Rico. *Arts and Humanities in*

Higher Education, 12 (2-3), 161-168. Doi: 10.1177/1474022212473524.

Renshaw, P. (2015, October). *Remaking the conservatorium agenda.* Retrieved from http://musicinaustralia.org.au/index.php?title=Remaking_the_Con servatorium_Agenda

Webster, P. (2014). Effects of musical experience on the creative thinking of adult non-musicians: Architects, industrial designers, and chefs. Paper presented at the *International Society of Music Education Conference* (ISME). Porto Alegre, Brazil.

Glocal Group Creativity: Mapping the Creative Process of a cappella in Hong Kong and the United Kingdom using the Musical Creativities Framework

Chi Wai Chen

The Education University of Hong Kong

cwchen@ied.edu.hk

Abstract

A cappella is a musical performance genre with a long history. Although many people compose and arrange a cappella works, the connection between a cappella and musical creativity has not yet been considered. This study examines the background of the musical creativities framework (Burnard, 2012). Based on interviews conducted with two professional a cappella groups in Hong Kong and the United Kingdom, it uses this framework to map the creative process of a cappella from east and west. Furthermore, it provides insights to music teachers, a cappella lovers and performance group members, especially those who compose and arrange a cappella pieces and organise a cappella groups in both schools and communities.

Keywords: Musical creativity, a cappella, group creativity, multi-identities, glocalization

Focus of this Study

In the past few decades, musical creativities have been considered a major topic in the field of music education. Burnard (2012), a scholar of music education and musical creativities, published a book entitled *Musical Creativities in Practice*. The book reveals an advanced framework of musical creativities characterised by social, cultural and habitus aspects. The framework was mapped using singer-songwriters, musical compositions, improvised music, DJs, original bands and interactive audio design. This study maps two a cappella groups from Hong Kong and the United Kingdom to compare the creative process from east and west, and discusses the framework's implications for music education and the music industry.

Burnard's Framework of Musical Creativities (2012)

This study adopts Burnard's (2012) framework of musical creativities, which is characterised by social, cultural and habitus aspects. The framework has its roots in Csikszentmihalyi's three-pronged system model of genre creativity. Csikszentmihalyi (1999) stated that creativity is a process that can be observed only at points where individuals, domains and fields intersect. Burnard's framework (2012) can be applied to different types of musical creativities.

The framework is significant in that it shows how multiple musical creativities are observable and can be located in practice.

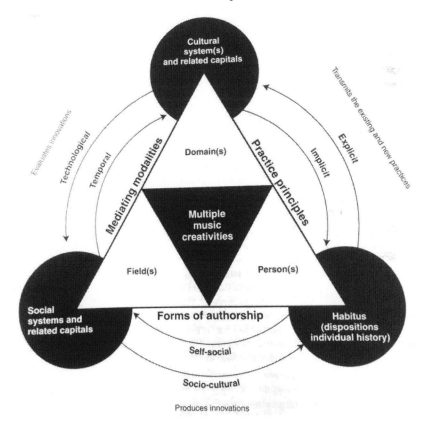

Figure 1. Burnard's (2012) synthesised framework for understanding multiple musical creativities

Research Questions

This study maps the three-pronged system of music creativities based on two a cappella groups. A case study approach is used to highlight the groups' creative processes. The following research questions are posed:

1. How do the focus groups respond to the three aspects of musical creativity?

2. What implications do mapping musical creativities have for the related issues of music, culture and pedagogy?

Method

This study focuses on how the three intersecting aspects of a cappella groups affect the mapping of musical creativities. Semi-structured focus group interviews were conducted with two a cappella groups. The interviewees were permitted to introduce new ideas during the interviews. Fifteen open-ended questions were asked. The researcher mapped the interview data according to Burnard's (2012) musical creativities framework. Interview scripts were analysed according to emerging themes based on grounded theory. Different themes were further selected to map the framework according to the interview data. The selection criteria of these two a cappella groups was that each group was representative of its origins and cultures, and was internationally renowned.

Profile of the Hong Kong a cappella group

The *Yat Po Singers* (http://yatposingers.org/en) was the first professional a cappella choral theatre company in Hong Kong to focus on developing original theatrical works. The company's first original a cappella theatre production, "Rock Hard", received both popular and critical acclaim in 2008. The re-run of "Rock Hard" was presented as the closing event of the Hong Kong 2010 International A Cappella Festival. The work was also selected to represent Hong Kong as the opening event at Shanghai Expo 2010.

Profile of the UK a cappella group

The *Oxford Gargoyles* (http://www.theoxfordgargoyles.com) were founded 15 years ago and have toured Europe, the United States and recently Hong Kong and Macau. In 2007, the *Gargoyles* won in the European category of the International Championship of Collegiate A Cappella (ICCA), and competed in the finals at New York's Lincoln Center. The group also won the Voice Festival UK competition in 2010, and were the Open Category Winners of the BBC Choir of the Year competition in 2012, starring in the final which was broadcast on BBC television.

Mapping Results in Hong Kong

The mapping results of the Hong Kong a cappella group are detailed as follows.

Three Aspects

Domains

Member A stated that '*mixing local culture into our music is the domain that our artistic directors intend to focus on*'. Chinese, Western and local music cultures are included in the group's musical creativities.

Fields

Member A identified two typically related fields used when the group composed or arranged a cappella music, including the cultural and social spaces used for entertaining people and the cultural production used to produce the work: '*Some of them are commissioned to compose for a commercial event. For example, a commercial performance may ask for a theme like "Hero" by Mariah Carey as a gimmick, and we will arrange that song as an a cappella performance*'. He also mentioned that '*at educational events, the score is rearranged as a simplified version to make it easier for the students to understand*'.

People

Member A was interested in a cappella when he was studying in secondary school and realised that human voices could imitate different kinds of sounds. He used to sing madrigals at school music festivals at an early age. Member B approached classical a cappella and began learning beat boxing after graduating from university. Member C sang his first a cappella song, a medieval song called "Kyrie", while studying as a vocal major at university. However, he used to listen to popular-style a cappella songs. Member D approached a cappella in secondary school and listened to popular oldies. The members clearly have diverse musical backgrounds, as exemplified by their academic training and musical interests.

Member C claimed that academic training sometimes restricts people when composing: '*It is good sometimes because we do not have a whole lot of musical rules to restrict us*'. When an individual focuses only on music, previous training and experience can be beneficial for musical creativity. However, they can also constrain and restrict the imaginations of professional players and composers.

Three Intersections

Forms of authorship

The focus group clearly identified two forms of authorship: *self-social* (intrinsic motivation) and *socio-cultural* (extrinsic motivation).

Self-social. The group holds *brainstorming sessions* with its artistic directors, indicating that collaboration and collectivism are part of its authorship. According to Member C, '*beat box is a kind of jamming during practicing. … I may write beat box sometimes on my own. However, sometimes I may not*'. Collaboration was also identified as an element of improvisation during performance.

The group also identified enterprise culture as one of its influences. The *Yat Po Singers* formed the first professional a cappella choral theatre company in Hong Kong, and their co-operators include artistic directors and managers seeking input in the field. The personal, collectivist, collaborative and enterprising forms of authorship fall into the *self-social* category.

Socio-cultural

Cultural practice is included in the *socio-cultural* form of authorship. The group also observed that it considers the tastes of Hong Kong audiences, and mixes Chinese and Western cultures into their music.

Mediating modalities

Temporal. Member A observed, '*I will re-harmonise some new chords for the original melody that would change into another mood*'. Improvisation is also a common modality in the musical creativities of an a cappella performer. According to Member C, '*we may have to ad lib or improvise in a performance … because these changes give both audiences and the group a kind of freshness*'. Performing on stage involves four temporal modes: composition, arrangement, improvisation and performance.

Technological. Member B observed, '*technologies help a lot in recording. For example, we can have audio effect processing when we are singing live, and we usually use YouTube as a medium of promotion*'. Member A also mentioned, '*we can adjust the tone quality of each person and blend different voices by using equalisers'.* Therefore, computer-mediated production and recording are included in the creative process.

Practice principle

Implicit. Member A stated that '*the vocal range in our group would only consist of 3–4 octaves. Since there are lots of unisons in Chinese music, it seems quite impossible for us as a group of four to create the similar effect'.* The group focuses mainly on mixing Chinese and Western music in their theatre works. Member C observed, '*not many people are willing to write or rearrange Cantonese songs for a cappella because a cappella music is still an emerging genre in Asia. Up to now, no one has rearranged Chinese instrumental music for a cappella either. Therefore, we intend to combine two concepts together and develop a new style that no one has tried before'.*

Explicit. The group arrives at new practices, compositions and possibilities through the creative thinking process. It sometimes experiments to determine whether the social and cultural systems will accept their new ideas.

Table 1: Results of the three a cappella intersections in Hong Kong

Form of Authorship		Mediating Modalities		Practice Principles	
Self-social	Socio-cultural	Temporal	Technological	Implicit	Explicit
Personal Collaborative Collective Enterprise	Concert based Audience based Education based Cultural practice	Composition Arrangement Improvisation Performance	Production Computer mediation Recording	Artistic Positioning Musical Possibilities	Innovation Experimental

Professional a cappella in Hong Kong: a practice perspective

Figure 2 shows a synthesised framework of the Hong Kong a cappella group's musical creativities, and indicates the intersections between the three perspectives.

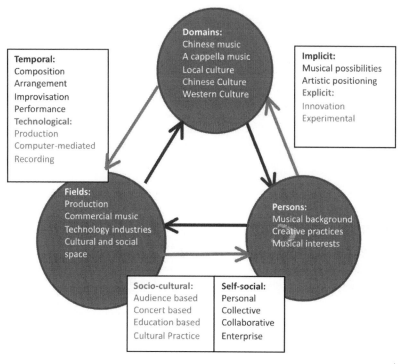

Figure 2. Synthesised framework of the Hong Kong a cappella group's musical creativities

Mapping Results of the UK Group

The mapping results of the *Oxford Gargoyles*, a UK a cappella group, are detailed as follows.

Three Aspects

Domains

As Member A observed, the '*best arrangers often listen to lots of different versions of pieces and incorporate or quote other songs or genres in their arrangements*'. The group attempts to include different musical styles, as well as elements such as beat boxing and even choreography. It explores new interpretations of music by opening itself up to different creative possibilities.

Fields

Member B stated that although the group is mainly rooted in jazz music, it performs other, more recognisable, genres due to their cross-cultural appeal and high entertainment value. The group has a tradition of performing one Disney arrangement each year. For its first Asia tour, it performed a piece by local Hong Kong band *Beyond*. It is the goal of the Musical Director to arrange pieces that can be sung to many different audiences.

People

As the group is self-organised, with members frequently contributing suggestions or improvisations, management is important. Member C was the group's Musical Director during his final year of high school, and served as its tour manager during the 2014 Asia tour. He believes that his experiences with different a cappella group management teams has contributed to his creativity.

Three Intersections

Form of Authorship

Member D said, '*when arranging a new piece, the arranger certainly must take into account location, occasion and audience preference*'.

Mediating modalities

The UK a cappella group typically relies on various modalities when creating music.

Temporal

Member E claimed that unlike other a cappella groups, the Oxford *Gargoyles* divert from a song's original arrangement: '*It is good to make an arrangement distinct from the original ... a cappella offers many possibilities ... it can offer new interpretations of music*'. Improvisation is also part of the essential element in the group's works: '*We are very egalitarian, and distribute solos as evenly as possible to showcase the diverse talents of our singers*'.

Technological

Technology assists with the group's musical creativity, including pianos or other instruments and the notation software *Sibelius* for score arrangements. Technology is crucial because it offers instant playback through

MIDI, and notation software allows the group to edit and distribute music more easily. Member F mentioned that the members learn music better by ear than by reading music.

Practical principle

Implicit Member G pointed out that the arranger's biggest challenge is to '*consider which voice parts we have available, the jazz tradition of the group, the various musical interests and talents available in the group, soloists, and the tempo and demeanour of each song*'. In this way, the music can be performed up to hundreds of times without becoming dull.

Explicit Member H stated that '*it is important to ... keep our performance authentic*'. The group is trying to make its arrangements distinct from the originals rather than copying them directly.

Table 2

Form of Authorship		Mediating Modalities		Practice Principles	
Self-social	Socio-cultural	Temporal	Technological	Implicit	Explicit
Individual	Audience based	Arrangement	Notation	Creativity	Authenticity
Egalitarian	Location based	Interpretation	Distribution	Fun	New Inter-
Originality	Cross-cultural	Improvisation	Practice	Musical	pretation
Sustainability	based	Performance		Possibilities	

Professional a cappella in the United Kingdom: a practice perspective

Figure 3 shows a synthesised framework of the UK a cappella group's musical creativities, and indicates the intersections between the three perspectives.

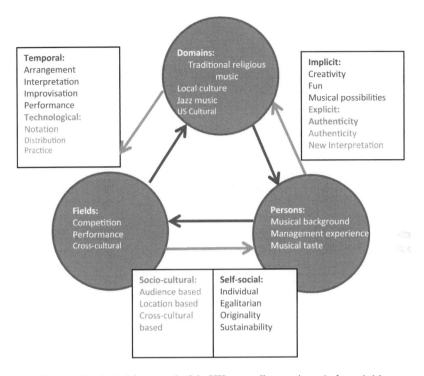

Figure 3. Synthesised framework of the UK a cappella group's musical creativities

Discussion

Group creativity

Group creativity can be found in a wide range of everyday human social activities (Sawyer, 2003). In this study, the UK group expressed that improvisation is also an essential element in its work: *'We are very egalitarian, and distribute solos as evenly as possible to showcase the diverse talents of our singers'.* In self-social forms of authorship, both egalitarian and individual characteristics are parts of the a cappella creative process. A cappella groups attempt to balance individual and group creativity. The process of *group creativity* evolves from individual creativity, and involves the achievement of originality and sustainability as a group. The *group creativity* process is also commonly found in jazz combos or rock bands, in which the members attempt to transform their creativity into a unique *musical identity* in the field.

The members of the Hong Kong group present their compositions and arrangements out of their *group creativity*. Their self-social forms of authorship are personal, collective, collaborative, and enterprise related. Furthermore, the composition or arrangement is made *explicit* to cultural practice to determine whether it is accepted. From a *socio-cultural* standpoint, group creativity must consider audience needs, concerts, education and cultural practices as their practice principles both *implicitly* and *explicitly*.

Multiple identities

Individuals take on different roles in different fields. However, the results of the Hong Kong and UK musical creativities frameworks identify *multiple identities* of composer, arranger, performer and improviser.

These identities can be found at different intersections in the frameworks. For instance, in *self-social* terms, one's identity is a composer or an arranger, and a performer in relation to the interview. One Hong Kong group member observed, *'performance is presenting what I think in my mind through my arrangement'*. One UK group member mentioned that *'it is good to make an arrangement distinct from the original ... a cappella offers many possibilities ... it can offer new interpretations of music'*. In *social-cultural* terms, they are considered performers, artists, teachers or administrators by the people in the production, cultural and social fields. In *explicit* terms, they are clearly functioning as cultural promoters, as they are promoting new concepts of a cappella that mix cultures.

Glocalization

Preserving traditional local culture is hard work in the current globalised world. Maintaining a separate traditional identity is often very difficult because it is virtually impossible to define the characteristics of a particular culture (Weiner, 2000). In music culture, it is even more difficult to preserve traditions separately, as the music in locations such as Hong Kong and the United Kingdom has been globalised.

People around the world are tasked with finding a balance between tradition and change (Weiner, 2000). In this study, the Hong Kong group serves as an example of how to integrate local Chinese culture into Western music. This kind of musical creativity is not restricted to a cappella, but can be adapted to any type of performance including choir, band and orchestra. Mixing local culture into music can create a sense of cultural identity and belonging, and teach audiences about local music. The UK group blends traditional church music with jazz. Although the group is mainly rooted in jazz music, it performs other genres that are more recognisable and have cross-cultural appeal and a high entertainment value. It has a tradition of performing one Disney arrangement each year, and during its first tour of Asia performed a piece by local Hong Kong band *Beyond*.

Co-curricular activities in schools/communities

Organising a cappella as a co-curricular activity in schools is vital for its promotion in Hong Kong and the UK. According to the Hong Kong group, *'teaching a cappella is like sowing seeds. When you give a performance in school, youngsters will have the opportunity to sing with the group and create a sense of belonging, and they may develop afterwards'*. Therefore, implementing a cappella in schools as a co-curricular activity can promote group creativity, multiple identities and glocalization. A cappella is an emerging genre that embraces musical uniqueness.

Moreover, based on the framework, it is clear that a cappella groups not only focus on performance, but also foster musical creativity. When students are involved in a cappella groups, they benefit not only from singing but also developing into creative people. Other performing groups like choirs, concert bands and orchestras are robbed of a certain amount of creativity, as their creative thinking is restricted by well-established genres and scores. Studying a cappella according to a musical creativity framework brings students into music and improves their musical creativity. Therefore, a cappella should be implemented as a new type of co-curricular activity in schools.

Limitations

As this study focuses on Hong Kong and the United Kingdom, its results cannot be generalised and applied to all a cappella groups worldwide.

References

Burnard, P. (2012). *Musical creativities in practice*. Oxford: Oxford University Press, Inc.

Csikszentmihalyi, M. (1999). Implications of a systems perspective for the study of creativity. In R. J. Sternberg (Ed.), *Handbook of creativity esthetics*, pp. 313-335. Cambridge, MA: Cambridge University Press.

Sawyer, R. K. (2003). *Group creativity: music, theater, collaboration.* Mahwah, NJ: Lawrence Erlbaum Associates, Inc.

Weiner, R. (2000). *Creativity and beyond: cultures, values and change.* Albany, NY: State University of New York Press.

Perception of Benefits Derived From Participation in Italian and American Community Bands

Deborah A. Confredo

Department of Music Education and Therapy, Temple University, Philadelphia, PA, USA

debconfredo@temple.edu

Abstract

Study of community bands as sociological phenomena have gradually emerged. Benefits from music participation into adulthood have been linked to health, well-being, and personal growth. Researchers are examining these factors as they pertain to community band musicians worldwide. Given the robust history of the Italian town band, its influence in Italian-American town bands, and American community bands, it is beneficial to study training, perceptions of benefits, and reasons for participation in and devotion to town bands in both countries. Survey content from three recent studies was pooled to investigate similarities and differences in degrees to which Italian and American community band musicians agree that certain benefits are derived from band participation. Surveys were constructed in English and Italian and emailed to conductors and other leadership of the Association of Concert Bands (US) and Associazione Nazionale Bande Italiane Musicali Autonome – Piemonte (Italy), inviting them and their musicians to participate. Respondents (N = 3269) ranked perceptions of personal improvement drawn from playing in band with focus on education, performance experiences, and attitudes towards community band experiences. Data show that the community band has global appeal and musicians derive a multitude of benefits. Italian and American views were remarkably similar despite vast differences in music education experiences. Most overwhelmingly agreed that band participation positively impacts all musical skills and strongly agree that community band is beneficial to aspects of their health and happiness, personal growth, and well-being. Religious and spiritual life were not as impacted. There was general agreement that these experiences are vital to certain sociocultural issues. Connection to cultural heritage was more important for Italians than Americans due, perhaps, to familial Italian communities and family units who perform together in the bands. Results support previous research generated from international samples. Perceptions parallel attitudes of New Horizons band populations. Italian respondents indicated that

their school experiences did not prepare them for community band participation; most received instruction from within the ensemble. Even so, Italian ensembles are ubiquitous and poised to proliferate. In the US, school
instrumental instruction is typical; respondents indicated that schools prepared them well for community band experiences. There is merit in both
systems. Americans can learn more about fostering lifelong music participation from Italians; Italians can learn more about school instrumental
music instruction from Americans. Continued research must focus on best
practices in lifelong music learning and connecting schools and communities.

Keywords: community band, adult learning, community music

Introduction

Although its existence enjoys worldwide popularity, focus on wind bands
as sociological phenomena has been slow to emerge. Once Eurocentric,
wind bands are prevalent in many countries (Dubois, Méon, & Pierru,
2013; Sheldon, 1998). The United States and Italy share the spirit of
community in town bands. Italian traditions date to the mid 1800s. Bands
are considered derivatives of the military band, an Italian nationalist em-
blem (Koehler, 1996). The stature of Italian bands during time of development was equal to if not greater than the orchestra (Koehler, 1996).
Important in Italian culture, bands continue traditions of ceremonial performance. They are mostly comprised of amateur musicians with a wide
range of ages. Also considered derivatives of their European counterparts
and the military, American community bands in the 19th and early 20th
centuries performed functions similar to Italian bands; even now, Italian-
American bands continue Italian traditions (Johnstone, 2011; Kreitner,
1990; LeCroy, 1998; Rocco, 1990). Today, they are outlets for social interaction and enjoyment from making music with others (Cavitt, 2005).
Adult community musicians report positive effects on self-esteem, quality
of life, cognitive skills, mood and emotions, and mental health (Coffman,
2006; Hallam, Creech, Varvarigou, & McQueen, 2012; Kostagiolas, 2015;
Kruse, 2012).

Rates of participation in Italian and American community bands differ.
Currently, 514 community bands hold membership in the American Association of Concert Bands (ACB) (Community Band and Orchestra
Contact Info, 2014). Though this seems substantial (many bands do not
hold membership in the ACB), given the size of the US, total population,
and number of ensembles per state, differences in participation rates between the US and Italy are clear. Italy consists of about 58 million in a
116,000 square mile area. The Piemonte, this study's targeted region, con-

sists of 4.4 million in a 9800 square mile area. Current Associazione Nazionale Bande Italiane Musicali Autonome (ANBIMA) organization membership is 270 (50° Anniversario ANBIMA, 2005). The US population is about 315 million, 5.5 times that of Italy. The square mileage of Italy is comparable to 2.5 times the size of Pennsylvania. Since Pennsylvania has one of the largest US community band populations given square mileage, it provides a good point of comparison with Italy. In 2014, 108 Pennsylvania community bands were ACB members. Multiplied by 2.5, mirroring Italy's size, the total 270 ensembles match only the number of those in the Piemonte, an area about 8.5% of Italy. Per capita, and in relation to the geographic size, community ensemble participation in the Piemonte exceeds the US.

Instrumental music education differs in Italy and the US. Italian community ensembles are often educational venues for the membership (Delfrati, 1990). Compared to Italy, US community bands are less important to young musicians' instrumental music instruction. Most American community bands are adult performance organizations. Except for New Horizons bands[11], they are less likely to provide private or small group instruction to cultivate new members; most instruction occurs in schools and private instruction is supplementary. While this system has advanced musical skills of millions of American school children, many discontinue performance after high school graduation (Coffman, 1996).

Italians promote participation through communal individual and small group instruction with performance-oriented teachers affiliated with the ensemble. Instruction is designed to help children attain success in readiness to perform in community ensembles. Emphasized are musicianship, community, and camaraderie. Americans promote participation through musical skills development as a function of public, institutionalized individual and small group instruction with education-oriented teachers. Instruction is designed to help children attain success as an individual performer and ensemble member. Large ensembles are school-centered and comprised solely of student musicians. Emphasized are musicianship and personal musical growth. These are complementary approaches.

For a long time and in many reaches across the globe, community music making has been an integral part of social being (Cross, 2006; Higgins, 2008; Leglar & Smith, 2010; McIntosh, 2009). Participants seem to de-

---

[11] Ensembles characterized as "…entry points to music making for adults, including those with no musical experience at all and those who were active in school music programs but have been inactive for a long time" (New Horizons International Music Association, 2015).

rive value from communal activities that range from enjoyment, to en-hancement of self-worth, to the advancement of creative skills (Rohwer & Rohwer, 2009; Shansky, 2010; Sheldon, 1998). While the approaches that frame instrumental community music practice in Italy and the US are complementary, differences exist in the development and nurturing of the musicians who end up populating community ensembles, calling in to question whether these distinctions influence social benefits derived from participation or identity attached to community music involvement. It is, therefore, necessary to understand more about the similarities and differ-ences of these approaches based on musicians' perceptions. This study focuses on training, perceptions of benefits, and reasons for participation in and devotion to Italian and American town bands.

Method

Data were collected via web-based survey using rosters of the ACB and ANBIMA Piemonte. Concepts and questions derived from three related studies (Coffman, 2008; Jutras, 2011; Mantie, 2012) were used. Im-portance of band participation benefits had been determined in the model studies; I used those findings to compare degrees to which Italians and Americans agree that those benefits are derived from band participation. Respondents ranked perceptions of personal improvement drawn from band participation with focus on education, performance experiences, and attitudes towards experiences in their community band. In addition to demographics, the survey was organized into six sections: *Music Instruction and Performance Habits*; *Musical Skills*; *Health*; *Personal Growth and Well-Being*; *Sociocultural Perspectives*, and; *Musical Experiences*. Response type was dependent on the question. In most cases, a 1-5 Likert-type scale was used (*Strongly Agree – Strongly Disagree*). Open-ended questions were asked, however, due to space limitations of the manuscripts, data from these questions are not reported.

The English version was piloted, modified, translated into Italian, and evaluated by two native speakers. Via email, conductors and other admin-istrative band officials of ACB and ANBIMA Piemonte member organi-zations were invited to encourage musicians to participate. The invitation included instructions for participation and a link to the survey (powered by SurveyMonkey®). Study instructions were the same for each group and were repeated on the first survey page. Because of the nature of how par-ticipants were invited, I could not determine how many were made aware of the project. Total respondents are skewed towards the US.

Results

Demographics

Italian responses (*n* = 225) were primarily from the Piemonte region of Italy (72.1%). US responses (*n* = 3044) were relatively evenly distributed throughout and represented all but two of the US states. Age range was greater and mean age older for US musicians (US: 13-94, M = 53.69; IT: 13-72, M = 36.02). Gender favored men (US: 54.6% male, 45.4% female; IT: 61.5% male, 38.5% female). More US musicians reported being married (71.2%) compared to Italian (50.3%). More than half reported having children (US: 63.9%, IT: 52.3). Difference in age range probably accounts for numbers who have played an instrument for more than 20 years (US: 72%, IT: 38%). However, Italians reported more having been members of their band for that long (35%) compared to the US (16.5%). Nearly all reported owning their band instrument.

Music Instruction and Performance Habits

Evidence of a striking difference between practices of these countries, when asked if they learned how to play in school, Italians indicated *No* (70.4%) and Americans *Yes* (87.2%). Most Italians reported learning with instruction provided by teachers affiliated with their local band. The majority from each country reported having taken private instruction (US: 87%, IT: 61%).

Instrumentalists' musical development sometimes include vocal and ear training as well education on other instruments. Piano instruction was more prevalent among Americans (US: 68%, IT: 29%); the difference in having sung in a choir was not as great (US: 86%, IT: 53%). Fewer than 22% reported singing regularly with a choir. Many play additional instruments (US: 66.5%, IT: 40.8%).

Questions about performance habits revealed that fewer Italians have been paid to play their instrument (US: 55.8%, IT: 34.1%) and only a small percentage have performed for pay on another instrument (US: 21.9%, IT: 7.6%). Most do not perform in a chamber ensemble (US: 41%, IT: 27.4%), suggesting the primary focus is the community band.

Musical Skills

Several questions focused on development of musical skills as an outcome of playing in the band. It is no surprise that most musicians reported improvement in several areas of musicianship based on band experiences (See Table 1). Although differences between the countries are noted, most indicated that performing in their band helped them improve skills.

Table 1: Impact of Band Participation on Musical Skills

		Strongly Agree	Agree	Neither	Disagree	Strongly Disagree
General Music Knowledge and Abilities	Italy	45.5	45.9	8.5	.5	.5
	US	64.8	40.00	4.0	1.0	.4
Technical Abilities	Italy	35.5	46.0	16.1	2.0	.5
	US	58.7	33.2	6.8	1.0	.4
Music Reading	Italy	46.5	44.6	8.0	1.0	0.0
	US	58.3	29.8	9.9	1.4	.7
Sense of Rhythm	Italy	41.2	43.6	14.2	1.0	0.0
	US	46.5	38.7	11.8	2.3	.65
Blend Sound With Others	Italy	54.3	40.0	6.6	1.0	0.0
	US	60.1	33.7	5.1	.7	.5
Music Theory	Italy	23.7	46.0	32.7	5.7	2.0
	US	25.8	33.5	29.2	9.3	2.3
Perform in Front of Others	Italy	43.6	43.1	10.0	2.8	.5
	US	45.3	37.7	14.3	18.4	.8
Understand More About Music I Listen To	Italy	33.2	42.7	20.0	2.8	1.4
	US	34.5	42.6	18.2	4.1	.7
Play Music I Could Not Play Before	Italy	37.4	41.7	18.5	1.9	.5
	US	38.5	33.8	19.4	6.7	1.6

Health

It is generally agreed that music can nourish the soul, mind, and body. Health benefits derived from music participation have been noted in numerous settings and circumstances. These benefits were cited among adult participants in New Horizons bands (Coffman, 2008; Mantie, 2012). Questions in this section were patterned after New Horizons studies, though current participants were inclusive of a wide age range. Using a 5-point scale ranking agreement concerning perceived health benefits of their band experience (*Strongly Disagree - Strongly Agree*), outcomes were highly positive for both countries. A majority indicated agree or strongly agree for all questions: *Mentally Challenging* – US: 90%, IT: 77%; *Physically Challenging* – US: 60%, IT: 56%; *Improves Focus and Concentration* – US: 85%, IT: 75%; *Improves Memory* – US: 64%, IT: 70%; *Improves Mood* – US: 93%, IT: 92%; *Improves Mental and Emotional Health* – US: 92%, IT: 78%; *Improves Spirit* – US: 92%, IT: 74%; *Improves Coordination and Physical Skills* – US: 68%, IT: 75%.

Personal Growth and Well-Being

Along with the many musical and health benefits of music participation, personal traits are sometimes affected. Using the same 5-point scale, a majority indicated agreement to statements focusing on impact of band participation on personal characteristics: *Improves Creativity* – US: 64%, IT: 51%; *Increases Appreciation of Beauty* – US: 67%, IT: 84%; *Improves Self-Confidence* – US: 78%, IT: 70%; *Improves Self-Discipline and Organization* – US: 73%, IT: 69%; *Increases Self-Esteem* – US: 75%, IT: 70%; *Relaxes* – US: 85%, IT: 80%; *Reduces Stress* – US: 83%, IT: 80%; *Evokes Happiness* – US: 97%, IT: 93%; *Fun* – US: 97%, IT: 96%; *Motivates Achievement* – US: 73%, IT: 74%; *Inspires Imagination* – US: 58%, IT 59%; *Nostalgia* – US: 77%, IT: 54; *Example for Children* – US: 86%, IT: 81%; *Meaningful* – US: 97%, IT: 95%; *Important (self)* – US: 97%, IT: 94%; *Important (family)* – US: 54%, IT: 63%; *Escape Routine* – US: 93%, IT: 87%; *Sense of Accomplishment* – US: 95%, IT: 54%; *Personal Value to Ensemble* – US: 81%, IT: 72%. Responses to influence on spiritual and religious life contrasted these results: *Spiritual Life* – US: 47%, IT: 49%; *Religious Life* – US: 29%, IT: 21%.

Sociocultural Perspectives

Town bands fill musical and social desires of their membership. Similarities in Italian and American perspectives are remarkable and may speak to the universality of community ensembles. With the same 5-point scale, a majority indicated agreement to statements focusing on the influence of community band participation on sociocultural aspects: *Improves Arts/Cultural Understanding* – US: 69%, IT: 72%; *Improves Cooperation* – US: 83%, IT: 92%; *New Friends* – US: 93%, IT: 97%; *Increased Social Support* – US: 73%, IT: 61%; *Positive Social Life Influence* – US: 78%, IT: 91%; *Sense of Community* – US: 81%, IT: 82%; *Sense of Camaraderie* – US: 93%, IT: 57%; *Connect to Others With Common Interest* – US: 99%, IT: 94%; *Sharing Similar Values* – US: 93%, IT: 90%; *Important to Town* – US: 75%, IT: 70%; *Help Each Other Learn* – US: 70%, IT: 74%; *Well-Known in Community* – US: 70%, IT: 91%; *Well Respected in Community* – US: 74%, IT: 78%; *Social Interaction With Musicians is Important* – US: 77%, IT: 89%. When asked whether the band is an important part of cultural heritage, a considerable contrast between countries appeared. While 90% of Italians agreed or strongly agreed, this was true of only 48% of Americans. Despite the strong town band culture in both countries, agreement that the activity honored ancestors was quite low (US: 32%, IT: 35%).

Musical Experiences

Aspects of the repertoire, conductor, and instruction are important to community band musicians in both countries but more differences in magnitude were demonstrated in this category than any other in the study. Most notably, in the question that speaks most directly to the differences in Italian and American systems of music education, Americans overwhelmingly agreed that school music experiences prepared them well for participation in their community band (90%); only 31% of Italians felt the same. Both groups agreed that private instruction helped in preparation (US: 86%, IT: 71%). Americans enjoy the experience more than Italians as a function of repertoire (US: 88%, IT: 57%). Americans' enjoyment was more influenced by the conductor (94%) compared to Italians (75%). There was agreement that level of enjoyment is affected by performance type (US: 79%, IT: 82%). Americans were more agreed that enjoyment depends on the musical interest of their part (60%) compared to Italians (44%). Neither group felt that enjoyment was tempo dependent (US: 25%, IT: 31%). Both agreed on the importance of the ensemble's musical proficiency (US: 89%, IT: 79%). Differences were evident in other areas of importance; Italians felt rehearsals were more important than performances (64%) compared to Americans (43%). Likewise, Italians indicated that, outside of work and family, playing in the band is more important than other activities to a greater degree than Americans (US: 51%, IT: 69%).

Discussion

Participants rated degrees to which they agree that previously identified benefits are derived from band participation. Respondents' views were markedly similar despite differences in music education experiences. Most overwhelmingly agreed that band has great impact on all musical skills and felt that it helps many aspects of health and happiness, personal growth, and well-being. Religious and spiritual life were not as impacted. There was general agreement that these experiences are vital to certain sociocultural issues. Cultural heritage was more important for Italians than Americans due, perhaps, to largely familial Italian communities and that many family units perform together. Results support previous research generated from international samples (Coffman, 2006, 2008; Jutras, 2011; Mantie, 2012). Although respondents' age range is large, data show parallels with the older New Horizons populations.

Dubois et al., (2013) identified the continuum, "four poles of the wind band world" (p.57). One anchor is described as largely insular. Intensely connected to its locale, it is highly social and unconnected to institutional instruction. Bands at the opposite pole are more concerned with musical

proficiency than sociability and are highly connected to institutional instruction. They caution that membership of the former is graying and
ranks are diminishing; they attribute this to lack of school involvement.
These data refute this finding. Although caution must be exercised due to
sampling bias, results suggest that Italian ensembles are strong and poised
to proliferate based on age range and prevalence of participating family
units, even though they are generally unconnected to school instruction. In
the US, institutionalized music education is the norm; schools prepared
them well for their community band experience. While US bands are not
directly tied to institutions, schools are important in preparing American
adult bandsmen for continued involvement. Both systems are meritorious,
as indicated by perceptions of benefits derived from the community band
experience.

Because there is no process of instrumental music teacher education in
Italy that parallels US practices, quality and type of instruction likely vary.
Musicians from both countries reported that their musical skills grow because of band participation. Implementation of systematic music instruction with instructors trained in music education practices may improve the
community band experience and further music achievement. One Italian
bandsman shared, "*I hope that more people can understand the importance of
teaching music in the schools. It is important for children's development of morality, friendships, and socialization*".

In the US, the system that prepares musicians for adulthood band participation could be a factor in why community bands are not as prevalent in
the US compared to Italy. This requires greater inquiry. Music educators
may need to provide information about adult community performance
options for their students. One respondent commented:

When I graduated from high school, I thought that it may be the end of
my music career. I was not unlike a lot of folks that the horn was set aside
as I didn't know of opportunities to play. I would play some things by ear
from time to time, but the loss of having an ensemble to play in was quite
disappointing. It was the formation of a community band at our local university that my sister heard about and convinced me to join. This turned
out to be a major turning point in my life.

Music educators might connect with community bands to perform stu-
dent-adult side-by-side concerts. Community band members or directors
could be invited to school rehearsals to observe, perform, or conduct. Students could attend rehearsals as observers. Providing contact information
and recordings for students is useful. Involvement of family units could be
developed within school settings, which may lead to participation post-

graduation. Students could teach parents, parents could teach students, and all could participate together in performances. Band directors can lead by example, performing in area community groups.

This study underscores the global appeal of community band and the multitude of benefits derived from participating. One musician described sentiments commonly shared in this study, *It has enriched my life greatly...at a time in my life when things were difficult, community band helped me through...the kinship I have developed with my friends in the band is very important. Music is an integral part of each day in my life.* Another stated, *"I like to learn new things, and play with other people. I meet people who have the same interests, I enjoy their company, and like working together with others for one purpose: making good music".* Americans can learn more about fostering lifelong music participation from Italians; Italians can learn more about school instrumental music instruction from Americans. Continued research must focus on best practices in lifelong music learning and connecting schools and communities.

References

50° Anniversario ANBIMA. Cinquant'anni di musica, storia e tradizioni (2005) San Vittore Olona (IT): La Tipotecnica.

Cavitt, M.E. (2005). Factors influencing participation in community bands. Journal of Band Research, 41(1), 42-59.

Coffman, D. (1996). Musical backgrounds and interests of active older adult band members. Dialogue in Instrumental Music Education, 20(1), 25-34.

Coffman, D. (2006). Voices of experience: Interviews of adult community band members in Launceston, Tasmania, Australia. International Journal of Community Music, 6(1), 1-23.

Coffman, D. (2008). Survey of New Horizons International Music Association musicians. International Journal of Community Music, 1(3), 375-390. doi:10.1386/ijcm.1.3.375_1

Community Band and Orchestra Contact Info (2014). Retrieved from: http://www.community-music.info/groups.shtml.

Cross, I. C. (2006). Music and social being. Musicology Australia, 28, 114-126. doi:10.1080/08145857.2005.10415281

Delfrati, C. (1990). Music education in Italy: Organization, achievements, and problems. The Quarterly, 1(4), 22-31.

Dubois, V., Méon, J., & Pierru, E. (2013). The sociology of wind bands: Amateur music between cultural domination and autonomy. Surrey, England: Ashgate.

Hallam, S., Creech, A., Varvarigou, M., & McQueen, H. (2012). Perceived benefits of active engagement with making music in community settings. International Journal of Community Music, 5(2), 155-174.

Higgins, L. (2008). Community music and the welcome. International Journal of Community Music, 1(3), 391-400. doi:10.1386/ijcm.1.3.391_1

Johnstone, J. (2011). A southern Italian band tradition lives in northeastern Ohio: Michael Lucente and the Lowellville Mount Carmel Band. Journal of Band Research, 46(2), 39-60.

Jutras, P. J. (2011). The benefits of New Horizons band participation as self-reported by selected New Horizons band members. Bulletin of the Council for Research in Music Education, 187, 65-84.

Koehler, E. C. (1996). Banda Minichini: An Italian band in America (Doctoral dissertation). Peabody Conservatory of Music, Baltimore, MD.

Kostagiolas, P. A., Lavranos, C., Korfiatis, N., Papadatos, J., & Papavlasopoulos, S. (2015). Music, musicians and information seeking behaviour: A case study on a community concert band. Journal of Documentation, 71(1), 3-24. doi:10.1108/JD-07-2013-0083

Kreitner, K. (1990). Discoursing sweet music: Brass bands and community life in turn-of-the-century Pennsylvania. Chicago: University of Illinois Press.

Kruse, N. B. (2012). Adult community musicians' self-esteem of music ability. Research Studies in Music Education, 34(1), 61-72.

LeCroy, H. F. (1998). Community-based music education: Influences of industrial bands in the American south. Journal of Research in Music Education, 46(2), 248-264. doi:10.2307/3345627

Leglar, M. A., & Smith D. S. (2010). Community music in the United States: An overview of origins and evolution. International Journal of Community Music, 3(3), 343-353. doi:10.1386/ijcm.3.3.343_1

Mantie, R. (2012). A study of community band participants: Implications for music education. Bulletin of the Council for Research in Music Education, 191, 21-43. doi:10.5406/bulcouresmusedu.191.0021

McIntosh, J. (2009). Indonesians and Australians playing Javanese gamelan in Perth, Western Australia: Community and the negotiation of musical identities. The Asia Pacific Journal of Anthropology, 10(2), 80-97. doi:10.1080/14442210902852831

New Horizons International Music Association. (2015). Concept and philosophy. Retrieved from http://newhorizonsmusic.org/concept-and-philosophy/

Rocco, E. S. (1990). A history of Italian-American bands in western Pennsylvania. Journal of Band Research, 26(1), 59- 85.

Rohwer, D., & Rohwer, M. (2009). A content analysis of choral students' participation perceptions: Implications for lifelong learning. International Journal of Community Music, 2(2&3), 255-262. doi:10.1386/ijcm.2.2-3.255_1

Shansky, C. L. (2010). Adult motivations in community orchestra participation: A pilot case study of the Bergen Philharmonic Orchestra (New Jersey). Research and Issues in Music Education, 8(1), 1-23.

Sheldon, D. A. (1998). Participation in community and company bands in Japan. Update: Applications of Research in Music Education, 17(1), 21-24.

Infant home soundscapes: A case study of 11-month-old twins

Eugenia Costa-Giomi
The Ohio State University, USA

costa-giomi.1@osu.edu

Abstract

We studied the home musical environment of a family with three young children Each of the 11-month-old twins wore a digital processor/recorder for an entire day that provided an assessment of their home language environment and allowed the analysis the incidence, characteristics, duration, and context of home music activities. We found the infants were immersed in music played by digital devices almost every instant of the day. They heard recorded children's music for more than eight hours and were exposed to live singing for approximately 20 minutes throughout the day. The infants heard live singing by an adult for as little as one minute. Overall, the results show the potential for music engagement afforded by the infants in the family. The parents were attentive to their children, provided them with plenty of instruments, toys, and devices to facilitate their engagement with music, and demonstrated to be competent singers and knowledgeable about music. Yet, they rarely initiated music activities, including listening and singing. We reflect on these findings and discuss their implications for research and music education.

Keywords: early childhood, home environment, parenting, musical development

Infants pick up cues from their environment to make sense of the sounds that surround them. Through daily exposure to language and music they learn to understand these complex aural communication systems rapidly and seemingly without effort. We know, however, that the way in which they learn to organize sounds is dependent upon the content and characteristics of their soundscapes. For example, infants' acquisition of vocabulary and grammar is affected by the amount, content, and delivery of the speech they hear at home (e.g., Hurtado et al, 2008). Language research has revealed the long lasting effects that the quantity and quality of exposure to speech has on their language skills (e.g., Otero et al., 2012). However, there's limited research about infants' music environment and their and its effect on musical development.

Information about infants' music environment is based almost exclusively on parental reports (e.g., Barrett, 2009; Custodero, Britto, & Brooks-Gunn, 2003; Custodero & Johnson-Green, 2003; De Vries, 2007; Koops, 2014; Ilari, 2005; Mehr, 2014; Young, 2008). According to these reports, young children hear music up to 80% of the day and the majority of music activities involve recorded music most often played by a TV or other media device (Lamont, 2008). The accuracy of these estimates is unknown. Also unknown is the amount of exposure to live music that infants experience in their daily lives. Parents all over the world report singing to their infants (Custodero, Britto, & Brooks-Gunn, 2003; Custodero & Johnson-Green, 2003; De Vries, 2007; Ilari, 2005; Mehr, 2014; Young, 2008) but the frequency and characteristics of parental singing seem to vary widely across families. Although observations of infant-mother dyads at home (Merkow, 2013) and in a lab settings (Costa-Giomi & Merkow, 2014) showed that mothers rarely sang to their infants during joint music play, videotapes and diaries prepared by parents to document their children's musical experiences at home suggest that they do so regularly (Barrett, 2009; Koops, 2014). There may be a disconnect between what parents believe happens at home in terms of singing and music engagement and what they actually do on a day to day basis.

The purpose of the present case study was to study the music environment of infants, through the analysis of the continuous recording of their home soundscapes.

Methodology

Participants

We completed the case study with a middle-class family with three young children, 11-month-old twins Emily and Austin, and 3-year-old Sasha. Both parents held university degrees, worked from home, and had taken music lessons. Only English was spoken in the home. The children didn't attend daycare but Sasha participated in a playgroup that met twice a week.

According to the mother, there was always music playing in the household and the parents sang "all the time." The family owned instruments, children's CDs, and many digital multimedia devices and toys.

Apparatus

The data was collected using a digital language processor (DLP) that registers and records sounds continuously up to 16 hours. The DLP fits in the chest pocket of a specially designed infant vest and captures sounds from the vantage point of the child.

Procedures

The parents received two DLPs and vests, one for each infant. They were asked to turn on the DLPs when the infants woke up and let the children wear them in the vests throughout the day. The device was to be used during a weekend when no unusual activities were planned. During a second visit to the lab, the mother returned the clothing and DLPs, provided the log of the infants' activities during the day data was collected, completed an interview about the musical interests, activities, and resources of the family.

Analysis of music environment

The sound files of the infants lasted eleven hours and seven minutes each. We listened to the files using high fidelity headphones multiple times to (1) become familiar with the sounds of the household particularly the voices of the family members; (2) identify and time the events listed in the infants' activity log; (3) develop a timeline and map of the activities of the family members; and (4) identify and categorize any sounds that could be interpreted as music including live singing, recorded music played by toys, TV, radio, and other electronic devices, rhythmic speech (i.e., rhymes), percussive sounds (e.g., tapping), instrumental sounds, and infant babbling; (5) gather information about the content, duration, and context of the music events. We consolidated the data into narratives of each music episode to facilitate the understanding of the content, context, and integration of musical experiences into the lives of the infants.

Results

Because of space considerations, only the analysis of selected activities is included in the paper. Language assessments and interview data are not reviewed. Table 1 displays the duration of the music activities we observed including singing.

Table 1: Frequency or duration (in Hours:Minutes:Seconds) of music episodes

	Emily	Austin
Singing		
Mother to baby	0:35	0
Mother and sibling	1:12	1:00
Grandfather to sibling	0:08	0
Grandfather and sibling	3:27	0
Grandmother to baby	0:08	10:08
Sibling to baby	0:32	0:45
Sibling singing	15:23	15:55
Father to adult	0	0:05
Baby singing	1:53	0:40
Adult singing total	5:30	1:05
Sibling singing total	20:34	17:40
Infant-directed singing total	1:15	0:45
Singing total	**21:25**	**17:53**
Recorded music		
Toys and game consoles	1:35:53	1:52:12
TV	8:03:24	8:25:51
Radio	24:45	0
Recorded music total	**8:28:09**	**8:25:51**

1 Austin heard the grandmother recite a rhyme to Emily

Listening to recorded music

Music was an ubiquitous component of the home environment. Recorded music played for most of the day (Table 1). In fact, the only time during which the infants were not exposed to recorded music was during naptime and the morning car ride to the store. Shortly after the infants woke up, the parents turned on the TV at Sasha's request and left it on until the end of the data-gathering period. There were many occasions in which other devices such as video games and toys played music along with the TV. It was not always possible to identify these devices individually but the game console and a few toys were easily recognizable. Overall, the analyses showed that multiple sources of sound played music simultaneously for extended blocks of time throughout the day.

The TV was tuned to children's programming and children's movies for most of the day. The shows were filled with music including songs, melodic and rhythmic motives, and instrumental sounds. Although the TV shows didn't broadcast music continuously, there was hardly a minute during which no TV music was heard. Most of the time the TV sounded softly in the background, yet, there were instances in which the infants clearly responded to it. For example, Emily babbled excitedly when the movie that Sasha was watching in the morning burst into music.

Austin was exposed to the sounds of the TV for all his waking hours with the exception of a few minutes early in the morning and for the duration of the trip to the store with the whole family. However, it was Emily who heard the most recorded music of the two infants simply because she was awake longer. While her brother slept, she heard music during a car ride to the store with dad who tuned the radio to a rock station. This was the only opportunity that Emily had to listen to music other than children's songs and children's programming. Austin didn't have such an opportunity.

Besides the recorded music broadcasted by the TV, the infants heard a substantial amount of music played by toys and game consoles. In general, the sounds of the toys were louder and more distinct than those of the TV. Sasha activated the toys during periods of play quite often but the twins also triggered the music when manipulating them. Overall, the infants were exposed to the music played by toys and digital devices other than the TV for more than an hour and a half the day in which data were gathered.

Infant music making

The infants made music by playing small percussion instruments. Both Emily and Sasha played maracas, shakers, and a wood block while in the playpen. The instrumental episodes occurred sometimes in isolation while playing with a variety of other nonmusical toys and sometimes as a response to or extension of a music activity. For example, in the afternoon, Austin spent a few minutes moving around the playpen manipulating various toys as well as a woodblock and a shaker. Emily noticed his brother's actions and took the shaker from him amidst his complaints and her mother's pleas to be kind to him. Undeterred, Emily started manipulating the shaker. The erratic and sporadic sounds of the shaker suggest that she was exploring the instrument rather than making music intentionally. However, when the loud and upbeat music of Sasha's video game started playing, Emily shook the instrument energetically and continuously until the music stopped. Her instrumental accompaniment restarted with the next iteration of the music and ended with a coda of loud and rhythmic vocalizations.

The infants babbled by themselves and in response to others throughout the day. Although it is impossible to determine whether their intent was to speak or to sing, there were instances in which the babbling could be interpreted as singing based on its context and content. For example, Emily participated in one of the longest singing episodes of the day by joining her grandfather and older brother in the singing of a children's song. Her babbling was reactive, controlled, and pitched and, for a couple of seconds, her pitch matched that of the song. Emily produced similar pitched babbling at other times, usually in response to a music activity developing around her such as Sasha singing to her, her mother singing with Sasha, or a toy or TV playing music. But sometimes she also engaged in musical babbling spontaneously rather than as a response to the sounds around her. For example, while alone in her playpen, during a relatively quiet moment, she babbled for approximately a minute and a half modulating and sustaining certain pitches with much vocal control. At times the babbling sounded more like speech because of the reduced range and recurring small pitch intervals, and at times it sounded more like singing because of the intensity of the sounds, the variety of the melodic contour, and the larger pitch range of the vocalizations. The mother responded to this babbling from afar by imitating some of Emily's speech sounds. Throughout the day, Emily "sang" for a total of almost two minutes.

Austin was not as vocal as his sister and engaged in only one babbling episode that could be interpreted as singing. This happened during a busy afternoon hour when everybody, including the grandparents, were together entertaining the children, preparing dinner, and talking to each other. Austin got a few minutes of undivided attention from his grandmother while playing a shaker. She picked him up, talked directly to him, asked him questions, and kissed him noisily multiple times as in a game. Austin touched her glasses, her nose, and her mouth, so she responded with a long pitched "Aaaaaah." Austin replied with his own long "Aaaaah" which got transformed into a recurring rhythm as he covered and uncovered his mouth rapidly with his hand. The grandmother laughed and imitated his "singing" a few times and then observed him in obvious amazement (i.e., she asked the mother to pay attention). Austin continued his long rhythmic vocalizations for an entire minute sometimes changing the pitch and timbre of the sound. Although at times, the vocalizations sounded more like muffled screams, it was clear that he was manipulating his voice purposefully and exploring the timbral and frequency changes that he could produce with it.

The infants had access to many toys that played music. By pressing buttons and sliding the toys' movable parts, the infants triggered the toys' programmed sounds and melodies and, in a way, made music. Both infants played with music toys purposely for extended periods of time. One such period occurred in the afternoon when the twins were in their playpen. Between 3:00 and 4:00 pm the infants were engaged in play with toys individually and with each other, and interacted with Sasha and the parents occasionally. Emily manipulated two toys, one that played children's songs with and without lyrics, and another one that played short musical motives embedded in sounds effects (e.g., gliding whistle, ding-dong bells, and percussive rhythms). It was clear that Emily remained engaged with these toys even in the presence of a multitude of competing sounds. Mom and dad talked to each other and to Sasha, a show on TV played rhythmic music, Sasha sang in response to the TV, Austin babbled and made lots of percussive sounds, yet, Emily continued to trigger the musical sounds of her two toys with a regularity and stillness suggestive of focused attention.

Discussion

We found that the infants had opportunities to participate in music activities throughout the day. They listened to music played by the TV, vocalized, played small percussion instruments, explored timbres including those produced by their own voices, triggered the onset of music in digital devices and toys, heard family members sing children's songs, and interacted musically with others. These activities didn't occur often or systematically and were not planned or prompted by the parents; they seemed to develop spontaneously amidst or in parallel to other nonmusical activities. Sometimes the music episodes were triggered by things, such as a toy that played music or the onset of music on the TV, and sometimes by people – the sibling humming or mom singing with Sasha. Many of the activities, particularly those involving instruments and toys, were initiated by the infants themselves. Overall, the infants experienced music in a variety of ways, even if they did so for short periods of time.

There was a notable scarcity of infant-directed singing in the data collected. Most of the singing the infants heard was produced by their 3-year-old brother Sasha, who hummed distractedly throughout the day or purposefully when interacting with the infants and adults. In fact, Sasha was the only member of the family who sang to each of the infants individually. Austin didn't hear any adult sing directly to him and the mother sang to Emily for just over half a minute in the entire day. Although episodes of infant-directed singing were few and short, the infants became engaged every time they occurred. They expressed their enjoyment of these episodes through giggles and vocalizations. The engaging and communicative nature of infant-directed singing was evident during these episodes.

There were few moments of silence in this busy family's soundscape. Music was heard throughout the day, broadcasted by the TV almost permanently, and produced by video games and music toys sporadically. Although recorded music filled the house at all times, there was not a single moment in which listening to recorded music became a purposefully shared experience for the infants. The only instance in which listening became the focus of attention was when the grandfather engaged Sasha with the music played by a digital device. Together, they listened to the songs it produced, sang along with it, and manipulated it intentionally to hear specific songs. Emily witnessed this listening experience that her brother shared with the grandfather but Austin did not have such an opportunity.

Shared musical experiences were short and sporadic in this household yet, they were spontaneous and rich in communicative content. Most of them were initiated by three-year-old Sasha, or by an adult as a response to the need of a child (e.g., singing to distract and entertain a restless child). They seemed unplanned and emerged and developed naturally throughout the day often in combination with other activities. The musical experiences shared by the family members seemed guided more by the social context of the moment than by a music goal. For example, none of the singing episodes initiated by adults resulted in a complete song performance; the singing often dissolved into verbal interactions that extended the communication triggered by the song. In fact, singing episodes were surrounded by and even interweaved into other forms of communication such as speech, nonsense vocalizations, and touch. Perhaps in this household, music was used as one more tool to establish communication, social bonding, and joint attention between the members of the family. The episode in which the mother sang to Emily while changing her diaper is a good example of the communicative nature of the shared musical experiences we observed. Mother and baby became immersed in an exchange of vocal sounds that developed easily and moved freely from singing to humming to talking to babbling and that evolved from a mother-initiated activity to a participatory dialogue. Not even Sasha's requests and questions could break the intimacy of this private "conversation" between Emily and her mother. It is clear that this singing episode was effective in establishing fluid communication and joint engagement between mom and baby even if it only lasted 35 seconds. Music educators may lament that the infants didn't have more opportunities to participate in the rich and engaging musical experiences we observed. But given that we know so little about the effects that the quantity or frequency of such experiences have on children's musical development and engagement, it is difficult to define what constitutes the "ideal musical environment."

The mother's overestimation of the amount and frequency of singing in the home raises an important question for researchers regarding the accuracy of parental reporting. Previous studies on children's soundscapes have been based on information provided exclusively by the parents through interviews, questionnaires, and diaries, as well as their self-selected videos and recordings of family musical activities (Barrett, 2009; Koops, 2014; Tafuri, 2009). Here we propose a methodology that provides a glimpse into young children's musical environment devoid of the interpretative lens of the parent. The unobtrusive observation of a home soundscape from the children's perspective may add a new dimension to our understanding of their musical environment and help us maximize the opportunities for music learning and music engagement afforded by young children.

As music educators, we may consider reaching out to parents and asked them to try to perceive their home soundscape from the perspective of their children. By listening to the sounds their children hear -- as opposed to the sounds they would like them to hear -- parents may become more aware of the opportunities for music participation they provide on a daily basis. The comparison of what they believe they do in terms of singing and other music activities to what they actually do, would help them set realistic expectations for themselves and shape the music home environment to match the one they envision for their family.

References

Barrett, M. S. (2009). Sounding lives in and through music: A narrative inquiry of the 'everyday' musical engagement of a young child. *Journal of Early Childhood Research, 7*, 115-134. doi: 10.1177/1476718X09102645

Costa-Giomi, E. & Merkow, C. H. (2014). It's child's play: playing with electronic music toys during the first years of life. In S. O'Neill (Ed.) *Music and Media Infused Lives: Music Education in a Digital Age*. CMEA/ACME Biennial Book Series on Research to Practice. Canadian Music Educators' Association: Toronto

Custodero, L. A., R. Britto, P., & Brooks-Gunn, J. (2003). Musical lives: A collective portrait of American parents and their young children.

Journal of Applied Developmental Psychology, 24, 553-572. doi:10.1016/j.appdev.2003.08.005

Custodero, L. A., & Johnson-Greeen, E. A. (2003). Passing the Cultural Torch: Musical Experience and Musical Parenting of Infants. *Journal of Research in Music Education, 51*, 102-114. doi: 10.2307/3345844

DeVries, P. (2007). The use of music CDs and DVDs in the home with the under-fives: what the parents say. *Australian Journal of Early Childhood, 32* (4), 18–21.

Hurtado, N., Marchman, V. A., & Fernald, A. (2008). Does input influence uptake? Links between maternal talk, processing speed and vocabulary size in Spanish-learning children. *Developmental Science, 11*(6), F31-F39. doi:10.1111/j.1467-7687.2008.00768.x

Ilari, B. (2005) 'On musical parenting of young children: musical beliefs and behaviours of mothers and infants'. *Early Child Development and Care, 175*, 647–60.

Koops, L. H. (2014). Songs from the car seat: exploring the early childhood music-making place of the family vehicle. *Journal of Research in Music Education, 62*, 52-65. doi:10.1177/0022429413520007

Lamont, A. (2008). Young children's musical worlds: Musical engagement in 3.5-year-olds. *Journal of Early Childhood Research, 6*, 247-261. doi:10.1177/1476718X08094449

Mehr, S. A. (2014). Music in the home: new evidence for an intergenerational link. *Journal of Research In Music Education, 62*, 178-88. doi:10.1177/0022429413520008

Merkow, C. H. (2013). Measurement of infants' behaviors with electronic music toys. *Texas Music Education Research*. Retrieved from http://www.tmea.org/resources/teaching-resources/research.

Otero, N., Hurtado, N., Weisleder, A., & Fernald, A. (2012). Linking Early Language Experience to Processing Efficiency in Low-and High-SES Spanish-Learning Infants in the U.S. and Mexico. Poster presented at the International Society for Infant Studies (ISIS) 2012

Tafuri, J. (2008). *Infant musicality: New research for educators and parents.* Surrey: Ashgate Publishing. ISBN 978-0-7546-6506-9.

Young, S. (2008) 'Lullaby light shows: everyday musical experience among under-two year- olds'. *International Journal of Music Education 26*, 33–46. doi: 10.1177/0255761407085648

Who is music education for? Student voices from plural communities

Andrea Creech
University College London, Institute of Education, London, UK

andrea.creech@ioe.ac.uk

Jo Saunders
University College London, Institute of Education, London, UK

jo.saunders@ucl.ac.uk

Graham F. Welch
University College London, Institute of Education, London, UK

graham.welch@ucl.ac.uk

Abstract

The research reported here, funded by English Music Hubs representing three plural Local Authorities, focuses on the student voice, interrogating student perceptions and experiences relating to the relevance of music education. "Plural" is a term used in discussions about how government policies might change when the population is so ethnically mixed that no one group is the majority. Some challenges have been noted with regards to the implementation of the English National Music Plan. In particular it has been argued that persistent barriers to student engagement with music education intersect with social, ethnic and geographic factors. Twenty-eight focus groups were carried out, involving a total of 112 students in Years 7, 8 and 9, from seven state secondary schools serving ethnically diverse communities. The focus groups were transcribed and an inductive thematic analysis was carried out, with emergent themes grounded in the words of the students themselves. Identification of themes was guided firstly by their perceived salience with regards to values in music education; and secondly by their predominance in the text. The analysis revealed some tensions in the discourses relating to the students' experiences and values in music education. While music was thought to be for everyone, a range of barriers prevented access for many students. Similarly, while music was valued within schools, students found they had difficult choices to make between music and other activities or subjects. Finally, while the wider benefits of music were valued, there were tensions with regards what counted as acceptable musicing. Overall, while music was valued and was clearly a part of students' family and community lives, there were many challenges in translating this into participation and engagement in formal music education. It is argued here that "student voice" must be at the heart of re-shaping the interpretation of a National Music Plan in such a way as to facilitate all students in navigating, and deeply engaging in, their rich musical landscapes, in and out of school.

Keywords: Multicultural, Inclusive Music Education, Student Voice

Introduction

"Plural" is a term used in discussions about how government policies might change when the population is so ethnically mixed that no one group is the majority. In England, within multicultural "plural" contexts, particular challenges have been experienced with regards the interpretation and delivery of the National Music Plan (NMP) (DfE & DMCS, 2011), which aims to "enable children from all backgrounds and every part of England to have the opportunity to learn a musical instrument; to make music with others; to learn to sing; and to have the opportunity to progress to the next level of excellence" (p.9). It has been argued, however, that the NMP is unevenly delivered, with its implementation characterised by fragmented progression routes and persistent barriers to access related to social, ethnic and geographic factors (Derbyshire, 2015). Critics argue, furthermore, that the NMP does not align well with principles of inclusion and that it promotes approaches to musical learning that downgrade informal learning and assume the existence of homogenous groups with common aims (Spruce, 2013). Finally, the integrity of the NMP has been debated, with some arguing that its underpinning values are compromised by the Department for Education's new English Baccalaureate proposals which exclude the arts from the compulsory subject areas for study at GCSE.

Since 2012, central government funding for implementation of the NMP in England has been channelled through 123 Music Hubs – "federations of local organisations with an interest in music education" (Ofsted, 2013). The core roles of Music Hubs are to: ensure that every child aged 5-18 has the opportunity to learn a musical instrument through whole-class ensemble teaching; provide opportunities to play in ensembles and perform; ensure clear progression routes are available and affordable to all young people; develop a singing strategy (ibid). However, the Office for Standards in Education, Children's Services and Skills (Ofsted) reported in 2013 that few Music Hubs were challenging and supporting school leaders to bring the benefits of music education to *all* students. Their report highlighted generally low expectations of students in music, lack of coherence between whole-class instrumental lessons and other music teaching in schools, little impact of singing strategies, as well as non-existent or irregular Music Hub/school partnership work.

Within England's multicultural context and in accordance with the principles of inclusion, it is therefore of crucial importance that Music Hubs develop deep understandings of how best to serve their communities, participants and stakeholders in music education. The research reported here, funded by Music Hubs representing three plural Local Authorities, focuses on the student voice, interrogating student perceptions and experiences relating to the relevance of music education.

Background

Increasingly, policy-makers, teachers and scholars within multicultural contexts have turned their attention to the idea of inclusive music education that welcomes students in to a diverse range of musical practices (Elliott and Silverman, 2015) and provides equitable access to music's wider benefits (Hallam, 2015) and creative career pathways (Gibb, 2015). Inclusive music education, in this sense, is thought to be underpinned by practices concerned with lifting barriers and shifting perceptions, structures and practices so as to "benefits the entire diversity of students" (Bahou, 2011, p.5).

Three principles of inclusive music education have been proposed (Spruce, 2013, p.117):

1. The right to be included in a music curriculum that respects and meets students' musical needs, interests and aspirations;
2. The right for students' voices to be included and heard;
3. The right to a curriculum that includes a diversity of musical practices, cultures, and traditions, including those with which children themselves engage outside of school.

In accordance with Spruce's principles, a dynamic and inclusive multicultural curriculum offers scope for young people to engage in music-making that encompasses familiar as well as unfamiliar musical cultures (ibid). Several benefits of such a curriculum have been highlighted. For example, students stand to benefit musically from exposure to a wide palette of sounds and musical idioms. A multicultural music curriculum may also foster intercultural understanding, whereby students learn that there are many diverse yet equally valid and sophisticated forms of musical expression and musical construction, around the globe (Anderson & Campbell, 2010).

Successful delivery of a multicultural curriculum is thought to be reliant upon knowledge of the musical cultures and activities in which students are involved, in-school as well as out-of-school (Cooke, 2011). In this vein, Derbyshire (2015) highlights that an inclusive music education land-scape must accord equal status to informal, non-formal and formal musical contexts and progression routes, providing young people with the infor-mation and resources that will support informed choices relating to en-gagement with music education. However, Elliott and Silverman (2015, p.449) caution that an approach is required that is inclusive in preserving the integrity of diverse musical cultures and practices, yet also expansive in that it "goes beyond local preferences and ethnocentric notions of music".

Student voice

"Student voice" conceptualises students as "expert witnesses" (Flutter & Rudduck, 2004, p.4) in research concerned with educational experiences and change (Bahou, 2011). Student voice can contribute to "a cultural shift that opens up spaces and minds not only to the sound but also to the pres-ence and power of students" (Cook-Sather, 2006, p.363). In its most par-ticipatory version, student voice can empower students, acting as a vehicle for shaping their own education in line with their aspirations, social and cultural lives and needs (Smyth, 2006).

In the context of plural communities, student voice offers an opportunity to interrogate the student perspective with regards to experiences and val-ues in music education and the ways in which these may intersect with cultural background or ethnicity. Accordingly, the research reported here focuses on student voice in exploring the relevance of the NMP as imple-mented within these multicultural communities, and the extent to which it potentially "looks unfamiliar, unattractive or out of reach to many stu-dents" (Silva, 2001, p.98).

Methods

Twenty-eight focus groups, exploring student perceptions and experiences relating to the value and place of music education in their lives and com-munities, were carried out. The focus groups comprised students (total n = 112) recruited through seven case study state secondary schools in three "plural" English Local Authorities. Six of the seven schools were mixed gender, while one was boys only. The seven schools had demographic pro-files that included high proportions of students with English as a second language; high proportions of students from poor socio-economic back-grounds and high proportions of students with special educational needs.

The students were in Years 7, 8 and 9 and therefore entitled to music as a compulsory curricular subject. The participants in the focus groups were selected by Heads of Music in the seven case study schools, the criteria being that they should be representative of the ethnic profile of the school and that they should include students who had demonstrated a range of levels of engagement with extra-curricular music.

The focus groups were recorded and later transcribed. The interview transcripts were imported into NVivo, a qualitative software analysis tool. A thematic analysis was carried out, the rationale being that this is a flexible tool for analysis of qualitative data, with the potential to yield complex and nuanced accounts. Identification of themes was guided firstly by their perceived salience with regards to values in music education; and secondly by their predominance in the text (Braun and Clarke, 2006). An inductive approach was taken, with emergent themes grounded in the words of the students themselves. Segments of text were coded under each theme; these chunks of coded text are referred to as 'coded references' in the findings, below. The initial coding structure, monitored by two additional researchers, was subsequently organised into overarching discourses and agreed amongst the research team.

Findings

The focus groups revealed some competing discourses relating to the students' experiences and values in music education (Figure 1). The following sections will set out examples of each of these pairs of ideas.

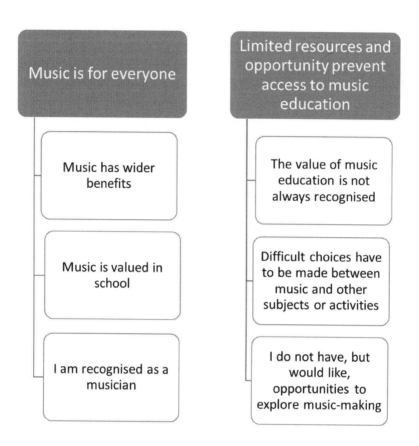

Figure 1. Overarching themes

"Music is for everyone" vs "limited resources and opportunity prevent access"

The idea that *music is for everyone* was articulated within every focus group, with a total of 249 coded references. As one student said, "everyone, somehow, will always find a different type of music through their life" (Y9 student). There was a widespread and predominant view that music was universal and that everyone could participate, in schools, homes and communities. "It's universal ... You can't go wrong. There's no wrong way" (Y9 students).

Students explained that they "grew up with music" (Y9 student) and that "we have like a tradition here that people like Indian music, so there's like

Harmonium, Tabla all together..." (Y8 student). Some students focused on the value of music-making in groups: "you can experiment with different ideas and what other people's tastes are" (Y9 student) while others spoke about music-making on their own: "I can freely do whatever I want and like put it in my own way" (Y8 student).

However, this view that "music is for everyone" was tempered with barriers to participation posed by limited resources: "yeah we can't do it because of the techno, we ain't got the techno, that's what we need though" (Y8 student). Intrapersonal and structural barriers were also highlighted. For example, students explained that "one of the main issues is that we're sort of left to our own devices ...I guess we need just a sort of push to get into it ... Afterwards everything is easy, but the first step is probably the hardest bit" (Y9 student).

For some students, learning musical instruments was something that only a few people had access to. "Only a few people got the chance." Some students thought they had already "missed the boat" and that starting to learn an instrument in secondary school was difficult. "I think because we didn't learn instruments at primary, it affected us because we didn't know like what we were good at" (Y9 student).

Limited financial resources was the most predominant barrier, with 50 coded references representing 27 focus groups. As one Year 9 student summarised: "I'd definitely be able to go and do it like outside of school, but it's like the money ...it's money I don't have" (Y9 student).

"Music has wider benefits" vs. "the value of music education is not always recognised"

Alongside the idea that *music is for everyone*, there was a strong and predominant view that *music has wider benefits*. One hundred and sixteen references were made, concerned with a belief in the wider benefits of music. However, an equally strong theme was that *the value of music education is not always recognised*", with 115 references that coded at this theme.

The most frequently cited benefit of music was its perceived potential to regulate emotions. Students explained that "when I'm sad I like listening to sad music and like, sometimes I listen to happy music and it changes my mood, like how I feel ..." (Y7 student). Furthermore, "you can actually like express your feelings, like you don't want to tell anyone else" (Y9 student).

Music was also thought to help to overcome social barriers. "Like, the more you get to like learn about music it's like the more you get to learn about other people as well" (Y8 student). Music-making offered opportunities for students to interact within new social groups: "It boosts people's confidence and it helps socialise with other people because you can work with other people in a group and you can have fun as well as doing something that's in school" (Y9 student). In this vein, musical activities offered a safe space for young people, where they could feel good about themselves. "I think it is important because it makes you feel good about yourself ... you get like a kind of happy buzz that feels good" (Y8 student).

Finally, there was also a widespread view that engagement with music had cognitive benefits, potentially enhancing students" academic performance in other subjects. "It helps with like academics too, multi-tasking, and surprisingly helps me with my maths homework (Y9 student).

Notwithstanding these attribution of wider benefits to music participation, there were some tensions. Students debated what was permissible in music-making, according to religious or cultural beliefs: "but they say, yeah, in our religion if you play with strings you're calling the Satan" (Y9 student). Some struggled to navigate competing values: "they disapprove a bit, but at the end of the day they can't really stop me from doing it because it's something I love and I'm not going to stop ... It's not really accepted in my religion, but it's something that I have a passion for" (Y9 student).

For some students, the transition from primary to secondary school had clearly been a vulnerable point. Owing to limited support for transition, many students had left instrumental learning behind. "I used to do some music when I was little but I stopped doing it because it is boring" (Y9 student). Others said they had lost interest in school music, generally. Some described secondary school music as "boring" and emphasised that they were "just not interested". "It kind of gets boring always, every day, like every lesson you've got to use piano all the time" (Y8 student).

"Music is valued in schools" vs. "difficult choices have to be made between music and other subjects or activities"

A predominant view was that music was easier to access when it was in school. For some this was because other out-of-school commitments (e.g. Mosque) were a priority. "I know I'd like to play but it's after school and I can't" (Y8 student). For others it felt "safer" to be within their own schools. "Yeah if it was more school based, because you'd be around people more of your age and you kind of have a more insight of the people you know" (Y8 student).

However, students were often faced with difficult choices between participation in music and other extra-curricular activities or curriculum subjects. "I'm also kind of sad that I have to give up because I would love to continue" (Y9 student). Some explained that faced with choices for optional subjects in Y10, music did not have the status of other subjects: "some of my friends, they wanted to do a GCSE in music but they can't, because their parents said "oh do proper GCSEs" ... her dad said there's no point in music ..." (Y9 student).

'I am recognised as a musician' vs 'I do not have, but would like opportunities to explore music-making'

Finally, some young people articulated a strong musical identity and spoke about being recognised as a musician (132 coded references), contrasting with others who expressed a strong desire to access opportunities where they could explore their as-yet undeveloped musical identities (130 coded references).

Amongst those who elaborated on their musical identities, a range of extra-curricular musical activities were described, in and out of school. For example, one Year 8 student explained, "at this school we have a music club that you can go to and play some music at lunchtimes, I do that there and at home ... in extra music you play like Indian kind of like instruments, so like Harmonium and the Dahl and the Tabla and everything." Another student described her rich involvement in musical ensembles. "On Tuesdays it's so much fun, the concert band ... we do more challenging stuff that really like boosts ... like you wouldn't have done" (Y10 student).

Some described how they had taught themselves instruments at home. This involved experimenting with music technology or using on-line videos. "I teach myself. Basically I do like music production. I have like an iPad at home ... Yeah, like I make beats. That's what I do" (Y9 student).

A sense of making progress was a key factor in supporting continuing engagement with music-making. "I started from one finger playing with my thumb and now to well-advanced fret work and all of this ... It's really great, like I'll just sit there and listen to a song, I'll pick out the guitar part and then I'll pick out the drum part and whatever part. Like I listen to Reggae music and I like that, then I can move on to Pop, and then I can move on to any sort of music (Y10 student).

However, in contrast to those for whom music education could resonate with an established or developing musical identity, other pupils seemed to identify in a very limited way with music – although many expressed a wish to explore music-making. "Now what I think should happen, is that we create a kind of workshop for more concerts where people can go in and try a few instruments and maybe, and maybe find their inner passion for music" (Y7 pupil).

Conclusion

A predominant view amongst the students in these plural communities was that music, in its many and diverse forms, is for everyone and that wider benefits could be attributed to participation in music. Generally, neither lack of provision nor lack of interest amongst pupils was seen as the main barrier to participation. Rather, barriers to participation were posed by financial constraints; limited resources, unclear progression pathways on entry to secondary school, intrapersonal barriers and tensions relating to the value and status accorded to music education. Overall, while music was valued and was clearly a part of students' family and community lives, there were many challenges in translating this into participation and engagement in formal music education.

The insights articulated by students reinforce the view that socioeconomic factors intersect with engagement with formal music education, as expressed in the NMP (Derbyshire, 2015). Students within the plural communities represented in our research were navigating complex tensions, some of which related to debates around what 'counted' as legitimate and acceptable musical practices, others relating to the structures and interpersonal support that was needed to facilitate sustained engagement with music education. Plural communities offer a rich context for shaping an inclusive and multicultural music curriculum. In line with proposals for inclusive practice (Spruce, 2013) such a curriculum must have the *student voice* at its heart, with students as lead "reform participants" (Silva, 2001). Participatory student voice (Bahou, 2011) offers the potential for shaping the interpretation of the NMP in such a way as to facilitate young people in navigating rich and culturally diverse and musical landscapes, embracing musical challenges that acknowledge formal and informal musicing both in and out of school.

Acknowledgements

We gratefully acknowledge the support of Luton, Leicester and Slough Music Hubs. We also acknowledge the generosity of the many students who contributed to the research.

References

Anderson, W. M., & Campbell, P. S. (2010). *Multicultural perspectives in music education*. Lanham [Md.: Rowman & Littlefield Education.

Bahou, L. (2011). Rethinking the challenges and possibilities of student voice and agency. *Educate, Kaleidoscope Special Issue, January 2011*, 2-14.

Braun, V., & Clarke, V. (2006). Using thematic analysis in psychology. *Qualitative Research in Psychology, 3*(2), 77–101.

Cooke, C. (2011). Promoting an inclusive music classroom. In G. Spruce, N. Beech & J. Evans (Eds.), *Making music in the primary school: Whole class instrumental and vocal teaching.* (pp. 33-44). London: Routledge.

Cook-Sather, A. (2016). Sound, presence, and power: "student voice" in educational research and reform. *Curriculum Inquiry, 36*(4), 359-390.

Department for Education and Department for Media, Culture and Sport (DfE and DMCS) (2011). *The importance of music: A national plan for music education*. Retrieved 31 July, 2012 from http://publications.education.gov.uk/

Derbyshire, S. (2015). *Musical routes: A landscape for music education*. London: Royal Philharmonic Society.

Elliott, D. J., & Silverman, M. (2015). *Music matters* (Second ed.). New York: Oxford University Press.

Flutter, J., & Rudduck, J. (20014). *Consulting pupils: What's in it for schools?* London: Routledge Falmer.

Gibb, N., & Department for Education. (2015). Speech: Arts Council England's "cultural education challenge". Retrieved 17 November, 2015, from https://www.gov.uk/government/speeches/arts-council-englands-cultural-education-challenge

Hallam, S. (2015). *The power of music*. London: UCL Institute of Education for the Music Education Council.

Ofsted. (2013). *Music in schools: What hubs must do. The challenging conversation with schools*. Manchester: Office for Standards in Education, Children's Services and Skills.

Silva, E. (2001). Squeaky wheels and flat tyres: A case study of students as reform participants. *Forum, 43*(2), 95-99.

Smyth, J. (2006). Educational leadership that fosters 'student voice'. *International Journal of Leadership in Education, 9*(4), 279-284.

Spruce, G. (2013). 'The National Music Plan' and the taming of english music education. *Arts Education Policy Review, 114*(3), 112-118.

Music teacher biography and its impact on teaching practice

Christopher Dalladay

University of East London, UK

cdalladay@aol.com

Abstract

This paper describes research carried out as part of a wider doctoral study on 'the biography of music teachers, their understanding of musicality and the implications for secondary music education'. Music teachers will come from a range of diverse backgrounds, though research data would suggest that most seem to have been educated as 'classical' music performers, which will have an effect on what they perceive to be central competencies in the development of young musicians. In turn, this will determine, to some extent, what is taught and learned in the secondary music classroom. This study explores the impact of the biography of secondary music teachers as they seek to develop the musicianship of their pupils and present the activities in which the young people will be expected to participate. A mixed methods approach has been taken, including surveys, observation and interviews. Surveys amongst a sample of experienced and trainee teachers have produced a range of quantitative data on respondents' experience of and values related to music education; whilst qualitative data in the form of lesson observation notes and transcription of semi-structured interviews have been the result of working with a small sub-set of participants. The outcomes have suggested a clear link between biography and classroom practice, but that there are also other potential tensions which arise, such as in the subject knowledge development of practitioners as they move from musician to teacher. Implications for a variety of stakeholders in secondary music education include a consideration of the development of subject knowledge together with potential review of national and local education policy, the nature of undergraduate music study and the 'shape' of initial teacher training in England.

Introduction: 'setting the scene'

We can all be considered products of our biography as who we are is a result of the life-histories that we each possess, with all the cultural, experiential and relational aspects that contribute to them (Brofenbrenner, 1979; Welch, 2012; Woods, 1984). In addition, whilst there is little that one can do to alter our life-histories, we can be agents in recognizing and, if necessary, changing our biographies as they are formed and considering how far the experiences of the past need to impinge on the activity of the now and future (Tudge *et al*, 2009, discussing the work of Brofenbrenner). An important part of biography is that of identity: biography being the 'historical counterpart' of identity, and identity is shaped by our life-histories (DeNora, 2000; Harrison, 2008). Kidd and Teagle (2012) go further by arguing that we can mould our identities and that this can shape our future lives (Kidd & Teagle, 2012:78). It can further be argued that, for a teacher, there is a clear relationship between biography and identity, and classroom practice; that the former impacts and shapes the latter (Dalladay, 2014). The study described in this paper seeks to explore the possible impact a teacher's biography has on their practice in the classroom. Music teachers in England would seem to come from a quite limited range of the musical population as a whole with backgrounds principally as white, Western classical music performers and/or singers, going into teaching straight after studying for a degree, and whose education in music has come more from private tuition, extra curricular activities, and music services rather than from in-class school music education (Rogers, 2002; Welch *et al*, 2011; York, 2001). It is possible to discern from this how 'conservative' and academic many music teachers' development as musicians is likely to have been and that this can potentially pose difficulties in the classroom where the musical interests and experiences of young people are frequently more contemporary and less formalised (Dalladay, 2011; Macdonald *et al*, 2002). It is the hypothesis at the centre of this study that this may affect the content, delivery and attitude of teachers in schools and their overall understanding of the development of musicianship in young people which may well be part of the reason for the continuing criticism of pupil progress noted frequently by official bodies such as Ofsted (2009; 2012).

Research methods

As an initial stage in developing the research described in this paper, a series of twelve competencies required for the development of musicians was drawn up along with a further twelve contexts within which musicians develop. These were determined through debate with music teacher trainees entering on teacher training courses and through a study of the related literature (e.g. Department of Education, 2013; Green, 2002; Hallam, 2006; Hargreaves *et al*, 2002; MENC, 1994; Pflederer, 1963; Swanwick & Tillman, 1986). The musical competencies include the ability to (1) perform on a musical instrument, (2) develop compositions, (3) improvise, (4) use musical terminology appropriately, (5) read from staff notation, (6) sing, (7) use ICT to develop musical 'events', (8) perform by ear, (9) harmonize melodies, (10) have a general knowledge of a range of musics, (11) relate to the expressive content of music, and (12) aurally analyse relationships between sounds. The learning contexts include (1) from a teacher, (2) through performing with others, (3) stimulated by role models and musicians we admire, (4) from family and/or friends, (5) through regular practice, (6) by being a teacher to others, (7) through devising our own music, (8) through attending live musical performances, (9) through academic musical studies (gaining qualifications), (10) through listening to recorded music, (11) through performing to an audience, and (12) through jamming/improvising with others by ear.

The research question of the study was 'is there any relationship between what is taught in class music and a music teacher's biography?' The research involved a mixed-methods approach with a range of data sources:

1. An exploration with teachers and trainees of the competencies for developing musicians and the contexts in which musicians develop with the resultant 'lists' described above;

4. The prioritisation/ranking of the competencies and contexts for importance according to personal values by participants (n=39, the 'sorting activity' participant group - SPG); these activities have been termed the 'sorting' activities;

5. A more general exploration of views on musicianship, music education (including one's own education and background) and personal philosophies on the place of music through a survey (n=64);

6. In-depth exploration of 'practice' through observation of teaching, using a unique observation 'tool' (n=11, the core participant group - CPG). The observation tool allowed for notes to be made by the observer and a timeline to be created on how far various aspects were evident. In addition, during observations, each competency was given an 'observed significance score' (OSS) where a score of 1 was awarded if the competency/context was evident in the lesson but not a major feature (e.g. short or cursory). A score of 2 was awarded where the competency/context was evident and with a degree of significance (e.g. singing takes place but with little emphasis on improvement), and a 3 awarded where it was strongly evident in the lessons.

7. Semi-structured interviews to explore the relationship between life history/musical development and practice observed in the classroom (n=10, selected from the observed group above). Interviews were recorded on audio with semi-transcriptions being made with time-coding for ease of location within the recording.

The participants have principally included Post-Graduate Certificate in Education (PGCE) and Graduate Training Programme (GTP) teacher trainees from a London Initial Teacher Education (ITE) provider, together with their music teacher-mentors within practice placement schools from the provider's secondary ITE partnership.

An exploration of the participants' understanding of musicality and the extent to which musicianship was being developed in the classroom became a central element within the research study. Other studies would suggest that personal biography can impact on values and, in particular, on the priorities of music education (e.g. performing, reading notation) (Burnard, 2011; Georgii-Hemming, 2011; Spruce, 2012).

Research findings and discussion

The mean rankings of the musical competencies and the learning contexts of the 'Sorting Participant Group' (SPG) have been compared with the observed significance rankings of each of the same competencies and contexts in teaching observation of the 'Core Participant Group' (CPG). The results of this comparison can be seen in Table 1.

Of note when considering the data at table 1, for example, is the case of 'the use of ICT to develop and enhance musical events': the SPG placed this musical competency in the lowest position, yet, in teaching and learning in practice amongst the CPG, it would seem to take on much more significance – 4th position (though, with quite a low mean 'observed significance score' (OSS) of 1.0).

Table 1: A comparison of the perceived importance of musical competencies and learning contexts with observed significance scores (OSS) in class music lessons (1=High, 12=low); also showing the percentage of participants placing aspects in the top 3 ranking positions (T3R%) and the relative mean OSS (max.3).

Musical competences	Sorting Activity mean rank (T3R%)	Sorting Activity overall ranking	OSS ranking (mean OSS /3)	Learning contexts	Sorting Activity mean rank (T3R%)	Sorting Activity overall ranking	OSS ranking (mean OSS /3)
Performing on an instrument	3.21 (64)	1	1 (2.0)	Performing with others	4.28 (39)	1	2 (1.5)
Performing 'by ear'	3.97 (46)	2	2 (1.5)	Regular music practice	4.36 (44)	2	7 (0.8)
Singing with accurate intonation	4.23 (56)	3	7 (0.5)	A teacher (class or instrument)	4.38 (51)	3	1 (2.6)
Aural analysis between sounds	4.52 (56)	4	7 (0.5)	Listening to recorded music	5.31 (36)	4	5 (0.9)
Composing	4.67 (36)	5	6 (0.7)	Role models / musicians I admire	5.54 (28)	5	3 (1.4)
Improvising	5.05 (33)	6	9 (0.4)	Family and/or friends	5.59 (39)	6	4 (1.0)
General knowledge of range of musics	5.69 (39)	7	3 (1.1)	Performing to an audience	5.67 (26)	7	5 (0.9)
Relate to expressive content	6.15 (33)	8	11 (0.1)	Attending live musical perfs.	5.92 (26)	8	8 (0.5)
Reading from staff notation	6.67 (13)	9	9 (0.4)	Being a teacher to others	7.03 (15)	9	11 (0.3)
Use of musical terminology	7.46 (21)	10	5 (0.9)	Jamming / improvising	7.12 (15)	10	11 (0.3)
Harmonization of melodies	8.03 (8)	11	12 (0.0)	Composing	7.18 (18)	11	10 (0.7)
Use of ICT to develop music	8.10 (10)	12	4 (1.0)	Academic musical studies	7.87 (18)	12	8 (0.5)

[The relative mean has been taken as an average across all lessons observed, where 'null' OSSs are counted a zero.]

Again, there is a difference in the place of singing, with most participants regarding this as an important musical competency (3rd in ranking with 56% of participants ranking the activity in the top 3 positions), yet comparatively little singing was observed in lessons – ranked in 7th position and with an OSS of 0.5. Performing on a musical instrument is consistently ranked in 1st position in terms of both personal values and observed significance, though it is, perhaps, notable that in most observed lessons, performing was restricted to the electric keyboard but that aspects of keyboard performance technique (e.g. fingering, phrasing) were rarely observed being covered; hence a mean OSS of just 2.0.

Other data would suggest that, in some cases, there does seem to be a clear link between the results presented in table 1 and teacher biography. The data to support this assertion largely comes from post-observation interviews with the CPG but also, to a lesser extent, from survey data. This is particularly the case (in the examples above) for singing and performing, and even the position of composing, but less the case for ICT for which other reasons may be likely for the discrepancy between value and practice (e.g. the desire to make use of equipment in which a large amount of investment has been made). The vast majority of the trainees' and teachers' participant group (n=55) come from a background in which instrumental performance has been a significant part of their training as musicians. 100% of the participants have had some training on a musical instrument and/or the voice with 57% as 1st or 2nd study pianists and 45% as vocalists (20% as 2nd study only within the CPG). 64% of the sample attained at least Grade 8 on their instrument (from, for example, the Associated Board of the Royal Schools of Music) and 78% started to learn their instrument before the age of 12. This data would tend to corroborate that of previous studies (e.g., Rogers, 2002; York, 2001). In contrast to these findings, 45% of the sample acknowledge that they have composed music for amateur or professional public use with fewer positive responses from Western classically trained musicians than other-than-classically trained musicians (50% by number within each group in the CPG) by a factor of nearly 1:2.

Focusing on the Core Participant Group who had been observed and interviewed, most had taken a traditional music/ music performance first degree though one had a degree related to 'world' music and another did not have a degree related to music at all. Half were from a classical music background and the rest from a contemporary popular music background.

Many of the group talk of having picked up musical instruments at quite a young age with other members of the family acting as a catalyst and then playing in school and local music service groups throughout primary and secondary school ages. Some have developed a profile which has included performing in community music groups such as brass bands and some continue to do so. Several speak rather disparagingly of their secondary school 'standard' music-class education (50%) though all have participated in a selection of extra-curricular musical activities at school. There was a more positive response, however, in the survey to the question, "I usually enjoyed music lessons in key stage 3 when a pupil at school" (60% strongly agreeing) than to the question, "My secondary school music teachers were very good at helping less musical pupils to develop" (20%). In terms of influence from families, all but one participant attested to family members being musicians or being a strongly influential figure in their musical development.

It is, perhaps, worth noting at this point that those participants who had 'dabbled' most widely in musical genres and traditions in their development (30%), would seem to have a more 'open' and less 'traditional' approach to music education. One, for example, who had experienced periods of non-attendance whilst at secondary school and differences with teachers, some family support issues and long periods of music-making with peers disconnected from education and family circles completely, had in observation a highly creative, practical approach in which student views were important and music making came alive for them by introducing activities which they found relevant and motivating. Again, another participant, with a background in an eclectic mix of popular, folk and world musics, wanted the students in his classes to enjoy the social aspects of music-making through developing group as well as individual, improvisation and performing activities based on traditions such as West African drumming and with an interest in developing inclusivity and authenticity.

During the course of this study, five aspects related to the effectiveness of secondary music teachers have suggested themselves: (1) the subject knowledge of the teachers, (2) their understanding of musicality, (3) processes and practices prevalent in individual schools, (4) curricular issues, and (5) teachers themselves understanding the impact of their own biographies on classroom delivery and lesson content. Looking at some of the life-histories of teachers can have a profound impact on what we and they can understand of their own interaction with music and their students (Barrett & Stauffer, 2012; Pitts, 2012). It has also become evident that those who have grown up with music from an early age (especially as Western classical musicians) can tend to have a 'narrower' view of what a musician looks like. This is evidenced, for example, in the participant who comes from a very musical home (mother is a music teacher) who entered her teacher training year with a 'narrow-minded' (her words) image, though her view of musicianship has changed over the year. This contrasts with another participant, not from a particularly musical home, who has a broad image of a musician, supporting all his students to reach their full potential including using ICT to support those who do not play an instrument.

Perhaps, one of the most significant aspects to come out of this study has been that of the subject knowledge of the music teacher: 'classical' musicians who struggle to include more contemporary styles within their teaching or ICT in a musical way; a non-keyboard player (a woodwind specialist) who struggles to support pupils working on electric keyboards in lessons; music technology or contemporary musicians who find it a challenge to support pupils in musical theory and score reading. However, the routines and practices of schools can also be problematic when teaching music. Data from this research has suggested that, on average, just 57% of lesson time is devoted to teaching and learning related to any one or more of the musical competencies with much of the rest of the time being taken up with practices such as setting and reviewing targets, ensuring that exercise books have notes in them and issues such as behaviour management.

Figure 1 shows a framework for the development of the music teacher identity which has been suggested by this current research study and which might form a point of consideration when planning for the training of music teachers and their continuing professional development, as well as act as a vehicle to stimulate reflection by teachers themselves.

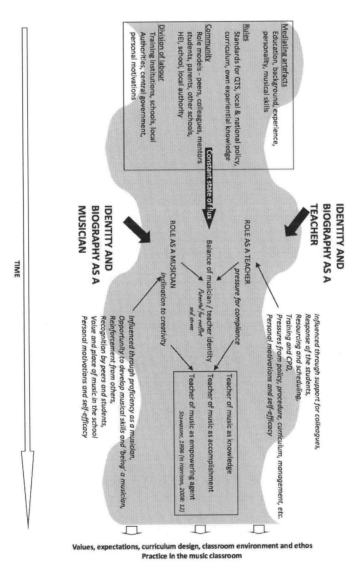

Figure 1. A model of the developing musician-teacher identity

Implications

There are a wide range of implications for an equally wide range of 'stake-holders': teachers, universities and conservatoires, initial teacher education, schools and their managers, government and other official bodies.

One of the most clearly demonstrated issues arising from the research has been that of the subject knowledge and skills of the music teachers themselves. Most teachers have come from a background centred on Western classical music and instrumental performance skills, yet the curriculum as laid out in the National Curriculum (DfE, 2013) places considerable emphasis, for example, also on devising skills – composing and improvising. Activities related to the development of these skills are quite often observed in the classroom, yet the teachers do not always have the skills in composing to be able to teach it with confidence. For instance, one research participant, an experienced music teacher, set his pupils off on a composing task but without providing much guidance on the 'how' of composing. Even in developing performing-related activities, teachers can still be 'at a loss' as demonstrated by the participant described earlier who had no piano/keyboard skills struggling to support pupils in playing the electric keyboard. Universities, Conservatoires and ITE programmes, even employing schools themselves, need, perhaps, to pay greater regard to the broader skill-set required of music teachers than in some other musical professions. This may involve funding and time for continuing professional development (CPD), increased opportunities during ITE for subject knowledge development as well as pedagogical aspects, and timetabling and deployment of music teachers in schools.

Another important implication from this study would suggest that music teachers and those responsible for delivering ITE and CPD programmes need to pay greater regard to what teachers bring to the classroom in terms of biography, identity, values and understanding. Opportunity might be provided for those involved to reflect on these and how they might impact on, or offer bias to, the teaching and learning in their classrooms.

Thirdly and finally, the music curriculum in schools (and the preparation for teaching it in ITE programmes) may benefit from an increasing focus on musical competencies in the development of young peoples' musicianship. There is the view that our role as music teachers is to seek to develop musicians rather than present a range of music-related activities which simply give young people a 'taster' of the subject. More in-depth learning will frequently take place in extra-curricular activities, the instrumental/vocal lessons (which can be an additional financial burden to families and schools) and the work of music services and community music groups

– all of which can play an important role, but which might also result in promoting exclusivity rather than inclusivity (Wright, 2012).

References

Barrett, M. & Stauffer, S. (Eds.) (2012) Narrative soundings: an anthology of narrative inquiry in music education. New York: Springer.

Brofenbrenner, U. (1979) The ecology of human development: experiments by nature and design. Cambridge, MA: Harvard University Press.

Burnard, P. (2011) Rivers of musical experience: a tool for reflecting and researching individual pathways. In C. Harrison & L. McCullough (Eds.) Musical pathways. Solihull: National Association of Music Educators (NAME), 168-178.

Dalladay, C. (2011) The biography of music teachers and their understanding of musicality. Research in Secondary Teacher Education, 1 (1), 10-16.

Dalladay, C. (2014) The biography of music teachers, their understanding of musicality and the implications for secondary music education. Unpublished PhD Thesis: University of East London.

DeNora, T. (2000) Music in everyday life. Cambridge: Cambridge University Press.

Department for Education (DfE) (2013) The National Curriculum in England: framework document. London: Department for Education.

Georgii-Hemming, E. (2011) Shaping a music teacher identity in Sweden. In L. Green (Ed.) Learning, teaching and musical identity: voices across cultures. Bloomington: Indiana University Press, 197-209.

Goodson, I.F. & Ball, S.J. (Eds.) (1984) Defining the curriculum: histories and ethnographies. London: Falmer.

Green, L. (2002) How popular musicians learn: a way ahead for music education. Aldershot: Ashgate.

Green, L. (Ed.) (2011) Learning, teaching and musical identity: voices across cultures. Bloomington: Indiana University Press.

Hallam, S. (2006) Musicality, in McPherson, G. (Ed.) The child as musician. Oxford: Oxford University Press

Hargreaves, D., Lamont, A., Marshall, N. & Tarrant, M. (2002) Young people's music in and out of school: a study of pupils and teachers in primary and secondary schools. Retrieved 16/03/2005, page since removed.

Hargreaves, D.J., Miell, D.E. & Macdonald, R.A.R. (Eds.) (2012) Musical imaginations: multidisciplinary perspectives on creativity, performance and perception. Oxford: Oxford University Press.

Harrison, C. & McCullough, L. (Eds.) (2011) Musical pathways. Solihull: National Association of Music Educators (NAME).

Harrison, S.D. (2008) Music teacher attributes, identity and experiences. Saarbrucken: VDM Verlag Dr Muller.

Kidd, W. & Teagle, A. (2012) Culture and identity (2nd ed.). Basingstoke: Palgrave Macmillan

Macdonald, R., Hargreaves, D. & Miell, D. (2002) What are musical identities, and why are they important. In R. Macdonald, D. Hargreaves & D. Miell (Eds.) Musical Identities. Oxford: Oxford University Press, 1-20.

McPherson, G. (ed.) (2006) The child as musician. Oxford: Oxford University Press

MENC (1994) National Standards for music education. Reston: VA, The National Association for Music Education.

Office for Standards in Education (Ofsted) (2009) Making more of music: an evaluation of music in schools, 2005/08. London: Ofsted http://www.ofsted.gov.uk

Office for Standards in Education (Ofsted) (2012) Music in schools: wider still, and wider; quality and inequality in music education 2008-11. London: Ofsted http://www.ofsted.gov.uk

Pflederer, M. (1963) The nature of musicality. Music Educators Journal, 49 (6), 49-52.

Pitts, S. (2012) Chances and choices: exploring the impact of music education. Oxford: Oxford University Press.

Philpott, C. & Spruce, G. (Eds.) (2012) Debates in music teaching. London: Routledge.

Rogers, R. (2002) Creating a land with music: the work, education and training of professional musicians in the 21st century. London: Youth Music.

Spruce, G. (2012) Musical knowledge, critical consciousness and critical thinking. In C. Philpott & G. Spruce (Eds.) Debates in music teaching. London: Routledge, 185-196.

Stowasser, H.M. (1996) Creative students need creative teachers. 100 Years of Music: Centennial Conference of the Faculty of Music,

The University of Melbourne, 1895-1995, pp. 545-555, Centre for Studies in Australian Music.

Swanwick, K. & Tillman, J. (1986) The sequence of musical development: a study of children's composition. British Journal of Music Education, 3 (3), 305-339

Tudge, R.H., Mokrova, I., Hatfield, B. & Karnik, R. (2009) Uses and misuses of Brofenbrenner's Bioecological Theory of Human Development. Journal of Family Theory and Review, 1, 198-210.

Welch, G., Purves, R., Hargreaves, D. & Marshall, N. (2011) Early career challenges in secondary school music teaching. British Educational Research Journal, 37 (2), 285-315.

Welch, G. (2012) Musical creativity, biography, genre and learning. In D.J. Hargreaves, D.E. Miell & R.A.R. Macdonald (Eds.) Musical imaginations: multidisciplinary perspectives on creativity, performance and perception. Oxford: Oxford University Press, 385-398.

Woods, P. (1984) Teacher, self and curriculum. In I.F. Goodson & S.J. Ball (Eds.), Defining the curriculum: histories and ethnographies. London: Falmer, 239-261.

Wright, R. (2012) Policy and practice in music education: a sociological perspective. In C. Philpott & G. Spruce (Eds.) Debates in music teaching. London: Routledge, 20-32.

York, N. (2001) Valuing school music: a report on school music. University of Westminster & Rockschool Ltd.

Factors Influencing Independent Instrumental Music Teachers' Use of Improvisation and Composition Activities with Young Students

Francis Dubé
Faculty of Music, Laval University, Québec City, Canada

francis.dube@mus.ulaval.ca

Isabelle Héroux
Department of Music, UQAM, Montréal, Canada

heroux.isabelle@uqam.ca

Noémie L. Robidas
ISDAT, Toulouse, France

noemie.robidas@isdat.fr

Benjamin Bolden
Faculty of Education, Queen's University, Kingston, Canada

ben.bolden@queensu.ca

Susan O'Neill
Faculty of Education, Simon Fraser University, Vancouver, Canada

sao@sfu.ca

Abstract

Research has demonstrated that it is advantageous for young music learners to engage in improvisation and composition activities. However, such creative activities remain largely absent in instrumental music teaching practices. This article reports survey research carried out with 130 independent instrumental music teachers in the province of Quebec in Canada. The study was designed to explore the extent to which teachers engage beginning instrumentalists in improvisation and composition activities; the degree to which teachers find improvisation and composition activities relevant; factors that influence teachers' use of improvisation and composition; the reasons why some teachers do not include these approaches in their pedagogical practice; and the extent to which teachers have experimented with improvisation and composition in their own instrumental practice. Data were analyzed using descriptive statistics and non-parametric tests (Chi-Square: Gamma and V of Cramer tests).

Improvisation. 78.9% of the teachers reported having previous experience with improvisation and 59.3% engaged in their own improvisation activities more than once a week or at least once a month. Male teachers reported more frequency in improvisation activities compared to female teachers. 70.4% of the teachers think it is very relevant or relevant to integrate improvisation activities into the teaching of young instrumentalists. This belief was found to be stronger among male teachers than female teachers. However, only 28.7% of the teachers reported including improvisation activities each week or each month in their teaching.

Composition. 83.1% of the teachers had composed their own music. However, their practice of composing was much less frequent than improvising; 36% of the teachers practised improvisation at least once a week, whereas only 9.6% composed. Male teachers reported composing more often than female teachers. 56.2% of the teachers felt it was relevant or very relevant to carry out composition activities with young instrumentalists. (This view was significantly higher among male teachers than among females.) However, 86.8% of the teachers engaged students in composition activities only a few times a year or not at all.

Through qualitative thematic analysis of survey responses we identified four main reasons why teachers do not engage students in improvisation and composition activities: 1) they do not feel competent enough to integrate improvisation/ composition in their teaching; 2) they do not have time to integrate improvisation/ composition activities into their lessons; 3) they are not interested in improvisation/ composition; 4) they do not believe that the student is at an advanced enough level on the instrument to improvise/ compose.

Keyword: Improvisation, Composition, Pedagogy, Instrumental Music Teachers, Young Students

Introduction

Several researchers over the past decade have investigated integrating creative music activities such as improvisation and composition into formal notation-based music teaching practices. For example, studies have concluded that learning to improvise can promote the acquisition of certain musical concepts (McPherson, 1993), precision in reading music (Azzara, 1992; Montano, 1983), a sharpening of auditory perceptions (Teixeira dos Santos & Del Ben, 2004; Whitman, 2001; Wilson, 1971), creativity

(Koutsoupidou & Hargreaves, 2009), as well as the quality of interpretation (Azzara, 1992). Composition has been seen as a meaning-making process and a means of expressing one's self emotionally and creatively, with studies suggesting that composition helps to promote and demonstrate musical thinking and students' understanding and development of higher order thinking skills (Barrett, 2003; Gromko, 2003; Hickey, 2003; Kaschub & Smith, 2009; Lewis, 2012; Miller, 2012; Moore 2003; Stauffer, 2003). Composing also promotes curiosity, courage, openness, observation, interpretation, reflection and risk taking (Miller, 2012). Moreover, the composition process reinforces understanding of musical concepts (Guderian, 2012; Miller, 2004; Miller, 2012; Stevens, 2011), and provides authentic opportunities for learners to apply the knowledge and skills they learn in theory workbooks and exercises (Miller, 2012).

Given the many positive effects of such activities on students' learning, we were interested in collecting information from independent instrumental music teachers in the province of Quebec in Canada about the pedagogical practices they use with young students that are related to improvisation and composition. This article reports this research and some of the key findings.

Improvisation

Improvisation in music can be defined as an instrumental or vocal realization in which a musician generates the musical material in real time while being capable of anticipating the sonoral consequences of his or her actions on the basis of past experiences (Dubé & Després, 2013). As we have mentioned, previous research suggests that integrating improvisation into music pedagogy will provide positive effects on a number of aspects of student development (Azzara, 1992; Kenny & Gellirich, 2002; Koutsoupidou & Hargreaves, 2009; McPherson, 1993; Teixeira dos Santos & Del Ben, 2004). Given the positive effects of improvisation and its interdependence with other competencies that an apprentice musician needs to develop, it seems likely that improvisation would be an integral part of the classical music curriculum. However, this is not the case (McPherson, Bailey, & Sinclair, 1997). Indeed, improvisation is almost absent from Western classical instrumental teaching (Azzara 2002; Bitz, 1998; Burrows, 2004). Various reasons have been offered for this situation. One reason relates to the value placed on reproduction of musical notation in Western classical music that requires musicians to be interpreters with great technical skills (Biesenbender, 2001; Riveire, 1997). Teachers often believe that the effort required to achieve technical skills leaves little time for working on other activities, such as improvisation (Robidas, 2010). Another reason is that teachers may lack the knowledge and skills necessary to teach improvisation to their students, especially if they had no experience of improvisation during their own training (Robidas, 2010).

Composition

Composition is the process of creating a new piece of music. There are thought to be wide-ranging benefits (musical, social, intellectual and emotional) for young children who learn how to compose (Barrett 2003; Hickey, 2003). For instance, the composition process challenges students to think creatively (Barrett, 2003; Hickey, 2003; Miller, 2012; Moore, 2003). Stauffer (2003) says that young composers begin this creative process from a place inside of themselves that represents the whole of who they are at that particular moment. In other words, students' compositions are meaningful to them as their work is directly related to their actions, feelings and thoughts – a reflection of their experiences (Gromko 2003; Stauffer, 2003).

Despite the acknowledged benefits of including composition in music learning (Barrett 2003; Gromko 2003; Moore 2003), there is evidence to suggest that it remains largely absent in instrumental music teaching practice (Stevens, 2011). Research indicates that there are two primary factors hindering music teachers from including composition: time restrictions and lack of teacher confidence or experience with composing (Hickey, 2003; Lewis 2012; Robinson, Bell, & Pogonowski, 2011; Stevens, 2011; Winters, 2012). Even though the past decade was characterized by a large increase of research on composing in the classroom context (Armstrong, 2012; Bolden, 2007; Bush, 2007; Espeland, 2003; Gromko, 2003; Guderian, 2012; Hickey, 2003; Kaschub & Smith, 2009; Lapidaki, 2007; Randles & Sullivan, 2013; Rutlumann, 2007; Saetre, 2011; Strand, 2007; Strand & Newberry, 2007; Strand, 2009; Wiggins, 2003; Winters, 2012), far less attention has been given to research on composition teaching and learning in the context of individual music lessons with young children (Barrett & Gromko, 2007; Miller, 2012; Stevens, 2011). There is thus a need for further research in this area.

Context for the Study

In Quebec, instrumental music teachers of young people work most often in private studios or private music schools. They follow instructional programmes offered by a number of organizations in Quebec (for example, the Anna-Marie Globenski Preparatory School of Laval University and the Music Preparatory School of the University of Quebec in Montreal). These programmes are divided into goal-oriented grades and students typically complete one grade per year. On the whole these programmes reflect a very traditional approach to music teaching, consisting of classical music solo repertoire from the Baroque period to the twentieth century, a strong emphasis on instrumental technique (scales, arpeggios), sight-reading exercises, and so on.

Since, for the most part, these programmes do not encourage instrumental music teachers to integrate improvisation and composition activities into their teaching practice, it seemed important to discover whether teachers in Quebec were in fact engaging students in composing and improvising activities. Given the benefits of integrating improvisation and composition activities into students' music learning, such as motivation, acquisition of skills, and musical and personal development, we see a pressing need for a systematic study designed to explore the use of such practices by instrumental music teachers in Quebec. We hope that the results of this study will aid in the rethinking of music teaching practices and training programmes for instrumental music teachers.

Research Questions

The main aim of the study is to determine the factors that influence independent instrumental music teachers' use of improvisation and composition activities with young students in their teaching practice. More specifically, we targeted teachers in Quebec, Canada who provide individual instruction to students (aged 5 to 10 years) outside of their elementary schools. We were interested in addressing five key areas:

o The extent to which teachers use improvisation and composition;

o The degree to which teachers find improvisation and composition activities relevant in teaching five-to-ten-year-olds who are beginning a musical instrument;

o The factors that influence teachers' use of improvisation and composition;

o The reasons why some teachers do not include these approaches in their pedagogical practice;

o The extent to which teachers have experimented with improvisation and composition in their own instrumental practice.

Method

The data was collected in the winter of 2014, using an online questionnaire sent to independent instrumental music teachers in Quebec who give individual lessons in a private studio or in the province's private music schools. To recruit teachers, we sent an email message to all the organizations in Quebec that sponsor music programmes outside the main school system and asked them to disseminate the information about the research project to their teaching members. We also used the database of the *Centre d'excellence en pédagogie musicale* of the Faculty of Music of Laval University. To verify the internal validity of the data collected, we piloted the questionnaire with five teachers and found that they understood the intention of the questions and were able to provide relevant information in response to the questions. The questionnaire was divided into four separate parts. The first part was designed to collect information about the personal profile of the teacher: age, gender, instrument taught, education and teaching experience, and the teaching programme used. The other two parts, namely those related to improvisation and composition, were designed to discover whether these teachers were already familiar with or had used these approaches and with what kind of frequency, and whether they found them relevant to teaching beginning instrumental students and, if so, the frequency with which they used them. Lastly, for those who did not use these approaches in their teaching, we asked them to explain briefly why they did not use them.

Most questions were answered using a Likert scale rated from 1 to 4. Data was analyzed using descriptive statistics and non-parametric tests (Chi-Square: Gamma and V of Cramer tests). Qualitative data, for its part, was analyzed using a thematic content analysis approach (Paillé & Mucchielli, 2012).

Participants

A total of 130 instrumental music teachers completed the questionnaire. Demographic and background information is shown in Table 1.

Table 1: Demographic data of respondents

Age	20 to 30 years 26.9%	31 to 40 years 34.6%	41 to 50 years 13.8%	More than 51 years 24.6%	
Teaching experi-ence	Less than 5 years: 10.8%	6 to 10 years: 25.4%	11 to 19 years: 22.3 %	20 to 29 years: 20%	More than 30 years: 21.5%
Gender[12]	Women: 80.8%	Men: 19.2 %			
Last academic qualification in music obtained	Diploma – Bachelor's De-gree: 59.3%	Graduate studies: 38.5%	Other: 2.3 %		
Formal music education cours-es	Yes: 60.8%	No: 39.2%			
Instrument taught	Piano: 62.3%	Other: 37.7 %			

Results

The results have been divided according to the two activities studied: im-provisation and composition.

Improvisation

The majority of the teachers (78.9%) reported having previous experience with improvisation as musicians. Furthermore, 59.3% of these teachers engaged in their own improvisation activities more than once a week or at least once a month. There was a significant gender difference between male and female teachers as to the frequency with which they used im-provisation, as shown in Figure 1. Male teachers reported more frequency in improvisation activities compared to female teachers, χ^2 =8.056 (df=3), p=0.045, V=0.306

---

[12] This division between females and males seems to be typical of the current situation in the field if one compares the list of the members of the Quebec Association of Music Teachers. For this reason, it was decided to present the significant statistical differences for any gender difference obtained.

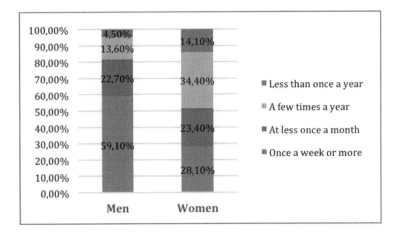

Figure 1. Frequency of male and female teachers' own improvisation activities

In relation to their teaching practice, the majority of instrumental music teachers (70.4%) think that it is very relevant or relevant to integrate improvisation activities into the teaching of young pupils who are beginning to study an instrument. This belief was found to be more relevant among male teachers than female teachers, χ^2 =13.337 (df=3), p=0.004, V=0.351. However, only 28.7% of the teachers reported including improvisation activities each week or each month in their teaching of young, beginner instrumentalists.

In order to identify the reasons why some teachers do not integrate improvisation activities into their teaching, we asked those who *never* use them in their teaching (28.7% of our sample) to share their reasons for not doing so. Through qualitative thematic analysis, we found four main reasons, as indicated below.

- o Reason 1: They do not believe they are competent enough to integrate improvisation in their teaching.

- o Reason 2: They do not have time to integrate improvisation activities into their lessons.

- o Reason 3: They are not interested in improvisation.

- o Reason 4: They do not believe that the student is at an advanced enough level on the instrument to improvise.

Composition

As in the case of improvisation, the majority of the teachers questioned (83.1%) had already composed some of their own music. However, their practice of composing was much less frequent than their improvising. Indeed, 36% of the teachers questioned practised improvisation at least once a week, whereas this percentage drops to 9.6% for composition. Further, our analysis revealed a significant gender difference between male and female teachers in the frequency of their composition activities, x^2=6.433 (df=1), p=0.011, V=0.278. Male teachers reported composing more often than female teachers.

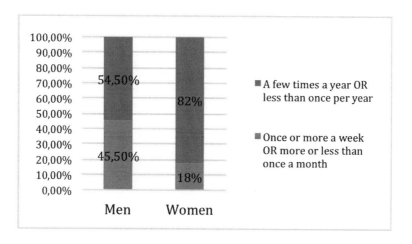

Figure 2. Relation between the frequency at which men and women compose

In terms of their teaching practice, 56.2% of the teachers reported that it was relevant or very relevant to carry out composition activities with young students beginning to learn to play an instrument.[13] This view was significantly higher among male teachers than among female teachers, x^2=4.471 (df=1), p=0.034, V=0.206.

As with improvisation, the teachers surveyed reported doing few composition activities with their beginning instrumental music students. In fact, 86.8% of our sample did composition activities only a few times a year or not at all with their students. However, 56.2% of teachers stated that it was relevant or very relevant for composition activities to be included in their students' programme of learning.

---

[13] The percentage was 70.4% for improvisation.

To better understand the reasons why some teachers do not integrate composition activities into their teaching, we asked those who *never* use them in their teaching practice (41.5% of our sample) to share their reasons for not including them. The reasons emerging from our thematic analysis were similar to those identified for not using improvisation.

- o Reason 1: They do not believe they are competent enough to integrate composition in their teaching.

- o Reason 2: They do not have time to integrate composition into their lessons.

- o Reason 3: They are not interested in composition.

- o Reason 4: They do not believe that the student is at an advanced enough level to compose.

Discussion

The aim of this study was to obtain a first level of knowledge about the use of improvisation and composition in the teaching practices of instrumental music teachers in Quebec who give individual lessons outside of school to young people aged five to ten years. Our results show that these teachers rarely use improvisation and composition with this student population, even if they consider these approaches to be relevant or indeed very relevant in terms of music teaching pedagogy. How are these results to be interpreted? We offer several possible explanations.

First, in referring to the comments of the teachers who never use improvisation or composition activities with their students, it can be seen that these are the teachers who state that they have not been trained to use these approaches with students. This finding supports the findings of previous studies (Azzara 2002; Bitz, 1998; Burrows, 2004; Robidas 2010). In fact, almost none of the Quebec institutions (faculties or departments of music, music conservatories) offer or require formal courses in improvisation or composition for students engaged in instrumental music study. Consequently, never having had experiences of this kind during their training, these teachers may have difficulty in forming a clear idea of what these approaches might look like when integrated into instrumental music instruction. They may also lack interest or understanding of relevance of these activities for teaching and learning to play an instrument.

We observed no significant difference between teachers who either use or do not use a specific teaching programme and the frequency at which they employ improvisation and composition in their instruction of young beginning students. Therefore, it does not appear to be the teaching pro-gramme per se limiting the teachers' use of these activities; rather, it is the value that the teachers ascribe to these kinds of activities, their lack of training, or their lack of tools that would enable them to use composition and improvisation with their students. These reasons emphasize the need for improvisation and composition activities to be included in music per-formance studies so that musicians who become involved teaching instru-mental music will appreciate the relevance of these activities and will be able to integrate them effectively into their teaching practice. Other rea-sons given by the teachers suggest that they place more value on the con-cepts and skills necessary to reproduce notated musical repertoire effective-ly than they do on improvisation based on playing by ear (without a score) or on activities involving composition.

Finally, teachers also suggested that they believe it is difficult or indeed impossible to improve students' instrumental music skills through the use of improvisation or to include the practice of composition with students who do not have a certain amount of music theory background. And yet, growing evidence indicates that it is quite possible and even useful for be-ginning students to practise various kinds of improvisation and to compose music, especially with the aid of music technologies; and, as was stated earlier, doing so can reinforce the acquisition of musical concepts (Guder-ian, 2012; Miller, 2004; Miller, 2012; Stevens, 2011).

It is also noteworthy that significant gender differences were found be-tween male and female teachers in both their personal practices of improv-isation and composition and in how they view the relevance of using these activities in teaching beginning instrumental music students. Male teach-ers reported experimenting more often with these kinds of activities in their personal music practice and they seem to find these activities more relevant to their teaching practice than the female teachers. However, we recognize the need for caution in interpreting this finding for various rea-sons. In particular, we point out that our sample comprised 80% female teachers and 20% male teachers. It is therefore possible that this strong representation of female teachers within the sample may have influenced the results. It is possible, for example that this result could be attributable to the respective experiences of male and female teachers during their own music education. Further research is needed to explore in more detail the music education experiences of instrumental music teachers in relation to their beliefs and practices about using improvisation and composition ac-tivities in the teaching and learning of young musicians.

Finally, even though some of our results are not surprising, the main contribution is to offer precise measures on several phenomena related to improvisation and composition pedagogy in extra-curricular music education context.

References

Armstrong, B. J. (2012). Niagara symphony's composer in the classroom. *The Recorder, 54*(3), 8–9.

Azzara, C. D. (1992). *The effect of audiation-based improvisation techniques on the music achievement of elementary instrumental music students* (Unpublished Ed. Doctoral dissertation). University of Rochester, Rochester, New York.

Barrett, M. S. (2003). Freedoms and constraints: Constructing musical worlds through the dialogue of composition. In M. Hickey (Ed.), *Why and how to teach music composition: A new horizon for music education* (pp. 3–27). Reston, VA: The National Association for Music Education.

Barrett, M. S., & Gromko, J. E. (2007). Provoking the muse: A case study of teaching and learning in music composition. *Psychology of Music, 35*(2), 213-230.

Biesenbender, V. (2001). *Plaidoyer pour l'improvisation dans l'apprentissage instrumental* (C. Barret, Trans.). Fondette, FR: Van de Velde.

Bitz, M. E. (1998). *A description and investigation of strategies for teaching classroom music improvisation* (Unpublished Ed. Doctoral dissertation). Columbia University Teachers College, New York City, New York.

Bolden, B. (2007). *Teaching composing in the classroom: what teachers know* (Unpublished Ed. Doctoral dissertation). University of Toronto, ON, CA.

Burrows, J. (2004). Resonances: Exploring improvisation and its implications for music education (Unpublished Doctoral dissertation). Simon Fraser University, B.-C., CA.

Bush, J. (2007). Composing and arranging in middle school general music. *General Music Today, 20*(4), 6-10.

Dubé, F., & Després, J.-P. (2013). Proposition d'un cadre conceptuel pour aider le professeur d'instrument à intégrer l'improvisation musicale à son acte pédagogique. *Intersections: Revue Canadienne de Musique, 32*(1-2), 143-166.

Espeland, M. (2003). The African drum: The compositional process as discourse and interaction in a school context. In M. Hickey (Ed.),

Why and how to teach music composition: A new horizon for music education (pp. 167–192). Reston, VA: The National Association for Music Education.

Gromko, J. E. (2003). Children composing: Inviting the artful narrative. In M. Hickey (Ed.), *Why and how to teach music composition: A new horizon for music education* (pp. 69–90). Reston, VA: The National Association for Music Education.

Guderian, L. (2012). Music improvisation and composition in the general music curriculum. *General Music Today, 25*(3), 6-14.

Hickey, M. (2003). Creative thinking in the context of music composition. In M. Hickey (Ed.), *Why and how to teach music composition: A new horizon for music education* (pp. 31–54). Reston, VA: The National Association for Music Education.

Kaschub, M. & Smith, J. (2009). Minds on music: Composition for creative and critical thinking. *Research and Issues in Music Education* 7(1), 3.

Kenny, B. J., & Gellrich, M. (2002). Improvisation. In R. Parncutt & G. McPherson (Eds.), *The science and psychology of music performance* (pp. 117-134). New York: Oxford University Press.

Koutsoupidou, T., & Hargreaves, D. J. (2009). An experimental study of the effects of improvisation on the development of children's creative thinking in music. *Psychology of Music, 37*(3), 251-278.

Lapidaki, E. (2007). Learning from masters of music creativity: Shaping compositional experiences in music education. *Philosophy of Music Education Review, 15*(2), 93-117.

Lewis, R. (2012). Composing the curriculum: Teacher identity. *British Journal of Music Education, 29*(2), 153-161.

McPherson, G. (1993). Evaluating improvisational ability of high school instrumentalists. *Bulletin of the Council for Research in Music Education, 119*, 11-20.

McPherson, G. E., Bailey, M., & Sinclair, K. E. (1997). Path analysis of a theoretical model to describe the relationship among five types of musical performance. *Journal of Research in Music Education, 45*(1), 103-129.

Miller, B. A. (2004). Designing compositional tasks for elementary music classrooms. *Research Studies in Music Education, 22*, 59-71.

Miller, B. A. (2012). Student composition in a private studio setting: Rethinking assumptions. In M. S. Barrett & S. L. Stauffer (Eds.), *Narrative soundings: An anthology of narrative inquiry in music education*, (pp. 305-327). New York: Springer.

Montano, D. R. (1983). *The effect of improvisation in given rhythms on rhythmic accuracy in sight reading achievement by college elementary group piano students* (Unpublished Doctoral dissertation). University of Missouri, Kansas City: Missouri.

Moore, B. (2003). The birth of song: The nature and nurture of composition. In M. Hickey (Ed.), *Why and how to teach music composition: A new horizon for music education* (pp. 193–207). Reston, VA: The National Association for Music Education.

Paillé, P., & Mucchielli, A. (2012). *L'analyse qualitative en sciences humaines et sociales*. Paris: Armand Colin.

Randles, C. & Sullivan, M. (2013). How composers approach teaching composition: Strategies for music teachers. *Music Educators Journal, 99*(3), 51-57.

Riveire, J. H. (1997). *California string teachers' curricular content and attitudes regarding improvisation and the national standards* (Unpublished D.M.A. dissertation). University of Southern California, US.

Robidas, N. (2010). *Élaboration d'un outil pédagogique facilitant l'intégration de l'improvisation dans l'enseignement du violon au cours des trois premières années d'apprentissage* (Unpublished Doctoral dissertation). Laval University, QC, Canada.

Robinson, N., Bell, C., & Pogonowski, L. (2011). The creative music strategy: A seven-step instructional model. *Music Educators Journal, 97*(3), 50-55.

Rutlumann, A. (2007). The composers' workshop: An approach to composing in the classroom. *Music Educators Journal, 93*(4), 38-43

Saetre, J. H. (2011). Teaching and learning music composition in primary school settings. *Music Education Research, 13*(1), 29-50.

Stauffer, S. (2003). Identity and voice in young composers. In M. Hickey (Ed.), *Why and how to teach music composition: A new horizon for music education* (pp. 91–112). Reston, VA: The National Association for Music Education.

Stevens, W. (2011). Tapping into creativity: Using composition to energize your studio. The American Music Teacher 61(1), 25-27.

Strand, K. (2007). 5 steps for leading students in classroom composing. *Teaching Music, 14*(5), 42-47.

Strand, K., & Newberry, E. (2007). Teachers share practical advice on classroom composing, *General Music Today, 20*(2), 14-19.

Strand, K. (2009). A narrative analysis of action research on teaching composition. *Music Education Research, 11*(3), 349-363.

Teixeira dos Santos, R. A. & Del Ben, L. (2004). Contextualized improvisation in solfège class. *International Journal of Music Education, 22*, 271–282.

Wiggins, J. (2003). A frame for understanding children's compositional processes. In M. Hickey (Ed.), *Why and how to teach music composition: A new horizon for music education* (pp. 141–166). Reston, VA: The National Association for Music Education.

Winters, M. (2012). The challenges of teaching composing. *British Journal of Music Education 29(1)*, 19-24.

Whitman, G. G. (2001). *The effects of vocal improvisation on attitudes, aural identification skills, knowledge of music theory, and pitch accuracy in sight-reading of high school choral singers* (Unpublished Doctoral dissertation). University of Missouri: Kansas City.

Wilson, D. S. (1971). *A study of the child voice from six to twelve* (Unpublished Doctoral dissertation). University of Oregon: Eugene.

"It does make a difference!" A follow-up CRDI study on contemporary music, music scores and aesthetic experience

Ana Lucia Frega
Academia Nacional de Educación, Argentina

analuciafrega@yahoo.com.ar

Ramiro Limongi
Music Department, National University for the Arts, Argentina

Dionisio Castro
Escuela Municipal de Bellas Artes "Carlos Morel", Subsecretaría de Educación y Participación Ciudadana; Secretaría de Gobierno, Educación y Seguridad; Intendencia Municipal de Quilmes, Florencia Varela, Argentina

mg.dionisiocastro@gmail.com

María Gabriela Galante
Music Department, National University for the Arts, Argentina

mggalante@hotmail.com

Abstract

CRDI (Continuous Response Digital Interface) studies on aesthetic responses to music have a long history. However, when regarding reception of non-traditional or avant-garde pieces, the field is still relatively new. A previous study with undergraduate music students revealed that new music, particularly that with the most original and perceptively harsh proposals, could yet be strongly rejected and incomprehensible. It was hypothesized that listeners found it so alien because they could not make sense out of the stimulus and, consequently, that music reading could lead to a significantly different experience. Introducing this variant, as a first stage, several possible designs were tested for a subsequent study. The present paper reports on this second phase where Music Education majors (N=30) listened to NN, a solo guitar piece by Argentinian composer Carlé Costa, while manipulating a CRDI dial. After having read the work's sheet music, this experience was repeated. Pre- and post-reading CRDI curves are compared and results interpreted in the light of answers to exit questionnaires that reflect on both the CRDI-listening experience and that which combines listening and reading. Generalizations should be avoided, particularly because of the nature of certain aesthetic proposals and their place in a cultural context,. However, it could be affirmed that, in the case of NN, the use of the music score provided a more meaningful listening experience, thus enhancing the subjects' aesthetic response to it.

Keywords: aesthetic response to music, CRDI, new music, music reading, meaningful listening

Introduction

In the last thirty years, CRDI (Continuous Response Digital Interface) studies on aesthetic responses to music have been extensive, varied, and fruitful (Madsen, 2011). However, as far as we are aware, issues regarding responses to contemporary music stimuli had not previously been addressed.

Selection of well-known pieces or excerpts, or, in any case, proposals that are at least clearly inserted within Western tonal traditions, has been an explicit choice of researchers using this tool in relation to aesthetic experiences (Madsen, Byrnes, *et al.*, 1993; Madsen, 2011).

Likewise, in 2012, replications of already published pieces of research were proposed in the context of a relatively newly transformed Argentinian university, both in order to explore equivalences between U.S. musicians and music students and our local counterpart, and to introduce research perspectives in an institution with almost a century of Conservatoire performing and composing tradition.

Soon after this initial and rewarding stage (Castro *et al.*, 2013; Galante & Limongi, 2013; Galante, 2014), a certain void was detected when considering reception of avant-garde music. This presented a relatively new field to be explored.

On the other hand, Frega (1997) has largely researched the perception of music scores with so-called "alternative signs" to traditional staff notation.

The first design was the same as previous studies, moving the CRDI stimulus to a really challenging solo guitar piece, NN, by Argentinian composer Carlé Costa. The composition employs extended techniques that considerably alter the instrument's timbral identity, and adopts some of the most demanding grammatical aspects of the 20th-century music, as well as its harshest aesthetic features (Carlé Costa, 2015).

Because of the radical divergence with other instances in this line of research, an extra item was added in the exit questionnaire that followed CRDI manipulation [*Do you consider having listened to the music?*] (see Madsen, Brittin, and Capperella-Sheldon, 1993, p. 63; Limongi *et al.*, 2014, p. 202). Even with that in mind, preliminary results were shocking. Many students strongly rejected this music that felt unusually alien to them. This probably happened because, besides any specific school training, when listening to tonal music, music students count on every tool provided by cultural experience and plenty of opportunities for (informal) music making and learning. On the contrary, although contemporary music has gradually gained a place within curricula, and higher education schools provide occasional chances to perform in new music ensembles, non-traditional musical aesthetics are still unfamiliar (Phelps, 2014).

At that point, we hypothesized that outraged listeners could make little sense out of the stimulus. Therefore, it was decided to introduce a methodological variant and, since the study focuses on undergraduate music majors, explore the effects of music reading on aesthetic response.

Although the NN score is as experimental as the music itself, presenting graphic notation beyond any established convention (Figure 1), our hypothesis was that responses would change with the additional visual representation.

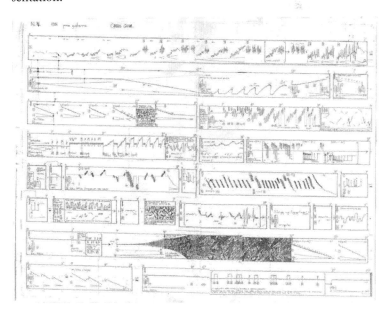

Figure 1. NN by Carlé Costa (music score).

The new elements of the sheet music and a new questionnaire (see Limongi *et al.*, 2014, p. 202) reflecting on the music reading experience, demanded a new sequential design for data gathering. Through trial and error, several possibilities were tested in different contexts, including students at Music Education programmes in different institutions. A preliminary report on this stage (Limongi *et al.*, 2014) was presented at the ISME Research Commission Seminar 2014. Since the sample for this study was too small to attempt reliable conclusions, the decision was taken to make a 30-person data collection, following actual conventions on sample size, applying the last sequence design whose results are reported below.

Methodology

Participants

For stage two, participants (n=30) were students at a Music Education programme offered by the High Council for Catholic Education (CONSUDEC) in Buenos Aires, Argentina. The majority were male (76.67%). Their mean age was 24 and 53% of them were taking introductory courses. Another 30% were undergraduates who had not yet taken half of the required credits to complete the programme. However, 40% of the subjects already worked in Education. Just 30% were full-time students.

Test

On September 4, 2014, a regular school day, students were brought in groups of seven or eight to a computer lab at CONSUDEC facilities were CRDI equipment (as described in Limongi *et al.*, 2014) was installed around a long table. Each group listened to a cassette recording of NN, for solo guitar, played by its composer, while each participant manipulated a CRDI dial according to her/his aesthetic response to the music. Afterwards, they completed Questionnaire 1 answering questions about frequency, duration, location, and magnitude of perceived aesthetic experience as well as their assessment of the stimulus.

Next, participants listened to the piece once more whilst reading the corresponding music score. Finally, they repeated the CRDI experience and answered Questionnaire 2, reflecting on the effects of music reading as modifier of their aesthetic response.

Results and Discussion

Out of the 30 participants, 40% reported an aesthetic experience in Questionnaire 1 whilst listening to what they thought of already as music during the first listening. Another 30% also reported an aesthetic experience, but in these cases, listeners held the stimulus just as 'sound', not as 'music'. Assessing NN as music, 23.3% of the students did not have any aesthetic experience, while the remaining 6.7% neither had any aesthetic experience, nor estimated that they had listened to music.

Regarding the use of the score, 66.67% (n=20) of the participants found it helpful for *understanding, following the structure, as guidance or reference,* for *ordering, identifying elements and their graphic representation,* or *building expectations,* among the most frequent answers. For 16.67% (n=5), the reading experience was partially useful, while 6.67% (n=2) made little or very little use of the sheet music. These seven subjects stated notation was hard to decipher. Two students (6.67%) found no use at all for the music score. One of them reported that they could make no sense out of it, while the other seems to have completely disliked the music. He later commented that seeing the score might have made the listening more endurable. Finally, although one person declared he did not know how the sheet music could be useful, he later elaborated in the lines of *comprehending, following,* or *understanding,* evaluating the whole experience as *unconventional.*

While 36.7% of the subjects (n=11) considered that the stimulus was not music, most of these (n=9 out of 11) declared they had an aesthetic experience. Even those that responded they did not (n=2), gave a considerably high score when evaluating the magnitude of *what happened* (5 and 7 points). While these marks were stated before the reading stage of the study, both subjects' CRDI responses were consistently more intense in terms of variation in response, even reaching the top of the dial (marked "positive") several times, once they had had contact with the music score.

Reading the sheet music was definitely useful for seven of these participants For the remaining four,, although it helped as a guiding reference, the visual code was not always clear and they had some trouble relating the graphic representation with the heard sounds.

Two cases are particularly remarkable. One of the students, even when he did not think of the stimulus as music, expressed having an intense experience (scored 9), and considered the score as a helpful reference that made the music more enjoyable, which shows when contrasting his CRDI curves (Figure 2c). The other, describing the score as guidance for understanding, stated that, after the reading experience, in fact he could consider parts of the stimulus as music.

On the other hand, most of the students (63.3%, n=19) thought they had indeed listened to music. Of these, seven declared that they had no aesthetic experience, although—strikingly—three subjects graded *what happened* with high scores: 5, 7, and even 9 points.

For the first of these cases, the CRDI curve after the reading experience exhibits notably higher values. For the second one, values are higher and especially much more differentiated (higher peaks and lower valleys). Both subjects considered that reading the score was useful for "*understanding what I am listening to*", and "*ordering the parts of the piece, becoming more aware of my aesthetic experience*".

Case number three presents two different curves with similar general tendencies and maximum (234 before reading; 237 after reading) and minimum values (0), although the mean value after reading is slightly lower (152.9 to 154.3). The participant considers the use of the score as little help since the notation is not clear for him to read and the language is strange, new, and unknown.

The others rated the experience between 1 and 4, based on a ten-point scale. For those who gave the highest marks, the sheet music was reported as useful in order to identify elements, comprehend the work's organization, generate expectations, and to relate sound to graphic representation and performing techniques. The student grading the event with 1 found very little use for the score, since he considered the notation to be strange and the music difficult to understand. However, all of them showed higher, or at least slightly higher, values and more contrasting peaks and valleys in their CRDI curves after the reading experience, within similar general tendencies.

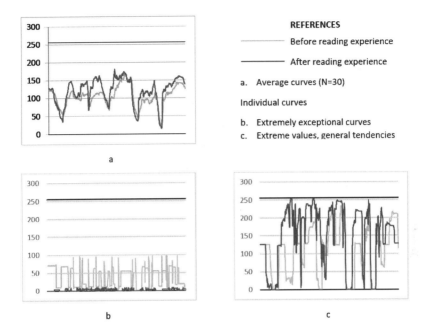

Figure 2. CRDI curves.

For most participants who had what they considered to be an aesthetic experience (n=8), the score was useful as a reference that helped understanding, creating order, identifying materials, relating sound and notation, and finding coherence. Half of them rated the experience 5 or 4. The rest went as high as 7, 8 and 9. In general, after reading, CRDI curves show higher values and/or more differentiated moments. Only one of the students presents lower values for her second CRDI curve and, stating that reading helped her to connect sound and writing, thus she was trying to comprehend the piece, and she expressed that, whilst listening, her feelings were constantly of complete displeasure.

The last four participants had different assessments for the use of the score. Two of them found the sheet music partially helpful for identifying elements and following the structure. The one who rated the experience with a 7 produced a second CRDI curve with much higher values. The one whose grade was just 4 presented very particular curves (Figure 2b) going from extremely low values with many peaks and valleys within a small range to almost flat zero. He declared the music gave him a headache.

One student indicated that he did not know how the score could be useful. However, he later developed his answer considering possibilities of guidance and predictability. After reading, his CRDI curve exhibits higher values, as does the curve of the final participant, in this case, even reaching once the top of the scale, although he considered the score was not useful because he could not understand it and assessed the music as mostly noise for its lack of harmony.

Conclusions and Suggestions

In a recent research meeting[14], where the 2014 study was described, Argentinian composer Teodoro Cromberg pointed out how this kind of music still presents individual and separate perceptual challenges, especially when there is such a multifarious amount of compositional aesthetic proposals with no definite referential system functioning as a general framework. Further investigation is required in this field, exploring other pieces and different and larger groups; hence, we must avoid any generalization at this point.

However, for NN, we can positively confirm our hypothesis. The use of the music score does certainly make a difference. Meaningful listening implies a cognitive process and musicians, both professionals and students, are used to find the consequent conceptual constructs in an encoded written pattern. That being said, the effect of immediately consecutive auditions remains to be evaluated.

Experimental aesthetics avoid *a priori* strong definitions.Accordingly, we may consider aesthetic experience as *"more or less any reaction that any person might have to any work of art, defined in the broadest possible terms [...] trying to account for everyday likes and dislikes in music rather that rarified reactions"* (Hargreaves & North, 2010, p. 517). If we further specified it as *"the composite emotional and intellectual responsiveness to music"* (Madsen & Madsen, 1970, p. 44), music reading provided music students who were NN listeners a valuable possibility to make sense out of the stimulus enhancing their aesthetic response (Figure 2a).

References

Carlé Costa. (2015, January 2). *NN (1986), Carlé Costa. Performed by Dionisio Castro* [Video file]. Retrieved from https://www.youtube.com/watch?v=4K9ABF1nc5Y

Castro, D., Galante, M. G. & Limongi, R. (2013). La experiencia estética y su medición: Una prueba piloto en cátedras de Estética de la Música, DAMus, IUNA. *Enseñar música: Revista panamericana de*

---

[14] National University for the Arts 1st Researchers Meeting, Buenos Aires, October 9, 2015.

investigación, 1(1), 19-31.
http://artesmusicales.org/web/index.php/tapa/149-tapa.html

Frega, A.L. (1997). *Metodología comparada de la educación musical*, (PhD dissertation). Buenos Aires: Collegium Musicum.

Galante, G. & Limongi, R. (2013). El sujeto promedio: la experiencia estética medida por el CRDI. Un análisis estadístico detallado. In C. Poblete Lagos (Ed.), *Actas de la 9ª Conferencia Latinoamericana y 2ª Panamericana de la Sociedad Internacional de Educación Musical, ISME* (pp. 357-366). Santiago, Chile.

Galante, M. G. (2014). Investigación sobre experiencia estética en el DAMus, IUNA. Historia de un proceso, relato de una experiencia. In Centro de Pedagogía Musical (Ed.), *Actas del 1° Simposio Internacional "Enseñar y aprender música: Un tema de músicos", CePeM, DAMus, IUNA* (pp. 164-172). Buenos Aires, Argentina.

Hargreaves, D. J. & North, A. C. (2010). Experimental aesthetics and liking in music. In P. N. Juslin & J. A. Sloboda (Eds.), *Handbook of music and emotion. Theory, research, applications* (pp. 515-546). Oxford: Oxford University Press.

Limongi, R., Frega, A. L., Galante, G., & Castro, D. (2014). Contemporary music, music reading and aesthetic response: A CRDI study at undergraduate school. Preliminary report. In O. Odena & S. Figueiredo (Eds.), *Proceedings of the 25th International Seminar of the ISME Commission on Research* (pp.194-208). João Pessoa, Paraíba, Brazil: Federal University of Paraíba.
http://issuu.com/official_isme/docs/2014_11_10_isme_rc_ebook_final_pp37?viewMode=magazine&mode=embed

Madsen, C. K. (2011). Nonverbal measurement of responsiveness to music. In P. Madura Ward-Steinman (Ed.), *Advances in social-psychology and music education research* (pp. 53-62). Farnham, England: Ashgate.

Madsen, C. K., Brittin, R. V., and Capperella-Sheldon, D. A. (1993). An empirical method for measuring the aesthetic experience to music. *Journal of Research in Music Education, 41*(1), 57-69.

Madsen, C. K., Byrnes, S. R., Capperella-Sheldon, D. A., & Brittin, R. V. (1993). Aesthetic response to music: musicians versus nonmusicians. *Journal of Music Therapy, XXX*(3), 174-191.

Madsen, C. K. & Madsen, C. H. Jr. (1970). *Experimental research in music.* Englewood Cliffs, New Jersey: Prentice-Hall.

Phelps, R. P. (2014). *Development of musical preference: A comparison of perceived influences* (Master's Thesis). Available from Electronic Theses, Treatises and Dissertations database. (Paper 8869)

Tempo Preferences for Fast and Slow Music Excerpts of Diverse Styles: Jazz, Western Classical, Pop/Rock, and Brazilian Pop

John M. Geringer
Center for Music Research, Florida State University, Tallahassee, FL, USA

jgeringer@fsu.edu

Ruth V. Brittin
Department of Music Education, University of the Pacific, Stockton, CA, USA

rbrittin@pacific.edu

Deborah A. Confredo
Department of Music Education and Therapy, Temple University, Philadelphia, PA, USA

debconfredo@temple.edu

Abstract

We examined tempo preferences of university music and non-music students for different styles of music. Slow and fast tempo examples of four styles (jazz, western classical, popular rock, and Brazilian popular) were presented to 108 listeners in three regions of the United States. Participants used a recently developed audio sort and rank procedure to indicate tempo preferences for four versions of each excerpt differing only in tempo. Tempos were presented at the original level, and altered by magnitudes of 6% (both tempo increases and decreases) and a 12% change (increase if originally slow, decrease if originally fast). Listeners preferred the popular rock excerpts at the original recorded tempo. However, originally fast examples of the other styles were preferred at slower tempos (6%), and originally slow tempo examples were preferred at faster tempos (6%). Tempo preferences of music majors and non-majors were not significantly different, but majors indicated greater familiarity with the examples, especially the two jazz excerpts. Present results appear consistent with earlier studies showing listener preferences for unaltered tempos in well-known popular music and for faster tempos of slow excerpts and for slower tempos of fast excerpts in less well-known examples of western classical, jazz, and other styles.

Keywords: Music Listening, Music Preference, Tempo, Music Style, Jazz, Rock, Classical

One of the most salient features of music concerns the rate of presentation, that is, the performed tempo. Obviously there are many factors to consider in the decision for a particular tempo including the composer's intention, conductor and performer interpretations, performer abilities, and so on. To what extent do such decisions and tendencies of performers affect listeners' perceptions of the music? Are listener tempo preferences similar across styles? We designed this study to investigate whether music examples chosen from diverse music genres would affect tempo preferences of listeners in similar or differential ways.

Researchers have demonstrated that tempo affects listener preferences. Multiple investigations by LeBlanc and colleagues found that faster tempos corresponded to higher preference ratings in comparisons between excerpts from different pieces (LeBlanc, 1981, LeBlanc & McCrary, 1983; LeBlanc, Colman, McCrary, Sherrill, & Malin, 1988). LeBlanc, Jin, Chen-Hafteck, Oliviera, Oosthuysen, and Tafuri (2000/2001) noted that tempo of jazz examples accounted for almost half of the variance in preference of listeners (ages 10 – 14 years) across five countries. Sims (1987), Montgomery (1996), and Brittin (2000) noted that children apparently acquire an association between increased preference and increased tempos by third or fourth grade. Wapnick's (1980) listeners preferred faster tempos of familiar piano excerpts. Geringer and Madsen (2003) found that music students listening to an entire symphonic movement showed higher levels of aesthetic response during the latter part of the movement in a version with gradual tempo increases compared to versions that were unaltered or with gradual decreases in tempo.

However, investigators have noted exceptions to the pattern of increased preferences for faster tempos. Yarbrough (1987) showed that musicians and non-musicians preferred slower tempos for fast pieces and faster tempos for slow pieces of Mozart and Chopin. Geringer's (2010) music major listeners heard symphonic excerpts and manipulated tempos to preferred levels. They increased tempos for the relatively slow excerpts and decreased tempos for fast examples relative to original levels.

Researchers have provided additional evidence by considering tempos of popular music. Geringer and Madsen (1987) altered tempos of familiar recorded popular music and presented excerpts to 500 listeners from fifth grade to university age. Participants showed marked preferences for unaltered versions compared to increased and decreased tempo versions. These results were attributed to possible effects of excerpt familiarity or style differences. Similar results were found recently among participants from the United States, Mexico, and Brazil (Geringer, Ilari, & Johnson, 2014). Moreover, Levitin and Cook (1996) reported that non-musicians produced tempos from memory of popular songs within 8% of the recorded tempo in 72% of trials. Results of these popular music studies suggest that listeners are able to remember tempo levels of music that typically is heard repeatedly at the identical tempo.

Listeners have preferred familiar popular and rock songs in their original unaltered tempos. In contrast, unfamiliar and western classical excerpts seem preferred at faster levels, unless they are perceived to be fast already in which case they are preferred at slower tempos. The purpose of this study was to replicate and extend previous work and further explore differences noted between popular, classical and other styles of music. We investigated whether music major and non-major listeners would show similar tempo preferences across relatively familiar examples of western popular rock, western classical, jazz, and Brazilian pop music.

Method

Participants

Volunteer participants were convenience samples of university students. Because of conceivable regional differences in familiarity with popular music styles, and therefore to increase possibilities for generalization, we included listeners in three regions of the United States. Students were drawn from universities in California, Florida, and Pennsylvania. We obtained approximately the same numbers from each region in our total sample (N = 108) including both music majors (*n* = 54) and students with majors other than music (*n* = 54).

Musical Stimuli

We incorporated excerpts from eight pieces for this project, representing four stylistically diverse genres: western popular rock, western classical, jazz, and Brazilian popular. Two examples from each genre were chosen: one with a relatively slow tempo and one with a fast tempo. We chose pieces regarded as familiar to most general listeners in the United States.

All pieces are ranked highly (within genre) in multiple lists of best-selling recordings.

Digital files of the eight pieces were edited to provide excerpts of 15—25 seconds in duration. We chose these extracts from familiar sections of the pieces. Tempo manipulations were prepared with software (Amazing Slow Downer, *v.* 3.5), which produced tempo changes without artifact or altering other music elements. We created a total of 32 stimuli: four versions of each excerpt that varied only in tempo. One version was not altered from the performed tempo of the original recording. Two of the changed versions were alterations of six percent from the original tempo: tempo increases (+ 6%) and tempo decreases (-6%). The third alteration was a change of 12%. For the fast excerpts, the alteration decreased tempo by 12%, and slow excerpts were increased in tempo by 12%. Table 1 displays the excerpts and alterations.

Procedures

We collected tempo preference data using a recently developed sort and rank procedure (Geringer & Bridges, 2015). The method facilitates direct comparisons of auditory stimuli so ratings are more efficient than presenting a series of paired comparisons. Earlier implementations using similar procedures have been used with diverse auditory stimuli (Granqvist, 2003; McAdams, Vieillard, Houix, & Reynolds, 2004). For example, variations of the sort task were used to study perception and classification of regional accents and non-native speech (Atagi & Bent, 2013; Clopper, 2008).

Our participants completed the task on their own personal computers. They were sent eight PowerPoint® slides with sound files embedded: Each slide contained the four tempo variations of one of the eight excerpts. The four sound files per slide were identified with a unique icon replacing the default PowerPoint® sound icon. We chose symbols from the character viewer in Microsoft Office® (e.g., ¶, §, ≅, ฿) to avoid possible associations participants might have with typical alphanumeric characters. Listeners were asked to use headphones to hear stimuli more clearly.

We used a 9-point scale for preference ratings (see Figure 1). Slides were presented in two sets of four, in alternate orders to balance conceivable effects of order. Listeners controlled the number of times they listened to each sound icon and could go back and forth between the slides. They could place icons anywhere on the continuum, including stacking icons on the grid in the same horizontal space if they had no differential preference.

We also used a 9-point scale for familiarity ratings. When listeners completed the task, they emailed the file back to us.

Results

Table 1 shows mean ratings and standard deviations for the eight excerpts. Listeners preferred the original recorded tempo for only the two popular rock examples, *Imagine* and *Satisfaction*. For the three other styles, listeners preferred a slower tempo (6%) for the fast examples (*William Tell Overture, Take Five, and Mais Que Nada*), and a faster tempo (6%) for the slow examples (*Ave Maria, My Funny Valentine, and Girl from Ipanema*). Across excerpts, standard deviations were lowest for the preferred tempo, except for *My Funny Valentine*, which exhibited near identical deviations for the preferred and original versions.

Mean familiarity ratings also are shown. The *William Tell Overture* was the most familiar (M = 8.20 on the 9-point scale). The two classical examples and the two popular rock examples were judged more familiar than the jazz and Brazilian pop examples. We calculated Pearson correlations between preference ratings for the original version and the familiarity rating scale. The popular rock examples were the only two exhibiting a significant relationship ($p < .05$), however, correlations were small with coefficients less than .20 except for *Imagine* ($r = .279$). There was a significant difference between music majors (M = 6.39) and non-music majors (M = 5.10) in familiarity, $F (1, 106) = 19.10$ $p < .001$, *partial* $\eta2 = .153$, and a difference between examples, $F (7, 742) = 69.96$, $p < .001$, *partial* $\eta2 = .398$. However, the interaction between major and excerpts was also significant, $F (7, 742) = 4.41$, $p < .001$, *partial* $\eta2 = .040$. Although music major familiarity means were higher than the non-major means for all examples, mean differences of the two jazz excerpts *My Funny Valentine* (4.32 versus 2.75) and especially *Take Five* (6.41 compared to 3.24) were considerably larger than for the other styles.

We screened preference data to test assumptions of the analysis of variance. Correlations between the slow and fast tempo examples were low ($r < \pm .20$), not significant, and scatterplots showed nonlinear relationships. We therefore computed separate analyses for the fast and slow tempo examples, using three-way analyses of variance with one between-subjects factor (music major students and non-majors) and two within-subjects factors (the four styles and the four tempo change conditions). We set a conservative alpha level of .01 for these analyses. The assumption of sphericity was violated for tempo change conditions, consequently we used the Greenhouse-Geisser adjustment to degrees of freedom.

Analysis of the fast tempo examples showed no difference between the music major and non-major groups, F (1, 106) < 1, p > .6. We found significant differences between the styles, F (3, 318) = 6.87, p < .001, *partial η^2* = .06, and between tempo change conditions, F (2.42, 256) = 80.11, p < .001, *partial η^2* = .43. None of the two-way or the three-way interactions were significant. Across styles, tempo change preferences for fast tempo excerpts were highest for tempo decreases of 6% (M = 6.49). This mean was significantly different from tempo increases of 6% (M = 4.47) and decreases of 12% (M = 4.26), but not different from the original tempos (M = 6.24) of the fast tempo examples.

The slow tempo examples also exhibited no difference between the music major and non-major groups, F (1, 106) < 1. There were significant differences between the styles, F (3, 318) = 4.44, p < .01, *partial η^2* = .04, and between tempo conditions F (2.36, 250.47) = 41.55, p < .001, *partial η^2* = .28. Across slow tempo examples, both the original tempo (M = 6.09) and tempo increases of 6% (M = 6.03) means were significantly different from the decreases of 6% (M = 4.53) and increases of 12% (4.83). One of the two-and three-way interactions was significant, between the variables of style and tempo change condition, F (7.54, 799.69) = 11.98, p < .001, *partial η^2* = .10. As may be observed in the Table, listeners preferred the original tempo (M = 6.98) of the slow popular rock example (*Imagine*) more than original tempos of the three other styles and more than tempo increases of 6% (M = 5.38) for that example. In contrast, tempo increases of 6% were rated higher than the original for the other styles: *Girl from Ipanema* (M = 6.71 compared to 6.25), *Ave Maria* (M = 6.13 versus 5.71), and *My Funny Valentine* (M = 5.90 versus 5.45). Across the tempo decreases of 6%, the most preferred was *Ave Maria* (M = 5.44) and least preferred was *Girl from Ipanema* (M = 3.46). Tempo increases of 12% were most preferred in *My Funny Valentine* (M = 5.58).

Discussion

University music majors and non-music majors preferred original tempos for the two excerpts representing well-known western popular rock examples. However, for examples representing jazz, western classical, and Brazilian pop styles, listeners preferred tempos that were slower (by 6%) for originally fast examples, and faster tempos (6%) for originally slow examples. Familiarity ratings were highest for the popular rock and classical excerpts; however, the degree of association between familiarity and preference for the original tempo was generally low and not significant except for the two popular rock examples. Differences between music majors and students with other majors were not significant regarding tempo preferences, but were different on the familiarity scale. Music majors indicated a higher degree of familiarity for all examples, particularly for the two jazz examples.

These results are consistent with those of tempo preference studies using popular music and others using western classical excerpts. Geringer and Madsen (1987), Geringer et al. (2014), and Levitin and Cook (1996) presented evidence that listeners may remember tempos of popular excerpts and prefer unaltered tempos. On the other hand, a number of studies have established an overall preference for faster tempos of western classical and less well known examples of jazz, popular, and other styles (Geringer & Madsen, 2003; LeBlanc et al., 2000/2001). Further examination of western classical examples and unfamiliar popular rock music indicates that although listeners prefer faster tempos for slow pieces, they prefer slower tempos for fast pieces (Geringer, 2010; Geringer et al., 2014; Yarbrough, 1987).

One of the reasons listeners tend to prefer well-known popular music at the original tempo appears related to not only familiarity but to the many repetitions heard at the same tempo. A popular rock piece, such as *Imagine* or *Satisfaction*, is most always heard at the same tempo and pitch with the same performers. Other musicians who play such well-known songs as "covers", affirm that audiences want to hear it played as closely as possible to the original. In contrast, most other styles are regularly performed with a variety of differences in fundamental elements, such as different tempos, performers, and instrumentation. For example, *Ave Maria* or *My Funny Valentine* may be heard with male or female singers, with a variety of solo instruments or ensembles, and in different keys. There is no "original" tempo, except for the tempo at which a particular version was recorded. This may also help account for the lack of relationship between familiarity and recorded tempo for the styles other than popular rock. Although listeners were familiar with *Ave Maria* and *William Tell*, they likely have heard them performed across a range of tempos.

The preference for moderated tempos, that is, faster tempos for slow music and slower tempos for fast music, is an interesting aspect. This result may be similar to outcomes in visual perception of human faces in which a statistical average or composite prototype of a category is perceived as more attractive than less typical individual faces (e.g., Langlois & Roggman, 1990). The argument has been made that the prototype has the smallest distance from the average perceiver's aesthetic ideals, referred to as the "minimal distance hypothesis". Repp (1997) found that the average of piano performances varying only in expressive timing and tempo was rated high in quality, albeit low in individuality. Johnson (2003) reported similar results with listeners who rated solo cello performances. His music major listeners judged the quantitatively averaged timing performance as the most musical. Perhaps our listeners when presented with both faster and slower versions of an excerpt tended to prefer tempos perceived to be more average. These results have implications for music teachers. Research literature has been reasonably clear that listeners prefer faster tempi for unfamiliar music, thus encouraging positive student responses. However, this study provides evidence that examples that are already very fast, even familiar ones, tend to be preferred at slightly slower tempos.

We used a recently developed technique to ascertain listener preferences. Listeners could listen individually on their own schedules, hear the examples as many times as they wished, and compare examples directly. This appears to facilitate increased discrimination between stimuli compared to typical Likert-type ratings of individually presented aural examples (Geringer & Bridges, 2015). A number of listeners used the entire scale, which often does not occur with rating scales. Indeed, standard deviations for the various tempo options were relatively high generally (over 2.0 on the 9-point scale), indicating diversity in tempo preferences. A small number of participants were not able to follow the suggested instructions, for example, a few participants appeared (by clustering all icons at one end of the scale) to be judging preference for the excerpt itself rather than for the various tempos. However, most all respondents appeared to place icons differentially based on tempo variations. Some listeners commented that they enjoyed the procedure and appreciated being actively involved in making preference judgments.

Table 1: Descriptive Data for Music Examples

Excerpt	Tempo	Ratings *M*	SD	Familiarity	Correlation[‡]
Imagine (slow Popular Rock)	**Original**	**6.98**	**1.86**	7.66	.279^
	Tempo +6	5.38	2.29		
	Tempo - 6	4.71	2.5		
	Tempo +12	4.19	2.36		
(I can't get no) Satisfaction (fast Popular Rock)	**Original**	**6.47**	**1.82**	6.12	.194^
	Tempo +6	4.37	2.45		
	Tempo - 6	6.02	2.06		
	Tempo -12	3.86	2.24		
Ave Maria (slow Classical)	Original	5.71	2.02	7.28	0.177
	Tempo +6	**6.13**	**1.77**		
	Tempo - 6	5.44	2.12		
	Tempo +12	4.98	2.68		
William Tell Overture (fast Classical)	Original	6.15	2.25	8.2	0.141
	Tempo +6	4.14	2.35		
	Tempo -6	**6.65**	**1.87**		
	Tempo -12	4.5	2.5		
My Funny Valentine (slow Jazz)	Original	5.45	2.11	3.54	0.137
	Tempo +6	**5.9**	**2.12**		
	Tempo - 6	4.5	2.55		
	Tempo +12	5.58	2.51		
Take Five (fast Jazz)	Original	6.26	1.99	4.82	0.088
	Tempo +6	4.64	2.31		
	Tempo -6	**6.68**	**1.63**		
	Tempo -12	4.73	2.08		
The Girl from Ipanema (slow Brazil Pop)	Original	6.25	1.88	4.69	0.186
	Tempo +6	**6.71**	**1.69**		
	Tempo - 6	3.46	2.22		
	Tempo +12	4.55	2.49		
Mais Que Nada (fast Brazil Pop)	Original	6.07	2.14	3.67	0.069
	Tempo +6	4.74	2.44		
	Tempo -6	**6.63**	**2**		
	Tempo -12	3.95	2.18		

Notes: ‡ Correlation between preference for original tempo and familiarity rating scales, ^ indicates $p <$ .05. Bold indicates preferred tempo.

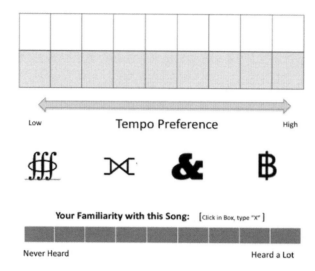

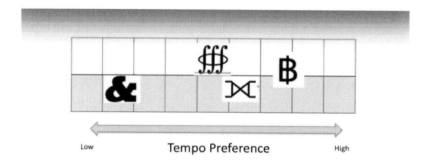

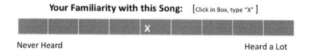

Figure 1. Example of slide before (top) and after (bottom) participant had moved sound icons

References

Amazing Slow Downer (version 3.5) [Computer software]. Retrieved from http://ronimusic.com/index.html/ : Roni Music®.

Atagi, E., & Bent, T. (2013). Auditory free classification of nonnative speech. *Journal of phonetics, 41*(6), 509-519. doi:10.1016/j.wocn.2013.09.003

Brittin, R. V. (2000). Children's preference for sequenced accompaniments: The influence of style and perceived tempo. *Journal of Research in Music Education, 48,* 237-248. doi:10.2307/3345396

Clopper, C. G. (2008). Auditory free classification: Methods and analysis. *Behavior Research Methods, 40*(2), 575-581. doi:10.3758/BRM.40.2.575

Geringer, J. M. (2010). Musicians' preferences for tempo and pitch levels in recorded orchestral music. *Journal of Research in Music Education, 58,* 294-308. doi:10.1177/0022429410380464

Geringer, J. M., & Bridges, C. (2015, May). Perception of amplitude modulation in vocal vibrato. Paper presented at the 44th annual symposium on the Care of the Professional Voice. Philadelphia, PA.

Geringer, J. M., Ilari, B., & Johnson, C. M. (2014). Preferences for tempo and pitch levels in classic rock music of the United States and Latin America. *Proceedings of the twenty-fifth international seminar on research in music education,* 98–113.

Geringer, J. M., & Madsen, C. K. (1987). Pitch and tempo preferences in recorded popular music. In C. K. Madsen and C. A. Prickett (Eds.), *Applications of research in music behavior* (pp. 204-212). Tuscaloosa, AL: The University of Alabama Press.

Geringer, J. M., & Madsen, C. K. (2003). Gradual tempo change and aesthetic responses of music majors. *International Journal of Music Education, 40,* 3-15. doi:10.1177/025576140304000102

Granqvist, S. (2003). The visual sort and rate method for perceptual evaluation in listening tests. *Logopedics Phonatrics Vocology, 28*(3), 109-116. doi:10.1080/14015430310015255

Johnson, C. M. (2003). Effect of rubato magnitude on the perception of musicianship in musical performance. *Journal of Research in Music Education, 51,* 115-123. doi:10.2307/3345845

Langlois, J. H., & Roggman, L. A. (1990). Attractive faces are only average. *Psychological Science, 1,* 115-121. doi:10.1111/j.1467-9280.1990.tb00079.x

LeBlanc, A. (1981). Effects of style, tempo, and performing medium on children's music preference. *Journal of Research in Music Education, 29*, 143–156. doi:10.2307/3345023

LeBlanc, A., Colman, J., McCrary, J., Sherrill, C., and Malin, S. (1988). Tempo preferences of different age music listeners. *Journal of Research in Music Education, 36*, 156-168. doi:10.2307/3344637

LeBlanc, A. & McCrary, J. (1983). Effect of tempo on children's music preference. *Journal of Research in Music Education, 31*, 283–294. doi:10.2307/3344631

LeBlanc, A., Jin, Y. C., Chen-Hafteck, L., Oliviera, A. J., Oosthuysen, S., & Tafuri, J. (2000/2001). Tempo preferences of young listeners in Brazil, China, Italy, South Africa, and the United States. *Bulletin of the Council for Research in Music Education, 147*, 97-102. Retrieved from http://www.jstor.org/stable/40319395

Levitin, D. J., & Cook, P. R. (1996). Memory for musical tempo: Additional evidence that auditory memory is absolute. *Perception & Psychophysics, 58*, 927-935. doi:10.3758/BF03205494

McAdams, S., Vieillard, S., Houix, O., & Reynolds, R. (2004). Perception of musical similarity among contemporary thematic material in two instrumentations. *Music Perception, 22*, 207-237. Retrieved from http://www.jstor.org/stable/10.1525/mp.2004.22.2.207

Montgomery, A. P. (1996). Effect of tempo on music preferences of children in elementary and middle school. *Journal of Research in Music Education, 44*, 134-146. doi:10.2307/3345666

Repp, B. H. (1997). The aesthetic quality of a quantitatively average music performance: Two preliminary experiments. *Music Perception, 14*, 419-444. doi:10.2307/40285732

Sims, W. (1987). Effect of tempo on music preference of preschool through fourth-grade children. In C. K. Madsen and C. A. Prickett (Eds.), *Applications of research in music behavior* (pp. 15-25). Tuscaloosa, Al: University of Alabama Press.

Wapnick, J. (1980). Pitch, tempo, and timbral preferences in recorded piano music. *Journal of Research in Music Education, 28*, 43-58. doi:10.2307/3345052

Yarbrough, C. (1987). The effect of music excerpts on tempo discriminations and preferences of musicians and non-musicians. In C. K. Madsen & C. K. Prickett (Eds.), *Applications of research in music behavior* (pp. 175-189). Tuscaloosa: University of Alabama Press.

Drawing music sounds good: A new approach to representation of sounds and music in school

Vicent Gil Asensio

Son Rullan State Middle School, Palma, Spain

vgilasensio@gmail.com

Abstract

The purpose of this study was to examine the effects of a technology-enhanced learning environment (TELE) on middle school students' meta-representational competence (MRC) in the domain of music. Particularly, we aimed at determining whether an educational intervention influenced the accuracy with which middle school students matched sounds (sonic fragments) to symbols (graphic representations). The students were randomly allocated to the experimental condition. An intervention was set up so that the experimental group students (E) were provided with scaffolding aimed at enhancing their use of constructive resources to generate representations and their critical capabilities to judge them. On the other hand, the control group students (C) followed a similar educational programme lacking in such scaffolding. Both E and C groups were administered the same pretest and posttest, which measured the students' MRC by means of six representational criteria. One month after the posttest, a retention test took place. We hypothesized that the experimental programme would have a positive overall effect on the students' MRC, which was partially supported, since that positive effect happened irrespective of the intervention. We also predicted a lasting effect of the intervention for the students who received scaffolding during the intervention, and that finding was also confirmed. As to the students' perception of the TELE, the E group students overall scored their experience with the lesson in a more positive way than the C group, despite this trend was not confirmed for all the subscales of the survey. Theoretical, methodological, and educational implications are discussed.

Keywords: Graphic representations, meta-representational competence, music-listening task, sound-to-symbol relationship, technology enhanced learning environment.

Introduction

In the early 1970s, pioneer works highlighted the educational potential of music for all pupils (Paynter, 2008) and claimed a new approach to music education alternative to representing music by means of standard music notation (SMN). Recently, Verschaffel, Reybrouck, Jans, and van Dooren (2010, p. 476) argued that the 'representational landscape' had changed for most sciences, and therefore "it [did] not make sense any longer to teach only a few standard representational forms".

In subsequent studies (Reybrouck, Verschaffel, & Lauwerier, 2009; Verschaffel, Reybrouck, Degraeuwe, & van Dooren, 2013; Verschaffel, Reybrouck, Jans, et al., 2010; Verschaffel, Reybrouck, Janssens, & van Dooren, 2010), the authors "gradually became aware of the potential relevance of the theoretical notion of 'metarepresentational competence' [MRC]" (Verschaffel, Reybrouck, Degraeuwe, et al., 2013, p. 692), as decribed by diSessa and associates (diSessa, 2002, 2004; diSessa, Hammer, Sherin, & Kolpakowsky, 1991; diSessa & B. L. Sherin, 2000).

In a pilot study (Gil, Reybrouck, Tejada, & Verschaffel, 2015), the influence of subject variables (age, music experience) and task variables (educational intervention) on middle school students' MRC was explored. In this respect, the authors suggested—as further research—designing and implementing a technology-enhanced learning environment (TELE). This has been addressed in the current study.

This research explores the extent to which an educational intervention can enhance a learner's representational skills. One of the main concepts in this study is MRC, described as "the faculty to generate, critique, and refine representational forms" (diSessa, Hammer, et al., 1991, p. 118). Two main concepts are important within the context of representational design: a) 'constructive resources' refer to a set of ideas and strategies for generating representations; and (b) 'critical capabilities' entail judging the effectiveness of the result and redesigning to ameliorate limitations (diSessa, 2002, p. 107).

In the course of their research on MRC, diSessa, Hammer, et al. (1991, p. 148) observed that students seemed to follow a regular pattern in designing representations for motion, and put forward a series of meta-representational criteria. The following is a list of definitions of the six meta-representational criteria that will be used for purposes of this study (Verschaffel, Reybrouck, Jans, et al., 2010, p. 482–483):

Correctness: "A representation is considered to be correct when it accurately shows the articulation of certain sonic parameters over time".

Completeness: "A representation is considered to be complete when it represents the whole of the music fragment, and not only a part".

Transparency: "When a representation contains an additional element that shows or suggests systematic variation that does not refer to any corresponding variation in the sound fragment that is to be represented, the representation is considered as misleading. When such misleading elements are absent, the representation is called transparent".

Formality: "A representation is considered to be formal when it uses signs, symbols, rules, and/or conventions that belong to a formal notational system".

Parsimony: "A representation is considered parsimonious when it contains no redundant information".

Beauty: "This criterion refers to the presence or absence of a pleasant visual effect".

The primary concern of this study was to examine the effects of a TELE on middle school music students' MRC. Our first hypothesis was that the experimental programme would have a positive overall effect on students' MRC. Our second hypothesis was that the positive effect of the experimental program would be lasting. We also hypothesized that the students allocated to the experimental group would experience the TELE in a more positive way than the students allocated to the control group.

Methods

Design

A pretest-posttest control group design was used in this study, with stratified random assignment of participants to the experimental condition, and pretest and posttest assessment of units. Between the pretest and the posttest, an educational intervention was carried out by means of a MoodleTM virtual classroom so that the students allocated to the experimental (E) group were provided with both fixed and adaptive scaffolding, while the control (C) group students did not. Such a scaffolding consisted of small hints and reminders provided by the teacher to help students carry out tasks. In addition, a retention test was performed around one month after finishing the intervention in order to measure the lasting effect of the program.

Participants

One hundred students aged 11–12 enrolled in the 1st grade music course in a state middle school in Palma (Balearic Islands, Spain) took part in the study. Twenty-five students were removed from the study for not attending to two or more sessions of the experimental programme. As a result, the analysed sample consisted of 75 students.

Variables

The study was designed so as to test hypotheses regarding the extent to which an educational intervention would improve the students' MRC, as measured after (pretest) and before (posttest and retention test) that intervention took place. There were two main independent variables or factors, namely 'Allocation to the experimental condition' (experimental, control), and 'Time' (pretest, posttest, retention test).

The dependent variables were generated by combination of three sound parameters (pitch, duration, and loudness) and six representational criteria (correctness, completeness, transparency, formality, parsimony, and beauty). Therefore, there were 18 dependent variables for each measurement (pretest, posttest, and retention test). All of these were qualitative and dichotomous.

Instruments

MRC measurement

Verschaffel, Reybrouck, Jans, et al. (2010) devised an 18 item paper-and-pencil test to measure children's MRC. For each item, only one representation was considered to be best matched to a given sonic fragment, generated by the researchers so as to enhance a salient musical parameter (pitch, duration, and loudness). Our version of this instrument closely followed the original one, albeit we made it available for students in an electronic way, by means of a MoodleTM virtual classroom. Random procedures were followed so as to guarantee that the three versions of the instrument (pretest, posttest, and retention test) would be parallel.

The Constructivist On-Line Learning Environment Survey (COLLES)

The COLLES (Taylor & Maor, 2000) was designed so as to measure students' perceptions of the TELE in which they are involved. The instrument consisted of 24 Likert-type items, distributed into six subscales: a) relevance, b) reflective thinking, c) interactivity, d) tutor support, e) peer support, and f) interpretation.

Materials

- o SamsungTM 10" netbooks (Model N145 plus) were available for the students to use during the time allocated for the experiment

- o SMART BoardTM 77" interactive whiteboard (Model SBM680) was available in the music classroom

- o TrustTM flex ultra-thin design 7.5" tablet with ergonomic wireless pen was used in connection with the classroom desktop computer

Procedures

In outline, this study proceeded chronologically as follows:

Pretest

The students were seated in the classroom as usual according to their school group, and they were provided with individual netbooks. The pretest consisted of three sections, namely 'pitch', 'duration', and 'loudness', each one containing six items with a more and less appropriate representation of a brief sonic fragment (see example in Figure 1).

Figure 1. A less appropriate (left) and more appropriate (right) representation of a crescendo-diminuendo

Educational intervention

The educational intervention consisted of eight sessions of 55 minutes each, distributed within four consecutive weeks, according to the weekly timetable scheduled for music in the middle school:

- o First week: Sessions 1 to 3 were common to both E and C groups. The students were introduced to the representational criteria. Brief explanations were followed by practical examples of sound-to-symbol matching.

- o Second week: Session 4 consisted of a MoodleTM task, different for students allocated to the E and C groups, so that scaffolding was only provided for the students belonging to the E group.

- o Third week: Session 5 was somewhat a review of the contents already dealt with, and Session 6 was a practical task in which the students were requested to draw a picture according to a given sonic fragment.

- o Fourth week: Session 7 consisted of a review of concepts about representational criteria, and Session 8 proceeded by retaking the drawing task from Session 6.

Posttest

The posttest took place once the educational intervention finished, and followed the same procedure as the pretest.

Retention test

The students were given a retention test around one month after finishing the educational intervention, with identical procedure to the pretest and the posttest.

COLLES

After the retention test, the students were invited to participate in a survey about their experience in the lesson. It was made clear to them that this task was not a regular (music) school test, but a survey to know their opinion.

Results

The analysed sample (N = 75) consisted of 36 boys (48%) and 39 girls (52%), who were randomly allocated to the E group (n = 41) and the C group (n = 34). No significant differences were found between the E and the C groups with respect to gender (x^2 = .02, df = 1, p = .882) and music experience level (x^2 = .22, df = 2, p = .897).

With respect to Hypothesis 1, a GEE analysis revealed significant differences between the pretest and the posttest, irrespective of the treatment (Wald $x^2(2)$ = 29.588, p = .000), what means that both the E and the C group benefited from the educational intervention. Therefore, our Hypothesis 1 was only partially supported (Figure 2). Regarding hypothesis 2, although the C group yielded slightly better results than the E group in the pretest, the latter outperformed the former during the posttest, and this difference in favour of the E group continued to exist on the retention test. Therefore, Hypothesis 2 was accepted (Figure 2). Further to Hypothesis 3, an overall effect of the intervention on students' perception of the TELE was found, with a significant difference between the E and the C group (x^2=16.45, df=4, p=.002). Significant differences were also found for the subscales 'Reflective thinking' (x^2=14.24, df=4, p=.007) and 'Tutor support' (x^2=10.78, df=4, p=.029).

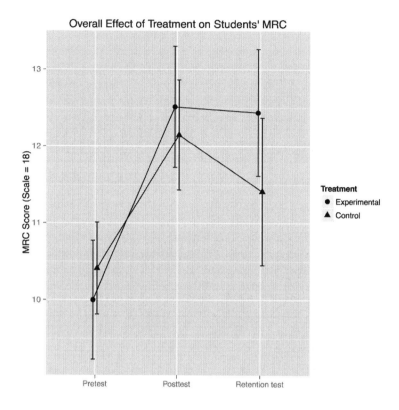

Figure 2. Mean scores and 95% confidence interval on the three tests by treatment.

Conclusions and discussion

Taking the treatment and the lasting effect as an overall measure of our educational intervention, two main conclusions arise: a) despite there not being a significant difference between the treatment groups in the posttest, there is a undeniable instructional value of our current outcome, since our mission as teachers is to enable all the students to improve, irrespective of their allocation; and b) a significant difference by treatment was found between the pretest and the retention test, which supports the effectiveness of the intervention insofar as the students' acquired knowledge was retained.

Two main outcomes due to the treatment deserve attention: a) the online learning environment significantly stimulated the experimental students' critical reflective thinking; and b) the role of the teacher to enable the students to participate in online learning was significantly acknowledged by the E group. With respect to the former, despite reflective thinking not being a sufficient condition for self-regulated learning, it is clearly a necessary condition. Therefore, we must consider such an influence as derived from our results, insofar as the students allocated to the E group were provided with scaffolding. As to the latter, it seems that the members of the E group acknowledged that "computers make it possible to give more personal attention to individual students, without which the coaching and scaffolding of apprenticeship-style learning are impossible" (Collins, Brown, & Newman, 1989, p. 491).

Theoretical implications

Previous studies on children's graphical representation of music have provided evidence for two main claims, namely the broad range of representational strategies that children employ (Barrett, 2001, p. 34; Barrett, 2005, p. 127; Elkoshi, 2004, p. 77; Upitis, 1990, p. 89; Upitis, 1993, p. 52), and the influence of musical tasks on those strategies, which do not seem to follow a developmental path (Barrett, 2000, p. 45; Barrett, 2002, p. 56; Barrett, 2005, p. 130; Reybrouck et al., 2009, p. 204). With respect to the former, taking the students' self-generated pictures that we collected in Session 6 as a snapshot of their drawing skills, the fact is that they did not display a broad palette of representational strategies. As to the latter, regarding the influence of the musical task on the students' representations, it seems that using a drawing tablet instead of paper and pencil constrained the students' graphical choices, which proved to be somewhat conservative.

Methodological implications

Technology enhancement allowed us to randomize our sample without altering the natural allocation of the students to the middle school classrooms, which would have been extremely difficult, if not impossible, to perform (De Corte, Verschaffel, & Masui, 2004). In addition, "[t]echnology has motivational benefits as a 'hook' that gets students to participate" (Blumenfeld et al., 2002, p. 484). Our approach, however, entailed some limitations as well. First, we did not collect any verbal reaction from our students, neither requested them to describe or explain their drawings in writing. The main reason for that decision was that the actual teaching was in English and we did not consider the students proficient enough to do this task. Second, "[b]ecause of the aims and scope of this study, it was not possible to borrow existent instruments with well-documented and widely acknowledged psychometric qualities" (Verschaffel, De Corte, et al., 1999, p. 224). Instead, we designed instruments whose internal consistency did not reach the level of standardized tests.

Educational implications

In considering implications for music education, what emerges from our findings is that children's self-generated representations of sound should be regarded as an integral part of the school curriculum, instead of focussing on SMN. That would provide a chance for students to increase their self-efficacy beliefs, and therefore to benefit from education in general, since transfer across multiple domains would be enhanced.

References

Barrett, M. S. (2000). Windows, mirrors, and reflections: A case study of adult constructions of children's musical thinking. *Bulletin of the Council for Research in Music Education, 145,* 43–61.

Barrett, M. S. (2001). Constructing a view of children's meaning-making as notators: A case-study of a five-year-old's descriptions and explanations of invented notations. *Research Studies in Music Education, 16*(1), 33–45. doi:10.1177/1321103X010160010401

Barrett, M. S. (2002). Invented notations and mediated memory: A case-study of two children's use of invented notations. *Bulletin of the Council for Research in Music Education, 153–154,* 55–62.

Barrett, M. S. (2005). Representation, cognition, and communication: Invented notation in children's musical communication. In D. Miell, R. MacDonald & D. J. Hargreaves (Eds.), *Musical communication* (pp. 117–142). Oxford, UK: Oxford University Press.

Blumenfeld, P. C., Kempler, T. M., & Krajcik, J. S. (2002). Motivation and cognitive engagement in learning environments. In R. K. Sawyer (Ed.), *Cambridge handbook of the learning sciences* (pp. 475–488). West Nyack, NY: Cambridge University Press.

Collins, A., Brown, J. S., & Newman, S. E. (1989). Cognitive apprenticeship: Teaching the crafts of reading, writing, and mathematics. In L. B. Resnick (Ed.), *Knowing, learning and instruction: Essays in honor of Robert Glaser* (pp. 453–494). Hillsdale, NJ: Erlbaum.

De Corte, E., Verschaffel, L., & Masui, C. (2004). The CLIA-model: A frame- work for designing powerful learning environments for thinking and problem solving. European *Journal of Psychology of Education, 19*(4), 365–384. doi:10.1007/BF03173216

diSessa, A. A. (2002). Student's criteria for representational adequacy. In K. Gravemeijer, R. Lehrer, B. van Oers & L. Verschaffel (Eds.), *Symbolizing, modeling and tool use in mathematics education* (pp. 105–129). Dordrecht, the Netherlands: Kluwer Academic.

diSessa, A. A. (2004). Metarepresentation: Native competence and targets for instruction. *Cognition and Instruction, 22*(3), 293–331.

diSessa, A. A., Hammer, D., Sherin, B. L., & Kolpakowsky, T. (1991). Inventing graphing: Meta-representational expertise in children. *The Journal of Mathematical Behavior, 10*(2), 117–160.

diSessa, A. A., & Sherin, B. L. (2000). Meta-representation: An introduction. *The Journal of Mathematical Behavior, 19*(4), 385–398. doi:10.1016/S 0732-3123(01)00051-7

Elkoshi, R. (2004). Interpreting children's invented graphic notation. *Arts & Learning Research Journal, 20*(1), 61–84.

Gil, V., Reybrouck, M., Tejada, J., & Verschaffel, L. (2015). Improving the representational strategies of children in a music-listening and playing task: An intervention-based study. *Research Studies in Music Education, 37*(1), 77–92. doi: 10.1177/1321103X15589337

Mills, J. & Paynter, J. (Eds.). (2008). *Thinking and making: Selections from the writings of John Paynter on music in education.* Oxford, UK: Oxford University Press.

Reybrouck, M., Verschaffel, L., & Lauwerier, S. (2009). Children's graphical notations as representational tools for musical sense-making in a music-listening task. *British Journal of Music Education, 26*(2), 189–211. doi: 10.1017/S0265051709008432

Taylor, P., & Maor, D. (2000). Assessing the efficacy of online teaching with the constructivist on-line learning environment survey. In A. Herrmann & M. Kulski (Eds.), *Flexible futures in tertiary teaching: Proceedings of the 9th annual teaching learning forum.* Curtin University of Technology. Perth, Australia. Retrieved from Curtin University of Technology: http://goo.gl/PeU59T

Upitis, R. (1990). Children's invented notations of familiar and unfamiliar melodies. *Psychomusicology: A Journal of Research in Music Cognition, 9*(1), 89–106. doi:10.1037/h0094156

Upitis, R. (1993). Children's invented symbol systems: Exploring parallels between music and mathematics. *Psychomusicology: A Journal of Research in Music Cognition, 12*(1), 52–57. doi:10.1037/h0094117

Verschaffel, L., de Corte, E., Lasure, S., van Vaerenbergh, G., Bogaerts, H., & Ratinckx, E. (1999). Learning to solve mathematical application problems: A design experiment with fifth graders. *Mathematical Thinking and Learning, 1*(3), 195–229. doi:10.1207/s15327833mtl0103_2

Verschaffel, L., Reybrouck, M., Degraeuwe, G., & van Dooren, W. (2013). The relative importance of children's criteria for representational adequacy in the perception of simple sonic stimuli. *Psychology of Music, 41*(6), 691–712. doi:10.1177/0305735612442975

Verschaffel, L., Reybrouck, M., Jans, C., & van Dooren, W. (2010). Children's criteria for representational adequacy in the perception of simple sonic stimuli. *Cognition and Instruction, 28*(4), 475–502. doi:10.1080/0737 0008.2010.511571

Verschaffel, L., Reybrouck, M., Janssens, M., & van Dooren, W. (2010). Using graphical notations to assess children's experiencing of simple and complex musical fragments. *Psychology of Music, 38*(3), 259–284. doi:10.1177/0305735609336054

An exploration of the relationships between practice, motivation and examination outcomes

Susan Hallam

University College London, Institute of Education, UK

s.hallam@ioe.ac.uk

Abstract

There has been relatively little research exploring the relationships between the quality of practice, levels of motivation and examination outcomes. Such research as has been undertaken has suggested that self-efficacy is the best predictor of examination success. The research reported here aimed to further that research exploring whether there were differences between those who had failed, passed, been commended or highly commended in their most recent examination in their responses to a series of statements relating to practice and motivation. 2131 young musicians, aged 6-19, across a wide range of expertise (from Grade 1 to higher education conservatoire entry level) and with a range of examination outcomes from fail to highly commended, playing a wide range of instruments responded to a series of statements on a 7 point Likert scale. These related to practice and motivation including: practice strategies; organisation of practice; enjoyment of practice; self-beliefs; enjoyment of musical activities; enjoyment of performance; level of support received from parents, friends and teachers; attitudes towards playing an instrument and perceptions of its value; and beliefs about the importance of musical ability. The findings showed that those who had been awarded a pass mark in their examinations (with the exception of those who had taken Grade 1) undertook less practice than those who had failed or who had higher marks. Factor analysis of the Likert scale responses revealed seven factors relating to practice and six to motivation. Multivariate analysis of variance revealed that there were no statistically significant differences between those with different examination outcomes in relation to the adoption of systematic practice strategies, ease of concentration, immediate correction of errors, support and social affirmation and disliking practice. In relation to the organisation of practice, the use of recordings and the metronome, the adoption of analytic strategies, social life and self-belief in musical ability the students who had passed their last examination were those responding least positively to the statements assessing these factors and not those who had failed their examination. Those who failed were most likely to adopt ineffective practice strategies and were less likely to enjoy performing, playing, lessons and practice. The findings are discussed in relation to earlier research and in terms of their educational implications.

Keywords: Music, education, motivation, practice, instruments, examination outcomes

Introduction

There has been relatively little research considering the practice strategies and motivation of students who have achieved different examination outcomes. An exception to this is the work of McPherson and McCormick (2000, 2003, 2006) who explored the predictors of examination outcomes using structural equation modelling. In a series of studies, which included measures of cognitive strategy use, practice regulation, practice time, grade level, informal practice, formal practice and self-efficacy they showed that self-efficacy was the strongest predictor of performance outcome. The research reported here continues this strand of research with a larger sample and a wider range of input variables.

Explanations of achievement in learning to play an instrument have been framed largely within the expertise paradigm which suggests that the amount of time spent practising is the single strongest determinant of the level and quality of expertise attained (Ericsson et al., 1993). While there is extensive evidence that the length of time playing an instrument makes a major contribution to the level of expertise attained, time spent practising alone is not a strong predictor, in part, because the quality of the practice undertaken is important (see Jorgensen and Hallam, forthcoming for a review). There has been less focus on the quality of learning outcomes at each specific level of expertise. Such research as has been undertaken has not found strong consistent relationships between the amount of practice and the quality of performance at any specific level of expertise (Williamon and Valentine, 2000; Hallam, 1998; 2013; Hallam et al., 2012).

When motivational factors are considered having a positive musical self-concept is related to high levels of attainment and successful task performance (Asmus and Harrison, 1990; Vispoel, 1993) as are high levels of self-efficacy (McPherson and McCormick, 2000, 2003, 2006). Those who give up playing tend to have lower expectations of success (Pitts et al., 2000; Chandler et al., 1988) and are less confident about future outcomes largely through disappointing earlier experiences where they have not been successful (StGeorge, 2010). Research within the expectancy-value paradigm supports this demonstrating that students' beliefs about their competence predict learning outcomes (Eccles and Wigfield, 2002).

The research reported here attempts to build on previous work comparing the responses of learners whose most recent examination outcome was failure, a pass mark, being commended or highly commended in relation to their self-reports of adopting effective practice strategies, being motivated and having high levels of self-belief.

Method

A self-report questionnaire was used to collect data from a large sample of learners. The questionnaire was devised based on the research evidence relating to practice and motivation (for reviews see Jorgensen and Hallam, 2016 and Hallam, 2016) and a smaller scale prior study (Hallam, 2013). The questionnaire sought information about the level of expertise attained as assessed by the highest examination grade achieved in independent graded instrumental examinations from grade 1 to Grade 8 and the level of performance in the most recent examination (fail, pass, commended, highly commended). Participants were asked about the number of days they carried out practice and for how long. The questionnaire also included a range of statements relating to various elements of practice including the strategies adopted, the organisation of practice, and ease of concentration and statements relating to motivation including the support of family and friends; enjoyment of performing; the value placed on playing an instrument; listening to music; music as a social activity; enjoyment of practice; self-beliefs about musical ability and potential; beliefs about self-efficacy, effort and the importance of musical ability; and social affirmation. Respondents were requested to respond to these on a seven point Likert scale with seven indicating the strongest agreement, one the strongest disagreement.

The sample

Data were collected from young people representing all of the classical and popular musical instruments in a variety of settings, including two junior conservatoires, two Local Authority youth orchestras, two Local Authority Saturday Music schools, a conservatoire for popular music and three state comprehensive schools. The children who participated were receiving tuition on their instruments individually or in small groups of no more than four children.

A total of 3325 children, ranging in level of expertise from Preliminary grade through to Grade 8 level (minimum required for conservatoire entrance in the UK), completed questionnaires. Only those who had taken graded examinations could be included in the current analysis. This excluded all of those who were at the preliminary level. The age range was from 6 to 19 years. The instruments that they played were representative of the classical and popular instruments played in the UK. Overall, 230 reported having failed their most recent examination, 419 had passed, 818 had been commended and 664 were highly commended, a total of 2131.

The research was designed taking account of the ethical guidelines of the British Psychological Society and the British Educational Research Association and was approved by the ethics committee of University College London Institute of Education. The participating young people were told that they did not have to participate if they did not wish to do so and were assured that the data would remain confidential and that their parents and teachers would not have access to it.

Findings

Analysis of the relationship between level of expertise and examination outcomes showed that there was considerable variability in the nature of the examination outcome and grade level (see Figure 1). For this reason the multivariate analyses of variance which were undertaken used level of expertise as a covariate.

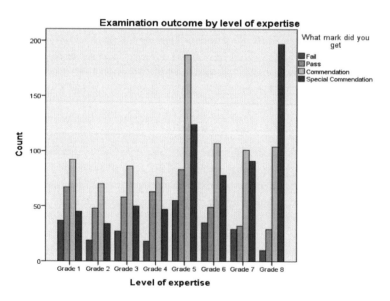

Figure 1. Examination outcome by level of expertise

Amount of practice

The overall mean for average weekly practice of those who had failed their most recent examination was 233 minutes (SE = 14.9), for those who had passed 177 minutes (SE = 11.1), for those with commendation 218 minutes (SE = 7.6) and for those who were highly commended 308 minutes (SD = 8.9). A multivariate analysis was undertaken and was statistically significant (F (1,3) = 31.8, p = .0001). At every grade level apart from grade 1 it was those who had only passed their last examination who did the least practice not those who had failed the exam. At Grade 1 the pattern was as might have been expected with those failing their examination doing the least practice.

Factor analysis of practice variables

To enable comparisons to be made taking account of the responses to all of the statements a Principal Components analysis was undertaken. This was selected as it affords an empirical analysis of the data set (Tabachnick & Fidell, 2001). Eigenvalues were retained if they were greater than 1 and the scree plot was used to identify those factors before the breaking point of the elbow of the plot. A varimax rotation was used to enable interpretation and description of results (Tabachnick & Fidell, 2001). Seven factors were identified: the adoption of systematic practice strategies, the organisation of practice, the use of recordings and the metronome, the adoption of analytic strategies, the adoption of ineffective practice strategies, perceived concentration and the immediate correction of errors.

Factor 1, the adoption of systematic practice strategies, had high weightings for statements relating to practising things slowly (.649); knowing when a mistake was made (.558); practising sections slowly when a mistake was made (.73); repetition when something was difficult (.68); and playing passages slowly to start with then speeding up (.59). Factor 2, the organisation of practice, had high weightings for making a list of what to practice (.62); starting practice with scales (.734); starting with warm up exercises (55); and starting practice with studies (.44). Factor 3, using recordings and the metronome had high weightings for getting a recording of the piece to be learned (.67); recording practice and listening to the tapes (.74); and practising with a metronome (.64). Factor 4, the adoption of analytic strategies, had high weightings for getting an overall idea of a piece before practising it (.66); trying to find out what a piece sounds like before playing it (.76); working out where the difficult sections are (.52); and analysing the structure of a piece before learning to play it (.43). Factor 5, the adoption of ineffective practice strategies, had high weightings for only playing pieces from beginning to end without stopping (.7); when making a mistake going back to the beginning of the piece and starting again (.64); and a negative weighting for practising small sections (-.41). Factor 6 focusing on concentration had a high weighting for finding it easy to concentrate (.70) and a negative weighting for being easily distracted when practising (-.77). Factor 7 relating to the immediate correction of errors had high weightings for when making a mistake, stopping, correcting the wrong note and then carrying on (.71); and a negative weighting for when making a mistake carrying on with correcting it (-.79).

Multivariate analysis of variance of the seven factors by examination outcome with level of expertise as a covariate was statistically significant ($F(21,5574) = 5.7$, $p = .0001$). Consideration of the statistical significance of each individual factor revealed that there were no statistically significant differences between those with different examination outcomes in relation to the adoption of systematic practice strategies, ease of concentration and immediate correction of errors. In relation to the organisation of practice, the use of recordings and the metronome and the adoption of analytic strategies the students who had passed their last examination were those with the least positive responses not those who had failed. Those who failed their examinations were the most likely to adopt ineffective practice strategies (see Table 1).

Factor analysis of variables relating to motivation

To explore the relationships between the motivational variables, factor analysis was undertaken. Six factors emerged from the data. Factor 1, support and social affirmation had high weightings for parents wanting the participant to play an instrument (.74); relations liking them playing a musical instrument (.66); most people thinking that they played their instrument well (.63); teachers at school liking them to play a musical instrument (.49); and brothers and sisters liking them playing a musical instrument (.46). Factor 2, social life and enjoyment of musical activities had high weightings for having lots of friends who played musical instruments (.72); enjoying going to concerts to listen (.61); believing it was valuable to play a musical instrument (.59); playing an instrument being an important part of participants' social life (.548); and enjoying playing in musical groups, orchestras and bands (.44). Factor 3, enjoyment of performing had high weightings for statements relating to finding it very satisfying to play in concerts (.79); and playing in concerts giving participants a real thrill (.83). Factor 4, self-belief in musical ability had weightings for statements relating to needing musical ability to succeed in playing an instrument (.74); participants having musical ability (.64); having the potential to be a good musician (.56); usually being successful in what they attempted to do on their instrument (.49); and to a lesser extent being able to achieve anything that they wanted if they carried out sufficient practice (.37); and most people thinking that they played their instrument well (.33). Factor 5, enjoyment of playing, lessons and practice had high negative weightings for hating having to play an instrument (-.84) and finding practice boring (-.56) and positive weightings for enjoying instrumental lessons (.72). Factor 6, disliking practice had high weightings for not wanting to practice on some days (.73), finding practice boring (.64) and a negative weighting for liking practice (-.66).

A multivariate analysis of variance of the six factors by examination outcome with level of expertise as a covariate was statistically significant $(F(6,1892) = 4.35, p = .0001)$.

There were no statistically significant differences in terms of examination outcomes with regard to support and social affirmation and disliking practice. In relation to social life and enjoyment of musical activities and self-belief in musical ability the students who had passed their last examination were those with the least positive responses not those who had failed. Those who failed their examinations were less likely to enjoy performing, playing, lessons and practice (see Table 1).

Table 1: Differences in factor scores by examination outcome with level of expertise as a covariate

	Fail		Pass		Commended		Highly com- mended		SIG
	Mean	SD	Mean	SD	Mean	SD	Mean	SD	
Adoption of systematic practice strategies	-.04	.93	-.12	.97	.02	.94	.05	.94	NS
Organisation of practice	.03	.94	-.09	.95	.01	.94	.15	1.0	.0001
Use of recordings and the metronome	-.03	.95	-.14	.92	.02	.99	.36	.97	.0001
Adoption of analytic strategies	-.01	.99	-.08	.92	.09	.95	.05	.94	.007
Adoption of ineffective practice strategies	.04	.92	.03	.93	-.22	.89	-.44	.91	.0001
Ease of concentration	.01	1.0	-.09	.96	-.01	.94	.09	1.0	NS
Immediate correction of errors	.02	1.1	.005	.97	-.10	.98	.0003	.94	NS
Support and social affirmation	-.01	1.0	-.07	.93	.02	.96	-.06	1.0	NS
Social life and enjoy- ment of musical activi- ties	.08	1.1	-.09	.98	.14	.92	.17	.94	.039
Enjoyment of perform- ing	-.13	.99	-.02	.93	.09	.89	.28	.83	.000
Self-belief in musical ability	-.01	1.0	-.09	1.1	-.05	.92	.21	.92	.000
Enjoyment of playing, lessons and practice	-.21	1.1	.01	.89	.07	.93	.04	.99	.006
Disliking practice	.04	.93	.15	.93	.14	.92	.07	1.0	NS

Practice and motivational factors as predictors of examination outcomes

A multiple regression was undertaken which included all of the factors relating to practice and motivation, with level of examination success as the dependent variable. The Multiple R was .42 accounting for 17% of the variance. This was statistically significant ($F(13,2053) = 33.84$, $p = .0001$). Standardised beta coefficients were statistically significant for organisation of practice (.1); use of recordings and the metronome (.14), the adoption of ineffective practice strategies (-.25), social life and enjoyment of musical activities (.06), enjoyment of performing (.15), self-belief (.08), enjoyment of playing, lessons and practice (.07) and disliking practice (.124).

Discussion

There are limitations to this research based as it was on self-report. As this limitation applied to all participants, and there is no reason to suppose that any bias introduced as a result of the self-report differed between those failing, passing or being commended or highly commended, the differences found can be assumed to be robust.

The findings revealed that for several of the factors it was those who had passed the examination rather than those who had failed who gave the most negative responses. They did less practice (apart from those having recently taken Grade 1), were less well organised in their practice, used recordings and the metronome less and were less likely to use analytic strategies. Music was not such an important part of their social life and they had lower beliefs in their musical ability. Why those who had passed their most recent examination should have given more negative responses in these areas than those who had failed is counterintuitive. Perhaps those who had failed were better supported by their teacher and significant others enabling them to continue to be positive about playing a musical instrument, while the need for such support when a participant had passed the examination was not recognised.

Those who had failed their examination were most likely to adopt ineffective practice strategies and were less likely to enjoy performing, playing, lessons and practice. Overall, this suggests that they were not strongly motivated which along with their ineffective practising strategies, contributed to their examination failure. This is supported by the multiple regression analysis which revealed that enjoyment of performing, adopting ineffective practising strategies and disliking practice were the strongest predictors of examination outcome.

While self-belief contributed to explaining differences in examination outcomes, in contrast to the findings of McPherson and McCormick (2000, 2003, 2006), it was not the strongest predictor. There are a number of reasons for these differences in the research findings. The current research did not include level of expertise in the regression analysis and the factors focused on more specific aspects of practice. As the examinations did not include improvisation informal practice was not included, the focus was on formal practice. A number of motivational factors were included and self-efficacy was only one element of a factor focusing on self-beliefs relating to music more generally. Further research could explore the impact of the separate elements of the self-belief factor providing a better comparison with the findings of McPherson and McCormick. Perhaps the most important difference relates to the timing of the research. McPherson and McCormick assessed self-efficacy prior the participants taking their examination. At this point, feedback, particularly from teachers, is likely to have influenced their responses to statements about how confident they were about the examination outcome. The current research asked participants to indicate the outcome of their most recent examination, so the data on practice and motivation related to a time when the outcome of the examination was already known. In some cases this may have been some time ago. Self-beliefs would therefore be based on current feedback from teachers and others which may have changed, positively or negatively, since the time of taking the examination.

Educational implications

The findings reported here indicate that it is not only failing an examination which may impact on motivation but also only gaining a pass mark. Teachers need to be aware of this and be ready to support students who may not have been as successful in examinations as they would like. The findings also suggest, implicitly, that for some young people performance anxiety can impact on examination outcomes. While this has been recognised at conservatoire level and appropriate guidance offered, this is not always the case for school aged children who also need to understand how best to manage their increased arousal level and use it to advantage to enhance their performance. The findings also indicate the importance of teachers modelling and discussing with their students how to practice effectively to maximise the time spent practising.

References

Asmus E.P. & Harrison C.S. (1990). Characteristics of motivation for music and musical aptitude of undergraduate non-music majors. *Journal of Research in Music Education, 38*, 258-268.

Chandler, D., Chiarella, C., & Auria, K. (1988). Performance expectancy, success, satisfaction, and attributions as variables in band challenges. *Journal of Research in Music Education, 35(2)*, 249-258.

Eccles, J.S. & Wigfield, A. (2002) Motivational beliefs, values and goals. *Annual Review of Psychology, 53*, 109-132.

Ericsson, K.A., Krampe, R.T., & Tesch-Romer, C. (1993). The role of deliberate practice in the acquisition of expert performance. *Psychological Review, 100*(3), 363-406.

Hallam, S. (1998) Predictors of achievement and drop out in instrumental tuition. *Psychology of Music, 26(2)*, 116-132.

Hallam, S. (2013) What predicts level of expertise attained, quality of performance an future musical aspirations in young instrumental players. *Psychology of Music, 41(3)*, 267-291.

Hallam, S. (2016) Motivation to learn. In S. Hallam, I. Cross & M Thaut (Eds.) *Handbook of Psychology of Music (2nd edition)*. Oxford: Oxford University Press (pp. 285- 294).

Hallam, S., Rinta, T., Varvarigou, M., Creech, A., Papageorgi, I., and Lani, J. (2012) The development of practising strategies in young people. *Psychology of Music, 40(5),* 652-680.

Jorgensen, H. & Hallam, S. (2016) Practising. In S. Hallam, I. Cross, I. & M. Thaut (Eds.), *Oxford Handbook of Music Psychology (2nd edition)* Oxford: Oxford University Press.

McPherson, G.E. & McCormick, J. (2000). The contribution of motivational factors to instrumental performance in a performance examination. *Research Studies in Music Education, 15,* 31-39.

McPherson, G.E. & McCormick, J. (2003).The role of self-efficacy in a musical performance examination: An exploratory structural equation analysis. *Psychology of Music, 31(1),* 37-51.

McPherson, G.E. & McCormick, J. (2006). Self-efficacy and performing music. *Psychology of Music, 34,* 322-336.

Pitts, S. E., Davidson, J.W., & McPherson, G.E. (2000b). Models of success and failure in instrumental learning: Case studies of young players in the first 20 months of learning. *Bulletin of the Council for Research in Music Education, 146,* 51-69.

StGeorge, J. (2010). *The subjectivity of musical learning: Understanding participation in instrumental music instruction.* Unpublished PhD, University of Newcastle, New South Wales.

Tabachnick, B.G. & Fidell, L.S. (2001). *Using multivariate statistics (Fourth Edition).* Boston: Allyn and Bacon, Pearson International.

Vispoel, W.P. (1993). The development and evaluation of a computerized adaptive test of tonal memory. *Journal of Research in Music Education, 41,* 111-136.

Wigfield, A., & Eccles, J. (1992). The development of achievement task values: A theoretical analysis. *Developmental Review, 12,* 265-310.

Williamon, A. & Valentine, E. (2000). Quantity and quality of musical practice as predictors of performance quality. *British Journal of Psychology, 91,* 353-376.

Effect of Related Instruction on Student Perceptions of Behavioral Characteristics and Instructional Patterns of Expert Teaching

Christopher M. Johnson
The University of Kansas

cmj@ku.edu

Lindsey R. Williams
West Virginia University

Rebecca L. Tast
Texas State University

Melissa Brunkan
Louisiana State University

Abstract

The purpose of this study was to investigate the effect of related instruction on student perceptions of behavioral characteristics and instructional patterns of expert teaching. Participants (N=76) viewed video segments from four consecutive swim lessons between an expert teacher and a new student. The first viewing of these videos occurred prior to a series of classroom lectures, discussions, and activities. Participants then viewed the videos a second time following the completion of coursework (15 weeks later). During both viewings, participants wrote observational comments. Results of a content analysis of 3,958 comments indicated that participants shifted their focus from listing activities observed and their opinion regarding the interactions to noting teacher behaviors, and resultant change in the student's behavior and affect. Qualitative analysis of those same comments indicated a shift from surface level statements to comments regarding purpose and effectiveness.

Keywords: expert teaching, perception, behavior, observation, affect

The primary goal of teacher education is to produce exemplary teachers. Significant time and resources are spent providing students with opportunities to develop teaching behaviors that they might employ to that end. One of the primary barriers to becoming an excellent teacher, however, is making the leap between newly acquired knowledge and skills and effective teaching behaviors. One might hope that students will obtain these characteristics of excellence from watching their daily models, or through some kind of educational osmosis, but there is little evidence to suggest that this is what actually happens. However, if students do not learn to adequately discriminate and / or perceive the presence of truly masterful teaching, it is unlikely that they will develop those skills in such a way that they might become most effective. The music teacher education literature is replete with high-quality research investigating what exemplifies good teaching, however, there is none on how students are able to identify and codify or define those examples.

Among the attributes contributing to effective teaching, it seems evident that students exhibit better learning and more willingness to learn in environments where teachers offer contingent feedback with an emphasis on approval, good eye contact, and well paced instruction (Duke, & Henninger, 1998; Forsythe, 1975; Hendel, 1995; Kostka, 1984; Price, 1983; Sims, 1986; Yarbrough, 1975; Yarbrough, Price & Bowers, 1991). Though the maxim "good teaching is good teaching" applies across disciplines, the specific situational aspects of the environment will undoubtedly modify delivery of reinforcement (Forsythe, 1975) and relate differently to instructor personas (Schmidt, 1989). There is also no doubt that different activities even in the same classroom (Yarbrough & Price, 1981), and teacher experience (Goolsby, 1996; Hedden & Johnson, 2008; Wagner & Struhl, 1979) impact the instructional atmosphere. It should be noted that while these independent attributes seem like common sense, this seemingly prima facies truth is the result of decades of substantially rigorous research.

Clearly being able to truly identify great teaching is not simply a byproduct of having sat in classes for most of one's life. Further, it has been said that the differences between good teachers and expert teachers might not be so much in what they do, but in when they do it (Duke, 2007). Of course, this observation is not on the same continuum as students who cannot even tell that the teacher is delivering misinformation. Previous research indicates that the observer needs to be extremely sophisticated in order to perceive all of the subtleties that occur in a teaching event. If we could get all students to the point where they are able to perceive, identify, and emulate great teaching, instruction of music teachers could be improved. The question becomes, how do we get students to move towards this more refined perception. The traditional fix for identified shortcomings has always been to have a class that addresses it, however there has been little documentation of how related instruction, such as that provided by a class, might help students become more refined in their ability to perceive, identify, and emulate great teaching. The purpose of this study was to investigate the effect of related instruction in undergraduate music education and music therapy training on student perceptions of behavioral characteristics and instructional patterns of expert teaching.

Method

Participants

Seventy-five university students in the Midwest USA completed both the pretest and the posttest tasks. Students were from two similar universities.

Stimulus Recordings

In a previous study, Claudine, a swimming teacher, was documented to be an exceptional teacher (Johnson, Williams, Parisi, & Brunkan, 2015). Claudine teaches swim lessons in a one-on-one paradigm at a pool in her back yard. She does not give students the typical one-hour lesson, but instead schedules lessons for 15 minutes over four consecutive days. The lessons recorded for that study were with Nicky, a two-year-old boy with no swimming experience.

In the previous research project, researchers viewed the lessons and a number of characteristics in Claudine's teaching were documented. Her pacing was remarkably quick, and her actions were extremely efficient in reaching target-learning behaviors. Perhaps the most striking characteristic of her instruction was the stable consistency of visual and verbal reinforcement. Until the student reacted appropriately to her instruction (not until the third lesson), Claudine's behavior was focused exclusively on the activity that needed to occur. She reinforced, but did not waver from the task at hand. At first, her reinforcement was constant, but not contingent. As trust was developed between teacher and student, the reinforcement became much more contingent on the child's behavior. Teaching cycles increased in number as the lessons progressed. Researchers also found that individual physical tasks were more fully linked in subsequent lessons. The amount of time swimming also increased from lesson to lesson, while the time spent reinforcing decreased. For this study, sample segments of 150-seconds were taken from each of the four recorded lessons. These segments were placed in chronological order so that participants could observe the progress of the swimming student over time. Each 150-second segment was followed by 90 seconds of blank time for continued reflection and data collection. Blank time on the video consisted of a black screen with no sound. The total time for the complete stimulus, with four teaching episodes, each followed by time for reflection, was 16 minutes in length.

Independent Variable

The independent variable for this study was a series of lectures designed to teach students classroom management, behavioral observation, and behavioral psychology techniques in a musical setting. To ensure that students from the two universities received as close to same instruction as possible, the two instructors agreed upon a set of goals and objectives for the course. In order to meet these goals and objectives, the instructors used the same syllabus, course calendar, textbook, lecture notes, classroom activities, behavioral observation training, self-actualizing activities, and assessments.

Procedure

The first viewing of these videos (pretest) occurred prior to the implementation of the independent variable. Participants were given a packet requesting their names (for matching purposes) and majors, and four blank sheets of paper for recording their observations. They were then read the following instructions:

You are about to see a DVD of four teaching episodes. The lessons are the first four swim lessons for a 2 year-old child. They are in chronological order. Each excerpt is 150 seconds long. For each lesson, please write your observations of the event. You may write about anything and everything you see. You may include any of your impressions. Please know that there are no correct or incorrect responses. Anything you write is indeed correct.

There will be a 90 second break between lessons for you to write or write more.

If you have any questions, please feel free to ask them now.

Participants then viewed the four teaching episodes and wrote comments regarding their observations both during and after each observation. After the implementation of the independent variable (15 weeks later) participants viewed the videos a second time (posttest) following the same procedures as the pretest.

Results

There were 3,958 comments classified using the categories in Table 1. Two researchers independently read the comments and created categories. Though previous research informed the project's starting point, researchers were free to interpret the comments as patterns emerged. They then met and negotiated a single group of categories for the submitted observations. After initial categorizations were assigned, all discrepancies were then viewed together until 100% agreement was reached on every comment. The total number of pretest comments categorized was 1,974. The total number of posttest comments was 1,984. A Chi Square analyses revealed significant differences in the nature of the comments made by participants from the pretest to the posttest (χ^2 (10) = 237.76, p < .001). One important difference noted in the nature of the comments was the dramatic increase in the number of comments directly related to Teacher Behavior overall and Teacher Approval to a lesser degree. Other differences noted in the posttest were decreased numbers of comments regarding Swimmer Behaviors, Observer Opinion, and Activity Identification.

Table 1. Pretest and Posttest Comment Classification

Category	Pretest		Posttest	
Teacher Behaviors				
Behaviors - general	350	17.70%	583	29.40%
Approval	157	8.00%	249	12.60%
Disapproval	2	0.10%	12	0.50%
Attitude/Affect	54	2.80%	91	4.60%
Swimmer Behaviors				
Behaviors - general	434	22.00%	205	10.30%
Feedback	30	1.50%	34	1.70%
Attitude/Affect	303	15.40%	386	19.50%
Participant Comments				
Observer Opinion	280	14.20%	188	9.50%
Activity Identification	283	14.30%	165	8.30%
Activity Intent	33	1.60%	28	1.40%
Miscellaneous	48	2.40%	43	2.20%
Pacing, Activity Order, Relative Comments, Setting, Student/Teacher Relationship				
Total Comments	**1,974**	**100%**	**1,984**	**100%**

Differences in the nature of the participant comments were also noted when examining the four different lessons (see Table 2). Though differences from lesson to lesson were expected as each lesson contained its own elements. These patterns might indicate shifts of attention paralleling activity shifts. For instance, categories of Teacher Behaviors had fewer and fewer comments progressively across the lessons, as Student Behaviors and Student Attitude/Affect showed a concomitant increase. Participant

Opinions also proportionally increased. The percentage of comments regarding teacher behaviors are about 15% higher in the posttest overall, but higher by far in Lesson One, and decreasing across the four lessons.

Table 2: Comment Classification Pretest and Posttest Percentages by Lesson

Categories	Lesson							
	1		**2**		**3**		**4**	
	Pre	Post	Pre	Post	Pre	Post	Pre	Post
	Teacher Behaviors (%)							
Behaviors - general	23.30	37.80	22.50	34.50	13.60	22.80	10.90	22.50
Approval	9.90	15.40	7.50	12.90	7.90	11.40	6.20	10.50
Disapproval	0.20	0.20	0.00	1.00	0.00	0.60	0.20	0.60
Attitude/Affect	4.40	7.90	1.90	5.30	3.40	3.20	0.90	1.90
	Swimmer Behaviors (%)							
Behaviors - general	15.20	3.00	19.20	9.50	25.50	12.40	29.10	16.50
Feedback	2.70	1.80	1.70	0.80	0.80	3.00	0.60	1.20
Attitude/Affect	10.10	15.40	12.70	16.60	19.40	26.80	19.90	18.60
	Participant Comments (%)							
Observer Opinion	11.70	5.90	14.60	7.50	15.30	9.50	15.60	15.40
Activity Identification	15.90	9.50	16.10	8.70	11.50	6.10	13.60	9.20
Activity Intent	2.40	1.50	1.90	1.60	1.20	0.80	1.10	1.70
Miscellaneous	4.20	1.60	1.90	1.60	1.40	3.40	1.90	1.90

Discussion

Although the number of comments participants wrote in the pretest and posttest were very close (1,974 and 1,984, respectively), the nature of the comments takes a definitive shift between the pretest and posttest. Participants went from focusing as much on their own opinions and identifying what activities were happening to noting all aspects of actual teacher behavior, teacher reinforcement, and the impact these had on the swimmer's behavior. This shift in focus seems to indicate that intervening instruction aided participants in modifying their observational behaviors. During the pretest, participants described what they saw and how they felt about it. One of our favorite comments was "Maybe he is a little nervous because some strange woman is almost letting him drown." While perhaps a legitimate concern from one perspective, this comment does not consider the complete picture. Most of the participants had similar reactions – they created a laundry list of activities and how they felt about that list at any given time. The comments were surface level, such that almost anyone in the general population could have written them. While previous research indicates that topics that are identified as crucial to good teaching include contingent feedback with an emphasis on approval, good eye contact, well paced instruction, delivery of reinforcement, intensity, and sequential patterns of instruction; very few participants noted these topics in their pretest comments. Some observational comments pointed at the soothing that the instructor did, but almost no other aspects of reinforcement were mentioned. It seemed that most participants were not aware of the actual cause and effect of behavior and reinforcement, much less teacher intensity, on/off-task, sequencing of instruction, or even eye contact, etc.

Posttest comments expressed a very different nature from the pretest comments. The comments focused more on topics of purpose and effectiveness. They used more technical terminology, and indicated understanding as opposed to reacting. For example, one participant stated "the teacher used a positive tone and approved behavior by the child." Yet another participant commented that "the teacher uses verbal positive reinforcement." There were many references to sequences as well as many comments that illustrated a viewing of the process, instead of a list of random observations. Participants saw patterns of behavior and sequences of instruction. The comments seemed to show a shift from outside observer to an instructor's point of view. For example, one participant first stated, "the child is very uncomfortable" whereas when viewing the same lesson in the posttest, the same participant's view seemed to shift with the comment "the teacher uses proper reinforcement and approval responses."

The patterns of comments noted from lesson to lesson (Table 2) are interesting. Certainly the lessons each had a different nature – one which the instructor anticipated based on prior experience. In her words, "the beginning of the second lesson is always the worst. In the first lesson the child does not know what is coming. The second lesson, they are not happy about what is about to happen." Usually by the third lesson things start to really break through. The comment emphasis as well as the content showed that the participants observed that the instructor's plan was reflected in the observations. There are some steady changes, but it is most notable in the second to third lesson, particularly in the posttest observations.

It seems that if we are to educate and develop excellent practitioners of music education and music therapy, we need them to be able to see an instructional episode and understand what is going on at a level more discriminating than listing the activities. They need to see the inner workings of the relationships – the behavioral causes and effects. If they can see those, it then follows that they will have a chance to eventually understand those complexities. Only then will they be able to wittingly use those techniques to become more effective educators and therapists. It is very unclear if this series of lectures and activities was able to get the participants to that level of sophistication, however the written comments do imply that the participants were further down that road after the intervention.

References

Duke, R. A. (2007). Intelligent music teaching: Essays on the core principles of effective instruction. Austin, TX: Learning and Behavior Resources.

Duke, R. A., & Henninger, J. C. (1998). Effects of verbal corrections on student attitude and performance. Journal of Research in Music Education, 46, 482-495.

Forsythe, J. L. (1975). The effect of teacher approval, disapproval, and errors on student attentiveness: Music versus classroom teachers. In C. K. Madsen, R. D. Greer, and C. H. Madsen, Jr. (Eds.), Research in music behavior (pp. 49-55). New York: Teachers College Press.

Goolsby, T. W. (1996). Time use in instrumental rehearsals. Journal of Research in Music Education, 44, 286-304.

Hedden, D. G., & Johnson, C. M. (2008). The effect of teaching experience on time and accuracy of assessing young singers' pitch accuracy. Bulletin of the Council for Research in Music Education, 178, 63-72.

Hendel, C. (1995). Behavioral characteristics and instructional patterns of selected music teachers. Journal of Research in Music Education, 43, 182-203.

Johnson, C. M., Williams, L. R., Parisi, J., & Brunkan, M. C. (2015). Behavioral characteristics and instructional patterns of expert teaching, and the transfer of those behaviors into a musical setting: Two case studies. The International Journal of Music Education: Research, doi: 10.1177/0255761415619060

Kostka, M. J. (1984). An investigation of reinforcements, time use, and student attentiveness in piano lessons. Journal of Research in Music Education, 32, 113-122.

Price, H. E. (1983). The effect of conductor academic task presentation, conductor reinforcement, and ensemble practice on performers' musical achievement, attentiveness, and attitude. Journal of Research in Music Education, 31, 245-257.

Schmidt, C. P. (1989). Applied music teaching behavior as a function of selected personality variables. Journal of Research in Music Education, 37, 258-271.

Sims, W. L. (1986). The effect of high vs. low teacher affect and passive vs. active student activity during music listening on preschool children's attention, piece preference, time spent listening and piece recognition. Journal of Research in Music Education, 34, 173-191.

Wagner, M., & Struhl, E. (1979). Comparisons of beginning versus experienced elementary music educators in the use of teaching time. Journal of Research in Music Education, 27, 113-125.

Yarbrough, C. (1975). Effect of magnitude of conductor behavior on students in selected mixed choruses. Journal of Research in Music Education, 23, 134-146.

Yarbrough, C., & Price, H. E. (1981). Prediction of performer attentiveness based on rehearsal activity and teacher behavior. Journal of Research in Music Education, 29, 209-217.

Yarbrough, C., Price, H. E., & Bowers, J. (1991). The effect of knowledge of research on rehearsal skills and teaching values of experienced teachers. Update: Applications of Research in Music Education, 9(2), 17-20.

Formative or cumulative? An autoethnographic study of slow and fast composing processes

Karlin G. Love

The University of Queensland, Australia

karlin.love@uqconnect.edu.au

Abstract

Many studies of creativity have proposed models of creative processes, identifying distinct stages. Music composition researchers, especially, have challenged the implicit linear nature of these models, proposing more recursive processes and recognising that exploration and inspiration occur throughout. Studying the creative process of another person is an investigation of those things which can be externalised: ideas written in verbal language, conventional or graphic musical notation or expressed through speech or performance. An autoethnographic approach, with a self-studying researcher, offers an additional body of less tangible information with which to interpret the experience of creating new work–experiences which, since they are exploring the new, may not be easily conveyed right away. This paper reports on a comparative case study of the author's processes of composing two chamber music works. One was composed very quickly; the other over a long period of time. Striking differences in the compositional processes were noticed, particularly in regards to preparation, research, and incubation. The process of slow composition appears to add to the composer's knowledge and skill in a 'formative' manner, whereas the quickly composed piece depended upon learning occurring in previous slowly composed works, and could be seen as a 'cumulative' work.

Keywords: creative process, stage model, composition, autoethnography, chamber music

Introduction

Amabile's (1983, 1996) model of creativity includes domain-relevant skills, creativity-relevant skills, and task motivation. Mastery of a domain ('domain-relevant skill') is considered necessary by many to make a creative contribution within it (Kaufman & Beghetto, 2009; Weisberg, 1999). Task motivation and persistence feature in descriptions of eminent creators (Csikszentmihalyi, 1996; Gardner, 1993; Gruber, 2005). Among their suggestions for fostering creative expertise, Bereiter and Scardamalia (1993) advocate sharing conceptual understandings of creativity. Learners need to know how to live with the process: what is normal, helpful, or negative; and develop awareness and repertoires of psychological and working techniques (Lubart, 2001; Schultz, 2009).

Much creativity research has attempted to aid understanding through models identifying parts of the process. Wallas' (1926) preparation-incubation-illumination-verification model has been widely used, adapted and criticised (Finke, Ward, & Smith, 1992; Lubart, 2001; Mace & Ward, 2002; Sawyer, 2006). Studies of music composition – understood as "making a revised piece over time" (Burnard & Younker, 2004, p. 62; Webster, 2003) – have challenged linear staged models. Harvey (1999), a composer, describes inspiration in all stages of his work. Katz and Gardner (2012) describe different kinds and functions of inspiration and observed ongoing experimentation and problem-solving. Students in Burnard and Younker's (2004) studies (drawn from composition teaching situations rather than controlled, short-term experiments) used a variety of processes, with many differing from linear staged models (also Collins, 2005; Seddon & O'Neill, 2003; Wiggins, 2007). Stage models highlight what may occur; but may not represent actual sequences of occurrences.

"Studies now show that creation of a substantial new work or idea involves problem-solving and reworking over time as opposed to one 'Aha!' moment" (Katz & Gardner, 2012, p. 108) as in Ward and colleagues' (1999) *geneplore* model of alternations between generating and exploring, restarts after partially successful attempts noted by Amabile (1996), or Bereiter and Scardamalia's (1993) notion of *progressive problem-solving* – using the solution to one problem to prompt new problems to solve, and thus develop expertise and creative practice. Burnard and Younker (2004), Collins (2005) and others conceptualise composition as a complex of problem-finding, -framing and -solving.

Most studies of established composers' creative processes are based on retrospective, generalised accounts (Camphouse, 2002; Gardner, 1993; McCutchan, 1999). Investigations of real-time composition processes commonly study novices or school students (Fautley, 2005; Seddon, 2006; Wiggins, 2003) on researcher-set tasks, sometimes in comparison with experienced composers (Kennedy, 1999; Younker & Smith, 1996). Researchers may be reluctant to impose upon established composers, and composers may be reluctant to divert attention from composing to report about it. Cultural expectations about how composers work, deeply entrenched in the classical music industry capitalise on mystery (Walton, 2014). Composers may feel they need to cater to these expectations; researchers may not trust them to tell the truth.

In novice studies, techniques used to access composers' creative process include saving progressive drafts (Nilsson & Folkestad, 2005), saving communications between collaborators (Seddon, 2006), passive observation (Stauffer, 2002) and recording musical sound and thinking-aloud (Wiggins, 2001). Collins' (2005) study of a professional composer's process used saved progressive drafts, spoken reflections at the end working sessions, and interviews.

Over the past 6 years I have been researching advanced composition teaching and learning (Love, 2014; Love & Barrett, 2014, 2015). I am also a composer and composition teacher. It has been important to stay alert to the influence of my own experience on my interpretations in the studies (Adams, Jones, & Ellis, 2014; Flyvbjerg, 2011). I kept notes in relation to nearly all of my composing, journaling after each working session in many cases. Because I am a researcher, my composition reflections engage with literature, observations and interviews from research projects. I frequently felt my own composition process did not fit theoretical models; I also noticed my approach sometimes resonating with and sometimes diverging from that of the participants in our studies.

This paper explores an issue emerging from these reflections: composition processes may vary substantially depending on the circumstances of composition – in particular, available time. While the music industry may love stories of fast composition, implying that writing quickly is evidence of true genius or divine inspiration, I suggest that the quickly-written piece may involve different creative processes than a slowly-written piece, and that a creative life's work may require both.

Method

I have chosen qualitative, reflexive methods to investigate interior phenomena–creative processes in music composition because they can yield abundant and direct data. This is a comparative case study of two compositions, selected from a 6-year body of work, because through reflection, issues emerged warranting further investigation (Stake, 1995). They are bounded, particular cases: separate composition projects within an ongoing creative practice; and within the culture of contemporary classical chamber music. I aim to provide clear descriptions of processes usually veiled in order that others may consider their own experiences in greater detail.

Adams, Jones and Ellis (2014) describe autoethnography as work that explores 'the interplay of introspective, personally engaged selves and cultural beliefs, practices, systems, and experiences' (p 17). While autoethnographers have typically raised oppressed *insider* voices in relation to cultural and power dynamics, an autoethnographic approach can also illuminate *inside* experience and knowledge – that which is not externally manifested – such as musical thought which occurs in un-representable, or not-yet-representable sound. 'Researching and writing from the lived, inside moments of experience allows autoethnographers to cultivate an "epistemology of insiderness," of being able to describe an experience in a way that "outside" researchers never could' (Adams, et al., 2014, p. 31). While this study is not social-justice oriented, disciplines from autoethnograhy – a method that has taken seriously the insider's story – offer much to the study of creative processes.

The primary research technique used was reflective writing in response to composing sessions. This occurred at different time intervals: shortly after a working session, after completion of a section of the piece, and after completion of the piece.

A secondary technique was artefact-elicited (Barrett & Smigiel, 2007) reflection – in many ways, a self-interview: reviewing sketches, exercises and drafts as memory triggers, to 'relive' the process. Written reflection, requiring more precision than mental reflection (John-Steiner, 1997), is a process of analysis and interpretation (Polkinghorne, 1995) especially when revisiting written musical material. In some instances this was the first time ideas were translated to verbal language.

Analysis of an autoethnographic case study is inherently subjective. Stake describes two approaches to analysis and interpretation in case study research. The first is *direct interpretation*, or simply, 'asking ourselves "What did that mean?"' (Stake, 1995, p. 78). In this study, data consists of present memories, written reflections, and artefact-elicited reflections. These rubbed against and challenged each other, and thus provide a degree of triangulation. Rigour comes through questioning one's interpretation. It must prove itself multiple times (Stake, 1995).

The cases (composition process experiences) were compared with each other and with theories of creativity. Theoretical critique provokes questioning of assumptions and interpretations. Within these processes lies Stake's other approach, *categorical aggregation*, leading toward prioritising and selecting, followed by *narrative analysis* (Polkinghorne, 1995) in which descriptions are formulated to communicate to others.

The two cases are described below. Quotations from reflective writing are italicized. These writings show that analysis was occurring during the composition and reflection process; indeed, the autoethnographic approach provoked the study (Adams, et al., 2014).

box 192 box

The cases

Case 1. Quartet:

A private commission from a family of competent players for a 10-minute work for piano and woodwind trio (ob, cl, bsn). The completion date was 8 months away. I predicted that it would take 6 weeks (fitting around my other work). I requested interviews with each player prior to composing and for a reading before producing the final version.

Quartet process, part 1

I had several other small projects in line, so although my mind was buzzing with ideas, I determined to let it incubate for 3-4 months before beginning serious work. One of the immediate projects was a set of educational trios for cellos, designed to develop chamber ensemble skills of leading, accompanying, and blending.

In the meantime, I listened to wind quintet and piano recordings, studied piano scores and wrote exercises. We did the interviews and I added repertoire recommended by the players to my study. Unrelated to their recommendations, I decided I wanted the last movement to be tango-influenced and added the tango collection to the CD stack.

Interruption

Case 2. Trio:

This was for a competition: a 7-10 minute work for piano trio (pno, vln, vc) for an elite performance competition. I usually avoid competitions, preferring to write to requests by performers I know personally. I chanced upon this one a week before its closing date and, uncharacteristically, by the next day I felt compelled to enter it. I had a 2-day commitment in the middle, leaving only 4 days to compose. Normally I average 20-30 seconds of music for a small ensemble per day (5-8 hours). This wasn't going to be normal. In fact, it felt impossible, but also inescapable: I felt I was 'supposed to' do it.

Piano trio process: (from post-composition reflective writing)

> I heard some ideas in my head, jotted them down, sat
> down at the keyboard and tried them, extended them a lit-
> tle. I felt then that I had the thematic material. I was ac-
> cepting of the material, not critical. It was my job to make
> it work. And to give it the best go I could in the time left.

> Another challenge was that each theme had a different
> pitch world. Thus to move between sections involved a
> kind of modulation to a new kind of scale. I don't think
> I've studied any other composers doing that.

> It's for a competition with some of the world's best per-
> formers. It was nice to be relatively free from the constraint
> of difficulty... There are some tough passages, and a lot
> that's easy. I think that's ok. It's a final round piece. It
> should be about interpretation and interaction, not just vir-
> tuosic execution.

I showed a late draft to a pianist and checked double-stops with my violist
son. Usually I get more player input than that.

My 2-day prior commitment was a family camping trip. I decided to go.

> I think I felt this project was so out of my control that if it
> was going to get completed it would get completed. My job
> was to show up and work on it when I could... I also
> thought the incubation time might be good. I usually build
> that in intentionally....That's an integral part of composing
> – it can't be only pushing out notes. If I don't have listen-
> ing and not-listening time it won't grow properly. Some-
> how it can't be forced, but it can grow quickly, if it wants
> to. My peace with the camping trip is evidence of my feel-
> ing it wasn't my responsibility for it to succeed.

Creating a coherent structure took a proportionately 'long time'.

> I didn't get to a point of imagining the total form until
> quite late in the process. None of my typical timelines for
> this piece. It was listening to the material and making sense
> of what I heard it could do.

> [On the last afternoon] I printed all of it and laid it out in a
> curly oval on the floor. I sat in the middle and wrote revi-
> sions. I could easily move to other pages and make compar-
> isons. ...It was the first time I felt I had a grasp of the
> whole thing.

A few hours later I completed the piece, and submitted it with 6 minutes
to spare.

> Still not panicking. It wouldn't be my failure if I didn't
> make it. It was an improbable if not impossible challenge

anyway. I wasn't in a failure/success mindset at all. Just 'do the work' 'I can do this' 'It is a good piece' 'Thank you' 'This piece has asked me to write it' Well almost thinking that. Probably feeling that.

I don't think of it as taking divine dictation. It's more like being given (or pointed towards) the pieces [musical materials] to make something from. And trusted to be able to do it.

Quartet process part 2

When I returned to the quartet project, I envisaged four movements, culminating in a final tango. Having decided it would be tonal with rich and surprising harmonies, I began exploring chord progressions. I found a phrase I liked but struggled to extend it. One day's solution sounded illogical the next. I decided to let it sit and took that phrase—a minor progression—and deleted the bass notes to produce a major progression. I improvised a melodic riff I liked which I broke into motifs and sequence-able patterns, then structured the movement in two days. Over 3 weeks I fine-tuned it, trialling voicings and transitions and play-testing parts. The structure felt clear; the energy was good. But it was four minutes long instead of the intended 2:30. Two movements must go. A single 6-minute slow movement could balance it. I returned to my chord progressions and sketches and assembled a draft with many empty, place-holding bars.

Reflection after the 2nd draft of slow movement (5 days after 1st draft):

I'm much more self-critical with this movement. I don't want to be held accountable to writing a real tango, and I don't think that's what they would have intended to commission.... I like borrowing the Michael Head progression, but was surprised to recognise a Bohemian Nights[15] song in what I'd done to it. That's more likely to be recognised, given the style, than the Head reference. Does that matter? Maybe.

Using the 3 woodwinds together, a la a bandoneon, was a nice surprise. I love the bandoneon and clarinet in David Orlowsky's 'Noema' klezmer disc....His work suits what I'm after.

---

[15] Tango, klezmer and gypsy duo.

I was more conscious of repertoire and the potential place for the quartet due to listening and study, but also due to time to critique. While composing I was concerned about innovation quality as well as technical quality. With the piano trio, I was rarely aware of thinking like that. I didn't have time.

Reflection near the end of quartet process:

> Composing quickly requires that you draw on what you know, the skills and technique you already have. There isn't time to explore new techniques, forms, languages etc. It's acting on the sum of what you know. It can flow quickly because – since there's no time to question, explore, look beyond – the uncertain and untried don't enter the picture. It's a different relationship to the process.

> Slow, exploratory, investigative composition is (partially) a different thing. You draw on what you know, but you are also consciously adding to it.

> When I wrote [the trio] in 4 days, I used techniques and harmonic dialects I already knew. I used the instruments in ways I knew worked from previous experience. This may be why there are great, well-loved pieces from the past that were written quickly, and why the mythology is so strong. They are the cumulative pieces. A synthesis of previous experience. The slow ones are the formative pieces.

> Working on [the quartet] is a different process. I've had lots of time to research and let what I've learned incubate. I've listened to other music....I mentally play with different configurations based on what [the players] told me about how they approach their instruments and each other. I'm mentally trialling many more possibilities than I did with [the trio].

Discussion

There were many similarities between fast and slow composition processes such as exploring and listening to the material to determine what to do with it, considering players' experiences, and discovery/inspiration throughout the process (Collins, 2005; Harvey, 1999). These are core to my individual preferred process (Burnard & Younker, 2004).

Overall, the fast process is not my preferred process. I sacrificed preparation: listening, score study, writing exercises, drawing structural timelines.

When I encountered problems along the way, rather than researching, I drew on the best I could come up with myself. Aside from the camping trip and sleep, I couldn't choose to let it incubate. Thus constrained, I didn't feel as in control of the quality of the trio. I had to trust the process, the material I was 'given', and trust that whatever I could offer would be adequate.

With the quartet I was more self-critical and strategic, looking for potential problems. These included considering particular players' abilities and tastes, and contemporary music culture and the place my piece might find in it. I had days and weeks to let the music and the doubts incubate. As I composed I was less trusting of the material and less willing to let go of outcomes. This suggests that my 'formative' pieces may incorporate more curiosity *and* more critique. They take bigger risks, yet also carry the weight of more judgment.

Expertise develops by means of progressive problem-solving (Bereiter & Scardamalia, 1993) – keeping one's eyes open to new problems to solve, never 'arriving' – and is considered essential to ongoing creative practice (Kaufman & Beghetto, 2009). I try to do something new to me in every piece, something I'm curious about, something I'm not completely certain will work. The 'cumulative' pieces can capitalise on the growth occurring during formative pieces. A creative life may require both kinds of processes to keep developing. It is neither total control nor total trust.

Conclusion

This study extends from Burnard and Younker's (2004) accounts of variations in different students' creative processes toward noting differences within an individual's practice. To help develop composers' conceptual understanding of creativity (Bereiter & Scardamalia, 1993) and creativity-relevant skills (Amabile, 1996) more descriptions are needed: from a wide range of composers at different stages of professional life, and descriptions of compositional processes for varied purposes and circumstances.

Popular cultural narratives tend to celebrate the mysterious – trust and cumulative processes; while narratives of academic research more often celebrate hard work and persistence – control and formative processes. Perhaps we can tell and hear both together.

References

Adams, T. E., Jones, S. H., & Ellis, C. (2014). *Understanding qualitative research : Autoethnography.* Oxford, GBR: Oxford University Press.

Amabile, T. (1983). *The social psychology of creativity.* New York, NY: Springer-Verlag.

Amabile, T. (1996). *Creativity in context: Update to The social psychology of creativity.* Boulder, CO: Westview Press.

Barrett, M. S., & Smigiel, H. (2007). Children's perspectives of participation in music youth arts setting: Meaning, value, and participation. *Research Studies in Music Education, 28,* 39-50.

Bereiter, C., & Scardamalia, M. (1993). *Surpassing ourselves: An inquiry into the nature and implications of expertise.* Chicago, IL: Open Court.

Burnard, P., & Younker, B. A. (2004). Problem-solving and creativity: Insights from students' individual composing pathways. *International Journal of Music Education, 22*(1), 59-76. doi: 10.1177/0255761404042375

Camphouse, M. (Ed.). (2002). *Composers on composing for band.* Chicago, IL: GIA.

Collins, D. (2005). A synthesis process model of creative thinking in music composition. *Psychology of Music, 33*(2), 193-216. doi: 10.1177/0305735605050651

Csikszentmihalyi, M. (1996). *Creativity: Flow and the psychology of discovery and invention.* New York, NY: Harper Collins.

Fautley, M. (2005). A new model of the group composing process of lower secondary school students. *Music Education Research, 7*(1), 39-57. doi: 10.1080/14613800500042109

Finke, R. A., Ward, T. B., & Smith, S. M. (1992). *Creative cognition: Theory, research, and applications.* Cambridge, MA: MIT Press.

Flyvbjerg, B. (2011). Case study. In N. K. Denzin & Y. S. Lincoln (Eds.), *The SAGE handbook of qualitative research* (4 ed., pp. 301-316). Los Angeles, CA: Sage.

Gardner, H. (1993). *Creating minds.* New York, NY: Basic Books.

Gruber, H. E. (2005). The creative person as a whole: The evolving systems approach to the study of creative work. In H. E. Gruber & K. Bödeker (Eds.), *Creativity, psychology and the history of science* (pp. 35-37). Dordrecht, The Netherlands: Springer.

Harvey, J. (1999). *Music and inspiration.* London: Faber and Faber.

John-Steiner, V. (1997). *Notebooks of the mind: Explorations of thinking* (Revised ed.). New York, NY: Oxford University Press.

Katz, S. L., & Gardner, H. (2012). Musical materials or metaphorical models? A psychological investigation of what inspires composers.

In D. J. Hargreaves, D. Miell & R. MacDonald (Eds.), *Musical imaginations: Multidisciplinary perspectives on creativity, performance, and perception* (pp. 107-123). Oxford: Oxford University Press.

Kaufman, J. C., & Beghetto, R. A. (2009). Beyond big and little: The four c model of creativity. *Review of General Psychology, 13*(1), 1-12. doi: 10.1037/a0013688

Kennedy, M. A. (1999). Where does the music come from?: A comparison case-study of the compositional processes of a high school and a collegiate composer. *British Journal of Music Education, 16*(2), 157-177.

Love, K. G. (2014). *Composer development: Learning from performance and performers.* PhD, The University of Queensland, Brisbane, QLD.

Love, K. G., & Barrett, M. S. (2014). Learning to collaborate in code: Negotiating the score in a symphony orchestra composers' school In M. S. Barrett (Ed.), *Collaborative creative thought and practice in music.* Farnham, UK: Ashgate.

Love, K. G., & Barrett, M. S. (2015). A case study of teaching and learning strategies in an orchestral composition masterclass. *Psychology of Music, 44(4)*, 830-846. doi: 10.1177/0305735615594490

Lubart, T. I. (2001). Models of the creative process: Past, present and future. *Creativity Research Journal, 13*(3), 295-308.

Mace, M.-A., & Ward, T. (2002). Modeling the creative process: A Grounded Theory analysis of creativity in the domain of art making. *Creativity Research Journal, 14*(2), 179-192. doi: 10.1207/s15326934crj1402_5

McCutchan, A. (1999). *The muse that sings: Composers speak about the creative process* New York, NY: Oxford University Press.

Nilsson, B., & Folkestad, G. r. (2005). Children's practice of computer-based composition. *Music Education Research, 7*(1), 21-37. doi: 10.1080/14613800500042042

Polkinghorne, D. (1995). Narrative configuration in qualitative analysis. In J. A. Hatch & R. Wisniewski (Eds.), *Life history and narrative* (pp. 5-23). London: Falmer.

Sawyer, R. K. (2006). *Explaining creativity: The science of human innovation.* New York, NY: Oxford University Press.

Schultz, A. (2009). Creativity and crisis: Some thoughts on self-management. *Resonate, 2009* (27 October). Retrieved from http://www.australianmusiccentre.com.au/article/creativity-and-crisis-some-thoughts-on-self-management

Seddon, F. (2006). Collaborative computer-mediated music composition in cyberspace. *British Journal of Music Education, 23*(03), 273-283. doi:10.1017/S0265051706007054

Seddon, F., & O'Neill, S. (2003). Creative thinking processes in adolescent computer-based composition: An analysis of strategies adopted and the influence of instrumental music training. *Music Education Research, 5*(2), 125-137. doi: 10.1080/1461380032000085513

Stake, R. E. (1995). *The art of case study research.* Thousand Oaks, CA: Sage.

Stauffer, S. (2002). Connections between the musical and life experiences of young composers and their compositions. *Journal of Research in Music Education, 50*(4), 301-322. doi: 10.2307/3345357

Wallas, G. (1926). *The art of thought.* London: Jonathan Cape.

Walton, C. (2014). *Lies and epiphanies: Composers and their inspiration from Wagner to Berg.* Woodbridge, Suffolk; Rochester, NY: University of Rochester Press.

Ward, T. B., Smith, S. M., & Finke, R. A. (1999). Creative cognition. In R. Sternberg (Ed.), *Handbook of Creativity* (pp. 189-212). Cambridge: Cambridge University Press.

Webster, P. R. (2003). "What do you mean, make my music different?" Encouraging revision and extensions in children's music composition. In M. Hickey (Ed.), *Why and how to teach music composition: a new horizon for music education* (pp. 55-65). Reston, VA: MENC.Weisberg, R. W. (1999). Creativity and knowledge: A challenge to theories. In R. Sternberg (Ed.), *Handbook of creativity* (pp. 226-250). Cambridge: Cambridge University Press.

Wiggins, J. (2001). *Teaching for musical understanding.* Boston, MA: McGraw Hill.

Wiggins, J. (2003). A frame for understanding children's compositional processes. In M. Hickey (Ed.), *Why and how to teach music composition: a new horizon for music education* (pp. 141-165). Reston, VA: MENC.

Wiggins, J. (2007). Compositional process in music. In L. Bresler (Ed.), *International handbook of research in arts education* (title in lower case letters?Yes) (Vol. 16, pp. 453-476). Netherlands: Springer.

Younker, B. A., & Smith, W. H., Jr. (1996). Comparing and Modeling Musical Thought Processes of Expert and Novice Composers. *Bulletin of the Council for Research in Music Education*(128), 25-36.

Competition for focus of attention: Attempts to multitask

Clifford K. Madsen

Center for Music Research, Florida State University, USA

cmadsen@fsu.edu

Chandler R. Bridges

Center for Music Research, Florida State University, USA

chandler.bridges@gmail.com

Abstract

The entire area of "multitasking" has received continued emphasis since the inception of modern devices that can be used "at the same time." The thrust of the current research is to test listeners in regard to their attentive music listening versus their attention to a GRE Reading Test when both are presented simultaneously. The current investigations constitute two replications of a study from over 30 years ago. The current investigation used exactly the same materials as the original study and replicated the three main groups from the original work. While there were six separate groups in the original study, three of these groups were intended as "control" groups for the main variable of experimental interest, which was testing the ability to multitask. Thereafter in the current investigations, only three groups were replicated: 1) students took a GRE-type Reading test only, during a 40 minute time limit, 2) students took only a music test, within the 40 minute time limit, or 3) students attempted to combine these two tests simultaneously during the same 40 minute time span. Results from the *post hoc* two investigations replicate almost exactly the same scores found 20 and even 30 years ago. Even though many students believe that they efficiently multitask, these studies demonstrate again that there is no such thing as effective multitasking. Whenever students attempt to accomplish two tasks during the same time period both of the tasks are diminished.

Keywords: Multitasking, focus, attention, replications over time

Introduction

It appears axiomatic that an important purpose for music performance and music education is that they have an attentive audience. The history of music education represents an extended chronicle of providing experiences in both performing and listening. Yet, background music is ubiquitous in society, and attempts to isolate attentive music listening are difficult because of the inherent difficulty assessing what attentive listening "produces." Therefore, attempts to define a dependent variable seem difficult.

Since the "digital revolution", the availability of devices capable of being "used" simultaneously has become problematic, especially for music educators. Regardless of research findings, many students actually believe that multitasking is "good" and also that they are good at it. Nass, a cognitive research scientist, has appeared across the country speaking about the deleterious effects of multitasking (Ophira, Nass, and Wagner, 2009). In one study designed to specifically test multitasking, Ophira, Nass, and Wagner (2009) surveyed 262 students on media consumption habits. Nineteen students who multitasked the most and 22 who multitasked the least then took two computer-based tests, each completed while concentrating only on the task at hand. Students had to remember the briefly glimpsed orientations of red rectangles surrounded by different numbers of blue rectangles. In a second task, they categorized a random string of words, and then did it again without categorizing words that were preceded by a beep. During a second test they were asked to remember whether letters had also been targeted in earlier trials. In a third test, a new cohort of 30 high- and low-multitaskers were asked to identify target letters on a screen. In every test, students who spent less time multitasking performed best.

Additionally, the long-term effects of multitasking are often not immediately apparent. Foerde Knowlton & Poldrack, (2006) suggested that distractions during learning can be harmful, even if the distractions do not seem to injure students' immediate performance on their tasks. Foerde and colleagues asked students to "predict the weather" based on cues they slowly learned over many computer trials. Initially distractions did not seem to harm the performance. Yet when they were later asked to describe the general probabilistic rules for that trial they did much worse than they did after the undistracted trials.

The field of music education and specifically, attentive listening to music is especially concerned with this phenomenon in that attentive listening is a primary goal of most instruction. Most people are accustomed to being "bathed in sound", as music is ubiquitous in society (Madsen & Madsen, 1978). Therefore, issues evident when a person phases music out of awareness in order to concentrate on a more important task need to be carefully investigated. Additionally, music listening skills (e.g., aural discriminations) might suffer from repeated situations where music is not "listened to" with a high degree of concentration, thus conceivably diminishing the full appreciation of the listening experience.

Researchers have studied music listening and attentiveness from many orientations. Some researchers have addressed aspects of music listening that are deemed important for students (Flowers, 1983, 1984). Others have attempted to specify attributes of music listening that give it meaning (Adams, 1994; Aiello, 1994; Berlyne, 1974; Madsen, Byrnes, Capperella-Sheldon & Brittin, 1993; Madsen & Fredrickson, 1993). Other ongoing research relates to competition for focus of attention. In these studies, music listening/performing activities are purposefully interspersed with other activity necessitating a competition for focus of attention (Madsen, 1987; Madsen & Coggiola, 2001; Madsen & Geringer, 1981, 1983; Madsen, Johnson, Geringer, Southall, & Brunkan, 2013; Madsen, Moore, Wagner, & Yarbrough, 1975; Madsen & Southall, 2004; Madsen & Wolfe, 1979; Martin, 1977; Wolfe, 1982, 1983).

In the current line of research concerning focus of attention, the first study addressing this issue was intentionally designed to investigate purposeful distractors (Madsen & Wolfe, 1979). Upon entering an experimental environment with a one-way mirror Wolfe asked advanced undergraduates and graduates to read a story by Flannery O' Conner. All participants were told that they would be asked questions afterward. Music was played during the entire time they read. However, every time a person would move any part of his/her body the music was immediately stopped for a short time period until the person stopped the movement. Upon exiting, all students were asked if they were aware of the music and any other aspects. Only one student out of 80 was aware that their bodily movement actually controlled the presence/absence of the music.

Another field of ongoing research has people listen to a piece of music and manipulate a Continuous Response Digital Interface (CRDI). The CRDI is specifically designed to record ongoing responses to music without necessitating a verbal response (Capperella, 1989; Gregory, 1989; Madsen, Brittin, & Capperella-Sheldon). Some of this research, more "qualitative" in nature, concerns what musicians as well as non-musicians consider to be the emotional content of music and addresses personally defined "aesthetic response". Other more "quantitative" research concerns focus of attention to salient musical elements.

The thrust of the current studies was to test the perception and performance of listeners in regard to their attentive listening versus their attention to other intellectually demanding tasks when both are presented simultaneously and they are asked to attend to both. The inherent difficulty in structuring such a situation is to provide a musical task that demands concentration and is capable of being measured as well as to provide another competing task that also can be measured. To accomplish both tasks, a recording consisting of musical examples and narration was presented simultaneously with a reading comprehension test taken from the Graduate Record Examination (GRE).

These series of studies were all designed to ascertain only one research question:

Is it possible to fully attend to a music listening task while simultaneously attempting to complete questions on a standardized examination?

Method

The present investigations are partial replications of the original study completed over 30 years ago. The original study consisted of two separate experiments; parts I & II.

The Original Experiments Parts I & II

In the original study (Madsen, 1987) three hundred undergraduates and graduates served as subjects. All were randomly assigned to one of six groups: (1) reading comprehension test, (2) music listening test, (3) simultaneous reading comprehension and music listening tests, (4) reading comprehension test with musical examples from music listening test as background, (5) music listening test without musical examples (script only), and (6) reading comprehension test with varied background music chosen by the experimenter and different for each student. In the original study, a GRE-type reading test was administered to all subjects in any of the reading groups 1, 3, 4, & 6. These subjects took an actual 40-minute timed GRE-type reading test. Participants assigned to music listening groups (2 & 5) listened to a music historical narrative describing over 100 years of audio technology with various examples and simultaneously took a test over the material seen and heard from the narrative. A third group attempted to do both tests still within the 40 minute time period. Additionally, another group, divided between a set of students that reported they regularly did study with music compared to another set that said they never studied with music, took the reading test with different background music, which was different for each person. When comparing these two sets of subjects those who reported regularly studying with music did slightly better compared to those who reported they did not.

Group 6 was comprised equally of subjects responding "Yes" and subjects responding "No" to the first question. The simulated GRE reading comprehension task was taken from *Barron's How to prepare for the GRE* (Brownstein & Weiner, 1982). The music listening task consisted of *"Technology—The Leader of Jazz and Pop"* (Wagner, 1978), presented via tape/visual recording. A 25-item multiple-choice test was developed from the tape script (narration over music) and the musical examples (reliability = .82, Spearman-Brown corrected). The musical examples used for the technology tape (Groups 2 and 3) and presented as background music (Group 4) covered a wide range of styles and performing media and are presented in the appendix. It is interesting that although some of the music material was obviously dated in subsequent replications, actual test scores were almost identical even across a 30 year time period. All aural stimuli were presented at dBA = 75.

Two multiple-choice tests, respectively, covering each task were also administered simultaneously to assess the relative gains attributable to either task. Possible scores on each test were 50 on the GRE and 25 on the music test.

Results of original experiments

Results of the original study (Part I) revealed that the mean score for subjects in Group 1 (reading only) was 31.74. The means for comparable groups with background music, Group 4 and Group 6, were 31.04 and 31.78, respectively. The small differences across these scores indicate that there is almost no difference among those subjects who took the reading test with music compared to those who did not. The scores for the music test including musical examples with narration was M = 18.94 (Group 2), and the mean for the group who received only the written narrative was 9.18 (Group 5), indicating that the music examples did contribute to increased scores on the multiple-choice music test. Total scores for Group 6 were almost identical to Group 4 scores, though it should be remembered that Group 6 was equally comprised of subjects who *usually* study to music (n = 25) versus those who *never* study to music (n = 25). A difference in scores between those who usually study with music compared to those who never study with music (33.92 vs. 29.64) indicates that music might be more distracting to those subjects who never study to music.

The above 6 groups constituted *separate individuals* being randomly assigned to one of the 6 groups. An additional experiment (Part II) used a different 100 students as their *own controls*. This related study constituted a second experiment and was completed by having subjects simultaneously deal with familiar material. Subjects in this experiment either took the reading test during one 40-minute period and then on a subsequent day took the music listening test or vice versa (split half rotation). Then, all 50 subjects took the exact same tests simultaneously during a third day (40-minute period). The design of this experiment was structured to determine if, having previously gone through the music and academic material, *subjects would be able to increase their score(s)*. Also, because materials were identical to those used in the previous experiment, comparisons could also be made between experiments.

Results of the second experiment (Part II) replicated almost exactly those two groups in the previous study that completed the reading test (Experiment 2, M = 31.63 vs. Experiment 1, M = 31.74) and the music test (Experiment 2, M = 18.96 vs. Experiment 1, M = 18.94). It is interesting that when subjects attempted both tasks simultaneously the scores for each of the two shared tasks were almost exactly the same as they had been for the two tasks independently. Therefore, it did not seem that subjects were able to increase their scores, though there was also not a consequential drop. It would appear that, even having gone through the material and therefore having the advantage of remembering the two tasks, listeners did not improve appreciably. Results of the questionnaire given to Groups 3 and 4 indicated that 21% of the subjects usually study with music. All subjects within these groups recognized some of the music, but could list only 11% and 13%, respectively, of the selections played during the reading test. This is consistent with previous research (Wolfe, 1983), which suggests that familiarity does not affect academic performance. Subjects in Groups 3 and 4 were also asked if the music interfered with the reading test. A total of 48 subjects in Group 3 and 25 in Group 4 responded -Yes." In Group 6, subjects were specifically selected on the basis of usually versus never listening to music. Questionnaire results for this group were approximately the same as for the other groups; all subjects recognized some of the music, with only 10% correct selections listed. Most importantly, total reading scores were almost identical for Groups 4 and 6 and even Group 1 that did not have music. It is interesting to note, however, that in Group 6, which was selected on the basis of "Yes, I usually study with music" versus "No, I never study with music," a difference in reading scores is observed (Yes, M = 33.92; No, M = 29.64). Also, while all of the subjects who never studied with music found it distracting, 18 of 25 subjects who usually study with music also found it distracting. It should be remembered that music for Group 6 was varied individually and chosen by the experimenter.

Replications # 1 & # 2

Results of the original study (Madsen, 1987) confirmed that the three most important groups concerning multitasking were Group 1 GRE only, Group 2 Music Test only and Group 3 GRE plus Music Test combined. Thereafter, subsequent replications of the original study (Madsen & Diaz, 2009) were done approximately ten years after the original study and 20 years after the original study in order to determine if students accustomed to digital advances got better at multitasking. The second and third replications were identical to the original study and these subsequent replications used the exact same materials as in the original study. However, in the two subsequent replications only the three "experimental" groups 1, 2, & 3 were used because all other groups in the original study had functioned as control groups. Subjects in Group 1 (N = 50) took the same practice version of the Graduate Record Examination (GRE) as used in the original study where the multiple-choice test that accompanied the GRE served as the test instrument. Students in Group 2 (N = 50) viewed and listened to the identical recording as used above and took the same multiple-choice test, as did the original group. Subjects in Group 3 (N = 50) attempted both tasks simultaneously to assess the relative gains/losses attributable to attempting both tasks simultaneously.

Results

Results are presented in the following table and represent scores on each of the three main groups of the original experiments and two replications of groups 1, 2, & 3.

It is seen that the mean score for subjects in Group 1 (reading only) is 31.74. The means for comparable groups with background music, Group 4 and Group 6, are 31.04 and 31.78, respectively. The small differences across these scores would indicate that there is almost no difference among those subjects who took the reading test with music compared to those who did not (see table below).

Table 1: Test Scores

	Test Scores	GRE	Music	GRE & Music	
Original Part I	31.63	18.96	16.48	15.72	p<.001
Original Part II (Ss as own controls)	31.74	18.94	_____	_____	
Replication # 1	31.72	18.98	16.40	15.82	p<.001
Replication # 2	31.70	18.62	16.64	15.70	p<.001
Bonferroni Corrected	-no sig difference-	-no sig difference-	-no sig difference-	-no sig difference-	-no sig difference

The most important experimental group was Group 3 in that it was considered to be the primary experimental group, with the two other groups functioning as controls. The scores for this group were: reading test, M = 16.48, music test, M = 15.72. Thus, when subjects were forced to complete two simultaneous (i.e., shared) tasks, their scores dropped appreciably when compared to the other groups. This finding was deemed to be the most important aspect of the study. In addition, subjects in Group 3 indicated via the questionnaire that they found the simultaneous task of having to go back and forth between tasks to be highly frustrating and extremely difficult. Only one student was positive in stating, "Once I got used to it, I found it a pleasant challenge."

Discussion

Certain music can mask other environmental sounds and may even help facilitate concentration compared to more distracting sounds or ambient noise. When music itself becomes distracting for any reason, it usually can be attenuated or cut-off. Yet, this usually is not possible in educational settings and might actively interfere with student learning. Therefore, teaching music in a quiet environment would seem most desirable. However, some students seem to not be concerned with focus of attention. The inconsistency between self-reported attitudes concerning distractibility and performance scores has been previously reported Moller, 1980; Ophira, Nass, & Wagner, 2009; Slater, 1968; Smith & Morris, 1976; Williams, 1961; Wolfe, 1982, 1983). This psychological component may be important in other ways. The psychological cost of having to force attention could be detrimental when structuring teaching/learning situations. Attending to and hearing a short musical phrase of a particular recording may serve as an adequate prompt for correct recognition, requiring only momentary attentiveness to a background environment. Or some other aspect within the total environment might momentarily capture attention. Regardless, it would seem that humans are capable of "timesharing" quite effectively. However, this might indicate a greater need for music educators to focus attention rather than encouraging conflicting attentiveness, though there does appear to be problems concerning fully operationalized replication, as discussed by Geringer & Madsen (1995/1996). Additional research should be primarily focused on addressing the issues of multitasking in all of its seemingly misguided implications not in continuing to test its veracity.

References

Adams, B. L. (1994). The effect of visual/aural conditions on the emotional response to music. Unpublished doctoral dissertation, *Florida State University, Tallahassee.*

Aiello, R. (Ed.) & J. A. Sloboda (1994). *Musical perceptions.* Oxford University Press: New York.

Berlyne, D. E. (Ed.). (1974). *Studies in the new experimental aesthetics: Steps toward an objective psychology of aesthetic appreciation.* New York: Halsted Press.

Brownstein, S.C., & Weiner, M. (1982). *Barron's how to prepare for the Graduate Record Examination* (6th ed). Woodbury, NY: Barron's Educational Series, Inc.

Capperella, D. A. (1989). Reliability of the continuous response digital interface for data collection in a study of auditory perception. *Southeastern Journal of Music Education, 1,* 19-32.

Flowers, P. J. (1983). The effect of instruction in vocabulary and listening on nonmusicians' descriptions of changes in music. *Journal of Research in Music Education, 31,* 179-189. doi: 10.2307/3345171

Flowers, P. J. (1984). Attention to elements of music and effect of instruction in vocabulary on written descriptions of music by children and undergraduates. *Psychology of Music, 12,* 167-24. doi: 10.1177/0305735684121002

Foerde, K., Knowlton, B. J., & Poldrack, R. A. Modulation of competing memory systems by distraction. 2006. *Proceedings of the National Academy of Sciences, 103*(31), 11778–11783.

Geringer, J. M., & Madsen, C. K. (1995/1996). Focus of attention to elements: Listening patterns of musicians and nonmusicians. *Bulletin of the Council for Research in Music Education, 127,* 80-87. Retrieved from http://www.jstor.org/stable/40318770

Gregory, D. (1989). Using computers to measure continuous music responses. *Psychomusicology, 8,* 127-134.

Madsen, C. K. (1987). Background music: Competition for focus of attention. In C. K. Madsen & C. A. Prickett (Eds.), *Applications for research in music behavior* (pp. 315-325). University of Alabama Press: Tuscaloosa, AL.

Madsen, C. K., Brittin, R. V., & Capperella-Sheldon, D. A. (1993). An empirical investigation of the aesthetic response to music. *Journal of Research in Music Education, 41,* 57-69. doi: 10.2307/3345480

Madsen, C. K., Byrnes, S. R., Capperella-Sheldon. D. A., & Brittin, R. V. (1993). Aesthetic responses to music: Musicians vs. nonmusicians. *Journal of Music Therapy, 30,* 174-191. doi: 10.1093/jmt/30.3.174

Madsen, C. K., & Coggiola, J. C. (2001). The effect of manipulating a CRDI dial of the focus of attention of musicians/nonmusisians and perceived aesthetic response. *Bulletin of the Council for Research in Music Education, 149,* 13-22.

Madsen, C. K., & Diaz, F. (2009) Background music: Competition for focus of attention. Poster presented at the *American Music Therapy Association, National Conference,* San Diego, CA. 2009.

Madsen, C. K., & Fredrickson, W. E. (1993). The experience of musical tension: A replication of Nielsen's research using the continuous response digital interface. *Journal of Music Therapy, 30,* 46-57. doi: 10.1093/jmt/30.1.46

Madsen, C. K., & Geringer, J. M. (1981). The effect of a distraction index on improving practice attentiveness and musical performance. *Bulletin of the Council for Research in Music Education, 66-67,* 46-52.

Madsen, C. K., & Geringer, J. M. (1983). Attending behavior as a function of in-class activity in university music classes. *Journal of Music Therapy, 20,* 30-38. doi: 10.1093/jmt/20.1.30

Madsen, C. K., Johnson, C. M., Geringer, J. M., Southall, J., & Brunkan, M. C. (2013). Effect of distractors purposefully placed in La Bohème: Replication and extension. Proceedings of the 24th *International Seminar on Research in Music Education. Thessaloniki, Greece.* pp 139-146.

Madsen, C. K., & Madsen, C. H. Jr., (1978). *Experimental research in music.* Raleigh: Contemporary Publishing.

Madsen, C. K., Moore, R. S., Wagner, M. J., & Yarbrough, C. (1975). A comparison of music as reinforcement for correct mathematical responses versus music as reinforcement for attentiveness. *Journal of Music Therapy, 12,* 84-95. doi: 10.1093/jmt/12.2.84

Madsen, C. K., & Southall, J. K. (2004). The Continuous Response Digital Interface:

Applications Pertaining to the Ongoing Measurement of Aesthetic Response to Music. Proceedings of the *Research Alliance of Institutes for Music Education, 7,* 27-35.

Madsen, C. K., & Wolfe, D. E. (1979). The effect of interrupted music and incompatible responses on bodily movement and music attentiveness. *Journal of Music Therapy, 16,*17-30. doi: 10.1093/jmt/16.1.17

Martin, M. (1977). Reading while listening: A linear model of selective attention. *Journal of Verbal Learning and Verbal Behavior, 16*, 453-463.

Moller, L. E. (1980). Performance of musicians under noise. *Perceptual and Motor Skills, 50*, 301-302.

Ophira, E., Nass, C., & Wagner, A. D. (2009). Cognitive control in media multitaskers. Proceedings of the *National Academy of Sciences, 106* (33), 15583-15587. Retrieved from www.pnas.org/cgi/doi.10.1073/pnas.0903620106

Slater, B. R. (1968). Effects of noise on pupil performance. *Journal of Educational Psychology, 59*, 239-243.

Smith, C., & Morris, L. (1976). Effects of simulative and sedative music on cognitive and emotional components of anxiety. *Psychological Reports, 38*, 1187-1193.

Wagner, M. (Speaker). (1978). *A forty minute audio presentation tracing one hundred years of science and sound.* Miami: Florida International University.

Williams, T. B. (1961). A study of the effect of music as a distraction on the mental test performance of certain eleventh grade students. *Dissertation Abstracts International, 22*, 168.

Wolfe, D. (1982). The effect of interrupted and continuous music on bodily movement and task performance of third-grade students. *Journal of Music Therapy, 19*, 74-85. doi: 10.1093/jmt/19.2.74

Wolfe, D. (1983). Effects of music loudness on task performance and self-report of college- aged students. *Journal of Research in Music Education, 31*, 191-201. doi: 10.2307/3345172

Appendix

"Rock Begins, Vol. I," "There Goes My Baby," The Drifters, ATCO, SD 33-314 Don Ellis, "Electric Bath," "Open Beauty," Columbia, CS 9585

"Rock Begins, Vol. I," "Tweedle-Dee," LaVerne Baker, ATCO, SD 3.3-314 Emerson, Lake, and Palmer, "Pictures at an Exhibition"

Quote—Paul Ackerman, jacket notes, "Rock Begins, Vol. I," ATCO, SD 33-314

"Electronic Music," Lewin-Richter, "Study No. 1," Turnabout, TV 30045 Disneyland, "Main Street Electrical Parade,"

"Fanfare and Ostinato," WD-4 "Switched-Off Bach," Glen Gould, Piano, "Two Part Invention in F," Columbia, MS 7241

"Switched-On Bach," Walter Carlos, "Two Part Invention in F," Columbia, MS 7194

"Country Moog," "Switched on Nashville," Gil Trythall, Athena, 6003 Tomita, -

Golliwog's Cake Walk," by Claude Debussy, RCA, ARL 1-0488

Thelma Houston, "I Got the Music in Me," title song, Sheffield Lab, SL7/SL8

Gasser, Urs. Palfrey, John. "Mastering Multitasking." Educational Leadership Mar 2009: Vol. 66, Issue 6. EBSCOHost. Web. 16 Apr. 2011.

Relationship between memory span and performance of successful students in melodic dictation

Ruth Cruz de Menezes

Laboratoire de recherche en formation auditive et didactique instrumentale (LaRFADI), Faculty of Music, Laval University, Quebec City, Canada

ruth.musica@gmail.com

Maria Teresa Moreno Sala

Observatoire International de création et recherche en musique (OICRM), Canada

maite.moreno@mus.ulaval.ca

Abstract

The purpose of the present study was to investigate whether the strategies used during dictation are related to short-term memory span in the students who perform better in a dictation task. In order to study that aspect, undergraduate music students were asked to transcribe a melodic dictation, and to write simultaneously the strategies that they were using to identify each note. Then, the subjects were exposed to an object recognition task to assess their visual short-term memory span, as well as a digit span task to assess their auditory short-term memory span. We present here the analyses undertaken with the most successful students (n=49). As in our previous studies, the strategies described by the students were classified into two main categories: the non-tonal and the tonal categories. The results indicate that the score in dictation is linked to the efficient use of non-tonal and tonal strategies. Moreover, the efficient use of tonal strategies is linked to both the auditory and the visual short-term memory span. The results of this study could help professors of aural skill classes and music teachers to understand what are the cognitive processes used by the most successful students on this task, which could help to develop better teaching strategies.

Keywords: auditory skills, cognitive strategies, memory span, musical cognition, musical transcription.

Introduction

In musical teaching, the importance of aural skill courses is major (Karpinski, 1990; Rogers, 1984; Langer, 1953). According to Rogers (1984), the skills developed during aural skill courses, such as inner audition, and the mastery of skills required to read, write, analyse, understand, appreciate, interpret or create music, are fundamental to the musician's education. As described by Karpinski (1990), these courses consist essentially of establishing mental relations between musical notes and their symbols, with a view to musical interpretation. Langer (1953) complements this view, as she considers that all musicians should listen to their own musical ideas before playing or writing, and the quality of their inner audition is the basis of all musical progress.

In aural skill courses, musical dictation is one of the main ways to develop this inner audition (Rogers, 1984). However, students show different levels of success in this task (Cruz de Menezes, 2010, Hedges, 1999; Hope, 1991). In fact, the exact underlining reasons for that difficulty are yet unknown, despite some interesting evidence in previous studies (Cruz de Menezes, 2010; Cruz de Menezes, Bissonnette, Guitton & Moreno Sala, 2009; Moreno Sala, Brauer, Cruz & Bissonette, 2008). This evidence concerns the optimal use of some cognitive strategies, especially tonal strategies (Moreno Sala et al., 2008), and an underlying relationship with mnenmonic capacities to solve musical melodic dictation (Cruz de Menezes, 2010).

However, music dictation is not solely a memory problem: it is also a problem-solving task. Performing a problem-solving task is to attempt to answer a question without having the answer at the moment the task starts (Ericsson & Simon, 1993), and this is what happens during a music dictation. To understand the difficulties students might have with these types of exercises, it is necessary to access and study the cognitive processes engaged during the act of problem solving (Greene Robertson & Costa, 2011; Ericsson, 2006, Van Someren, Barnard & Sandberg, 1994; Ericsson & Simon, 1993). One of the ways to gain access to cognitive processes is to ask people to verbalize the information they are processing while they are solving a problem (Van Someren, Barnard & Sandberg, 1994; Ericsson & Simon, 1993). Usually, this procedure called "think aloud" grants access to a person's cognitive processes through his or her loudly spoken verbal reports.

In previous studies, we adapted the "think aloud" procedure to a music dictation task: people had to verbalize their cognitive processes by writing down their thoughts during a dictation (Moreno Sala, et al., 2008; Moreno Sala & Brauer, 2007). The analysed descriptions showed meaningful results from different groups of students at different levels of performing this task (Cruz de Menezes, 2010; Cruz de Menezes et al., 2009). Two main categories of strategies emerged from the descriptions: non-tonal strategies and tonal strategies. Non-tonal strategies were defined as the strategies outlined by the subjects to identify the notes of the dictation, regardless of the each note's function and tonal context. For example, they compared one interval played on the dictation with a song to find out what type of interval there was. Tonal strategies were defined as the strategies outlined by the subjects who identified the notes by their association and/or comparison within the tonal context of the dictation. For example, the descriptions of tonal pillars as tonic as well as the descriptions of the degrees. Detailed and deeper explanations regarding these two types of strategies and their subcategories can be found in the complete study (Cruz de Menezes, 2010).

Moreover, a visual short-term memory test was conducted, and it suggests the existence of an underlying relationship between mnemonic capacities and the optimal use of certain cognitive strategies. Indeed, the efficacy of non-tonal strategies correlated with the visual memory span in a group of subjects who had difficulty on this task (Cruz de Menezes, 2010).

Consequently, after our results relating short-term visual memory span and the use of some types of strategies in subjects displaying difficulty with dictation, we wanted to analyse more deeply the underlying mechanism used by students with better results in musical dictation and their short-term or working memory characteristics. For that reason, we decided to analyse separately the best performing students in relation to the types of strategies they use, how they use them to solve a dictation, and their auditory and visual memory span in order to better understand comparatively their high-level performance in music dictation.

Material and Methods

Subjects

Our experimental sample was composed of undergraduate students enrolled in the programme of the Faculty of Music of Laval University. Experiments were performed during aural skills courses. Only subjects who obtained the best scores in dictation were selected for these analyses to better understand their cognitive strategies and their relationship with memory tasks. A previous study has already analysed and shown meaningful results from a group of students at different levels of difficulty on this task (Cruz de Menezes, 2010; Cruz de Menezes et al., 2009; Moreno Sala et al., 2008).

To collect data about the target students, we brought together students from two distinct groups. The first group was composed of students who were beginning the first level of the aural skills course, while the second was composed of students who were beginning the second level of this course. The homogeneity of this sample was reached at the time when we selected the 49 subjects by obtaining a score of at least 21 out of 24.

Experimental protocol

During the first week of the 1st and 2nd levels of the aural skills course, subjects had to perform a tonal musical dictation in the classroom context so that they could be studied in a real-life situation. The aim of this test was to collect data about the strategies the subjects use to solve a dictation task. To this end, they had to describe verbally the cognitive strategies used to solve the dictation as it progressed.

One week later, the subjects underwent two types of memory span tests: two short-term tests, one with an auditory "digit span" (Wechsler Memory Scale, WMS, 1987) and the other with a visual "objects recognition memory span" (Levy, Manns, Hopkins, Gold, Broadbent & Squire, 2003). These tests were spread over two days separated by 48 hours. We developed and adapted these tests in order for them to be used in group testing. On the first day, the visual "objects recognition" test was completed. On the second day, the auditory "digit span" test was done. The two memory tests require auditory processing information and/or visual processing information. This choice of task was made because taking dictation requires both kinds of information processing: auditory to hear the musical notes, and visual to transcribe the notes. All of the tests had been validated in a pilot study (Moreno Sala et al., 2008).

Musical dictation paradigm

The subjects were asked to write down in detail the mental processes they used during the transcription of the tonal melodic dictation while the dictation was proceeding. The subjects had first to write down the reasoning they used to find the notes and then to write the names of the notes (for example, D) without using musical notation (staff).

The dictation was an unknown eight-measure tonal melody (Figure 1) presented to the subjects using the same procedures as a musical dictation performed in the context of the standard aural skills course. The musical phrase was played on a vertical Kawai piano. The first note of the dictation was provided to the subjects, without indications regarding tonality or mode. The phrase was played twice straight through, and then each fragment of two measures (including the first note of the following fragment) was played three times. Each time a new fragment was added, the dictation was played again once from the beginning up to the end of the new fragment. This dictation included 24 notes. Each incorrect note removed one point from the score. Thus, the performance of the subjects was assessed with a scale ranging from 0 to 24. The testing session took about 30 minutes.

Figure 1. Musical dictation

Visual short-term memory span

A visual short-term memory span test called "Object recognition memory span" was adapted (Levy et al., 2003; Snodgrass & Vanderwart, 1980) using simplified cartoons of common objects. These pictures were presented on a computer screen in the following sequence. At first a black screen was shown, and then the automatized sequence of pictures to be displayed started when the subjects were ready. The first white screen displayed a single picture. Each white screen was separated from the next by a black screen. The following white screens displayed the same picture(s) as the previous one but added a new supplementary picture, up to the last screen with 24 different pictures (Levy et al., 2003). On each screen, the position of the pictures varied so as to make the position of the new picture unpredictable. From the 2nd to the 5th picture, each white screen was presented for 2s. From the 6th to the 10th picture, the white screens were presented for 3s. From the 11th to the 15th picture, they were presented for 4s. From the 16th to the 20th picture, the white screens were presented for 5s. From the 21st to the 24th picture, they were presented for 6s. Between two consecutive white screens, a black screen was presented for 3s; at that time, the subjects were asked to write on a piece of paper the name of the new object they had observed. A click was emitted 2s after the beginning of the black screen to indicate that the next picture would appear in 1s. Trials continued in this way, until the 24 pictures had been presented. Four consecutive sequences (of 24 pictures each) were presented to the subjects with a different set of pictures for each. For each trial, the score represented the largest number of pictures that were correctly recognized in sequence. For example, if an error was made during the presentation of the tenth picture, the score for that trial was nine. For each subject, the visual recognition memory span score was the average across the three last trials, because the first was a training session.

Auditory short-term memory span

This "digit span" test was derived from one of the standardized components of the Wechsler Memory Scale tests (WMS, 1987) to measure auditory short-term memory. The digit lists were selected for this study by the experimenters, taking the shape of 6 double lists with 5 to 10 digits each, which were read in a loud voice during the experiment. The choice to vary the digits present on the lists was made so as to have a scale around 7, the median number of items humans can retain in short-term memory (Miller, 1956). Each list of a different size was doubled in order to calculate the average and minimize data skewed because of possible interferences, such as a noise that could disturb the subject's concentration. The test was carried out in a group in a single session. A five-second break was given between the reading of each list and the instructions to write it down. For each double list, the score was the average of the number of correct digits in sequence.

Results

Score on the musical dictation

The average score on the musical dictation was 23.22. ± 0.3 (minimum: 21; maximum: 24). This sample consisted of 49 students (24 males and 25 females).

Utilization of strategies

The same two chief categories of strategies classified and explained in the main study (Cruz de Menezes, 2010) emerged from the descriptions: *non-tonal strategies* and *tonal strategies*. In order to explain the utilization of those strategies used to solve the dictation, two types of indicators were calculated for each subject: the number of different strategies used and the number of utilizations of each strategy. The first represents each strategy used by the subject counted only once, reflecting the variety of different strategies used. The second represents the total number of times that a strategy was described by the subject. The mean number of utilizations of non-tonal strategies used was 12.92 ± 1.13%, while the mean number of utilizations of tonal strategies used was 10.1 ± 1.08%.

To understand the relationship between the types of strategies used and the scores obtained on dictation, Spearman correlations were applied. No correlation was assessed between the scores of the dictation and the number of different non-tonal strategies (rs: 0.136, p=0.350), nor the number of utilizations of each non-tonal strategy (rs: 0.061, p=0.677). Similarly, there was no correlation between the scores of the dictation and the number of different tonal strategies (rs: 0.1590, p=0.275) nor the number of utilizations of each tonal strategy (rs: 0.134, p=0.357). These results show that the performance of the best students is not related to the type of the strategy used or to how often the strategies are used by them.

Efficacy of strategies

In order to explain the effectiveness of the strategies used to solve the dictation, the percentage of correct answers obtained following the utilization of each particular strategy was calculated. For each strategy, the results were first averaged for each subject before being averaged across subjects. The efficacy of non-tonal strategies was 97.94 ± 0.72% and the efficacy of tonal strategies was 98.97 ± 0.43%. Moreover, the score on the musical dictation correlates with the efficacy of non-tonal (rs: 0.577, p<0.001) and tonal (rs: 0.283, p<0.05) strategies. In fact, the performance of the most successful students is related to the efficient manner in which they use both types of strategies, non-tonal and tonal. This high performance in strategy use allows them to achieve better results.

Memory span tests and the efficacy of strategies

The purpose of comparing the short-term memory span tests with the efficacy of non-tonal and tonal strategies was to understand if the capacity of the visual or auditory memories was related to the efficacy of using both types of strategies.

Visual short-term memory span

Among the 49 subjects, 30 subjects did this test. The mean obtained in the visual recognition memory span test was 17.78 ± 0.8. A significant correlation was found between the efficacy of tonal strategies and this test (*rs*: 0.466, *p*<0.01). Accordingly, it seems that students who use the tonal strategies more efficiently have a tendency to have a larger visual memory span, which in turn probably allows them to better use this type of strategy.

Auditory short-term memory span

Among the 49 students, 32 subjects did the digit span test. Thus, there was a correlation between this test and the efficacy of tonal strategies (*rs*: 0.373, *p*<0.05). However, there was no significant correlation between this test and the efficacy of non-tonal strategies (*rs*: 0.104, *p*=0.569). Once again, there is the same tendency observed in the previous test. The capacity of auditory short-term memory is related only to the optimum utilization of tonal strategies. This supports the results of the visual recognition memory span: the larger the short-term memory capacity, the better the subjects use the tonal strategies.

Conclusion

The results of our study showed significant correlations between the efficacy of the strategies used by the most successful students and their results on music melodic dictation. In fact, the score on the music dictation correlated especially with the efficient use of tonal strategies. That means that the performance of the most-successful students on this task is related to the efficient manner in which they use tonal strategies.

Comparing short memory tests and the type of strategies used to solve a musical dictation also revealed very interesting results. A significant correlation was found only between the efficacy of using tonal strategies and the two short-term memory span tests (auditory and visual) in the most successful students. That probably means that the best performing students have a larger short memory span that allows them to use better their tonal strategies, which are a kind of associative reasoning.

Similar to these findings, previous studies in other fields (Barrouillet & Lépine, 2005; Camos, 2008) have shown a relationship between mnemonic capacities and the ability to write language dictation or to solve some mathematics questions. For example, eight-year-old children with a smaller working memory have more difficulty than others in writing simple words from dictation. Likewise, in mathematics they often recover less from memory when doing simple addition, and they are slower and less accurate than others in using algorithmic strategies (Barrouillet & Lépine, 2005). Additionally, recent studies with adults (Gonthier, & Tomassin, 2015) also support these findings between working memory capacity and the use of more effective strategies. Their results indicate that individual differences using strategies guide the predictive utility of working memory.

In music, there are several examples of situations during a dictation task in which a large memory span could help the most successful students to better use their tonal strategies. First, a larger auditory memory could help them keep in memory the notes of the dictation in order to compare them with the tonal context. They could compare a note with tonal pillars, tonic or dominant, to discover if the note is one degree higher than the heard tonal pillar. Secondly, a larger visual memory span could allow them to write down the found notes faster in order to be ready to hear the other fragments of the dictation.

Moreover, what is also interesting is that the correlation occurs with both kinds of short memory tests, auditory as well as visual. This could be explained by the fact that taking a dictation is both an auditory and a visual task, and to be good on both helps to perform better on this task. Consideration of the underlying type of thinking in the most successful students on dictation performance could guide teachers to better understand their students and to better make their pedagogical choices.

References

Barrouillet, P., & Lépine, R. (2005). Working memory and children's use of retrieval to solve addition problems. *Journal of Experimental Child Psychology, 91*, 183-204.

Camos, V. (2008). Low working memory capacity impedes both efficiency and learning of number transcoding in children. *Journal of Experimental Child Psychology, 99*, 37-57.

Cruz de Menezes, R., Bissonnette, J., Guitton, M., Moreno Sala, M. T. (novembre 2009). Stratégies cognitives mises en jeu dans les situations de transcription musicale complexe. Poster presented at the *Congrès de la Fédération des Associations de musiciens éducateurs du Québec (FAMEQ)*, Montréal, Canada.

Cruz de Menezes, R. (2010). *Les stratégies cognitives utilisées lors de la transcription musicale et des facteurs cognitifs pouvant influencer leur résultat.* Thèse de maîtrise inédite, Université Laval, Québec, Canada.

Ericsson, K. A. et Simon, H. A. (1993). *Protocol analysis: Verbal reports as data*. London: MIT Press.

Ericsson, K. A. (2006). *Protocol analysis and expert thought: Concurrent verbalizations of thinking during experts' performance on representative Tasks*. Dans K. A. Ericsson; N. Charness; R. R. Hoffman; P. J. Feltovich (Eds.), Cambridge Handbook of Expertise and Expert Performance (p. 223-241). Cambridge, UK: Cambridge University Press.

Greene, J. A., Robertson, J. et Costa, L. J. C. (2011). *Assessing self-regulated learning using think-aloud methods*. Dans B. J. Zimmerman et D. H. Schunk (Eds.), Handbook of Self-Regulation of Learning and Performance (p. 313-328). New York: Taylor & Francis.

Hedges, D. P. (1999). *The history, practice, and innovation of musical dictation in english and american aural skills pedagogy*. Unpublished Thesis, Indiana University, Illinois.

Hoppe, K. M. (1991). *The melodic dictation strategies of musicians and common pitch and rhythm errors*. Unpublished Thesis, University of Texas at Austin, Austin.

Karpinski, G. (1990). A model for music perception and its implications in melodic dictation. *The Journal of Music Theory Pedagogy, 4*, 191-229.

Langer, S. K. (1953). *Feeling and form*. New York: Charles Scribner's Sons.

Levy, D. A., Manns, J. R., Hopkins, R. O., Gold, J. J., Broadbent, N. J., & Squire, L. R. (2003). Impaired vision and odor recognition memory span in patients with hippocampal lesions. *Learning & Memory, 10*, 531-536.

Manns, J. R., Hopkins, R. O., Reed, J. M., Kitchener, E. G., & Squire, L. R. (2003). Recognition memory and the human hippocampus. *Neuron, 37*(1), 171-180.

Miller, G. A. (1956). The magical number seven, plus or minus two: Some limits on our capacity for processing information. *Psychological Review, 63*, 81-97.

Moreno Sala, M. T., & Brauer, V. (2007). Identificación de las estrategias utilizadas por los estudiantes durante la resolución de un dictado. Paper published in the proceedings of *II Jornadas de Educación Auditiva Universidad Pedagógica y Tecnológica de Colombia*, Colombie, 94-102.

Moreno Sala, M.T., Brauer, V. Cruz, R, Bissonnette, J. (2008). Musical Dictation Strategies. Conference presented at the *28th Internation-*

al Society of Music Education World Conference (ISME), Bologna, Italy.

Rogers, M. R. (1984). *Teaching approaches in music theory: An overview of pedagogical philosophies.* Carbondale: Northwestern University Press.

Snodgrass, J. G., & Vanderwart, M. (1980). A standardized set of 260 pictures: norms for name agreement, image agreement, familiarity, and visual complexity. *J Exp Psychol Hum Learn, 6,* 174-215.

Van Someren, M. W., Barnard, Y. F. et Sandberg, J. A. C. (1994). *The think aloud method: A practical guide to modelling cognitive processes.* London: Academic press limited.

Wechsler, D. (1987). Manual for the Wechsler memory scale-revised. San Antonio: The Psychological Corporation.

Acknowledgements

This research was supported by the Fonds de recherche du Québec– Société et culture FRQSC) and the Université Laval.

The perceived influences of private teachers on pianists' expertise in learning stages

Yuki Morijiri

Tokyo Gakugei University, Japan

yuki.m.h@gmail.com

Abstract

Most piano tuition is provided privately and individually, which becomes a personal matter in terms of the relationships between piano students and their teachers. When pianists look back on their piano learning from childhood to the present day, their memories about their teachers contain reflections on the subsequent influences and learner/teacher roles that were (are) adopted. This research investigates the reported influences of piano teachers on expert pianists and what they remember having learnt from such teachers. The participants in this study were sixty-eight pianists who were based in Japan and the UK (male = 28, female = 40; JP = 34, UK = 34). The average age at interview was 29.1 years old (SD=7.9) and the average age of beginning piano lessons was 5.7 years old (SD=3.0). The research used semi-structured interviews in which participants were asked to talk about each of their previous (and any current) piano teachers. The main foci of this interview were: length of time taking lessons, their experiences of the teacher, what the participants remembered learning, and how they were influenced by each teacher. Data analysis using Nvivo 10 revealed that the priority values that participants placed on the different musical components in piano performance were likely to have been cultivated primarily by teachers who had taught them either in their late adolescence (15 - 18 years), or as a young adult (18 - 25 years). An emphasis on technical issues to establish a solid foundation tended to precede a focus on coming to understand the music in greater depth and to consider the music on a macro scale. The most influential teachers were likely to teach how to understand music itself and demonstrate their own professionalism as pianists.

Keywords: pianists, private teacher, learning stage, influences, lesson

Background

Research studies have identified key factors in enabling someone to become a musician, such as parental involvement, musical parents, economic status, early education, sufficient practice, motivation, enjoyment, the quality of their teachers, the pedagogical environment, availability of private lessons and learning strategies (e.g. Creech & Papageorgi, 2014; Duke & Simmons, 2006; Fredrickson, 2007a; Macmillan, 2004; Manturzewska, 1990; Mills, 2003). Generally, pianists report taking piano lessons from early childhood, which turns out to be a life-long process (Jørgensen, 2001; Manturzewska, 1990). Jørgensen (2001) reviewed literature which investigated the starting age of private lessons for professional musicians or music major students, and then summarised that most of them started receiving private tuitions from early childhood, before the age of eight. He also found, in his own empirical studies, that the pianists started music lessons significantly earlier than other instrumental majors, e.g. compared to brass and woodwinds, except strings.

The key features that influence the quality of private tuition have been identified as personality, professionalism, content of lessons, expectations, approaches, level of skills, and aims of learning (e.g. Davidson, Sloboda, & Howe, 1998; Gaunt, 2010; McPhee, 2011; Mills, 2003). Successful learning was also reported when learners develop an intense relationship with their teachers through one-to-one lessons over a sustained period. A substantial body of research has addressed the relationships between students and their private music teachers to investigate the important features of private music lessons (Duke, Flowers, & Wolfe, 1997; Fredrickson, 2007b; Pellegrino, 2009). It is generally reported that an effective relationship between teacher and student is important (Duke, Flowers & Wolfe, 1997; Fredrickson, 2007a; Gaunt, 2010). Through the lessons, students can learn how to improve their performance, how to practise, how to overcome a problem raised, how to interpret feedback, and how to evaluate their own performances. The relationships with private music teachers can be intense and influential for future musicians' development (Duke et al., 1997). A large number of research studies have been conducted (see Schmidt, 1992) in terms of the content of private lessons, what teachers give, what students receive and the interactions between the two (e.g. Carruthers, 2008; Gaunt, 2010; Kostka, 1984; Speer, 1994). The findings indicate that teachers exert significant influence on students' perceptions, at least within a Western classical tradition, towards what counts as a good performance.

Regarding the relationships between student and teacher, Jørgensen (2000) asked the students in the author's academy about influences in developing their practice behaviour. The results revealed that 61% of the students thought that the influences by their teachers at the academy on their major instruments were 'high' or 'very high'. He also described that the relationships between student and teacher predominantly follow the pattern of a "master-apprentice relationship", where the teacher functions as a role model for their students (p.68).

As a result of interviews with young musicians and their parents, Howe and Sloboda (1991a) found that the quality of the first teacher was likely to be assessed as being poor, and half the children and their parents rated the first teacher as less than average. Howe and Sloboda (1991b) also reported that the children found at least one teacher in their career as learners that could be described as being touching, admirable and respectable, and who had influenced their instrumental learning. Howe and Sloboda (1991b) also highlighted that a major reason for changing from one teacher to another was the students' desire for a teacher with higher musical expertise. This research added that "the remarks of the older students quite often demonstrate a considerable degree of identification with a teacher" (p.56). Morijiri (2013) explored two professional musicians' learning histories, including their teachers' influences on piano improvisation, and found that their teachers influenced these musicians' paths and musical idiom to perform.

After becoming professional musicians, the learners still keep learning, trying to improve their skills, expanding their repertoire and developing as musicians. Most musicians play two roles in their professional careers: that of a performer and that of a teacher (Bennett & Stanberg, 2006; Watson, 2010). As well as performing, their role is to nurture future musicians and provide music education to other people. Not only being an educator, but also a great musician, can be influential as an ideal model for some learners, which might motivate and inspire them. Hence, what musicians have learnt and acquired through their teachers has been found to impact on their teaching.

Aims of the research
The aims of this research were to investigate perceived influences on pianists from the pianists' teachers in relation to their learning phases and to consider the potential impact on their expertise in developing their professionalism as a pianist.

Methodology
The number of participants in this study were sixty-eight pianists (mean age = 29.1, SD = 7.9) who were based in Japan and the UK (male = 28, female = 40). Thirty-four Japanese pianists and thirty four Europeans based in the UK participated in this research project. The age range was from 18 to 56 years old. They were either currently majoring in piano at

university (undergraduate/post-graduate), or were graduates of piano and professional-standard pianists. The mean age for beginning piano lessons was 5.7 years old (SD = 3.0).

The research approach used semi-structured interviews. The participants were asked to talk about each of their previous (and any current) piano teachers. The main foci of this interview were: length of time taking lessons, their experiences of the teacher, what the participants remembered learning and how they were influenced by each teacher. The participants also reported who they perceived as being their most influential piano teacher in terms of their own piano learning. With their permission and appropriate ethical approval, all interviews were recorded on a digital audio recorder by the researcher. The interviews were transcribed and then analysed thematically using NVivo 10.

Main findings

The descriptive analyses revealed that the average number of the participants' teachers since starting piano lessons, was 5.15 (SD = 1.97). The thirty-four participants who were born and started piano learning in Japan were compared with thirty-four participants who were European or based in the UK. Each group was compared in terms of the mean age of starting piano lessons. The independent t-test revealed a significant difference, $t(44.278) = -5.973, p < 0.001$. Japanese musicians started taking piano lessons (M = 3.9, SD = 1.3) significantly earlier than others (M = 7.4, SD = 3.1).

Three hundred and fifty teachers were reported from the sixty-eight participants. The extracted comments from all the participants were coded and classified by contents. The classification was in terms of what the participants remembered about the lessons and any significant features which they had learnt from each teacher. Nine categories emerged as follows: as a musician, interpretation, technique, how-to, tone quality, psychological aspects, fun, general musical expression, and repertoire. Forty-seven participants (69.1%) recalled teacher(s) who emphasized or taught techniques intensively in their piano learning. Forty-two participants (61.8%) reported that they had learnt how to interpret or understand music from specific teacher(s). Twenty-nine participants (42.6%) reported that they had at least one teacher who influenced them "as a musician". The category of "as a musician" includes a respect for the teacher as being a professional musician and his/her professionalism. Twenty-five participants (36.8%) remembered that they received tuition of "how to" manage their performances as a strategy. The category of "how to" indicates being taught the strategy of performance or practice, how to manage building up a performance and how to integrate both aspects of how a student would like to play and what he/she can. Twenty-four participants (35.3%) had met a teacher(s) who paid attention to "tone quality" or tone colour. The category of "tone quality" indicated suitable sound production, the quality of tone colour or paying attention to it in building up a performance. For example a participant reported: "The sounds he creates are like jewellery. Every single tone sounds so twinkle and beautiful. No edge, no attacked sounds. Like a pearl." Eighteen participants (26.5%) remembered that they got emotional support or received psychological encouragement from a teacher; these were labelled "psychological aspects". Twelve participants (17.6%) reported that their teacher helped them to expand their range of repertoire or gave them a different genre of music as a new experience. Eleven participants (16.2%) recollected a memory of having fun or feeling joy while in a lesson. Also, eleven participants (16.2%) reported that their teacher(s) prioritised musical sensitivity and general music expression within a performance, such as including their own emotion.

The distribution of the numbers of teachers by each category was also analysed regarding the students' ages. The reported teachers who contributed "having fun" to the learners were more distributed at a primary school phase of piano learning. Thereafter, "technical tuition" dramatically rose and seemed to be dominant, particularly from later childhood to adolescence. In adolescence and early adulthood, interpretation of music was emphasised in piano tuition and hit a peak at the age of twenty-one (student's age), in contrast to decreasing technical instruction. Interestingly, the distribution of "tone quality" matched that of "interpretation". The tuition of "how to" manage performance or integration of different skills was also assigned more frequently to ages in later adolescence and early adulthood. As well as "interpretation", the categories of "tone quality" and "how to" recorded the highest numbers of teachers' reports at the students' age of twenty-one. The influence "as a musician" appeared slightly later on. Regarding the category of "as a musician", the peak was at the age of twenty-three, with fourteen teachers reported.

The mean age of meeting the most influential teacher(s) was 18.5 years old (SD = 5.36). The mean duration of taking lessons from the most influential teacher(s) was 4.44 years (SD = 2.60). Eighty-five teachers were reported as the most influential teachers from across all the participants. At the age of eighteen, seventeen teachers of the total were reported as the participants' most influential teachers. This was 20% of the total number of the most influential teachers. It could be said that piano teachers who had taught either in the learners' late adolescence or young adulthood were likely to be reported as the most influential. 26% of the most influential teachers were recalled because of the student's respect for them as a musician. 21% of the teachers were reported as giving great guidance for interpretation and understanding music. The percentage of the influential teachers, who taught how to build up a performance or a strategy, was 16%. 13% of the most influential teachers emphasised technical aspects of performance. 12% of influential teachers tried to enhance learners' tone quality skills. The teachers who supported learners intensively by mental encouragement obtained 7%.

Sixty-five teachers (18.6% of all the teachers reported), which was a largest number by each category, were recalled as teaching technical aspects. However, 24.6% of the teachers were assigned as the most influential teachers. On the other hand, 68.6% of the teachers, who influenced the participants "as a musician", were reported as the most influential teachers. Similarly, the teachers who taught "interpretation" of music, "how to" manage a performance and "tone quality" were also highly likely to be the most influential, as these categories obtained more than 50 %. None of the teachers who were reported based on an experience of "having fun" with music were chosen as the most influential teacher.

Conclusions

From the results of the fieldwork, it seems that these performance dimensions might be also interrelated with the structural phases of education, based on piano learning in the context of one-to-one teaching. Learners can acquire any musical aspect at any stage. However, the main findings in this research suggested the related learning stages. Chaffin and Imereh (2001) suggested the stage of performance creation consists of three dimensions: basic, interpretative and performance. The data of teachers' influence in this study also seems to support these stages. The data also suggested that instructions in basic skills and technical development in one-to-one tuition were likely to be established and emphasised in the early stages of piano learning. The learners tended to be focused on technical enhancement in order to actually play the piano correctly (mainly at a higher level), and to expand technical potentialities for actualising their ideal performance in their mind as much as possible. Interpretative aspects in teaching become more intensely introduced after establishing these basic and technical foundations. The participants in this research reported that, in their later period of piano learning, they came to learn these strategies and developed how to manage their performance on stage, which could be perceived as a superior and progressive level of performance creation.

The values revealed in their prioritisation of musical components in piano performance were likely to have been cultivated by teachers who had taught them either in their late adolescence or young adulthood. An emphasis on technical issues to establish a solid foundation tended to precede a focus on coming to understand music in depth and to consider music on a macro scale. One reason why this age phase was considered important was due to its association with university entry. When the participants entered university, they were likely to take lessons from piano teachers who were much more qualified than hitherto, e.g., those who held a doctoral degree, had more experience of performance and/or tutoring outstanding pianists. The participants reported that the main reason why their teachers were perceived as influential was a respect for the teachers as being established musicians. This was considered as inspiring for young, developing musicians. Additionally, by the age of entry to higher education, it could be that the students had already established enough ability to recognise how the teacher could demonstrate their quality as a pianist. This relates to the studies by Johnson (1996) and Wapnick and Rosenquist (1991) which explored how music students at the university level could understand the quality of performance appropriately. Likewise, these studies imply that when the students are focusing on their musical development in relation to performance skills and advanced musical knowledge, they might be more able to understand accurately the quality of the performances by their teachers who were assumed to be good musicians. In addition to what the pianists learnt from their teachers, how to emotionally connect to their teachers and how they respect their teachers as a musician became remarkable points in deciding who the most influential teacher happened to be.

References

Bennett, D., & Stanberg, A. (2006). Musicians as teachers: Developing a positive view through collaborative learning partnerships. *International Journal of Music Education, 24*(3), 219-230.

Carruthers, G. (2008). Educating professional musicians: Lessons learned from school music. *International Journal of Music Education, 26*(2), 127-135.

Chaffin, R., & Imereh, G. (2001). A comparison of practice and self-report as sources of information about the goals of expert practice. *Psychology of Music, 29*(1), 39-69.

Creech, A., & Papageorgi, I. (2014). Concepts of ideal musicians and teachers: Ideal selves and possible selves. In I. Papageorgi & G. F.

Welch (Eds.), *Advanced musical performance: Investigations in higher education learning* (pp. 99-114). Farnham, UK: Ashgate.

Davidson, J. W., Moore, D. G., Sloboda, J. A., & Howe, M. J. A. (1998). Characteristics of music teachers and the progress of young instrumentalists. *Journal of Research in Music Education, 46*(1), 141-160.

Duke, R. A., Flowers, P. J., & Wolfe, D. E. (1997). Children who study piano with excellent teachers in the United States. *Bulletin for the Council of Research in Music Education, 132*, 51-84.

Duke, R. A., & Simmons, A. L. (2006). The nature of expertise: Narrative descriptions of 19 common elements observed in the lessons of three renowned artist-teachers. *Bulletin for the Council of Research in Music Education, 170*, 1-13.

Fredrickson, W. E. (2007a). Music major's attitudes toward private lesson teaching after graduation: A replication and extension. *Journal of Research in Music Education, 55*(4), 326-343.

Fredrickson, W. E. (2007b). Perceptions of college-level music performance majors teaching applied music lessons to young students. *International Journal of Music Education, 25*(1), 72-81. Retrieved from <Go to ISI>://WOS:000246594600007

Gaunt, H. (2010). One-to-one tuition in a conservatoire: The perceptions of instrumental and vocal students. *Psychology of Music, 38*(2), 178-208.

Howe, M. J. A., & Sloboda, J. A. (1991a). Young musicians' accounts of significant influences in their early lives. 1. The family and the musical background. *British Journal of Music Education, 8*(1), 39-52.

Howe, M. J. A., & Sloboda, J. A. (1991b). Young musicians' accounts of significant influences in their early lives. 2. Teachers, practising and performing. *British Journal of Music Education, 8*(1), 53-63.

Johnson, C. M. (1996). Musicians' and nonmusicians' assessment of perceived rubato in musical performance. *Journal of Research in Music Education, 44*(1), 84-96.

Jørgensen, H. (2000). Student learning in higher instrumental education: Who is responsible? *British Journal of Music Education, 17*(1), 67-77.

Jørgensen, H. (2001). Instrumental learning: Is an early start a key to success? *British Journal of Music Education, 18*(3), 227-239.

Kostka, M. J. (1984). An investigation of reinforcements, time use, and student attentiveness in piano lessons. *Journal of Research in Music Education, 32*(2), 113-122.

Macmillan, J. (2004). Learning the piano: A study of attitudes to parental involvement. *British Journal of Music Education, 21*(3), 295-311.

Manturzewska, M. (1990). A biographical study of the life-span development of professional musicians. *Psychology of Music,* 18(2), 112-139.

McPhee, E. A. (2011). Finding the muse: Teaching musical expression to adolescents in the one-to-one studio environment. *International Journal of Music Education, 29*(4), 333-346.

Mills, J. (2003). Music performance: Crux or curse of music education? *Psychology of Music, 31*(3), 324-339.

Morijiri, Y. (2013). The influence of learning history on musical approaches to piano improvisation. In M. Stakelum (Ed.), *Developing the musician: Contemporary perspectives on teaching and learning* (pp. 101-118). Surrey, UK: Ashgate.

Pellegrino, K. (2009). Connections between performer and teacher identities in music teachers: Setting an agenda for research. *Journal of Music Teacher Education, 19*(1), 39-55.

Schmidt, C. P. (1992). Systematic research in applied music instruction: A review of the literature. *The Quarterly, 3*(2), 32-45.

Speer, D. R. (1994). An analysis of sequential patterns of instruction in piano lessons. *Journal of Research in Music Education,* 42(1), 14-26.

Wapnick, J., & Rosenquist, M. (1991). Preferences of undergraduate music majors for sequenced versus performed piano music. *Journal of Research in Music Education, 39*(2), 152-160.

Watson, A. (2010). Musicians as instrumental music teachers: Issues from an Australian perspective. *International Journal of Music Education, 28*(2), 193-203.

Music Teacher Working Conditions

Valerie Peters
Université Laval, Québec, Canada

valerie.peters@mus.ulaval.ca

Abstract

This collaborative research study documents music teacher working conditions in one province in Canada. Five focus groups were conducted with primary and secondary music teachers. Different aspects of music teacher working conditions were discussed including time, frequency and continuity for music classes, material conditions and the educational reform. Data were analyzed and themes including the valuing of music education, power struggles and the ongoing battle of music teaching were perceived by participants as having an important impact on their working conditions.

Keywords: Music Teachers, Working Conditions, Collaborative Research, Focus Group

Introduction

This collaborative study sought to document in detail the challenges of music teaching in one Canadian province. While publications do exist that describe the necessary conditions in order to implement a quality music program (MENC, 1994), reality demonstrates that many music teachers leave the profession because of difficult working conditions in addition to the fact that music education is not valued by society (Scheib, 2004).

Research Questions

This study was designed to answer the following research questions:

1. Describe music teacher working conditions in one Canadian province.
2. Following the analysis of the data, propose collective and organizational solutions to challenges experienced by music teachers in schools.

Heron (1996) states that participative research involves phases of reflection and action. Therefore, the second phase of this research is on going, a collaborative effort to propose solutions to the challenges of music teacher working conditions.

Theoretical frameworks

We began with the premise that the music teachers' experiential knowledge would provide answers to our research questions (Schön, 1983, 1994). This participatory research study is based on collaborative research approaches that have their origins in Co-operative Inquiry (Heron, 1996) and Collaborative Inquiry (Bray et al., 2000). We therefore designed our research study based on these principles (Bourassa, Fournier & Goyer, 2013).

Bourassa et al. (2013) define collaborative research as bringing together people that share similar interests and who wish to analyze attentively and rigorously their experience and their practice in order to answer questions of importance to them. A collaborative research design allowed the researchers to dialogue *with* the participants in a particular context, facilitating the co-construction of a knowledge base about music teacher working conditions.

Literature Review

This inductive research design, inspired by grounded theory, requires researchers to suspend temporarily their consultation of the scientific literature. The authors of a study on grounded theory method explain:

"We start by collecting and analyzing data; then, and only then, do we turn to scientific literature to enrich the theory." What participants meant is that they refused to impose an explanatory framework on the empirical data, a framework preliminary to these data, not based on them. Once more, the fundamental logic is one of emergence. This logic works in opposition to the logic of application and deduction. (Luckerhoff & Guillemette, 2011, p. 403)

Grounded theorists systematically reject any survey of the literature prior to the actual research to avoid using a priori concepts for data analysis (Luckerhoff & Guillemette, 2011) and with the goal of optimal openness to what may emerge from the data (Glaser, 1998). Therefore, in order to respect the epistemological posture and method of grounded theory, the literature is consulted "for the purpose of finding 'ideas' to compare with those that emerge" (Luckerhoff & Guillemette, 2011, p. 405), enriching the analysis reported in the results section of this paper.

Method

A focus group method allowed the researchers to explore in depth the working conditions of music teachers. A focus group is a qualitative data collection method that brings together a small number of people around a conversation focusing on a subject or a defined area that is part of the existence of the group. This method favors a group dynamic in order to encourage the expression of perceptions, attitudes, beliefs, feelings, aspirations, resistances and interest present in the focus group (Lerclerc, Bourassa, Picard, & Courcy, 2011). Two groups of 15 participants (elementary music teachers in one school board) participated in 2 three-hour focus groups (June, October, 2014). One other focus group, made up of elementary and secondary music teachers from across the province was conducted during a provincial music education conference (November, 2014). Three important themes were discussed during the interviews: (a) organizational conditions (time, frequency, continuity); (b) physical conditions (classrooms, materials); and (c) conditions related to the curricular reform.

All interviews were recorded and transcribed. An inductive method oriented the coding procedures and therefore the themes that emerged were solidly grounded in the empirical data. A data analysis procedure was conducted using Nvivo 10 and based on the thematic coding procedures of Paillé & Mucchielli (2012). Two graduate students and the researcher read the transcriptions and analyzed the data. According to Patton (1999), *analyst triangulation*, which includes multiple observers and perspectives, enhances the quality and credibility of the data analysis. "Having two or more researchers independently analyze the same qualitative data set and then compare their findings provides an important check on selective perception and blind interpretive bias" (Patton, 1999, p. 1195).

Results

The themes that emerged from the data have been grouped into three larger categories: (a) Themes related to the interview questions: Power, Working Relationships, Working Environment and Budget, Elementary School Daycare, Music Curriculum and Legislation; (b) Expressed Feelings; and (c) Solutions. This section will also discuss an emergent overall theme, Ongoing Battle.

The theme of power is recurrent throughout the data. This power is defined as the person or people that have the authority to make decisions about a music teacher's workload, classroom environment, class schedule and ongoing professional development. Music teachers stated that the school principal holds this power and that the other classroom teachers, parents and the decision-making bodies in schools control the principal. The power of the music teacher depends on contract status and relationships with the principal and all the people that influence this person. The following two citations illustrate who decides whether music education will take place in schools. "A popular teacher who does not have problems and has good classroom management skills, well, this person has a better chance of keeping a job in our school because the classroom teachers have a say about your workload....They are the ones who decide whether there will be more time in the schedule for music or not" (Kathy, FG, November 2014).[16] "I find that this problem is very important because it should not be your colleagues who decide how many hours you teach year after year" (Kathy, FG, November 2014). It is clear that other teachers are making decisions about the time allocated to music education in schools.

Working relationships go beyond interactions with the principal and the teaching staff. Often, these relationships are influenced by factors not controlled by the music teacher such as stability, a constant presence in a school to create strong ties with staff and the school climate (cohesion or individualism). Relationships with staff were expressed as being negative (adversity, preconceptions about music, rivalry between subjects) or positive (diplomatic, good relationships). Here are two citations that describe these different relationships and how they impact music teacher working conditions. "If a person is well adjusted to their school context, it is much easier to interact with parents, school administrators and children and this contributes to the [creation of a musical school culture]" (Mark, FG, June 2014). "I have experienced different realities during the years. I realize after all these years that it all comes back to the relationships that we create with others and school administration" (Cara, FG, June 2014).

The themes Working Environment and Budget comprise the physical environment, teaching materials and financial resources in a school. For example, teachers described their physical working spaces in the following ways: absence of classroom space, nonfunctional space, sharing space with others and working in dirty and smelly workspaces. Access to materials is often difficult and when resources are available, they are often out dated. Quality materials are not readily available or are distributed unequally from school to school. The budget for music programs depends on the financial state of the school and the workload, influence and popularity of the

---

[16] Pseudonyms will be used throughout the study to protect the identity of the participants. All citations have been translated into English. A section of a citation in square brackets indicates an attempt to clarify meaning or an interpretation on the part of the author. All attempts were made to quote the participants voices *verbatim*.

teacher. Teachers mentioned having no place to work, not being able to set up in their classrooms, spending their own money to buy materials and investing a lot of work and energy to fund raise. In addition, many teachers experienced instability, fearing that they would lose their classroom space.

The working environment and budget varies greatly varies greatly from school to school. Music teachers need to cultivate good relationships with their colleagues and school administration in order to work in an acceptable environment, which is especially difficult for teachers that work in several schools. Music teachers must adapt, be creative and invest their own money in order to teach music. A few teachers speak their mind on this issue. "Honestly, if I experienced poor working conditions, I wouldn't be a teacher. I would work in a shop somewhere but I would simply not be a teacher" (Samuel, FG, November 2014). "I am well aware that I had to invest my own money and by doing so, this does not help the next teacher because I am leaving [with my material] and the person who replaces me will not have the necessary conditions [to teach music]" (Roger, FG, June 2014).

An unexpected theme connected to working conditions was Elementary School Daycares. The music teachers in elementary schools often share their classroom with the daycare service that uses the room in the morning, at lunch and after school. The teachers described the negative impact: Less teaching time, restricted access to their classrooms to prepare and being forced to work in a dirty, noisy, smelly environment. Music teachers felt that they were being treated unfairly compared to other teachers who do no have to share their rooms. In addition, some participants stated that this situation impacted the quality of their work as well as their mental and physical health. Here is one example: "Forty lunches heating up in your classroom…you have no idea how much it stinks!" (Terry, FG, June 2014). One silly solution proposed by several school administrators was for the music teachers to wear construction earmuffs in order to be able to work in their classrooms despite the noise.

The teachers proposed several solutions: Lobbying, maintaining good relationships with school administration, other teachers, school personnel, parents, and being involved in decision-making school committees. Music teachers must raise the profile of their discipline and continuously promote music. They are creative and adaptable to almost any situation because they want to share their passion for music. Several participants suggested that the music teachers' provincial association and the teacher unions should help them to advocate for better working conditions.

One of the interview questions concerned the provincial music curriculum and legislation. For most school subjects, there are a suggested number of hours per week in the Education Act. For the arts, there is no suggestion for the number of hours at the elementary level, leaving this decision up to schools. Powerful actors in schools manipulate this information or communicate misinformation in order to obtain their own goals (for example, less time for music). In terms of the curriculum document, teachers explained the problem of continuity between schools and the difficulty of evaluating the music competencies (performing, creating, listening-appreciating). There were diverse opinions about the curriculum, some favorable and others indifferent. According to the teachers, the problem in not the curriculum but the working conditions. As expressed by one teacher, "We use the method that we are comfortable with. We take the children [from A to B, help them progress], notwithstanding the curriculum guides that were in place during the 1980s, 1990s and 2000s etc. It is important to [help the students to progress]" (Terry, FG, October 2014).

The participants expressed negative and positive feelings about their working conditions. Negative feelings of humiliation helplessness, outrage, vulnerability and isolation were voiced. One teacher was outraged given the inequality of the current situation: "We have rights, it shouldn't be like that…When I look at the teacher beside me, I think: 'we don't discuss you teaching workload in front of everybody.' It's awful! It's humiliating!" (Andrea, FG, June 2014). The word "humiliation" was pronounced with emphasis multiple times during this discussion. On the other hand, there were also positive feelings of pride, respect and empathy expressed towards participants in the focus groups. Also, one teacher articulated feelings of pride concerning the place of music in his school: "[We have developed a musical culture in our school]. We are proud. The school is proud" (Jeff, FG, November 2014).

The overall theme that permeates the interviews is the feeling that music teachers are involved in an ongoing battle. Several citations illustrate this theme. "I still like my work and I want to retire, but I'm telling you, sometimes you have to fight. You have to really fight …in order to do our work adequately" (Terry, FG, June 2014). "Sometimes we feel like we are in a popularity contest" (Kathy, FG, November 2014). "Can I emphasize this point 'market yourself'? This is what we do every day as a music teacher. Do physical education, English and homeroom teachers need to 'market their subjects' to keep their jobs? No! But we have to do it or else we lose our job. We lose our place. This is the hard reality" (Kathy, FG, November 2014).

Discussion

A literature review was conducted following data coding in order to respect the inductive approach. There are few qualitative studies that describe in rich detail the actual working conditions of music teachers in
schools. According to Scheib (2004), "we need to look at the day-to-day
routine of music teachers, the struggles they face, and the systems under
which they operate" (p. 57).

Clearly, unsatisfactory working conditions are at the heart of role stress.
"Role stress occurs as a result of conflicting, overwhelming, or unsatisfactory expectations identified by the person holding an occupational role
within an organization (Scheib, 2006a, p. 6). For example, of the six role
stressors identified through research that negatively impact job satisfaction, resource inadequacy and nonparticipation are directly related to the
present study. Resource inadequacy requires a person to make things work
without the necessary tools and resources. Clearly, "creating something out
of nothing", adapting to any context and being courageous despite all the
challenges describes many of the teachers in this study (FG, June 2014).
While music teachers may be praised as "heros", perhaps "making do" with
inadequate resources sends the wrong message to school administrators, a
message that music teachers will accept the *status quo* and therefore,
schools do not need to invest in their music programs. This also penalizes
the next music teacher that takes a job in a school with no resources. As
Scheib (2004) states, "we [music educators] 'made do' with what is given
to us. But by doing so, we are enabling a system to continue to undermine
our efforts" (p. 57).

Nonparticipation means that teachers are not being included in decisions
affecting them. The participants expressed strong feelings of humiliation
when their workload is discussed publically in front of fellow teachers and
administration. Music curricular decisions are based on whether the music
specialist is popular, has no problems, demonstrates good classroom management skills and has developed the right political alliances with administration and colleagues (FG, November 2014).

An important theme that emerges from this study's data is related to the
role of school administration. In fact, Scheib (2004) notes that according
to the National Center for Educational Statistics in 1997, inadequate support from administration was one of the main reasons for feeing dissatis-
fied with teaching as a career. In addition, in Scheib's (2004) email survey
of instrumental music teachers planning to move to new positions or leave
the profession, difficult working conditions and the low priority of music
education within the school curriculum were two of the four general re-

sponse categories. One of the respondents stated: "It is very difficult to teach in a school system where the administration does not highly value music instruction" (Scheib, 2004, p. 55). In addition, the following comment of one of the respondents relates to the theme Ongoing Battle. "One major problem in teaching music is always having to justify our existence [to] other teachers, administrators, and boards. I had the feeling that I was a second-class program compared to math, reading, etc." (Scheib, 2004, p. 56). Many teachers in the focus groups expressed feelings of frustration that music is not valued. They are in a constant battle to justify music education in the curriculum. Aptly put by another of Scheib's participants, "People are fed up with justifying music all the time" (p. 56).

Gardner (2010) emphasizes the importance of school administration for music teachers. "Music teachers' perceived level of administrative support had the most prominent influence on both music teacher satisfaction and retention" (p. 112). In addition, "music teachers' perceptions of the level of support from their administrators exhibited the strongest influence on teacher satisfaction and job commitment in all analyses" (p. 119). Heston, Dedrick, Raschke and Whitehead (1996) confirm that the major concern of music teachers is the lack of support from school officials and the community at large. This study stresses the importance of positive interpersonal relationships between music teachers and administration and between music teachers and other teachers. The issue of power in the current study is related to administrative support and working relationships with other colleagues.

Many of the focus group participants gave examples of inadequate working environments. All over the world, music teachers face these same challenges. According to Octacioglu (2008), there are no assigned music rooms in schools for 70.7 % of the questionnaire study participants in Turkey. Fifty percent of schools did not have musical instruments and in general, instruments and equipment were insufficient. Schneider (2003) also conducted a study documenting how teachers perceived working conditions affecting job performance and teaching effectiveness in Chicago and Washington schools. In general, respondents described a lack of specialized facilities for music and a third of the teachers in Chicago and half of the teachers in Washington judged music and arts rooms to be somewhat or very inadequate. The school environment can impact teacher health and contribute to attrition. "Poor school conditions make it more difficult for teachers to deliver an adequate education to their students, adversely affect teachers' health, and increase the likelihood that teachers will leave their school and teaching profession" (Schneider, 2003, p. 5).

Clearly, working conditions are a challenge for music teachers around the world. It is difficult to advocate for the inclusion of music in the school curriculum and power issues are challenging music teachers to become politically savvy about how to win over administration and colleagues in order to keep their jobs. These ongoing battles take energy and time away from curriculum planning and students.

Conclusion

The music teachers in this study had a lot to say about their working conditions. The focus groups provided us with a deeper understanding of the situation and some clues to finding solutions. The results of this study will be communicated to our provincial music educators association to facilitate their ongoing battle to improve music education in schools.

Acknowledgements

We wish to acknowledge first and foremost all the music teachers who gave of their time to discuss these issues. We also wish to thank our different funding partners.

References

Bourassa, B., Fournier, G., & Goyer, L. (2013). Faire le point, comprendre et réviser sa pratique professionnelle: une recherche collaborative auprès d'intervenants d'un service de placement étudiant. In B. Bourassa, G. Fournier & L. Goyer (Eds.), *Construction de savoirs et de pratiques professionnelles: le double jeu de la recherche collaborative* (pp. 30-86). Québec, Canada: Presses de l'Université Laval.

Bray, J. N., Lee, J., Smith, L. L., & Yorks, L. (2000). *Collaborative inquiry in practice: Action, reflection, and meaning making*. Thousand Oaks, CA: Sage Publications.

Gardner, R. D. (2010). Should I stay or should I go? Factors that influence the retention, turnover, and attrition of K-12 music teachers in the United States. *Arts Education Policy Review, 111*, 112-121.

Glaser, B. G. (1998). *Doing grounded theory*. Mill Valley, CA: Sociology Press.

Heron, J. (1996). *Co-operative inquiry: Research into the human condition*. London: Sage.

Heston, M. L., Dedrick, C., Raschke, D., & Whitehead, J. (1996). Job satisfaction and stress among band directors. *Journal of Research in Music Education, 44*(4), 319-327.

Lerclerc, C., Bourassa, B., Picard, F., & Courcy, F. (2011). Du groupe focalisé à la recherche collaborative: avantages, defis et strategies. *Recherches Qualitatives*, *29*(3), 145-167.

Luckerhoff, J., & Guillemette, F. (2011). The conflicts between grounded theory requirements and institutional requirements for scientific research. *The Qualitative Report*, *16*(2), 396-414.

MENC (1994). *Opportunity-to-learn standards for music instruction: Grades PreK-12*. Reston, VA.

Otacioglu, S. G. (2008). Music teachers in Turkey: Their proficiency, working environments and problems. *Educational Studies*, *34*(3), 201-211.

Paillé, P., & Mucchielli, A. (2012). *L'analyse qualitative en sciences humaines et sociales*. Paris: Armand Colin.

Patton, M. Q. (1999). Enhancing the quality and credibility of qualitative analysis. *Health Services Research*, *34*(5 Pt 2), 1189-1208.

Scheib, J. W. (2004). Why band directors leave: From the mouths of maestros. *Music Educators Journal*, *91*(1), 53.

Scheib, J. W. (2006a). Policy implications for teacher retention: Meeting the needs of the dual identities of arts educators. *Arts Education Policy Review*, *107*(6), 5-10.

Schneider, M. (2003). *Linking school facility conditions to teacher satisfaction and success*. Washington, DC: National Clearinghouse for Educational Facilities.

Schön, D. (1983). *The reflective practitioner: How professionals think in action*. New York, NY: Basic Books.

Schön, D. (1987). *Educating the reflective practitioner: Toward a new design for teaching and learning in the professions*. San Francisco, CA: Jossey-Bass.

'The Ten Percent'. Young people's access to publicly-funded instrumental music tuition in England: findings from an idiographic geographical case study

Ross Purves

De Montfort University, UK

ross.purves@dmu.ac.uk

Abstract

This paper reports on research into the provision and take-up of publicly-funded musical instrument tuition by young people living in one English local government area ('local authority'). A range of possible 'hidden' barriers to accessing this tuition are explored, embracing socio-economic status, geographical distance between home and teaching sites, along with instrument size and weight.

The case study local authority's particular cultural and economic circumstances led to its instrumental music service receiving unparalleled levels of national government funding between 1998 and 2011. The then government's intention for this funding was to address a perceived decline in schools' instrumental tuition and to widen access. This came at a time of unprecedented political interest in all aspects of music making and learning. The provision of instrumental tuition within this particular district thus offers a valuable deviant, idiographic study of the impacts of this investment. Geocoded participant records and local-level data have been explored through the lens of spatial statistical analysis (e.g. location quotients, tests for spatial autocorrelation and distinct distributions, and associated regression models). This paper offers a brief summary of some of the underlying geographical and socio-economic trends in patterns of access and participation that emerged over the period of time covered by the data.

Introducing local authority music services

In England, the term 'local authority' refers to the tier of local government responsible for the provision of a range of municipal services, including aspects of education, within a town, city or county. Beginning in the 1940s, many local authorities appointed teams of 'peripatetic' music teachers, whose role was to travel between schools providing instrumental tuition *alongside* any music education that might be part of the school's classroom curriculum. In addition, local youth orchestras, wind bands, choirs and jazz orchestras were instituted, with rehearsals taking place in evenings and at weekends. This kind of provision has always been a non-statutory responsibility for local authorities. As a result, there have been frequent fluctuations in public funding and demand for tuition has rarely been met by supply.

By the 1960s, these local authority 'music services' were flourishing and musical performance expectations of pupils very high (Cleave and Dust, 1989). This was the period in which many of the UK's next generation of world-class musicians emerged, many of them later citing their local music service for initial inspiration and support. Yet whilst there were undoubtedly opportunities and resulting personal and professional successes for some, there was an acknowledgement in some quarters from the early 1950s onwards that these might come at the expense of opportunities for the many. An oft-repeated estimate was that only around ten percent of the school population was in receipt of local authority instrumental tuition at any one time (e.g. Mainwairing, 1951; Hallam, 1985, Thomson, 1989).

The Music Standards Fund (MSF)

Despite some commentators continuing to express concerns about perceived inequities (sometimes in vociferous terms, e.g. see Farmer, 1979), it was economics, and not changing attitudes regarding equal opportunities, which first began to challenge conventional practices within music services. A landmark court ruling in 1981, followed by radical reform of local government and education policy in the 1980s and early 1990s, resulted in many services experiencing serious financial difficulties and it is now estimated that approximately fifty closed down during this period (Annetts, 2010). Many others reduced provision or introduced significantly higher fees to parents and schools. Levels of provision, along with policies on fees and fee remission, varied very widely from locality to locality (Hallam and Prince, 2000).

The net result of such diversity was even greater inequities in young people's ability to access the remaining provision. In response, a group of high-profile musicians and educators lobbied the incoming 1997 Government, drawing on recent advances in neuro-psychological research to argue for the extra-musical benefits of musical engagement (e.g. Rauscher *et al*, 1993). This also coincided with political interest in the growth of the 'Creative Industries' as a means of supplementing GDP as traditional manufacturing declined (e.g. see NACCCE, 1999). This concerted effort was successful and the Government introduced the 'Music Standards

Fund' (MSF) from January 1999 in order to 'protect and expand' local authority music service provision. Subsequently, the Secretary of State for Education pledged that 'every child should get the opportunity to learn an instrument' (Blunkett, 1998: 13).

The MSF was central government's first ever direct financial support for local authority music services, and the sums of money involved were large. Between 1999 and the end of the MSF in 2011, over three-quarters of a billion pounds was distributed. Local authority bids were partially assessed on 'the number of young people benefiting from funded provision and 'the extent to which the bid improved equality of access to music services' (DfEE, 1998: Section 27a). As a result, Hallam *et al* (2002) concluded that, nationally, the MSF had enabled music services to halt the decline and focus resources on broader, more accessible and inclusive forms of provision.

Introducing the Case Study Local Authority

As funding from the MSF was beginning to make an impact on music services' work, I was working as a music teacher in a 16-19 college in a highly socio-economically- and ethnically-diverse, urban local authority in England (the 'case study authority'). In May 1997, the authority's music service employed 10 FTE staff but this figure was 47 FTE staff by June 2001 (Case Study Authority, 1997; 2001). Such expansion was possible thanks to this particular local authority receiving an allocation from the MSF representing £25.24 for each pupil in its schools. Nationally, the average per pupil allocation was £8.95 and so the case study authority had done particularly well from the MSF.

Case study authority records reveal a clear intention amongst elected officials to create a service as diverse and accessible as possible. By 2002 this vision was recognised publicly by both the education inspectorate and the National Music Council (Ofsted, 2002; NMC, 2002). Thus, the authority could certainly be said to have responded proactively to the MSF impetus to widen participation and support social inclusion in instrumental music. Yet, as a teacher whose pupils had formerly studied within twelve secondary schools across the town, it was anecdotally clear that there remained inequities in the profiles of individuals coming forward to study our music courses. Such observations led to the hypothesis that there may exist a range of 'hidden' factors which were impacting on some young people's ability to access and sustain engagement with instrumental tuition provision.

As outlined, this hypothesis was in itself not new. What *was* new was the possibility of testing it through reference to operational data held by the case study music service and through the application of novel geospatial statistics.

Methodology

The case study music service consented to provide its entire database of 12448 instrumental tuition records covering September 2003 to November 2010, anonymised through the removal of pupil names. A clustering algorithm revealed that these records were, in reality, associated with 6350 individual young people (on the basis of distinct combinations of birth date, gender and ethnicity). Using this data, it was possible to derive additional information about each pupil, such as the total time spent learning formally with the music service, the total number of instruments studied and primary/secondary schools attending during periods of tuition. Additionally, pupils' postal codes[17] allowed their geographical location to be pinpointed to street level. This, in turn, facilitated the referencing of a wide variety of Government datasets, 'geocoded' using the smallest spatial unit of resolution used to represent census data: the 'Lower Level Super Output Area' (LSOA). Typically, each LSOA in England has a population of c.1500 residents. The area of the case study local authority is divided into 121 LSOAs.

Documentary analysis: applying educational history to inform the present

Some writers have commented that the world of instrumental tuition is characterised by slow evolution, with teachers often continuing to practise pedagogies, and to hold beliefs, associated with *their* former teachers (Creech and Gaunt, 2012). Thus, historical documentary analysis (McCulloch, 2011) was employed to identify themes relating to implicit or 'hidden' assumptions regarding young people's access to the instrumental tuition on offer in music services. These were found present – to a greater or lesser extent – in discourse surrounding local authority music services over much or all of their entire history. The themes relating to the findings reported in this paper were identified as follows.

- o Socio-economic status of participants;
- o family vehicle ownership;

---

[17] In the UK, postal codes are termed 'postcodes' and, in America, 'zip codes'. A summary of many other international synonyms is given at
http://www.grcdi.nl/gsb/summary_%20postal%20code%20synonyms.html

o instrument size and weight; and

o distances between pupils' homes and teaching/rehearsing sites.

The 'deviant, ideographic' case study

The goal of the second phase of the research was to 'test' these implicit assumptions through the interrogation of the case study authority data. This approach drew upon the 'idiographic' case study, commonly used within the social sciences (George and Bennett, 2005; Mitchell, 2006). This seeks to 'emphasise place as unique assemblages where diverse processes and factors come together' (Crang, 1998: 192). The comparatively generous funding arrangements in the case study authority characterise it as a 'deviant' or 'outlier' case. These can be very valuable since the distinct circumstances under study can help identify hitherto unexplored hypotheses, variables and causal relationships which will perhaps lead to insights and theories with more general applicability (George and Bennett, 2005).

The analysis was chiefly quantitative, employing a range of recently-developed local spatial statistical techniques outlined below. In themselves, the themes derived from the documentary analysis are what Clinton refers to as 'unobservable quantities of interest' (2004: 879) thus was necessary to identify a range of proxy variables to represent these factors as closely as possible. These were then used as 'predictor variables' for the various geospatial tests. Overall, the intention was to occupy what Goodchild terms the 'middle ground' between the qualitative, idiographic case study and quantitative, nomethetic study in which, 'place-based analysis focuses on how the parameters of the model vary from place to place, and draws insights and conclusions from those variations' (2000: 177).

Selected results

In this short paper, only a few key 'highlights' of the research results are offered. These have been selected on the basis of both insights into impediments to music service participation and in order to demonstrate the range of geospatial analysis techniques employed.

Overall music service 'reach'

A first step in analysing young people's participation was to identify areas well-served and under-served by the case study music service. Simply counting the number of pupils living in each LSOA was too simplistic, since this would not have taken into account areas inhabited by fewer children to begin with (e.g. concentrations of small flats inhabited by young, childless professionals or retired people). Use was therefore made of 'location quotient' calculations. These compare local concentrations of a particular activity or characteristic prevailing national trends (St John and Richardson, 1989). The 'Service Reach Location Quotient' (SRLQ) was calculated using equation 1:

$$SRLQ = \frac{p_{lsoa} \div p_{all}}{P_{Hallam} \div P_{all}} \qquad (1)$$

Here *plsoa* refers to all young people receiving music service tuition in an LSOA each academic term[18], and *pall* refers to all young people aged 7-16 in that LSOA at the time of the 2001 census. *PHallam* refers to the total number of young people aged 7-16 receiving instrumental tuition nationally on February 1st 2005, according to Hallam *et al* (2005), and *Pall* refers to the total school population aged 7-16 in England in January 2005, according to school census data.

The resulting SRLQ scores were averaged over the 21 academic terms covered by the case study data and then plotted as a choropleth map (Figure 1). In general, LSOAs on the south-west of the case study authority were inhabited by far fewer music service pupils whilst areas in the north-east were often home to far higher numbers of participants, as scores of >2.0 demonstrate. The clustering of average SRLQ scores in adjacent LSOAs is visually quite clear but a Moran's I test allows the researcher to be sure that such visual clustering is evidenced statistically (Lloyd, 2010). In this case, a statistically-significant Moran's test ($I = 0.55$; $p < 1x$ 10-15) suggested a relatively high level of clustering (the maximum score for I in a Moran's test is 1.0).

Overall, the case study authority was bisected by a line extended from the north-west tip to the south-east side. This 'line' is, in fact, a major inter-city railway. One is reminded of the old folk saying, 'living on the wrong side of the tracks'. This describes the way that socio-economically distinct communities may be separated by physical features of the landscape (Price, 2011). Thus, in order to test whether the distribution of music service pupils' homes was related to the town's prevailing socio-economic landscape, the non-parametric test proposed by Syrjala (1996) was employed. This

---

[18] In the UK, the academic year is traditionally divided into three 'terms': Christmas, Easter and Summer.

compares the values of two geocoded datasets with shared coordinates. Here, the comparison dataset was for income deprivation data from 2010 edition of the UK 'Indices of Multiple Deprivation'. The test statistic was small (0.0393) and non-significant (p = 0.109). We may therefore conclude that these datasets were drawn from a common spatial distribution and that prevailing socio-economic conditions in the local authority *were* strongly related to music service tuition take-up.

Subsequently, a regression model was used to identify which socio-economic factors were most strongly associated with tuition take-up. A wide variety of proxy variables were initially explored as predictors for this module, with the ASV selection routine being used to assess which combination produced the best R2 score, and thus best explained the variance in the average SRLQ scores (Field, 2012). Post-hoc VIF tests were employed to ensure that the observed regression coefficients were accurate and not overly distorted by multicollinearity. Table 1 gives the final model for average SRLQ scores; this can explain over 60% of variance in these data. 'CYPSubDomScore' refers to an official measure of educational deprivation, with higher scores representing higher prevalence of truancy, school drop-out and low educational attainment. 'PC_DegHolders' refers to percentage of local adults holding university degrees and 'PC_NonWhiteBritish' refers to the percentage of the LSOA population hailing from non-White British ethnic backgrounds.

Table 1: Average SRLQ regression model

	Estimate	Standardised estimate	% of R^2 (LMG test)	Std. Error	t value	p
(Intercept)	1.44203			0.13715	10.51	$<1\times10^{-15}$
CYPSubDomScore	-0.01095	-0.326	19%	0.00226	-4.85	$<1\times10^{-5}$
PC_DegHolders	0.02053	0.208	8%	0.00646	3.18	<0.01
PC_NonWhiteBritish	-0.01377	-0.542	33%	0.00153	-8.99	$<1\times10^{-14}$

Residual standard error for model : 0.312 on 117 degrees of freedom
R^2 for model : 0.601
F statistic for model: 58.9 on 3 and 117 DF, p: $<1\times10^{-15}$

Of the three proxy predictor variables, PC_NonWhiteBritish explained the most variance: 33% of the total R^2 according to a post-hoc LMG test (Grőmping, 2006). As the percentage of non-White British people in the LSOA rose, the number of young people undertaking music service tuition decreased. A similar, albeit less pronounced, negative relationship was found between average SRLQ and CYPSubDomScore. PC_DegHolders made a positive, smaller still contribution, indicating that areas inhabited by more graduates also tended to have greater levels of instrumental tuition take up. Overall, Table 1 tells quite a clear story: Instrumental tuition was taken up more widely in case study areas populated by high numbers of degree-holders and white British people, whose children achieved better results in school examinations, exhibited lower levels of school absence and were more likely to stay on in post-compulsory education.

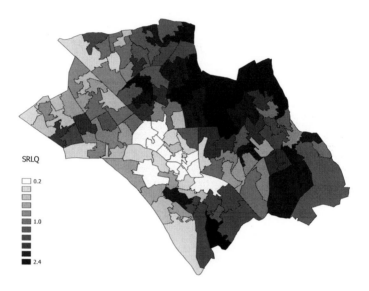

SRLQ

0.2

1.0

2.4

Figure 1. A choropleth map of mean SRLQ (Service Reach Location Quotient) scores for each LSOA within the case study authority. Increasingly darker red shading indicates below-national levels of music participation, whilst increasingly darker blue shading indicates above-national levels.

Home-school distance and the physical properties of instruments played

Literature dealing with local authority music service tuition has often highlighted concerns that pupils can be put off continuing their lessons in cases where they live farther from school or where they play a large or heavy instrument (e.g. see Artservice, 2005; Cleave and Dust, 1989; Long, 1959; Ofsted; 2004; SCAM , 1960). In order to investigate these issues within the context of the case study local authority, home-school walking distances were calculated using Google Map's Distance Matrix API (Google, 2015). Data on instrument weight and size were extracted, with permission, from Amazon's product database.

Amongst pupils who both began and ended their tuition whilst at primary school, a regression model revealed a small, statistically significant negative relationship between the total period of time over which tuition was received (in days) and the instrumental weight (β=-9.42; SE=2.05; t=-4.6; p=<1x10^{-5}). Home-school distance was found to make a non-significant contribution. Whilst the R2 for this model was small (0.09), this still implies that around 1% of total variance in tuition durations for primary school pupils can be explained through the weight of their instrument. Specifically, the coefficient estimate of -9.42 suggests that as instrument weight increases by 1kg, length of tuition reduces by 9.42 days. With larger instruments, the potential reduction of study time become quite large, suggesting instrument weight is a factor in children's decision to cease tuition. In the case of the 20KG tuba, 188 days is only two-days short of a full UK academic year:

- o   Saxophone (c.7.5KG): -70 days

- o   Cello (c.9.5KG): -89 days

- o   Baritone (10KG): -94 days

- o   Tuba (20KG): -188 days

Amongst music service pupils who commenced tuition at primary school but continued into secondary school, home-school *distance* was found to be a statistically significant factor. Again this was able to explain around 1% of variance in total duration of tuition (β=-30.6; SE=14.4; t=-2.13; p=<1x<0.05). As home-school distance increases by 1km, the total time spent in receipt of tuition on this instrument at secondary school drops by 30.6 days.

The mean geodesic home-secondary school distance in England is 2.44km (Burgess et al, 2006). Mean home-primary school distances are considerably shorter. Thus whilst distance might not be a critical factor for primary school pupils, once the secondary transition has taken place, the additional distances to school may begin to exert a greater influence on pupils' decisions to continue or cease tuition. That instrument weight is not a significant contributor in the second model suggest that as secondary-aged pupils become physically bigger and stronger they are better able to transport a larger instrument.

Conclusions

Even though only a few results from the dataset are presented above, it is clear that between 2003 and 2007 within the case study local authority, there remained significant inequalities regarding young people's ability to engage with, and sustain, instrumental tuition. The reasons for this are complex and involve far more than funding alone. Even in an area with plentiful MSF funding, participation was not even, and certain client groups benefited more than others. Hidden factors identified in historical literature may persist into the present and these should be considered at a strategic level when planning public instrumental tuition schemes in future. Some of these are far from obvious, e.g. physical properties of instruments and prevailing levels of educational achievement in the local area. These factors may be highly interrelated. Although not presented here, other strands of the research have revealed that pro-active attempts to address these inequities at a policy level can sometimes be effective, such as initiatives in England for some schools to become local leaders in arts provision through the 'ArtsMark' and 'Specialist College' schemes.

More generally, it is hoped that this paper has demonstrated the potential of both the deviant ideographic case study approach, alongside newly-developed geo-demographic/spatial statistics, as a means of facilitating further enquiries into educational access and equality.

References

Annetts, D. (2010). Fighting for the future. Keynote speech, Music learning live conference, Manchester, 26th February 2010. Retreived on 29.11.12 from http://www.ism.org/images/uploads/files/ISM_Deborah_Annetts_speech_MLL_Feb_2010.pdf

Artservice (2005). *Endangered species evaluation: Phase 2 report.* Hereford: Artservice.

Blunkett, D. (1998). Facing the music. *Times Educational Supplement,* 22nd May 1998, p. 13. Retrieved on 23.12.11 from https://www.tes.com/article.aspx?storycode=302022

Burgess, S., Briggs, A., McConnell, B. & Slater, H. (2006). *School choice in England: Background facts.* Bristol: Centre for Market and Public Organisation, Bristol Institute of Public Affairs, University of Bristol.

[Case study authority] (1997) 'Music service – Report of first year', paper to the Quality and Performance Sub-Committee of [the case study local authority].

[Case study authority] (2001) 'Best value review report: The music service'. England: [Case study local authority].

Cleave, S. and Dust, K. (1989). A sound start: the schools' instrumental music service. Windsor: NFER-Nelson.

Clinton, J. D. (2004). Proxy Variable, in MS. Lewis-Beck, A Bryman & T Futing Liao (Eds.) The SAGE Encyclopedia of Social Science Research Methods. London: Sage, p789.

Crang, M. (1998). *Cultural Geography*. London, Routledge.

Creech, A & Gaunt, H (2012). The changing face of individual instrumental tuition: Value, purpose and potential. In G McPherson & G Welch (Eds), *The Oxford Handbook of Music Education*. Oxford University Press, Oxford, pp. 694-711.

DfEE (1998) Circular 13/98: The Standards Fund 1999-2000. London: Department for Education and Employment.

Farmer, P. (1979). *Music in the comprehensive school*. London: Oxford University Press.

Field, A, Miles, J & Field, Z (2012). *Discovering Statistics Using R*. London: Sage.

George, A. L. and Bennett, A. (2005). *Case studies and theory development in the social sciences*, MIT Press.

Google (2015) The Google Maps Distance Matrix API. Retrieved on 16.12.15 fom https://developers.google.com/maps/documentation/distance-matrix/intro?hl=en

Grőmping, U (2006). Relative Importance for Linear Regression in R: The Package relaimpo, *Journal of Statistical Software*, Volume 17, Issue 1, pp. 1-27.

Goodchild, MF (2000) New horizons for the social sciences: geographic information systems. In OECD (Ed.) *Social Sciences for a digital world: Building infrastructure and databases for the future*. Paris: OECD Publishing, pp173-182.

Hallam, P. (1985). The development and influence of instrumental activity in schools during the twentieth century. Unpublished MA Dissertation, Institute of Education, University of London.

Hallam, S., & V. Prince (2000). Research into instrumental music services. Research report, Great Britain, Department for Education and Employment: 79.

Hallam, S & Rogers, L (2002) Survey of Local Education Authorities Music Services 2002 (Research Report RR478). London: Department for Education and Skills.

Hallam, S., L. Rogers, et al. (2005). Survey of Local Authority Music Services 2005. Nottingham, Department for Education and Skills: 99.

Lloyd, C.D. (2010). *Spatial data analysis*: New York: Oxford University Press

Long, N (1959). *Music in English education: grammar school, university and conservatoire*. London, Faber.

Mainwaring, J (1951). *Teaching music in schools*. London: Paxton.

Mitchell, J. C. (2006). Case and situation analysis. The Manchester School: Practice and Ethnographic Praxis in Anthropology. T. M. S. Evens and D. Handelman, Berghahn Books: 23-44.

McCulloch, G (2011). Historical and documentary research in education, in L. Cohen, L. Manion & K. Morrison (Eds.) *Research Methods in Education*. Abingdon: Routledge: 248-255.

McPherson, G. & Hallam, S. (2009). 'Musical potential'. In S. Hallam, I. Cross & M. Thaut (Eds.) *Handbook of music psychology*. Oxford: Oxford University Press

NACCCE (1999) All our futures: creativity, culture and education. Report to the Secretary of State for Education and Employment and the Secretary of State for Culture, Media and Sport. National Advisory Committee on Creative and Cultural Education

NMC (2002). The National Music Council Local Education Authority Music Awards - Report 2002, National Music Council.

Ofsted (2002). [Report on community cohesion in case study local authority]. London: Ofsted / Audit Commission.

Ofsted (2004). *Provision of music services in 15 local education Authorities*. London: Ofsted.

Price, S. D. (2011) *Endangered phrases: intriguing idioms dangerously close to extinction*. New York: Skyhorse.

Rauscher, F. H., Shaw, G.L., Ky, K.N. (1993) Music and spatial task performance, *Nature*, 365: 611.

SCAM (1960). The scope of instrumental music in schools: a report. London, National Council of Social Service for the Standing Conference for Amateur Music.

St John, P & Richardson, D (1989). *Methods of presenting fieldwork data*. Sheffield: Geographical Association.

Syrjala, S. E. (1996) A statistical test for a difference between the spatial distributions of two populations, *Ecology*, Vol. 77, No. 1, pp. 75-80

Thomson, W. (1989). Instrumental music teaching in schools 4: the future of peripatetic teaching, *Music Teacher*, May 40-41.

'The World Declaration on Higher Education for the Twenty-First Century' and perspectives for Music Education in Brazil

Luís Ricardo Silva Queiroz
Federal University of Paraíba, Brazil

luisrsqueiroz@gmail.com

Sergio Figueiredo
State University of Santa Catarina, Brazil

sergiofigueiredo.udesc@gmail.com

Abstract

This investigation is a documentary research which included UNESCO documents produced for higher education from the 1990s, and documents of Brazilian educational legislation covering the same period. Documentary research is the basis for understanding educational perspectives for music education. It provided important information for the analysis of different social contexts, given that documents produced in a particular time and for a specific group, reflect concepts, forms of action, and power. When linked to institutional dimensions, they show important political aspects, since they have definitions, guidelines, parameters and several determinations that directly impact on the social reality. We believe that the understanding of texts produced in this scenario represents conceptions of culture, education, art and music that have guided structural bases for higher education in music and music education in the country. The analysis showed the neoliberal dominance in the international and Brazilian documents, providing evidence that countries such as Brazil and some others with limited resources make choices about the educational profile to be reached, whilst privileging some educational levels and perspectives. The result has been an emphasis on the labour market and economic sustainability to align the design of a more targeted higher education with neoliberal tendencies. Through music education research, individual documents in more interrelated frameworks will allow us, in the future, to understand the complex world that characterizes educational policies and interpret concepts, visions and actions outlined under the dominant political power.

Keywords: music education, higher education, Brazilian educational policies, documental analysis, UNESCO.

Introduction

Since 1945, *The United Nations Educational, Scientific and Cultural Organization* (UNESCO) has had a major role in shaping global education, with proposals directed towards the development and consolidation of different educational levels of formal education in the world. These proposals aim to establish *a priori* parameters and guidelines that can support the strengthening of education, directing collective efforts to promote peace and equal rights and access, in order to minimize the boundaries and inequalities between countries of the world (UNESCO, 2015a; 2015b).

UNESCO propositions, especially for higher education and for basic education, consolidated more specifically from the 1990s, have significantly corresponded with educational directions in Brazil over the past three decades and, as a consequence, there has been a major impact on institutionalized music education in the country. This paper presents an analytical approach to a comprehensive research that has been undertaken since 2014 and which aims to understand UNESCO interrelationships between definitions for higher education and basic education in the international arena and the specificities of music at these levels of education in Brazil. We directed the analysis exclusively to higher education, with an emphasis on trajectories, advances and boundaries that mark such a scenario, especially since 1998 after the *World Declaration on Higher Education for the Twenty-First Century: Vision and Action* document approved at the *World Conference on Higher Education*, in Paris (UNESCO, 1998).

Documentary research included UNESCO documents produced for higher education from the 1990s, and documents of Brazilian educational legislation covering the same period. We focus on the analysis of the *World Declaration on Higher Education* (UNESCO, 1998) and interpretation of the interrelations of such declaration within the Brazilian Ministry of Education documents.

Documental research, educational policies and music education

The setting of public policy at local, national and international levels is being increasingly researched and analyzed in recent years. Different areas of expertise have been a significant body of knowledge about concepts, guidelines and actions that guide public policies, both within each country and in the broader context of the world.

In this paper, we understand public policy as the sum of conscious and deliberate uses, from action – or lack of action – in society to meet certain requirements through optimized use of available and fundamental human and material resources at a given time. From this perspective, public policies are made of "defined guidelines and actions and coordinated by municipal, district, state and mainly federal government departments, to plan, implement and evaluate developmental and improvement strategies for multiple segments of society" (Queiroz & Marinho, 2010, p. 1813).

In education, and more specifically music education, public policies define important bases of educational purposes for educational systems. Policies are designed, planned and implemented "in order to enable the quantitative and qualitative growth of education, providing access, but more than that, the full formation of individuals" (Queiroz, 2012, p. 37; Queiroz & Penna, 2012).

From the perspective of what is and how it is characterized in a public policy scenario today, this study aims to understand propositions for education internationally, in order to reflect on the impacts of those propositions in the Brazilian music education context. To achieve our goals, we defined documentary research as the methodological basis of the study.

There is some consensus that the fragmented primary sources in various documents are the main parts that can provide key interpretive links to the composition of representative frames of educational public policies in different dimensions and contexts. This perspective is applicable to research in music education, especially when it comes to studies dealing with the understanding and interpretation of public policies related to the realities of formal education (Figueiredo & Queiroz, 2010).

Dealing with documents produced at different levels, but interconnected in their concepts, objectives and proposals, enables the construction of panoramas of the music education scene. It is possible to understand more broadly and transversally the definitions that affect Brazilian educational policies, considering that they have been designed and generated in broader dimensions of the global educational scene.

Documentary research involves a wide range of media and has served as a basis for different studies, with both qualitative and quantitative approaches. In the field of music education such research has been used for different purposes, becoming an important methodology for studies that seek to understand historical, methodological, curriculum and policies, among others dimensions related to education and learning music in multiple contexts (American Educational Research Association, 2015). Documentary research is the basis for the study, analysis and understanding of educational perspectives for music education.

The use of documents for research provides important information for the analysis of different social realities, given that documents produced in a particular time and for a specific group, reflect concepts, forms of action, power disputes (Mogalakwe, 2006). When linked to institutional dimensions, they show important political aspects, since they have definitions, guidelines, parameters and several determinations that directly impact on the social reality. We are considering this perspective to guide our study on the universe of documents produced by UNESCO and by the regulatory educational agencies in Brazil, because we believe that the understanding of texts produced in this scenario represents conceptions of culture, education, art and music that have guided structural bases of higher education in music and music education in the country.

According to Le Goff (1996, p. 10), from a current perspective, the document is recognized as a record that "expresses the power of the past society on memory and future". This way of thinking, therefore, sees the document as a human production. In this study, the time refers to the last three decades, focusing on higher education from the groups set up by UNESCO and the institutions linked to the political and educational context of Brazil.

Documents selection, organization and analysis

We limit our analysis and interpretation of the international scene to the *World Declaration on Higher Education for the Twenty-First Century: Vision and Action* (UNESCO, 1998). Under the Brazilian education we include various official documents related to both the general *Plano Nacional de Educação* (National Education Plan) and the more specific universe of music education. These documents have been analyzed in detail, but are considered partially in this text. They were analyzed according to their content analysis (Mayring, 2000; Moraes, 1999).

World Declaration on Higher Education: Perspectives for inclusion and sustainability of higher education in music

The preamble of the Declaration is incisive in presenting higher education as a key element in the strengthening of different dimensions of the world's countries, giving to this level of education a fundamental responsibility in training professionals and producing high-level knowledge. This level of education, as the document points out, covers "all types of studies, training or training for research at the post-secondary level" (UNESCO,

1998). In higher education, undergraduate and postgraduate courses are important benchmarks especially to provide "essential components of cultural, socio-economic and environmentally sustainable development of individuals, communities and nation" (UNESCO, 1998).

The design that guides the Declaration is based on three large dimensions, permeating the views and actions presented in the document as prospects and guidelines for higher education in the third millennium.

[...] there is an unprecedented demand for and a great diversification in higher education, as well as an increased awareness of its vital importance for sociocultural and economic development, and for building the future, for which the younger generations will need to be equipped with new skills, knowledge and ideals (UNESCO, 1998, original griffins).

To meet the broad existing demand, to structure courses, activities, and to produce knowledge that can reach the diversity of contemporary society, and to take responsibility on socio-cultural and economic development, matrices are fundamental to the construction of a higher education contextualized to the needs and capabilities of today's world.

The analysis of the entire document shows that conceptions about the purpose of higher education are structured in two different ideologies, sometimes conflicting: 1) a conception linked to economic objectives and market, according to a neoliberal universal tendency, and 2) an ethical perspective, democratic, liberating, with an emphasis on human development, respecting and promoting the diversity and plurality of ideas, subjects and training contexts.

Without adequate higher education and research institutions providing a critical mass of skilled and educated people, no country can ensure genuine endogenous and sustainable development and, in particular, developing countries and least developed countries cannot reduce the gap separating them from the industrially developed ones (UNESCO, 1998, our griffins).

In this passage, there is a strong support for higher education as a way to reduce inequalities between countries, which is positive. However, there is an explicit assumption that reducing inequality is fundamentally linked to the industrial development.

Higher education itself is confronted therefore with formidable challenges and must proceed to the most radical change and renewal it has ever been required to undertake, so that *our society, which is currently undergoing a profound crisis of values*, can transcend mere economic considerations and incorporate deeper dimensions of morality and spirituality (UNESCO, 1998, our griffins).

In this quotation it is recognized that social crisis is not limited to developing and least developed countries, but includes even the rich countries, requiring training that transcends guidelines aimed at the labor market and economic sustainability. In this scenario, the arts, philosophy, anthropology, psychology, music, and other fields related to the sphere of training and production of human knowledge gain important connotation in the Declaration, guiding a representative portion of the visions and actions presented in the concluding part of the document.

Higher education has given ample proof of its viability over the centuries and of its ability to change and to induce change and progress in society. Owing to the scope and pace of change, society has become increasingly knowledge-based so that higher learning and research now act as essential components of cultural, socio-economic and environmentally sustainable development of individuals, communities and nations (UNESCO, 1998, our griffins).

These motions revealed by the content analysis create different impacts on policies of different countries that are guided by UNESCO propositions. The tendency, not only in Brazil, but also in different Latin American countries classified as developing or under-developed, is to pursue a higher education strategy that meets not only the UNESCO definitions, but international mechanisms such as those of the World Bank and the OECD, among others, who make educational policies as a reference to measure indicators of success or failure of such countries in the international arena.

Under this pressure of a neoliberal dominance, the tendency of countries like Brazil and some others with limited resources is to make choices about the education profile to be reached, privileging some educational levels and perspectives. The result has been to align to the first strand (labour market and economic sustainability) and therefore align the design of a more targeted higher education to such neoliberal tendencies.

Brazilian higher education in music and interrelationships with definitions of the international scene

UNESCO propositions have provided important bases for the definition of the Declaration, and had significant impacts in Brazil since the 1990s. In this sense, the introduction of the National Education Plan (PNE), approved by the Law 10172 in 2001, provides evidence that, in addition to the internal discussions and documents produced by the country, the aforementioned Plan "also considered previous achievements, especially the Ten Year Plan for Education for All, prepared according to the recommendations of the meeting organized by UNESCO and held in Jomtien, Thailand, in 1993" (Brasil, 2001, p. 6).

However, although UNESCO's propositions have impacts on public policies in Brazil for education since the 1960s and these impacts have been growing from the 1990s, only in the first decade of this century institution's proposals for higher education impact more decisively on the direction of education in Brazil. Analysis of concepts and guidelines for higher education present in the PNE - 2001 to 2011- reveals a considerable connection of the document with the proposals of the World Declaration.

Regarding the expansion of supply and the meeting of demands, the country, after a long period of stagnation in the 1990s, implemented a consistent policy of higher education in the first decade of this century, especially since the year 2004. With the design of a new political setting within the Federal Government, REUNI (Programme of Support for the Restructuring and Expansion of Federal Universities) was implemented in 2007, establishing actions in Brazil "[...] in order to create conditions for increased access and permanence in higher education at the undergraduate level, for the best use of physical infrastructures and human resources existing in federal universities" (Brasil, 2007). As a result of this policy, the following is highlighted by the document 'Analysis of the Expansion of Federal Universities: 2003-2012':

[...] Significant growth not only of federal universities, but also of campuses within the country. From 2003 to 2010, there was a jump from 45 to 59 federal universities, which represents an expansion of 31%; and 148 to 274 campuses/units, growth of 85%. Actions directed to the interior also provided an expansion in the country increasing the number of municipalities covered by federal universities from 114 to 272, an increase of 138%. Also as part of integration and regional development, it highlights the creation of 47 new campuses in the period between 2011 and 2014 [...]. (Brasil, 2007).

This data allows us to infer the size of growth that marked higher education in Brazil after the World Declaration. This scenario outlined in the country is linked to a complex network of variables that together consolidated the context of higher education in Brazil since the 2000s. But it is crucial to point out that the policies outlined in dialogue with the Declaration had, and still have, a strong impact on these settings.

In higher education in music, we can consider two main phases: 1) the first phase comprises a long period established between the 1960s and 1990s, which marked the creation of *Bacharelado* (Musicians preparation) and *Licenciatura* (Teacher preparation) in music in several universities in the country; from the 1980s postgraduate programmes have also been implemented; 2) from the 2000s, the undergraduate and graduate degrees in music grew dramatically; research shows 80 music courses (*Licenciatura*) in 2010 (Soares; Schambeck; Figueiredo, 2014), and today 115 undergraduate music courses are offered in the country; the graduate programmes increased from 8 in 1999, to 27 in 2015 (Brasil, 2015a).

From the 2000s, higher education covers new formats of courses, in addition to *bacharelado* and *licenciatura* degrees, that also encompass vocational and technological undergraduate education. Many of these courses are more aligned with the perspective of the Declaration, forming skilled people for the labour market, including the field of music.

One side of the Declaration is directed towards human development and is, therefore, committed to promote and develop an "advancing knowledge through research in science, the arts and humanities and the dissemination of its results" (UNESCO, 1998). This has had an important role in the consolidation of higher education in music in Brazil. However, the other aspect of the document, which protects remnants of a strong neoliberal bias, tends to establish a secondary place for higher education in music and in other areas that are not lined up directly and strongly to the industrial, economic and market development.

The *Ciência sem Fronteiras* ('Science without Borders') Brazilian programme illustrates very well the remnants of a higher education that focuses on areas considered strategic for economic development. The 'Science without Borders' seeks to "[...] promote the consolidation, expansion and internationalization of science and technology, innovation and Brazilian competitiveness through the exchange and international mobility." The programme includes undergraduate and graduate students, offering grants to "do internship abroad in order to contact with competitive educational systems in relation to technology and innovation" (Brasil, 2015b). This programme, in some sense, answers the call of the neoliberal strand of the Declaration, prioritizing knowledge and strategic actions to insert Brazil in the field of competitiveness and production of science, technology and innovation, focusing on industrial and economic development.

Areas such as music and the arts in general, philosophy, sociology, among others, are not priorities of this internationalization policy and scientific strengthening of Brazilian education. According to the Declaration: "Sharing knowledge, international co-operation and new technologies can offer new opportunities to reduce this gap." In the case of Brazil, these objectives are restricted to areas that are directly linked to the industrial and economic development. For the humanities, social sciences and the arts, this is an example of the perverse effect of this trend, highlighted in different UNESCO documents, privileging some areas.

Final considerations

This brief analysis allows us to highlight major tendencies in higher education in Brazil from the interrelationships of the national educational policies with the guidelines set by official international documents. Documents produced by UNESCO for different educational levels and contexts are important references for the understanding of policies and guidelines that support educational propositions from different countries in the world.

Documentary research and analytical procedures serve as important bases for reading, understanding and interpreting this powerful international scenario. Through music education research, individual documents in more interrelated frameworks will allow us, in the future, to understand the complex world that characterizes the educational policies and interpret concepts, visions and actions outlined under the dominant political power.

In Brazilian education, the two tendencies that guide the World Declaration on Higher Education – one of economistic nature and another of a more democratic basis – dialogue in a not always balanced way. The first tendency is quite dominant in various funding programmes related to educational contexts of the country, such as the 'Science without Borders' programme. The study, analysis and understanding of guidelines that permeate public policy, expressed in the plurality of documents that guide education, both globally and nationally, allow us to reflect comprehensively about problems, challenges and possibilities that characterize the insertion of music education in the context of current educational policies today.

References

American Educational Research Association (2015). *An introduction to documentary research*. Retrieved from http://www.aera.net/SIG013/ResearchConnections/Introductionto DocumentaryResearch/tabid/15485/Default.aspx.

Brasil. (2001). *Lei no 10.172, de 9 de Janeiro de 2001*. Aprova o Plano Nacional de Educação e dá outras providências. Retrieved from http://www.planalto.gov.br/ccivil_03/leis/leis_2001/l10172.htm

Brasil. (2007). *Decreto n. 6.096 de 24 de abril de 2007*. Institui o Programa de Apoio a Planos de Reestruturação e Expansão das Universidades Federais – REUNI. Brasília: Presidência da República. Retrieved from http://www.planalto.gov.br/ccivil_03/_ato2007-2010/2007/decreto/d6096.htm

Brasil. (2015a). Coordenação de Aperfeiçoamento de Pessoal de Nível Superior. Brasília: Ministério da Educação. *Cursos recomendados*. Retrieved from http://www.capes.gov.br/cursos-recomendados

Brasil. (2015b). *Ciência sem fronteiras*. Brasília: Ministério da Ciência, Tecnologia e Inovação (MCTI) e Ministério da Educação (MEC). Retrieved from http://www.cienciasemfronteiras.gov.br/web/csf

Figueiredo, S. L. F. & Queiroz, L. R. S. (2010). Educational policies and practices in the preparation of music teachers in Brazil. *Proceedings of the 29th ISME World Conference*. Beijing: ISME, v.1, p. 1-3.

Le Goff, J. (1996). *História e memória*. 4ª ed. Campinas: Unicamp.

Mayring, P. (2000). *Qualitative Content Analysis. Forum Qualitative Sozialforschung / Forum: Qualitative Social Research*, n. 1(2). Retrieved from http://nbn-resolving.de/urn:nbn:de:0114-fqs0002204

Moraes, R. (1999). Análise de conteúdo. *Revista Educação, 22* (37), 7-32.

Mogalakwe, M. (2006). The use of documentary research methods in social research. *African Sociological Review, 10* (1), 221-230.

Queiroz, L. R. S. (2012). A educação musical no Brasil do século XXI: articulações do ensino de música com as políticas brasileiras de avaliação educacional. *Revista da ABEM*, 20 (28), 35-46. Retrieved from http://www.abemeducacaomusical.com.br/revistas/revistaabem/index.php/revistaabem/article/viewFile/102/85

Queiroz, L. R. S.& Penna, M. (2012). Políticas públicas para a educação básica e suas implicações para o ensino de música. *Educação*. Santa Maria, *37*(1), 91-106. Retrieved from http://www.redalyc.org/pdf/1171/117123668007.pdf

Queiroz, L. R. S. & Marinho, V. M. (2010). Políticas públicas em educação musical: a atuação do Grupo de Pesquisa PENSAMUS. *Proceedings of the 19th Congresso Nacional da Associação Brasileira de Educação Musical*. Goiânia: ABEM, v.1, p. 1811-1820.

Soares, J., Schambeck, R. F., & Figueiredo, S. (2014). *A formação do professor de música no Brasil*. Belo Horizonte: Fino Traço.

UNESCO (1998). *World Declaration on Higher Education for the Twenty-first Century: Vision and Action and Framework for Priority Action for Change.* Retrieved from http://www.unesco.org/education/educprog/wche/declaration_eng.htm

UNESCO (2015a). *70 Anniversary: from past to future.* Retrieved from http://en.unesco.org/70years#past_to_future

UNESCO (2015b). *Draft preliminary report concerning the preparation of a global convention on the recognition of higher education qualifications.* Retrieved from http://unesdoc.unesco.org/images/0023/002328/232858e.pdf

Enacting reciprocal coauthorship as a creative, collaborative and ethical practice in music teaching and learning

Yaroslav Senyshyn

Faculty of Education, Simon Fraser University, Canada

senyshyn@sfu.ca

Susan A. O'Neill

Faculty of Education, Simon Fraser University, Canada

sao@sfu.ca

Abstract

The emphasis on relational and dialogical approaches in education has grown in recent years, particularly in response to participatory learning approaches within frameworks of 21st century education. New opportunities for engaging in musical creation, collaboration, and sharing are made possible through crowd-sourced digital media platforms and the participatory affordances of Web 2.0. As a result, previously recorded musical content has become increasingly viewed in terms of its evolving potential to be re-created or "recomposed". This dynamic and evolving form of music collaboration contrasts with older (pre-Web 2.0) forms of creative music making that had delineated roles and functions for the content creator, performer, and audience/spectator. Within today's participatory learning approaches there is a sense of equity and "distributed expertise" across a network of people, tools, and resources. However, online participatory approaches do not necessarily translate into, or offer a full or adequate account of, face-to-face "physically present" interactions during creative collaborations in the classroom. This paper aims to explore this issue by examining a particular form of participatory learning, what we refer to as *reciprocal coauthorship*, and elaborating its potential for meaningful and shared practices that evoke creative, collaborative, and ethical enactments in the music classroom. We begin by integrating a philosophical exploration of the concept of reciprocal co-authorship in music coupled with the process of maintaining *dialogue* and *coherence* that frame communication practices as they develop dynamically between participants engaged in collaborative music activities. To illustrate our theoretical approach, we draw on the current practice of "recomposing" advocated by the prestigious classical music label Deutsche Grammophon. We then examine a case study of four students aged 13-14 years engaged in a creative collaborative process of learning to play a previously recorded popular song 'by ear' during five 50-minute sessions as part of their band instrument ensemble classes. Each session was video recorded and interactions were coded using an inductive, narrative approach and a classification system. Through our conceptual lenses and analysis procedure it was possible to see the transformative aspects of participatory learning in collaborative music making whereby minute negotiations and student-led decisions about content, activities, and materials for collaborative work provided opportunities that opened up spaces for both creative and ethical practices as well as innovation, control, and a sense of personal and artistic freedom. We conclude with a discussion of the implications for music teaching and learning.

Introduction

The emphasis on relational and dialogical approaches in education has grown in recent years, particularly in response to the growing number of researchers with interests in socio-cultural approaches to creative collaboration (John-Steiner, 2000; Miell & Littleton, 2004). Barrett (2014) reminds us of how "the notion of the individual creator, a product in part of the Western Romantic ideal, has been troubled by accounts of creative thought and practice as a social construct" (p. 3). At the same time, participatory accounts of learning have grown within frameworks of 21st century education through online participatory cultures (Jenkins, 2009; Jenkins, Ito & Boyd, 2016) and the affordances and pedagogical models based on Web 2.0 in educational contexts (McLoughlin & Lee, 2007). Technological affordances make possible creative and collaborative learning opportunities that have not been available to music educators before. Young people who are interest-driven or have an intense commitment to musical creative pursuits via technology will seek out material and social resources (O'Neill, 2014). Within participatory learning approaches there is a sense of equity and "distributed expertise" across a network of people, tools, and resources (Warschauer & Matuchniak, 2010). However, as Rose (2007) argues, the internet also promotes "experiential expertise" of a multitude of "lay experts" (p. 128) who mediate professional expertise at a distance and who are, reciprocally, involved in "making up citizens" (p. 140). This is not to say that young people are not benefiting from these practices; rather, it draws attention to a new "style of thought" that has taken shape in the 21st century and one that emphasizes "making up" as a social practice that not only influences identity construction; it drives the production of experimental "hybrids" based on expert "texts" that are reshaped, recreated, or reinterpreted through technology-enabled tools, resources, and communities.

A key assumption of 21st century education is that it is possible to translate online participatory approaches into face to face "physically present" interactions during creative collaborations in the classroom. However, there is no evidence to support the idea that online participatory approaches offer a full or adequate account of classroom collaborative practices. Within today's participatory learning approaches there is a sense of equity and "distributed expertise" across a network of people, tools, and resources. And yet, we know the benefits and constraints of technology used in learning vary as a function of access, opportunity, and knowledge of the rapidly changing and evolving tools in the digital landscape (Livingstone, 2012). Add to this the beliefs and values of young people who find various features of school culture "do not fit comfortably" with the opportunities afforded by Web 2.0 in particular (Crook, 2012). And even in the absence of technology, collaborative music activities in the classroom might not be perceived by all students as equitable due to perceived or real power differences in expectations, knowledge, and experience. The effects of these power differences on students' sense of agency and autonomy may be particularly pronounced when music collaborations take place within teaching approaches that emphasize adherence to conventional musical practices, competition, or classical music traditions.

Keeping these ideas in mind, we wanted to explore a particular form of participatory learning related to creative collaboration, which we refer to as *reciprocal coauthorship*. We begin by examining its philosophical origins before exploring its potential for meaningful and shared practices in the music classroom.

Reciprocal coauthorship

Perceptions in music learning have drifted toward dialogical and thus reciprocal approaches inclusive of participatory accounts of learning that incorporate a sense of equity among learners. This notion and practice was originally conceptualized in the philosophical work of R. G. Collingwood's (1938), *The Principles of Art*. Collingwood referred to our contemporaneous terms of equal partnerships in collaborative, collateral opportunities and reciprocal experiences in terms of his coined notion of *coauthorship* of musical texts and scripts of literary dramas or plays via their actualization in musical or dramatic performances. In his terms, Collingwood argued that in fact "every performer is co-author of the work he performs" (p. 144). He felt that relying simply on traditionally inequitable and authoritative approaches to music learning stifled student or professional performances and would only result in learning-performing outcomes that would eventually exhaust aesthetic and imaginative states of experience in classrooms and concert halls alike (see also, Senyshyn, 2010).

Coauthorship in music may be defined as the learner-composer-performer's ability to modify a given musical resource which is frequently referred to as the *text*. Thus, co-authorship is the activity that takes place when any modification in compositional techniques, interpretative dynamics, phrasings, agogics, tempi, etc., are made by the performer(s) or other composers to aural resources that are or are not inherently "visible" as such. These changes or modifications would be prompted by subjective reactions to a text.

Coauthorship is an assumed activity in most forms of jazz, popular, and folk music because there is a living tradition that encourages its use abundantly. On the other hand, in more traditional forms of Western classical music there is at least an unhealthy resistance to coauthorship. In all genres of music, as Schonberg reminds us, there is "a dreadful uniformity" arising from a lack of coauthorship and individuality (Schonberg, 1981, p. 144-145). Further, Adorno (1981) reminds us that a "musical score is never identical with the work; devotion to the text means the constant effort to grasp that which it hides" (p. 144). The visible text of drama and music are for Collingwood and recreative artists but blueprints or approximations of the final product to be performed or interpreted. Perhaps more importantly for our purposes, Collingwood felt that the lack of great emotional feelings in artistic performances or renditions of art were due to the lack of coauthorship on the part of performer-composer-learners: "a translation into imaginative form of an emotion ... must pre-exist to the activity of expressing it" (p. 279).

Recomposing: Maintaining dialogue and coherence in creative collaboration

As mentioned previously, the 21st century has seen an increase in the production of experimental 'hybrids' by reshaping, recreating, or reinterpreting existing expert "texts" (cf. "mashups" or "blends" based on overlays of tracks from two or more pre-recorded songs). We draw on an illustration from the prestigious Deutsche Grammophon's *Recomposed Series,* whereby artists from film and club music scenes are invited to "recompose" classical repertoire by digitally reworking recordings from the Deutsche Grammophon archive. Taking up this challenge of co-authorship in 2012 was Max Richter, a British film composer, who "recomposed" Vivaldi's Four Seasons by "layering and looping familiar fragments to reinvigorate a work diminished by overuse in elevators, TV ads and as telephone 'holding music'" (http://www.recomposed.net). Richer aimed "to create a new score, an experimental hybrid, that constantly references 'Vivaldi' but also 'Richter' and that is current but simultaneously preserves the original spirit of this great work". He goes on to say "there's Vivaldi DNA in all of it […] I kept the gestures and shapes, the textures and dynamics.]…] There are bits of Vivaldi and bits of me daydreaming about the original, thinking aloud about it […] it was my way of having a conversation with Vivaldi".

In a video recording on the recomposed website, Max Richter describes his process of notating his recomposed version and "making a new score" in order to "really get inside [the piece] and start to work with the alchemy of the material itself. This gave me much more scope in terms of what I could do with it". He describes going through the piece and choosing his favourite "bits" and "turning those up and making new objects out of those". He also describes the process as similar to a sculpture having great raw material to work with and putting it together in a way that pleases. After the score was produced, the composer worked with virtuoso violinist Daniel Hope and Berlin's Konzerthaus Chamber Orchestra with conductor André de Ridder as part of a collaborative process of what Richter calls "making it come alive". He reflects on this process as follows, "Once you get the people in the room – human beings onto the material – you get a whole new dimension which you can't really predict". Daniel Hope the violinist described Max Richter's recomposition as "he goes to the soul of the piece and as a result we learn not just about a new concerto but we learn about the Vivaldi [Four Seasons] as well" as Richter is "bringing the piece into the 21st century".

In this illustration of recomposing, there are two prominent themes that relate to the reciprocal nature of the creative and collaborative process: dialogical encounters (e.g., "it was my way of having a conversation with Vivaldi"), and coherence with the original composition (e.g., "there's Vivaldi DNA in all of it"). Both of these practices are significant in terms of maintaining an ethical stance in relation to this work. Dialogue is a form of social practice that is advocated as a fundamental component of ethical education (Freire, 1970; Noddings, 2002). A key feature of dialogue is that it is open-ended: participants involved in dialogue do not know at the outset what the exact outcome will be. In this way, dialogue resembles a form of creative collaboration where a topic may shift and evolve through the process. Also, of fundamental significance for authentic dialogue is that participants need to attend to each other through episodes of what Noddings refers to as "interpersonal reasoning" where a participant "may pause to remind the other of her strengths, to reminisce, to explore, to express concern, to have a good laugh, or otherwise connect with the other as cared-for" (p. 17). As such, dialogue always implies a seeking to understand the "other" with whom one is in dialogue as "they reach across the ideological gap to connect with each other" (p. 17).

Integrity is also implied within the dialogical, and is sometimes referred to as maintaining a sense of *coherence*. Bohm (1996) refers to coherence in dialogue as a space of commonality and inclusivity, not to reach a consensus, but to embrace the 'between' of differing perspectives. Integrity is an ethical principle, which derives from the Latin *integer*, which mean 'whole' or 'complete.' There is a purposefulness to the notion of integrity and coherence that is also captured in Dewey's (1938) notion of *flexible purposing* as a process of shifting aims while engaged in the immediacy of one's work. Eisner (2004) argues that flexible purposing in arts education is *opportunistic*. It is not something that one can predefine precisely or predict in advance; rather, it emerges in the context of relationships within a flexible environment that encourages exploration, wonder, and surprise. Eisner refers to this emergent process as a key feature of artistically crafted work that provides an opportunity for artistic accomplishments and "temporary resting places to contemplate and create a space for change in understanding to happen" (O'Neill & Peluso, 2013, p. 118).

To explore these issues further, we now turn our attention to a case study of music students engaged in a collaborative process in the music classroom. Our aim is to use the conceptual lenses we have articulated to identify and elaborate related aspects of reciprocal coauthorship.

Case study

The case study consisted of four female participants aged 13-14 years from a class of 22 Grade 7 beginner band students engaged in Unit 9 "In at the Deep End" from *Musical Futures*. This unit asked students to form friendship groups of 3-5 students and to re-create a piece of music of their choice entirely "by ear" without the use of notation or direct instruction. The unit took place over five 50-minute sessions in which students engaged collaboratively in learning to play the piece. This case study is drawn from a larger study of student engagement that focused on the subjective experiences of creative music collaboration among 44 young people who took part in the study.

We selected our case study group for this paper because they engaged in a range of activities over the course of their work together. They were able to use their voices, a keyboard, and percussion instruments (tambourine, maracas; bongo drums) in addition to their band instruments (flute, trombone, drum set), and to engage with other resources such as iPods and a computer connected to the Internet to find and listen to different versions of the song they chose to learn to "play by ear," and to engage in research connected with learning about the song, such as information about the song writers and performers.

The students chose the song "Born This Way" by Lady Gaga, which was released in February 2011 and became one of the best selling singles of all time having sold 10.2 million copies worldwide. The students discovered in an interview with Lady Gaga that the song was "her freedom song" and was inspired by 1990s music for empowering women and the gay community (Werde, 2011). The students also discovered and discussed the controversy about the song being similar to Madonna's 1989 song, "Express Yourself" (Greenblatt, 2011). They therefore played both songs and made their own comparisons.

The five sessions were video recorded as well as a final performance of the song at the end of the unit. The analysis consisted of coding minute interactions using an inductive, narrative approach and a classification system similar to the one proposed by Lofland and Lofland (1984) for classifying "social phenomena" as acts, activities, meanings, participation, relationships, and settings. The coding was completed by two researchers working independently followed by a discussion of any discrepancies before reaching a consensus.

Themes relating to reciprocal coauthorship

Dialogical encounters

As the students gained more confidence with their re-creation they begin to engage in a process of recomposing that revealed similar characteristics to the Max Richter example. Inspired by the original song, the students began to incorporate their own ideas. They engaged in both independent work at times, but mostly their work was in pairs, threes, or with all four students engaging in what resembled a series of dialogical encounters. For example, each student could be seen at times to offer another student help and support in both practical ways (for example, Sally asks, "What is the fingering for 'B' again? Nadine quickly comes over and shows her) as well as in supportive and caring ways (see maintaining coherence below). The group became more cohesive as time progressed and more willing to try out ideas and ask for feedback from one or more group members. For example, at one point Claire plays a passage on the keyboard and Nadine responds by saying "I want to play it slightly differently to the recording, what do you think of..." (and she plays her version on the flute). This inspired further creative ideas by the others. There were also several "ah ha" moments when the students would work out something together and then realize at the same time that they had found a good solution, shouting "Yeah!" followed by big smiles.

Flexible Purposing and Maintaining Coherence

The students regarded making 'mistakes' as "part of the fun" and this created a light-hearted mood; they would laugh after a mistake and then work together to determine the problem and find a solution. This form of flexible purposing required a large amount of 'trial and error' as the students spent time going over different sound combinations trying to capture a sound that pleased them (their own creative input) and yet still maintaining a coherence with the original song. For example, one student Claire said, "When Sally is playing the drums, I need to play it this way to keep the same melody... wait can you try that again". At another point Nadine states, "We might add a bit in here [of new content they created] before going back to the main chorus of the song".

At one point in the third session, Sally said, "When I was looking online, I saw some of the different instruments being played [in the song] and wondered how we can create that harmony". Nadine quickly stated, "We're not doing harmony; that's way to too hard". This led to a brief impasse where the group separated (possibly to avoid a confrontation) and continued to experiment with sounds independently. After 5 minutes, Claire went over to Nadine and said, "could we listen to the harmony" and this prompted Nadine to ask the teacher if he could listen to the song with them and advise them on the harmony and how they might incorporate this into their version. There were also times when one student would show obvious signs of struggle or frustration and this was almost always followed by a purposive-rational action by another student to try to remedy the situation coupled with one or more of the other students providing support and encouragement. Even if this form of caring only resulted in attempts to 'lighten the mood,' it served the purpose of maintaining caring relations through acknowledging and being responsive to the student in need at that particular moment. These roles shifted among the students over the course of their collaboration.

Conclusion

We aimed to integrate a philosophical exploration of the concept of reciprocal coauthorship in music coupled with the process of maintaining *dialogue* and *coherence* that frame communication practices as they develop dynamically between participants engaged in collaborative music activities. We drew on Collingwood's philosophical notion of coauthorship and extended it through a conceptual enfoldment of dialogical encounters, flexible purposing, and maintaining coherence. This conceptual lens enabled us to illuminate deeper levels of the collaborative process as well as the ethical practice that unfolded as the students reciprocated with and supported each other in their creative and collaborative work vis-à-vis their chosen "text" or musical resource.

Our findings challenged the notion of collaboration as happening merely between students; rather, both the social and musical resources they were engaging with were reciprocal in the sense that they entailed or enacted and energized their collaborative music practice. When students were united in the meanings and actions of what they were working on because they understood the social uses of what they were learning in relation to the material resources they were engaging with, this contributed to the stability and focus of their collaborative music practices which in turn enhanced their music engagement and learning. Through our conceptual lenses and analysis procedure it was possible to see the transformative aspects of participatory learning in collaborative music making whereby minute negotiations and student-led decisions about content, activities, and materials for collaborative work provided opportunities that opened up spaces for both creative and ethical practices as well as innovation, control, and a sense of personal and artistic freedom.

References

Adorno, T. (1981). *Prisms, studies in contemporary German social thought.* [Translated from the German by Samuel and Shierry Weber]. Cambridge, MA: MIT Press.

Barrett, M. (Ed.). (2014). *Collaborative creative thought and practice in music.* Farnham, Surrey: Ashgate.

Bohm, D. (1996). *On dialogue.* New York: Routledge.

Collingwood, R. G. (1938). *The principles of art.* Oxford: Oxford University Press.

Crook, C. (2012). The 'digital native' in context: tensions associated with importing Web 2.0 practices into the school setting. *Oxford Review of Education, 38*(1), 63-80. doi: 10.1080/03054985.2011.577946

Dewey, J. (1938). *Experience and education,* Indianapolis, IN: Kappa Delta Pi.

Eisner, E. (2004). What education can learn from the arts about the practice of education? *International Journal of Education & the Arts, 5*(4), 1–12.

Freire, P. (1970). *Pedagogy of the oppressed.* New York: Continuum.

Greenblatt, L. (February 14, 2011). Lady Gaga talks Grammy egg, Madonna comparisons on 'Leno' tonight. *Entertainment Weekly.*

Jenkins, H. (2009). *Confronting the challenges of a participatory culture: Media education for the 21st century.* Cambridge: MIT Press.

Jenkins, H., Ito, M., & Boyd, D. (2016). *Participatory cultures in a networked era.* Cambridge: Polity Press.

John-Steiner, V. (2000). *Creative collaboration.* New York: Oxford University Press.

Livingstone, S. (2012). Critical reflections on the benefits of ICT in education. *Oxford Review of Education, 38*(1), 9-24. doi: 10.1080/03054985.2011.577938

Lofland, J., & Lofland, L. H. (1984). Analyzing social settings. Belmont, CA: Wadsworth.

McLoughlin, C., & Lee, M. J. (2007, December). Social software and participatory learning: Pedagogical choices with technology affordances in the Web 2.0 era. In *ICT: Providing choices for learners and learning. Proceedings ascilite Singapore 2007* (pp. 664–675).

Miell, D., & Littleton, K. (Eds). (2004). *Collaborative creativity: Contemporary perspectives.* London: Free Association Books.

Noddings, N. (2002). *Educating moral people: A caring alternative to character education.* New York: Teachers College Press.

O'Neill, S. A. (2014). Music and media infused lives: An introduction. In S. A. O'Neill (Series Ed. & Vol. Ed.), *Research to Practice: Vol. 6. Music and media infused lives: Music education in a digital age* (pp. 1–15). Waterloo, ON: Canadian Music Educators' Association.

O'Neill, S. A., & Peluso, D. (2013). Using dialogue and digital media composing to enhance and develop artistic creativity, creative collaborations and multimodal practices. In P. Burnard (Ed.), *Developing creativities in higher music education: International perspectives and practices* (pp. 142–162). Abingdon, OX: Routledge.

Rose, N. (2007). *The politics of life itself: Biomedicine, power, and subjectivity in the twenty-first century.* Princeton, NJ: Princeton University Press.

Schonberg, H. (1981). *Facing the music.* New York: Summit Books.

Senyshyn, Y. (2010). *The artist in crisis: Kierkegaard's philosophy of the aesthetic stage of existence and live musical performance.* Vancouver, BC: Platon Promotions Publishing.

Warschauer, M., & Matuchniak, T. (2010). New technology and digital worlds: Analyzing evidence of equity in access, use, and outcomes. *Review of Research in Education, 34*(1), 179–225.

Werde, B. (April 18, 2011). Lady Gaga 'Born This Way' Cover Story. *Billboard.* p. 4.

Angels and ogres: Online discourses of adult music learners, a corpus-based study

Rachel Shirley
Lancaster University, UK

sheffieldflute@gmail.com

Abstract

The purpose of this study is two-fold – to explore the potential of linguistic analysis techniques in music education research; and to use these techniques to investigate the discourses of adult learners in music, specifically those around learners and their teachers. Although music education research often uses text (interviews, autobiographical accounts, survey responses), linguistic analysis has barely been used in this area. Equally, the internet has become a source of support and expression for learners, using blogs and forum discussions, but these are an untapped data resource in music education research. Corpus linguistics techniques, which enable semi-automated analyses of databases of text, are increasingly being used in other discipline areas to identify patterns in large sets of textual data, and thus investigate recurring discourses, but have not yet been exploited in music education research. In this study, I use corpus techniques to investigate discourses of adult music learners using text from online sources. I begin by summarising current literature on adult music learners, which identifies them as an under-researched group, and the background to corpus-based discourse analysis. I discuss the ethical challenges of using online data, how corpus linguistics techniques may provide solutions, and my approach to these challenges. I use a corpus-based approach to explore the discourses around learners and their teachers, looking in particular at metaphorical language. Discourses around teachers suggest that the learner/ teacher relationship is crucial, but can be problematic – issues around control are evident, but there is a feeling that learners welcome some level of control. I conclude that corpus-based discourse analysis has the potential to enrich music education research, and suggest other ways in which it might be used. In the area of adult music education, this research has the potential to inform teachers, training and community organisations and exam boards, to help them better meet the needs of this group which often 'falls through the gaps'.

Keywords: music education, corpus linguistics, discourse analysis, adult learners, research methods

Introduction

An estimated 34% of adults (17.2m) in the UK play an instrument (ABRSM, 2014, p. 15) and another 23% would like to learn (NIACE, 2015). Many adults report "social, cognitive, emotional, and health benefits" from participating in musical activities (Hallam et al., 2013). Despite this, adult music learning is a relatively under-researched area. However, there is an increasing interest in the needs of adult music learners, reflected in the publication of specific tutor books (e.g. Hammond, 2008; Wedgwood, 2006) and the presence of online forums, communities and blogs where adult learners share their experiences and seek support. Although music education research often uses various types of texts (interviews, autobiographical accounts, questionnaire responses), linguistic analysis has barely been used in this area, and the wealth of online data has not been explored.

What is an adult learner?

For the purposes of this research, an 'adult music learner' is anyone who defines themselves as such, including adult beginners, restarters and continuers. They are predominantly amateur players, mainly in the classical tradition. Professional musicians and aspiring professionals (e.g. University/ Conservatoire students) tend not to be referred to as adult learners, suggesting a strong association of this label with amateur status.

Literature review

Adult music education

Forrester (1975, cited in Bowles, 2010, p. 51) described adult music education as a "new frontier" forty years ago. Today, music education research still primarily focuses on children, and there is "little... documentation of the extent of adult participation in the arts" (Pitts, 2012, p. 145). However, in the years since Forester's work, there has been a small but gradually growing body of research into adult music learning. In this literature review I focus on recent studies, reviewing current trends and findings.

These are generally small-scale studies, using participant interviews, questionnaires or autobiographical techniques such as 'life stories' (Pitts, 2012) or 'life paths' (Taylor, 2011). There is an emphasis on older adults (Bowles, 2010, p. 50), but Pitts (2012, p.141) highlights a "trend towards increased self-development between the ages of 35 and 65... [offering] a prompt to considering the motivation of adult learners" (Pitts, 2012, p. 141).

Researchers find varying attitudes, from it being 'never too late' to learn, to feeling restricted by age. Some learners feel limited by "assumptions about the optimal age for learning an instrument" (Pitts, 2012, p. 141), the "discourse around talent" (Lamont, 2011, p. 384) and a narrative of "regret about wasted time" (Lamont, 2011, p. 380). Many have "a constant awareness of their own perceived inadequacies" (Hobbs, 2014, p. 20) and "a relatively negative musical identity" (Lamont, 2011, p. 369).

Studies highlight adult learners' high levels of intrinsic motivation (Lamont, 2011, p. 380; Taylor, 2011, p.351; Hobbs, 2014, p. 20) but find that some struggle with "unrealistic expectations" (Taylor, 2011, p. 358). There are also "business issues" (Bowles, 2010, p. 56) around scheduling and cancelling lessons, and "making time to practise" (Taylor, 2011, p. 358).

Family and friends are a strong influence, including "the encouragement of friends [as] catalysts" to taking up or returning to music (Taylor, 2011, p. 345) and the importance of ongoing support from family and friends (Taylor, 2011, p. 351). Adult learners often show "a high level of trust and appreciation of teachers encountered in adulthood" (Pitts, 2012, p. 143). The ideal teacher has "an understanding of the wide range of responsibilities handled by adults, along with a steady insistence that students be challenged" (Roulston et al., 2015, p. 331). However, many teachers "lack confidence in dealing with a different kind of teaching challenge" (Hobbs, 2014, p. 20). Bowles (2010, p. 56) finds that 67% of music teachers would like specific training in teaching adults. This is supported by my own survey of music teachers which found that many considered teaching adults as "a separate skill" to teaching younger learners (Shirley, 2015, p. 9).

In summary, whilst these small-scale studies complement each other, there is a lack of large-scale research into adult learners. Most existing research is predominantly qualitative, involving interviews, autobiographical writing or questionnaire responses. These methods allow for "a greater degree of respondents' own interpretations" (Pitts, 2014, p. 192), influenced by the fact they are taking part in a research project, and they are also clearly subject to interpretation by researchers.

Although much existing research produces and uses textual data, there has been little use of linguistic analysis. In section 2b, I discuss corpus-based discourses analysis techniques which allow large textual data sets to be analysed and enable the use of anonymised data not specifically elicited for research purposes, potentially revealing different aspects of adult learners' 'stories'.

Data and methodology

Corpus-based discourse analysis

Discourse analysis, the approach that "choice of words expresses an ideological position" (Stubbs, cited in Baker 2006, p. 47), is particularly suited to investigating the use of language to express identities and attitudes. Recent developments in discourse analysis include the use of corpus-based techniques, using software to enable the analysis of larger data sets than could be handled 'manually'. Since patterns are identified by running searches and automated reports, these approaches potentially lessen the problem of researcher bias and subjective interpretation. Widdowson (1998, p. 148) describes corpus-based analyses as "grounded in systematic language description" seeing this as preferable to less structured approaches. However, as Baker (2006, p. 92) points out, corpus-based discourse analysis "is still a matter of interpretation… subject to the researcher's own ideological stance".

Corpus approaches are particularly suited to online texts. Computer-mediated communication can produce large quantities of text in a short period of time, and building a corpus offers a way to analyse this data and identify patterns in the text. Corpus linguistics techniques are increasingly crossing over into other discipline areas, for example in the interdisciplinary work of the ESRC Centre for Corpus Approaches to Social Science (CASS) which includes projects on online misogyny[19], language education[20], healthcare (e.g. Semino et al., 2015), and geography[21]. As yet, music education research has barely used these techniques, with only one published study using corpus-based discourse analysis (Mantie, 2012).

Data

The data for this study consists of a 500,000-word corpus of text posted online by adult music learners between January 2010 and April 2015. In order to compile a corpus of these postings, I searched for relevant web sites where adult learners describe and discuss their experiences of learning

---

[19] http://cass.lancs.ac.uk/?page_id=1022
[20] http://cass.lancs.ac.uk/?page_id=1327
[21] http://www.lancaster.ac.uk/spatialhum

music. I downloaded webpages as plain text files, and removed extraneous text such as web page headings.

Ethical considerations

Using online data raises ethical issues, primarily:

- o Expectations of 'participants' – although site contents are public, there is a sense of a private community/anonymity. It is important to consider whether the data "you want to study is publicly available and perceived as such by the participants" (Page, Barton, Unger & Zappavigna, 2014, p. 72). NatCen Social Research, exploring users' views on social media research, found that participants were aware of this 'sense of anonymity' but also displayed 'self-regulation' – they "only posted online what they were happy for others to access" (2014, p. 20).

- o Would informing 'participants' constitute interfering in this community or change the nature of postings? NatCen Social Research found that participants felt that "their answer will be influenced by the fact that they… know someone else is going to read [it]" (2014, p. 20). Meanwhile, Tusting (in Page et al., 2014, p. 77) found resistance from forum site owners to "post[ing] a thread to open up a conversation about my research."

My solution to these concerns was to use the data entirely anonymously. I felt that making an announcement or contacting site users would constitute interference – as well as influencing what people posted; it could, more importantly, disrupt communities that members see as a source of support. I do not identify the sites used, and quotations do not include personal or identifying information. In order to ensure that only publicly available data was used, I downloaded text without logging in.

Analysis

I analysed the corpus using AntConc[22], which can produce word lists (by frequency), concordances and collocate lists, with some statistical analysis. The word list showed that *teacher* was the 6th most frequent term in the corpus, suggesting prominent discourses around teachers.

I use corpus searches as a starting point for discourse analysis, in particular analysis of metaphor use, finding recurrence of "different expressions relat-

---

[22] Downloaded from http://www.antlab.sci.waseda.ac.jp/software.html

ing to the same broad source domain" (Semino, 2008, p. 22) – groups of related metaphors which represent how experiences are being described.

Adult learners and music teachers

Teacher(s) occurs 2785 times in the corpus. In order to investigate how teachers are described, I used AntConc to search for collocates of *teacher** – words frequently co-occurring with *teacher* or *teachers*. The parameters I used were as follows:

Span: 5L, 5R – includes words five places to the left and right of *exam** - I chose this wide span in order to capture a broad view of how adult learners describe exams, as this span includes pronouns, adjectives, intensifiers and verbs around the word being investigated.

Minimum collocate frequency: one (since even words used just once or twice may be part of a group of terms which represent a particular discourse, or may be significant as a 'dissenting voice').

Sort order: I sorted results by frequency, and also by MI ('mutual information') score. This statistical measure identifies words which occur more frequently than would normally be expected, which is useful for identifying patterns specific to these texts.

In the full corpus, *teacher** occurs 2785 times, and a collocate search shows 2267 collocates.

Table 1: Top thirty collocates of teacher* in order of frequency

Rank	Word	Frequency	MI score
1	tempting	7	8.77071
2	horrified	6	9.77071
3	unfailingly	4	8.77071
4	maternity	3	9.35567
5	hampering	3	9.35567
6	vibe	3	8.77071
7	tenterhooks	3	8.77071
8	treasure	2	8.77071
9	topped	2	8.77071
10	stunningly	2	8.77071
11	wows	1	8.77071
12	whinge	1	8.77071
13	vinyl	1	8.77071
14	unlucky	1	8.77071
15	tweaks	1	8.77071
16	treats	1	8.77071
17	toys	1	8.77071
18	thrilled	1	8.77071
19	thanking	1	8.77071
20	temper	1	8.77071
21	teatime	1	8.77071
22	swapped	1	8.77071
23	surmise	1	8.77071
24	stumped	1	8.77071
25	stray	1	8.77071
26	stilted	1	8.77071
27	steadier	1	8.77071
28	stacks	1	8.77071
29	spurred	1	8.77071
30	soonish	1	8.77071

Table 2: Top thirty collocates of teacher* in order of MI score

Rank	Word	Frequency	MI score
1	horrified	6	9.77071
2	maternity	3	9.35567
3	hampering	3	9.35567
4	wows	1	8.77071
5	whinge	1	8.77071
6	vinyl	1	8.77071
7	vibe	3	8.77071
8	unlucky	1	8.77071
9	unfailingly	4	8.77071
10	tweaks	1	8.77071
11	treats	1	8.77071
12	treasure	2	8.77071
13	toys	1	8.77071
14	topped	2	8.77071
15	thrilled	1	8.77071
16	thanking	1	8.77071
17	tenterhooks	3	8.77071
18	tempting	7	8.77071
19	temper	1	8.77071
20	teatime	1	8.77071
21	swapped	1	8.77071
22	surmise	1	8.77071
23	stunningly	2	8.77071
24	stumped	1	8.77071
25	stray	1	8.77071
26	stilted	1	8.77071
27	steadier	1	8.77071
28	stacks	1	8.77071
29	spurred	1	8.77071
30	soonish	1	8.77071

As Tables 1 and 2 show, an intriguing mixture of terms appear in association with *teacher**. Sorting both by frequency and by MI score shows some strongly negative words – *horrified, hampering, whinge, unlucky* – and some strongly positive – *wows, treasure, thanking* – ranking highly.

As MI score highlights terms which are particular to this text, I used the top 1000 collocates sorted by MI, to more fully investigate terms associated with teachers. These could be categorised mainly into three groups:

o   Emotions/ feelings

o   Verbal processes

o   Metaphors

The analysis below focuses on metaphorical language.

Metaphors

The metaphorical language apparent in collocates of *teacher** falls mainly into three groups - violence, injury and pain; metaphors of war; metaphors of religion.

Violence, injury and pain

Collocates of *teacher** include a number of metaphors of violent actions: *force, push, pushing, pushed, pushes, pounced, knocks, struck, torn, inflict, flogging, murdering, whip, shreds, struck, chucking* (some of these terms occur several times, making 38 tokens in total).

Many of these refer to actions by or attitudes of teachers, for example:

> 'my teacher pounced on my least favourite out of them'

> 'torn to shreds by your teacher'

> 'my teacher started to force me into weekly lessons'

> 'I wanted an easy lesson but my teacher pushed me over the edge'

These imply that some learners find their teachers slightly 'scary'. This idea could be compounded by the presence of *ogre* in the collocate list, but this turns out to be a learner stating that their teacher 'is not an ogre'. Equally there are instances which suggest that learners appreciate teachers' direction, with one learner stating 'I'm glad my teacher pushes me so hard'.

Some terms refer to actions by the learners themselves:

> 'didn't want to inflict it on my teacher'

> 'as soon as I have to play in front of anyone (including my teacher) I feel I'm murdering the piece'.

It seems that learners feel that playing 'badly' is somehow injurious to their teacher or to the piece of music itself.

There are also terms referring to pain and injury (7 tokens): *pains, bleed, dead, innards.* One of these turns out to refer to a real injury, where the learner didn't want 'to bleed on my teacher's piano' and another is a description of violin playing, referring to 'cat gut' strings – 'a cat's innards!'. The others are used metaphorically:

> 'my teacher was at pains to explain that'

> 'feel like I'm flogging a dead horse, my teacher suggests…'

These metaphors of violence and pain suggest that the learner/ teacher relationship can be difficult and learners can see their teachers' actions and their own limitations in quite severe terms.

War metaphors

Several metaphors (14 tokens) could fit into a 'war' theme - *battling, conflicting, lost, revenge, reinforcement* - overlapping with that of violence and injury. In the same way that learners depict themselves as 'murdering' pieces of music, there is a sense of fighting with difficult pieces, e.g.: 'my teacher has me battling with [a particular piece of music]'.

The use of 'my teacher has me' is especially interesting here, the image of the teacher 'sending the learner into battle' suggesting that the teacher is in control. Conversely, *revenge* is used in the sense of the learner regaining control: 'I have a plan to get revenge on my teacher for always finding something wrong with my playing'.

Religion

A number of collocates of *teacher** are religion-related terms: *angel, saint, saints, faith, spirit, soul, believes, praise* (24 tokens). Looking at these in context shows these are generally used in fairly conventional metaphorical ways such as 'my teacher is an angel' or 'has the patience of a saint'. The use of the plural *saints* is interesting, as it comes as part of a discussion around teachers showing their frustration with students: 'I think teachers would have to be saints not to let a hint of frustration show occasionally'.

Faith is used in variations of 'my teacher has faith in me/ my abilities/ my playing', often with an implication that the teacher thinks more highly of the learner's ability than they do themselves: 'my teacher has more faith in me than I do'. Likewise, *believes* appears in the context of 'my teacher believes I can…' and *soul* is used as part of the conventional phrasing 'my teacher is the soul of diplomacy'.

The use of these religious metaphors suggest that the 'belief' and opinions of teachers are important to adult learners, and that they recognise they often do not have the same confidence in their own abilities as their teachers have (or give the impression of having). They highlight qualities which the learners appreciate – patience and diplomacy – but also somewhat place the teachers on a pedestal, contributing to the discourse of teacher control.

Conclusions

The metaphorical language evident here - couching interactions in terms of violence, war and religion - suggests that learner-teacher relationships provoke strong responses. There is a clear sense that the teacher is in control, whether that is expressed through negative (war or violence) terms or more positive terms of admiration (religious metaphors). Learners appreciate support, patience and understanding from teachers, want to impress and please them, and feel ashamed of 'not doing well'. It appears that learners appreciate some aspects of teaching which might seem initially negative, such as 'strictness' and teachers making the decisions, but do seem to be issues around the balance of control between teacher and learner.

These findings have the potential to inform music educators, influencing individual teachers, music education training, and organisations who are seeking to engage with and support adults.

Limitations

The most obvious limitation to this study is that it excludes those who do not contribute to online content. It is also difficult to ascertain 'tone of voice' - unlike an interview situation, there is no opportunity to ask for clarification from participants. It could also be argued that the problems associated with biographical research approaches apply here – learners may 'self-edit' and present a particular identity online. These issues suggest that a combined approach may be useful, incorporating corpus-based analysis with traditional music education research techniques such as questionnaires or interviews.

AntConc, whilst far easier than manual searching, does have limited functionality. Corpus tools with part-of-speech and semantic tagging and more statistical analysis options would enable easier investigation of aspects such as passivisation, modality and transitivity in the text.

Potential for further research

Corpus-based analysis has the potential to contribute to a truly in-depth study of adult learners. It would be useful to investigate whether there are varying discourses amongst different groups of adult learners, for example taught versus self-taught learners or beginners versus returners, and to compare discourses in text written by music teachers.

These techniques could equally be applied in other areas of music education research, giving insights which could benefit educators, organisations and, most importantly, learners.

References

Anthony, L. (2011). AntConc (Version 3.2.4) [Computer Software]. Tokyo, Japan: Waseda University. Available from http://www.antlab.sci.waseda.ac.jp/

Associated Board of the Royal Schools of Music (2014). *Making Music: Teaching, learning & playing in the UK.* London: ABRSM.

Baker, P. (2006). *Using corpora in discourse analysis.* London: Continuum.

Bowles, C. L. (2010). Teachers of adult music learners: An assessment of characteristics and instructional practices, preparation, and needs. *Applications of Research in Music Education, 28, 50–59.*

Hallam, S., Creech, A., Gaunt, H., Pincas, A., Varvarigou, M., & McQueen, H. (2013). *Music for life project: The role of participation in community music activities in promoting social engagement and well-being in older people.* Sheffield, UK: NDA Research. Programme. Retrieved from http://www.newdynamics.group.shef.ac.uk/assets/files/NDA%20Findings_9.pdf

Halliday, M.A.K. & Matthiessen, C. (2004). *An introduction to functional grammar.* London: Hodder Education

Hammond, H. (2008). *Play flute: a course for adult beginners.* London: Kevin Mayhew Ltd.

Hobbs, E. (2014, March). Inspiring adult learners. *Libretto: ABRSM news and views,* 20-21.

Lamont, A. (2011). The beat goes on: music education, identity and life-long learning. *Music Education Research, 13(4),* 369-388.

Mantie, R. (2012). Music education and avocational music making: examining discourse using techniques from corpus linguistics. In Thompson, L. & Campbell, M. (Eds.), *Advances in Music Educa-*

tion Research, Volume 5 (pp. 119-146). Charlotte, NC: Information Age Publishing.

NatCen Social Research (2014). Research using Social Media; Users' Views. Retrieved from http://www.natcen.ac.uk/media/282288/p0639-research-using-social-media-report-final-190214.pdf

NIACE (2015, April 27). Festival of Learning survey finds that UK is a nation of 'wannabe' chefs and musicians. Retrieved from http://www.niace.org.uk/our-thinking/news/festival-learning-survey-finds-uk-nation-wannabe-chefs-and-musicians

Page, R., Barton, D., Unger, J. & Zappavigna, M. (2014). *Researching language and social media: a student guide.* Abingdon: Routledge.

Pitts, S. E. (2012). *Chances and choices: exploring the impact of music education.* New York: Oxford University Press.

Roulston, K., Jutras, P., & Kim, S.J. (2015). Adult perspectives of learning musical instruments. *International Journal of Music Education, 33(3),* 325-335.

Semino, E. (2008). *Metaphor in discourse.* Cambridge: Cambridge University Press

Semino, E., Demjen, Z., Demmen, J., Koller, V., Payne, S., Hardie, A. & Rayson, P. (2015). The online use of Violence and Journey metaphors by patients with cancer, as compared with health professionals: a mixed methods study. *BMJ Supportive and Palliative Care.* Published Online First: *2015(0),* 1–7.

Shirley, R. (2015). "You're never too old for music!": online discourses of adult music learners, a corpus-based study. (Unpublished master's dissertation). Available from http://www.sheffieldflute.co.uk/research.html

Taylor, A. (2011). Older amateur keyboard players learning for self-fulfilment. *Psychology of Music, 39(3),* 345-363.

Wedgwood, P. (2006). *It's never too late to play piano.* London: Faber.

Widdowson, H. (1998). The theory and practice of critical discourse analysis. *Applied Linguistics, 19(1),* 136-151.

Student, Parent, and Teacher Perspectives on Studio Music Instruction

Rena Upitis
Faculty of Education, Queen's University, Kingston, ON, Canada

rena.upitis@gmail.com

Philip C. Abrami
Centre for the Study of Learning and Performance, Concordia University, Montreal, Canada

abrami@education.concordia.ca

Julia Brook
Faculty of Arts & Sciences, Queen's University, Kingston, ON, Canada

julia.brook@queensu.ca

Wynnpaul Varela
Centre for the Study of Learning and Performance, Concordia University, Montreal, Canada

w_varela@education.concordia.ca

Karen Boese
Faculty of Education, Queen's University, Kingston, ON, Canada

boese.k@queensu.ca

Abstract

The purpose of the study was to describe the experiences of students, parents, and teachers engaged in one-on-one instrumental or vocal instruction. Three self-report surveys explored parental values, musical progress, the teacher-student relationship, the practice environment, teachers' views on student self-regulation, students' practising habits, and parent behaviours during practice sessions. The study aimed to determine the extent to which outcome measures, such as enjoyment and progress, could be predicted by the nature of parental involvement, students' intrinsic motivation, and teacher qualities. Results for 3,920 students, 2,583 parents, and 1,468 teachers indicated that the most salient predictor of enjoyment and persistence was the extent to which students were intrinsically motivated to pursue musical studies. In the case of the outcome measure of persistence, intrinsic motivation accounted for almost 40% of the variance. Parental involvement was also a significant predictor of student enjoyment, explaining 25% of the variance. There was evidence indicating that parents were deeply invested in their children's music lessons. Teachers identified that their greatest challenge was to motivate students to practice. The data also suggested that positive teacher-student relationships predicted both student enjoyment of music and musical progress. The paper closes with a discussion of the role of intrinsic motivation for lifelong musicianship and directions for future research.

Keywords: student self-regulation, parent-child-teacher triad, teaching strategies, music practice support

Introduction

Over two million Canadian children annually take extra-curricular music lessons (Upitis & Smithrim, 2002). Despite the pervasiveness of the independent studio model, studio music instruction is under-researched (Barry, 2007), and the current study was designed to fill that gap. The study examined the perspectives of students, parents, and teachers involved in one-on-one studio music instruction, using self-regulation in music learning (e.g., McPherson & Zimmerman, 2011) and the cultivation of deliberate practice habits (e.g., Hallam et al., 2012; Miksza, 2011) as the theoretical underpinnings for the design of the surveys.

Literature

The parent-teacher-student triad

Parental aspirations and values, parents' musical background, the home practice environment, and family dynamics positively affect students' musical outcomes (Creech & Hallam, 2003; McPherson, Davidson, & Faulkner, 2012; McPherson, 2009). Further when teachers, parents, and students share a mutual understanding of goals and purpose, music students are more likely to experience success (Duke, 1999). In a study involving 263 violin teachers, students, and parent(s), Creech (2009) examined the interpersonal interactions in the parent-teacher-student triad in terms of student self-efficacy, satisfaction, enjoyment, motivation, and self-esteem. Creech found the most effective teaching and learning occurred where parents, teachers, and students communicated well, demonstrated mutual respect, shared a sense of common purpose, and adopted child-centred goals.

Supporting practice and developing self-regulated learning

Children with parents who actively assist with practising are more likely to experience musical success (Brokaw, 1982; Spera, 2006). Creech (2001), found that a strong sense of parental self-efficacy helped parents (a) motivate their children, (b) support focused practice sessions, (c) communicate effectively with the teacher, and (d) respond to children's requests for support. Likewise, Davidson, Howe, Moore, and Sloboda (1996) concluded that parental beliefs in their children's abilities to succeed were critical in sustaining persistence and predicting long-term success.

While assistance is crucial, learning is ultimately more effective in the longer term when students take control over their learning processes by developing self-regulatory habits (Dignath, Büttner, & Langfeldt, 2008). Largely due to McPherson and his colleagues, self-regulation has been applied to music learning (e.g., McPherson, Davidson, & Faulkner, 2012; McPherson & Zimmerman, 2011). Initially, learners require support to emulate expert learners, progressing to scaffolded self-control, and ultimately, to self-regulation (Zimmerman, 2011). In the earliest stages parents often provide scaffolding between music lessons, where most engagement with the instrument occurs (Davidson et al., 1996; Varela, Abrami, & Upitis, 2014).

Self-efficacy, motivation, beliefs about musical abilities, and other psychological constructs

While self-regulation encompasses various psychological constructs, including motivation, some of these constructs, such as self-efficacy (Bandura, 1997), have been operationalized as discrete factors in the music learning literature, separate from self-regulation (e.g., McCormick & McPherson, 2003). Researchers have also focussed on beliefs about musical abilities (Hallam, 2011), and environmental elements (e.g., Davidson, Howe, & Sloboda, 1997) to describe musical engagement.

Researchers have also investigated the effects of accumulated practice over time (e.g., McPherson & Zimmerman, 2011; Hallam et al., 2012). Intuitively, more practice time should lead to better achievement. However, this is not always the case (Madsen, 2004). Indeed, despite an overall trend suggesting accumulated practice time predicts higher levels of performance, practice time alone does not consistently predict achievement outcomes (Hallam et al., 2012).

Bonneville-Roussy and Bouffard (2015) posited an integrative framework would predict musical achievement by combining accumulated practice, aspects of self-regulation, and deliberate practice strategies. Despite a small sample size, they found evidence for a latent variable they termed formal practice, comprising self-regulation, deliberate practice, goal direction, and focussed attention. They concluded formal practice was most effective when a highly positive motivational profile was combined with considerable practice time. This finding accords with studies where the nature of practising, the time spent practising, the motivation to practise, effort management, and beliefs about competency are combined to predict music achievement (e.g., Hallam, 2011; McCormick & McPherson, 2003; Renwick, 2008).

Research questions

The research questions were as follows:

1. What are the key features that characterize the teacher, student, and parent populations?
2. To what extent are student outcomes (e.g., enjoyment) predicted by parenting values and behaviours, time spent practising, physical environment, student self-regulation, student intrinsic motivation, teacher qualities, and quality of lessons?

Method

Development and deployment of the survey

The three self-report surveys were developed through a combination of prior questions relating to student self-regulation and teachers' use of technology (Abrami, Venkatesh, Varela, & Lysenko, 2012), deliberate practice (e.g., Hallam et al., 2012), and a survey of Australian Music Examinations Board students (Renwick & McPherson, 2009). Questions regarding demographics and music studio practices were based on interviews from an earlier study of 20 Canadian music studios (Brook, Upitis, Troop, Varela, & Abrami, 2014). Research was conducted in accordance with the Canadian Tri-Council Policy Statement governing research with human participants. The surveys were deployed through The Royal Conservatory (RCM), as well as through music schools across Canada. The survey was available in both English and French; surveys are archived at www.musictoolsuite.ca.

The RCM database was used to provide survey links to 14,547 teachers. Parents and students were contacted through a combined RCM database, containing 69,419 records. Two reminders were sent after initial requests. The teacher survey return rate was 17%, yielding 2,470 initial responses.

Parents returned 3,104 online surveys, and students returned 5,219 online surveys. Calculating a return rate for parents and students was not possible, given the combined database of emails.

Eighty-six other schools and conservatories across Canada were contacted and 30 agreed to participate. Music schools were provided with 155 paper surveys for teachers, 900 for parents, and 1,041 for students. Return rates were extremely low: 26, 54, and 94 responses for teachers, parents, and students respectively.

File preparation

Once the paper returns were added to the electronic file, anomalous responses were removed. We next removed files that were less than 90% complete, yielding 1,468 teacher surveys, 2,583 parent surveys, and 3,920 student surveys for analysis. We used maximum likelihood expectation-maximization to impute for missing values of interval and continuous variables (Cheema, 2014), and hot deck imputation for categorical variables (Young, Weckman, & Holland, 2011). The number of missing values per variable was less than 1%.

Analysis

Descriptive statistics were produced using SPSS (IBM, 2013). For the student and parent surveys, composite scales were developed through factor analysis of the predictor survey items, using oblique and Varimax rotation. Because of item collinearity concerns, the data files were randomly divided in half with analyses performed separately on each half, as well as the entire data file, thus ensuring the stability of the final factors and their item loadings. Factors and items that were inconsistent or that had weak factor loadings (<0.45) were excluded. A reliability analysis was conducted with each set of variables. A factor analysis was not performed for the teacher file, as the teacher survey contained no outcome measures.

The final set of 11 composite predictive scales for the parent survey comprised: (a) teacher characteristics, (b) quality of lessons, (c) parent practice monitoring, (d) parent practising assistance, (e) valuing music as a career path, (f) valuing music itself, (g) student SRL, (h) practice environment, (i) deliberate practice strategies, (j) supporting musicianship, and (k) explicit SRL support. Several unique items were also identified as predictors: (a) a question regarding whether parents valued music for fun (the only predictor that failed to load on the factor analyses), (b) two items measuring practising time, and (c) measures for time spent on out-of-school activities. The composite measures and unique items were used in step-wise regressions for two outcome variables: (a) the extent to which children made music for enjoyment, and (b) the satisfaction parents reported with their children's progress.

The same procedure was performed on the student file, yielding 12 predictive factors. Four factors related to *motivation*: (a) extrinsic motivation, (b) intrinsic motivation, (c) musical skill development, and (d) lifelong music-making. One factor represented *parenting behaviours during practising.* Two factors related to *practice components*: (a) technical and exam-related requirements, and (b) aural abilities. Five factors represented *self-regulation*: (a) being motivated to practice well, (b) poor motivation regarding practising, (c) planning with effective practising strategies, (d) effective dealing with mistakes, and (e) reflection combined with effective practising strategies. Several unique predictor items were identified: (a) parenting values, (b) time spent practising, (c) out-of-school activities, (d) practice environment, and (e) causal attribution.

An analogous process determined outcome variables for the student file. *Enjoyment* was represented by students' overall enjoyment of music learning, including practising, lessons, and playing repertoire. *Persistence* was represented by whether students would continue making music if they stopped taking lessons. *Performance skills* were represented by three composite outcome measures: (a) performing for others, (b) the employment of aural abilities in performance, and (c) practising skills. *Self-efficacy* was captured by the students' responses to questions regarding personal competency beliefs and externally influenced beliefs.

Results

The full results of the three questionnaires are reported elsewhere (Upitis, Abrami, Brook, Boese, & King, submitted; Upitis, Abrami, Brook, & King, submitted; Upitis, Abrami, Varela, King, & Brook, submitted). We describe some of the key features of the three data sets below.

Characteristics of teachers, parents, and students

Teachers responding to the survey were well-educated, with close to 40% having earned Bachelor's degrees in Music, a quarter (26.6%) with Bachelor's degrees in other disciplines, and another 18% with graduate degrees. Most of the teachers had been teaching between 11 and 30 years (47.1%), with another third (33%) having taught 30 years or more. Roughly a quarter of the teachers (23%) reported teaching fewer than 10 students, while another quarter (27%) reported teaching 30 students or more. Most students remain with their teachers for five to seven years (45%), and many stay with the same teacher for eight years or more (27%). Most of the parents and guardians who filled out the survey were female (86%) and well educated: 90% of the respondents had completed some form of post-secondary studies, with 38% reporting that they had completed five or more years of university training. Parents responding to the survey valued music: 73% had been involved in music lessons themselves, and of this group of parents, more than half (60%) were still playing an instrument. Nearly a fifth of the respondents (19%) had supported their children's involvement in music lessons for a decade or more. Nearly two-thirds of the students described by the parents were female (63%), and most were teen-agers (*Median*age = 13.1 years, age range: 6 – 24+ years). Their children began taking music lessons at quite a young age: 43% began taking lessons at the age of 5 years or younger. The most common instrument was piano (81%).

Most of the student respondents were teenagers (*Median*age = 15 years, age range: 6 – 24+ years) living in urban settings (85%), and identifying as female (72%). Approximately half of the students (50%) reported beginning lessons between the ages of six and nine, and a third of the respondents (32%) had been playing their instruments for 10 years or longer. Most of the students responding to the survey identified the piano as their primary instrument (81%), and over half of the students' parents played, or once played, a musical instrument (55%).

Lesson Components and Learning Goals

Nearly every teacher (99%) reported teaching repertoire from notated music. Well over half (58%) reported that they taught students to play by ear and half (49%) also reported that they taught their students composition and improvisation.

Parents valued music lessons as a means for their children to develop proficiency to enjoy music in adulthood (53%), for well-roundedness (44%), to develop self-discipline (42%), and for overall enjoyment (38%). 42% reported that they were extremely pleased with their child's progress, with another 51% selecting the upper end of the scale (5 or 6 on a 7-point scale). Most parents indicated that their children admired and respected their teachers: on a scale from *not true* (1) to *very true* (7), 85% selected 6 or 7. Similar patterns were found for the teachers' responsiveness to the students' needs and interests (79% selected 6 or 7), the teachers' encouragement and support (88% selected 6 or 7), and the students receiving clear expectations from teachers (84% selected 6 or 7).

Supporting practice and developing self-regulated learning

Parental responses indicated that their children became more capable of assuming responsibility for their own learning over time. For example, the least experienced students regularly set goals for the practice sessions 5% of the time, but those parents with children who had been studying for ten or more years reported that students regularly set goals for practice sessions 51% of the time.

We asked students to indicate what they practice and on a scale from *never* (1) to *always* (5), the most common practising activity involving learning new repertoire (M = 4.75, SD = 0.52), followed by playing pieces they already had mastered (M = 3.72, SD = 1.02), technical requirements (M = 3.71, SD = 1.05), and sight-reading (M = 3.02, SD = 1.06). Many students employed effective deliberate practice strategies, such as practising small sections of the pieces they were learning. Students indicated that their parents played an active role in supporting students' home practising. On a scale from *never* (1) to *always* (5), many parents reminded their children to practise (M = 3.95, SD = 2.09), and offered comments and suggestions (M = 3.81, SD = 2.17). On the whole, developing musical skills in general was highly valued by students.

More than a quarter (27%) of the teachers claimed to be *very comfortable* with the use of digital technologies. In terms of the impact of learning technologies, 68% of the teachers believed that technology could improve learning (choosing either *agree* or *strongly* agree), and 61% believed that technology helped motivate students. When asked how they currently used technology, the most common responses were: to compare performances by different musicians (56%) and to share performances and links (35%).

Enjoyment and Motivation

Using data from the parent survey, we conducted a regression analysis predicting enjoyment of music. Together, the following accounted for close to 25% of the variance: (a) monitoring practice sessions (with *less* monitoring leading to greater enjoyment), (b) valuing the benefits of music, (c) student self-regulation, and (d) "fun" as reason for taking lessons. Musical progress, as observed by the parents, was predicted by (a) teacher qualities and characteristics, (b) parenting behaviours in terms of supporting practising, (c) lack of distractions while practising, and (d) quality of lessons, which together accounted for close to 25% of the variance.

Similarly, we conducted a regression analysis using data from the student to predict students' enjoyment of music, 55% of the variance was accounted for by five variables (see Table 1), ranging from intrinsic motivation, which alone accounted for 44% of the variance, to students' abilities to self-regulate in terms of being motivated to practice effectively, the motivation to acquire musical skills, the extent to which students practised technical exam-related components, and the quality of teaching.

Table 1: Step-wise regression analysis for enjoyment composite outcome measure (student data)

Step	adjusted R2	R2 change	df	F-value change*
1 Motivation: Intrinsic	.439	.439	1/3918	3066.33
2 Self-Regulation: Motivated to practise well	.498	.059	1/3917	461.19
3 Motivation: Musical skills	.534	.036	1/3916	304.19
4 Practice Components: Technical/exam related	.550	.016	1/3915	139.47
5 Quality of teacher (single item: Q28.v)	.555	.005	1/3914	48.05

*$p < .001$

In terms of predicting persistence, the regression analysis indicated that four factors accounted for 48% of the variance, with intrinsic motivation being the most important factor, explaining 38% of the variance. Other factors were motivation in terms of lifelong music-making, self-regulation including reflection and effective practising strategies, and extrinsic motivation.

Two aspects of self-efficacy were analysed, based on the outcome scales described earlier. Regarding personal competency beliefs, 41% of the variance was accounted for by five variables: (a) intrinsic motivation, (b) likelihood of performing well in public, (c) extrinsic motivation, (d) a parent or guardian who also plays an instrument, and (e) the belief that the quality of music-making depends on a student's musical abilities. Nearly a third of the variance (29%) regarding externally influenced beliefs about self-efficacy was explained by five predictors: (a) intrinsic motivation, (b) extrinsic motivation, (c) likelihood of performing well in public, (d) self-regulation in terms of being poorly motivated to practise, and (e) self-regulation involving reflection and practising strategies. These results appear in Table 2.

Table 2: Step-wise regression analysis for two types of self-efficacy measures

Step	adjusted R2	R2 change	df	F-value change*
Personal competency beliefs				
1 *Motivation:* Intrinsic	0.239	0.239	1/3918	1231.27
2 Likelihood of performing well in public (single item: Q36)	0.358	0.119	1/3917	729.68
3 *Motivation:* Extrinsic	0.383	0.025	1/3916	160.56
4 Parent/guardian also plays an instrument (single item: Q9)	0.397	0.014	1/3915	89.66
5 Belief that the quality of music-making depends on a student's musical abilities (single item: Q28i)	0.409	0.012	1/3914	79.09
Externally influenced beliefs				
1 *Motivation:* Intrinsic	0.176	0.176	1/3918	835.92
2 *Motivation:* Extrinsic	0.243	0.067	1/3917	347.90
3 Likelihood of performing well in public (single item: Q36)	0.273	0.030	1/3916	162.62
4 *Self-Regulation:* Poorly motivated to practise	0.283	0.010	1/3915	52.26
5 *Self-Regulation:* Reflection/practising strategies	0.289	0.007	1/3914	35.98

*$p < .001$

Discussion

Parents of students involved in studio music instruction are clearly dedicated to their children's musical education, as demonstrated by the years spent supporting music learning, the active support of their children's evolution as self-regulating musicians, and the respect for their children's teachers. The teachers worked with students and parents, sharing responsibility for various music-learning activities in a co-regulatory fashion. The results also indicate that contemporary independent music teachers are highly professional. They are well educated and engage in practices to improve their pedagogy, musical skills, and content knowledge.

Perhaps most importantly, the results underline the central role of motivation in successful music learning. It seems enjoyment of music, persistence, overall performance skills, and self-efficacy, are predicted by students' overall intrinsic motivation to become musicians. In the case of persistence, intrinsic motivation accounted for an extraordinary 40% of the variance.

We share McPherson, Davidson, and Faulkner's (2012) view that one cannot "definitively and exhaustively explain what factors promote musical development ... because of the complexities that are actually involved in this agency in real musical lives" (p. 187). Our study provides a glimpse into the complexity of the parent-teacher-student triad. It also provides further empirical support regarding the role of parental support as mediated by teaching, and students' abilities to work with greater autonomy over time.

Given our findings, and the empirical studies cited earlier, it would be of value to concentrate our efforts on how factors that repeatedly surface – such as motivation, effective practice strategies, and beliefs about performance abilities – can best be supported and nurtured in lessons and home environments. We are aware that much is to be gained by broadening the sample of respondents to encompass students who have become disengaged from their musical studies.

One limitation of the present study was our inability to link the parent, teacher, and student surveys at the level of individual respondents. A powerful future study will involve direct links between each parent-teacher-student triad, echoing the approach of Creech (2009) described previously. Such cross-validation will allow us to continue to define the nuanced interplay between parents, teachers, and students who pursue musical studies.

Acknowledgements

Our thanks to the thousands of teachers, students, and parents who took the time to fill out the survey. We are also grateful for the funding from the Social Sciences and Humanities Research Council of Canada.

References

Abrami, P. C., Venkatesh, V., Varela, W., & Lysenko, L. (2012). The Student Learning Strategies Questionnaire, Version 3 (forms A & B). Unpublished instrument. Montreal, QC: Centre for the Study of Learning and Performance.

Bandura, A. (1997). *Self-efficacy: The exercise of control.* New York, NY: Freeman.

Barry, N. H. (2007). A qualitative study of applied music lessons and subsequent student practice sessions. *Contributions to Music Education, 34,* 51-65.

Bonneville-Roussy, A., & Bouffard, T. (2015). When quantity is not enough: Disentangling the roles of practice time, self-regulation and deliberate practice in musical achievement. *Psychology of Music, 43*(5), 686-704.

Brokaw, J. P. (1982). *The extent to which parental supervision and other selected factors are related to achievement of musical and technical-physical characteristics by beginning instrumental music students.* Unpublished PhD dissertation, University of Michigan.

Brook, J., Upitis, R., Troop, M., Varela, W., & Abrami, P. C. (2014). Considering the commonplaces: Developing responsive curricula in studio instruction. *Presented at the ISME (International Society for Music Education) World Conference*, Porto Alegre, Brazil.

Canadian Institutes of Health Research, Natural Sciences and Engineering Research Council of Canada, Social Sciences and Humanities Research Council of Canada, *Tri-Council Policy Statement: Ethical Conduct for Research Involving Humans (TCPS2)*, December 2010.

Cheema, J. R. (2014). A review of missing data handling methods in education research. *Review of Educational Research, 20*(1), 1-22. doi: 10.3102/0034654314532697.

Creech, A. (2001). *Play for me: An exploration into motivations, issues and outcomes related to parental involvement in their children's violin study.* Unpublished MA dissertation, University of Sheffield.

Creech, A. (2009). Teacher-parent-pupil trios: A typology of interpersonal interaction in the context of learning a musical instrument. *Musicae Scientiae, 12*(2), 163-182.

Creech, A., & Hallam, S. (2003). Parent-teacher-pupil interactions in music tuition: A literature review. *British Journal of Music Education, 20*(1), 29-44. doi: 10.1017/S0265051702005272

Davidson, J. W., Howe, M. J. A., Moore, D. G. & Sloboda, J. A. (1996). The role of parental influences in the development of musical performance. *British Journal of Developmental Psychology, 14*, 399-412.

Davidson, J. W., Howe, M., & Sloboda, J. (1997). Environmental factors in the development of musical performance skill in the first twenty years of life. In D. Hargreaves & A. North (Ed.), *The social psychology of music* (pp. 188-203). Oxford: Oxford University.

Dignath, C., Büttner, G., & Langfeldt, H.P. (2008). How can primary school students learn self-regulated learning strategies most effectively? A meta-analysis on self-regulation training programmes. *Educational Research Review 3*(2) 101-129.

Duke, R. A. (1999). Teacher and student behaviour in Suzuki string lessons: Results from the International Research Symposium on Talent Education. *Journal of Research in Music Education, 47*, 293-307.

Hallam, S. (2011). What predicts level of expertise attained, quality of performance, and future musical aspirations in young instrumental players? *Psychology of Music, 41*(3), 267–291. doi: 10.1177/0305735611425902

Hallam, S., Rinta, T., Varvarigou, M., Creech, A., Papageorgi, I., Gomes, T., & Lanipekun, J. (2012). The development of practising strategies in young people. *Psychology of Music, 40*(5), 652-680. doi: 10.1177/0305735612443868

IBM Corp. (2013). Released 2013. IBM SPSS Statistics for Windows, Version 22.0. Armonk, NY: IBM Corp.

Madsen, C. (2004). A 30-year follow-up study of actual applied music versus estimated practice. *Journal of Research in Music Education, 52,* 77-88.

McCormick, J., & McPherson, G. E. (2003). The role of self-efficacy in a musical performance examination: An exploratory structural equation analysis. *Psychology of Music, 31*(1), 37-51.

McPherson, G. E., (2009). The role of parents in children's musical development. *Psychology of Music, 37*(1), 91-110. doi: 10.1177/0305735607086049

McPherson, G. E., Davidson, J. W., & Faulkner, R. (2012). *Music in our lives: Redefining musical development, ability and identity.* Oxford: Oxford University Press.

McPherson, G. E., & Renwick, J. M. (2011). Self-regulation and mastery of musical skills. In B. J. Zimmerman & D. H. Schunk (Eds.), *Handbook of self-regulation of learning and performance* (pp. 327-347). New York, NY: Routledge.

McPherson, G. E., & Zimmerman, B. J. (2011). Self-regulation of musical learning: A social cognitive perspective on developing performance skills (pp. 130-175). In R. Colwell & P. Webster (Eds.), *MENC Handbook of Research on Music Learning, Volume 2: Applications.* New York: Oxford University Press.

Miksza, P. (2011). Relationships among achievement goal motivation, impulsivity, and the music practice of collegiate brass and woodwind players. *Psychology of Music, 39*(1), 50-67.

Renwick, J. M. (2008). *Because I love playing my instrument: Young musicians' internalized motivation and self-regulated practising behaviour.* Unpublished doctoral dissertation, University of New South Wales.

Spera, C. (2006). Adolescents' perceptions of parental goals, practices, and styles in relation to their motivation and achievement. *Journal of Early Adolescence, 26,* 456-490.

Upitis, R., Abrami, P. C., Brook, J., Boese, K., & King, M. (in press). Characteristics of independent music teachers. *Music Education Research.*

Upitis, R., Abrami, P. C., Brook, J., & King, M. (in press). Parental involvement in children's independent music lessons. *Music Education Research*.

Upitis, R., Abrami, P. C., Varela, W., Brook, J., & King, M. (in press). Student experiences with studio instruction. *Music Education Research*.

Upitis, R., & Smithrim, K. (2002). *Learning Through the Arts TM: National assessment—A report on year 2 (2000-2001)*. Toronto, ON: The Royal Conservatory of Music (78 pp.).

Varela, W., Abrami, P. C., & Upitis, R. (2014). Self-regulation and music learning: A systematic review. *Psychology of Music*. doi: 10.1177/0305735614554639

Young, W., Weckman, G., & Holland, W. (2011). A survey of methodologies for the treatment of missing values within datasets: limitations and benefits. *Theoretical Issues in Ergonomics Science, 12*(1), 15-43.

Zimmerman, B. J. (2011). Motivational sources and outcomes of self-regulated learning and performance. In B. J. Zimmerman, & D. H. Schunk (Eds.), *Handbook for self-regulation of learning and performance* (pp. 49-64). New York, NY: Routledge.

The Provision of Music in Special Education (PROMISE) 2015

Graham F. Welch
University College London, Institute of Education, London, UK

graham.welch@ucl.ac.uk

Adam Ockelford
University of Roehampton, London, UK

a.ockelford@roehampton.ac.uk

Sally-Anne Zimmermann
Royal National Institute of Blind People, UK

sally.zimmermann@rnib.org.uk

Eva Wilde
University College London, Institute of Education, London, UK

wilde-e@web.de

Keywords: music, special education, provision in England

Abstract

The paper reports the outcomes of a national survey of music in special schools in England that was conducted in the summer of 2015. The survey sought to uncover the current state of affairs in the sector, whilst also allowing a comparison to be made with the findings of a related study undertaken at the end of the last century. The survey outcomes also provide contextual data to inform the design of a current wider national initiative to improve the overall effectiveness of music education in the UK for all children (the *inspire-music* project). In total, fifty-seven special schools responded to the on-line survey. Findings suggest that music is taught at least weekly to 95% of children aged 2–13 years (noting that 5–13 are the statutory ages for music in mainstream schools), with slightly smaller proportions for 14–16 year-olds (83%), an age group for whom music becomes an optional subject in mainstream schools, and less for the oldest age group (66% of 16–19 year-olds). Eighty per cent of schools reported that they employed a specialist music teacher, which appears to be a much higher proportion of musically qualified staffing than almost two decades earlier. Where schools have a formal music curriculum, over half (59%) report that this is specially designed and adapted from existing models, such as the new *Sounds of Intent* framework. Music was also reported to be a common element in other lessons by 3:4 schools, and common at lunchtimes/break times (2:3). Regular and systematic input from outside music agencies was reported to be relatively common (3:4 schools). Four-fifths of schools had a dedicated music room, and music technology use was commonplace. Music therapy was reported to be available in 1:3 schools, a similar proportion to 1999–2000, but for relatively double the numbers of children (11%, compared to 5% earlier). In addition, virtually all schools (96%) reported children with a particular interest in music and almost all schools felt that music was important. The detailed data imply a clear positive shift since the late 1990s, with more musically qualified staffing, a broader range of resources for the music curriculum, more external organisations available to support music, increased use of music technology and improved music therapy provision. Nevertheless, given the small number of schools responding to the survey compared to those in total within the special schools sector, it is not yet possible to confirm that *all* children have access to an effective music education.

Introduction

The latest statistical data from the UK Government suggests that there are 1.5m children and young people of school age in England that have some form of special need, being approximately 18% of the total school population (DFE, 2014a). Of these, 232,190 pupils have formal 'statements of SEN' (2.8%), meaning that their special need is such that it requires some form of statutory support. Within this sub-group are a special school population of 41,585 children with *severe learning difficulties* (SLD) or *profound and multiple learning difficulties* (PMLD) in a ratio 3:1, collectively referred to here as pupils in special schools.

In the late 1980s, the first iteration of a statutory National Curriculum was emerging in England, with music being introduced in 1992 and quickly undergoing its first revision in 1995. However, despite these policy initiatives, there was a distinct absence of a national music education strategy for children and young people in special schools. Indeed, a schools' inspection summary report at that time (Ofsted, 1999) stated that one third of special schools had so few music lessons that it was impossible to make a judgment on their quality. Furthermore, where it was possible to make a judgment, only half of the schools demonstrated music provision that was satisfactory or better. Deconstructing these figures suggested that only one third of special schools in England at that time had observable effective music education provision. There was also little evidence about of music therapy in special schools.

As a consequence, the authors, funded by the Esmée Fairbairn Foundation with support from the RNIB[23], undertook a research-based enquiry into the provision of music in special education in England (termed the PROMISE enquiry, see Welch, Ockelford & Zimmermann, 2001). The research was conducted in three phases across the 1999–2000 academic year and included questionnaire sampling and school visits, supplemented by informal discussions with teachers and other professionals. A total of 53 schools participated, representing 2,758 pupils, and equating to approximately 10% of special schools. Although the research was exploratory in nature, the data suggested that there was considerable variation in the quantity and quality of music education and music therapy available to pupils. Nevertheless, there was evidence of examples of effective educational practice that could provide the basis for raising standards across this special school sector if these could be grounded in an appropriate, evidence-based national curriculum framework.

The outcome of the research, the 'PROMISE' report, offered evidence of a widespread recognition of the potential benefits of music for children in special schools, both as an area of development in its own right, as well as in supporting wider learning and well-being (Welch, Ockelford & Zimmermann, *op.cit.*). Schools reported that they would welcome clearer guidance on how to ensure high quality music provision for their pupils.

However, in the absence of official guidance at that time as to how to frame music education for this group of children and young people, the team secured further research funding from various sources[24] to address this need. The new funding led to the establishment of the *Sounds of Intent* project whose aim, firstly, was to undertake basic research to map the musical development of children and young people in special schools (see, e.g. Ockelford et al., 2005; Welch et al., 2009; Cheng et al., 2009; Vogiatzoglou et al., 2011; Ockelford and Zapata Restrepo, 2012) and, secondly, through applied research, to provide evidence-based guidance on appropriate music pedagogy for all children in special education (thus informing policy and practice).

---

[23] Royal National Institute for the Blind, since renamed as the Royal National Institute of Blind People (RNIB).

[24] External research funding for Sounds of Intent has been received from the Qualifications and Curriculum Authority (QCA), Esmée Fairbairn Foundation, Amber Trust, Soundabout and RNIB , alongside 'in kind' support from the Institute of Education, University of London (now UCL Institute of Education) and Roehampton University.

Once the mapping phase was complete, an interactive web-based version of the resulting developmental framework was designed, trialled and launched, with the intention of enabling practitioners and parents/carers to gauge their children's levels of musical attainment, to chart any changes that may occur over time and, in response to particular musical experiences and interventions, to record qualitative observations in the form of written, video or audio data, thus building up a profile of a child's experiences, achievements and development (see www.soundsofintent.org – Welch & Ockelford, 2015).

The official version of the website went live in February 2012. Since then, the online platform has had over 6.2 million unique visitors from all over the world, with 937,745 resources opened, streamed or downloaded (to 26 March 2016), comprising, for example, video and audio files, work-cards and pupil registration forms. There are currently over 630 registered practitioners, of whom 250+ are actively using the assessment tool. These represent over 190 special schools or schools with specialist SEN units/provision, with 3,586 pupils currently being assessed using the online system that holds over 9,000 recorded sessions. The framework, either in the original English or through translation, is being used to support music education for children with special needs in the UK, USA, Haiti, Spain, Portugal, Colombia, Taiwan, Japan, The Netherlands and Pakistan.

Notwithstanding the interest in the *Sounds of Intent* project and its official recognition by the English schools' inspection body, Ofsted, as an exemplar of good practice in music education[25], a recent independent review of school music education nationally (Zeserson et al, 2014) suggested that, in general, the place and status of music continues to vary widely across the country, despite being more inclusive, musically diverse and better quality than a decade earlier[26]. This finding was echoed at an expert meeting in London (February, 2015), called by the UK Music Education Council (MEC), to discuss the current status of music in the special school sector.

Consequently, given this background, alongside the interest in *Sounds of Intent* (and its new offshoot, *Sounds of Intent in the Early Years*, www.eysoi.org), it seemed appropriate to revisit the original PROMISE

---

[25] Ofsted (2012) published six exemplars of good practice in music education as part of a wider triennial review of music education and related professional development materials. See http://www.ofsted.gov.uk/resources/110158 and https://www.gov.uk/government/uploads/system/uploads/attachment_data/file/383377/Music_professional_development_materials.pdf

[26] See http://www.**inspire-music**.org for more details of the independent PHF-funded report into the nature and status of music education in England in early 2014.

research findings and to investigate more formally the perceptions of the current status of music education in special schools.

Methodology

Accordingly, an on-line survey was piloted, designed and (with appropriate ethical approval) distributed to special schools across England in June 2015, with responses requested by the end of the academic school year (July). The original PROMISE survey had been sent to a sub-section of special schools that were believed to cater specifically for children with learning difficulties—although we discovered subsequently that there was considerable overlap in school pupil populations across the sector. However, given the significant changes within the sector over the past two decades, with schools changing official designation and population and some being incorporated into larger units, the decision was made to survey all special schools in England in the Summer of 2015 rather than to go back to the original set of responders from the turn of the century. The team felt that the resultant data were likely to be more representative of the special school sector as a whole (101,500 pupils in 1,033 schools). In total, 57 schools responded, representing 7,306 pupils, and drawn from all nine English regions.

The focus for the PROMISE 2015 survey was on seeking information using the same general categories as in 1999–2000. Questions related to the nature and type of music education being offered, including staffing and resources, as well as music's place and perceived value in the curriculum.

Main findings

(i) Access to music education

There was a mix of pupil access to music education, with 91% (n=51) of schools providing whole class music lessons, 65% (n=36) offering sessions to small groups and just over half (57%, n=32) providing 1:1 lessons. In addition, 40% (n=23) provided instrumental lessons and over one-third of schools listed other kinds of regular, usually weekly, music-based education, including music therapy. A common comment concerned the use of, and opportunities for, music (including singing) throughout the school day.

Overall, music was being provided at least weekly for 95% of children aged 2–14 years, including all those required by statute to have music education from ages 5 to 14[27]. In addition, early years music provision was universal (100%), being at least weekly in schools that responded to this question (n=36). Encouragingly, 4:5 schools (83%, n=46) taught weekly class music lessons to pupils in Key Stage 4 (ages 14–16), an age phase for which music becomes optional in the National Curriculum; 2:3 (66%, n=32) provided music for their oldest pupils at least weekly (ages 17–19).

(ii) Music staffing

Specialist music teachers taught music in the majority of schools (80%, n=39) and class teachers taught music in half of the schools (51%). There appears to be a much higher proportion of musically qualified staffing compared to two decades earlier where under half (43%) of school music coordinators had a music degree, or had specialised in music in their teacher education. A fifth of schools also had music led by classroom assistants (which our previous observations had suggested to be more common with younger children). Two schools mentioned class teachers or classroom assistants who had received specialist training and had instrumental skills. These members of staff provided certain types of musical experience, such as resonance board activities. Instrumental teachers taught specific instruments, either in small groups, or 1:1. Two schools had a music technology specialist providing 1:1 sessions. Another had a braille music tutor.

In terms of staff music qualifications, the survey answers suggested that this was an aspect not widely known within schools and, consequently, the reporting was more varied. Where knowledge existed, as might be expected, specialist music teachers and instrumental teachers held qualifications in music, and three quarters of these also held Qualified Teacher Status (QTS). Overall, most schools were able to call upon someone with experience of music education on their staff, whether classroom teachers, specialist staff member, classroom assistant, and/or visiting instrumentalist. Additionally, between 43–55% of schools reported some form of music professional development in the previous twelve months, either led internally (43%, n=37), or by an external specialist, either at the school (55%, n=40), or by staff attendance at a local Music Hub[28] session (43%, n=37).

---

[27] Within the English school system, this pupil age range is divided into three phases, labelled Key Stages 1 to 3, ages 5-7, 7-11, 11-14.

[28] 'Music Education Hubs are groups of organisations – such as local authorities, schools, other hubs, arts organisations, community or voluntary organisations – working together to create joined-up music education provision, respond to local need and fulfil the objectives of the hub. Hubs are coordinated by the hub lead organisation, which takes on responsibility for the funding and governance of the hub. The total amount of hub funding from the Department for Education in 2015–16 is £75 million.' Retrieved 1

The majority of respondents had plans for professional development in 2015–2016, with one third (*n*=15) focused on music technology (e.g., iPads, Soundbeam, Beamz, Kaoss pads and Charanga resources). Other needs were more general (e.g., singing, support for music making by non-specialists, basic training for music lessons involving children with complex and moderate needs, and training using resonance boards through Soundabout). Five schools made specific mention of a need for new members of staff to be inducted into the use of *Sounds of Intent*.

(iii) Music curricula

Many schools that responded were not obliged to follow the English National Curriculum for Music. Responses (*n*=49) suggested that schools drew on a wide variety of curricular sources: over half (59%, *n*=29) devised their own music curricula, some (12%, *n*=6) adopted/adapted a local Music Hub curriculum, and/or a commercial scheme (20%, *n*=10). Only a small proportion (16%, *n*=8) did not having a documented curriculum.

(iv) Music in other areas of school life

Respondents (*n*=50) offered a wide range of comments on the use of music in other areas of school life, including supporting other aspects of the curriculum, such as topic work, literacy and drama (*n*=8), foreign languages (*n*=2), numeracy/mathematics (*n*=5), physical education and dance (*n*=10), humanities (*n*=5), religious education (*n*=3), science (*n*=3), and art (*n*=2). Music was also commonplace across early years activity.

In terms of incidence, music was reported as being evidenced regularly in non-music lessons by nearly three-quarters of respondent schools, i.e., daily (60%), *n*=30) or weekly (14%, *n*=7). Similarly, two-thirds of schools reported music at lunchtimes, either daily (36%, *n*=18) or weekly (32%, *n*=16). One third of schools also had music scheduled after school (such as group work, dance club, signing choir) and most (80%, *n*=40) had music at special events, including fundraising. Musical cues were used at transition points in the school day (*n*=10), including greetings, signifying the day of the week, lining up, tidying up, lesson changes and goodbyes. One school noted that their Early Years class sang and signed every day. Two others reported that "all lessons start with music of reference", and "We use music as a way to communicate with the pupils on a daily basis."

November 2015 from http://www.artscouncil.org.uk/what-we-do/cyp/music-education/music-education-hubs/

(v) Engaging with external organisations and musicians

Some schools used their local networks to engage in regular, termly projects with local mainstream schools ($n=18$, one of which was weekly) and/or other local special schools ($n=15$). Similar numbers ($n=15$) were involved in projects with local Music Hubs. Nevertheless, around half of the respondents either did not have such partnership music projects, or did not know if they did.

Thirty-seven schools (75%) named outside music agencies (Music Hubs ($n=12$), local or national disability organisations, e.g., Live Music Now[29] ($n=12$) and Jessie's Fund[30] ($n=3$)) or freelance musicians with whom they had worked in the previous twelve months; some schools had worked with several, with 41 other music organisations mentioned. These included regional and specialist music centres (such as Sage Gateshead, Royal Opera House, Purcell School, Liverpool Philharmonic Orchestra, London Symphony Orchestra, English Touring Opera, Opera North, Music for Youth), as well as specialist charitable organisations (including Music for Autism, Music for Life, Music in Hospitals, Live Music Now, Music in the Round, Amber Trust, YAMSEN). Most of these external agencies visited the school for a day, but some took residencies, usually of a term. Musicians (from organisations or freelance) might be called in to contribute to days when the whole school investigated a particular topic, as in one school that has regular "Enrichment Days" where a specific country becomes the school focus.

(vi) Music accreditation available to pupils and assessment

Because of pupils' special needs, the National Curriculum for music is likely to be disapplied (i.e., not required). As might be expected, therefore, relatively few children and young people within this respondent population had their music learning accredited. Nevertheless, some accreditation was evidenced, both internal and external. A small number of schools ($n=8$) presented children with their own, internal, music certificate. Two schools ran GCSE music classes. Eleven schools ran accredited vocational courses that included a musical element, and 17% ($n=7$) had some pupils taking graded instrumental examinations. In total, 21 different types of

---

[29] Live Music Now is a registered charity that has focused on live music education provision for disadvantaged people since the early 1980s, including older people and those within the special education sector. The charity draws its inspiration from the life and work of one its founders, Yehudi Menuhin. http://www.livemusicnow.org.uk/about-us

[30] Jessie's Fund was established as a registered charity in April 1995 with the aim of helping seriously ill and disabled children in all areas of the UK through the therapeutic use of music. http://www.jessiesfund.org.uk/our-aims/

external, national music learning accreditation were mentioned, such as ABRSM, BTec, GCSE, A-level, Rock School, and Trinity. There were also more vocationally-based qualifications that included music elements (available through ASDAN[31])[32].

This consideration was reinforced by another school that their pupils were only able to reach a standard for an internal certificate, implying that there is a gap in accreditation provision that could recognise music achievement at a special school level that was not just the application of a mainstream award designed for so-called 'neurotypical' pupils.

In terms of musical assessment, n=45 schools commented and 2:3 (65%, n=33) reported formally about music progress termly to parents. The most common assessment schemes were P Levels[33] (56%, n=32) and B Squared[34] (20%, n=11), reported termly (sometimes monthly). Where *Sounds of Intent* was being used, this tended to be more frequently (4 schools weekly, 4 monthly or termly).

(vii) Resources for making and listening to music – spaces and sound sources around the school

Overall, 86% (n=49) schools either had a dedicated music room (n=31) or a music room that was shared with other activities (n=18). Over four-fifths of schools had a hall with a sound system and keyboard, with similar numbers reporting a sound system in their multisensory areas. Half of re-

---

[31] ASDAN is a curriculum development organisation and awarding body, offering programmes and qualifications that explicitly grow skills for learning, skills for employment and skills for life. Developed and managed by practitioners, ASDAN grew out of research work at the University of the West of England in the 1980s and was formally established as an educational charity in 1991. http://www.asdan.org.uk/about

[32] One respondent wrote, "This is something that needs looking into. Music accreditation from the nationals – ABRSM and Trinity – does not allow for 'special needs' in the same way that a special needs school means. Giving extra time to someone that is autistic is not up to scratch for making it actually inclusive. There, for example, could be a SEND music medal scheme that could run alongside the ABRSM music medals."

[33] 'P Levels' are 'Performance – P Scale – attainment targets for pupils with special educational needs' aged 5 to 16 who are perceived to be 'unable to access the National Curriculum' (DFE 2014b). They emerged initially as part of a Government response in the early 1990s to the recognition that children in the special school sector (and some pupils in mainstream schools) were likely to need alternative official guidance on attainment. The first National Curriculum has been introduced in Primary schools in 1989, with music emerging in 1992. Although the English National Curriculum for Music no longer has levels of attainment in its latest (fifth) iteration (2014), P Levels continue as statutory guidance (a somewhat paradoxical situation). The *Sounds of Intent* project arose out of the perceived inadequacy in the design of the P Levels for music.

[34] B Squared (http://www.bsquared.co.uk) is a commercial assessment provider that offers software-based tools for measuring attainment in all National Curriculum subjects, as well as in the Early Years Foundation Stage (EYFS) and for P Levels.

spondents had a sound system for their hydrotherapy pool (where this existed) and similar numbers had musical instruments in an outdoor installation. Free text commentary suggested that other accommodation was being used flexibly for music-related activity, such as music therapy. One school had a sound system that fed into two playgrounds; another had a designated music area with instruments for the two early years' classes. Two schools mentioned having additional small music rooms for music therapy or intensive interaction, one of which doubled as the instrumental teaching room, and, for one school, a space for "song writing and composing".

(viii) Music technology and other resources

Music technology is commonplace, as might be expected with the widespread public availability of new technology-related media. The largest category was non-specialist, such as Apps on tablets. Four-fifths (79%, n=45) said that they had this kind of technology. There was widespread availability of music software available for pupil use (such as Garage Band and Audacity) in 2:3 schools (65%, n=36). Just under half (n=24) had digital percussion, with similar numbers having the means to record pupils' musical work in a studio, or with microphones. Alongside mainstream music technology, half (52%, n=30) had specialist switching devices that used sound, such as Skoog, BigMack and Jelly Bean, with slightly fewer (n=25) having beam systems, all traditionally considered specifically for people with "special needs". One caveat to these details is the extent to which, notwithstanding availability, schools regularly use such devices. Some comments suggested that this was not always the case.

In terms of other music resources, all school accessed music material online, and most used CDs (n=42) and songbooks (n=36). Two schools reported that having no access to YouTube restricted what could be used. Two schools said they made their own materials, such as Powerpoint, with song lyrics along with pictures "to help word recognition". The most frequently used resources were percussion (tuned and untuned) and other acoustic instruments, including keyboards and ukuleles. When asked to name a favourite song/soundtrack/type of music, all respondents had at least one, with popular music genres predominating.

(ix) Music therapy

One third of respondent schools (n=19) had some form of music therapy being provided for pupils. This represents a similar proportion of schools (1:3) to 1999–2000. There is an average provision of 5.5 hours music therapy reported per week across 293 pupils (range 2–60 pupils; mean n=15 pupils), representing approximately 11% of this respondent school population. This is double the level of provision reported in 1999-2000 (5%)[35]. Four schools offered 1:1 sessions for all children, whereas the others provided a mix of group and 1:1 sessions. Therapy provision was usually by referral or a child's Statement of Special Educational Needs. Therapy was mainly funded from school budgets, but this was an issue for some.

Summary

The survey data evidence suggests that there is a greater awareness of the potential significance of music in special education, with 96% schools reporting children and young people with a particular interest in music (including 100 pupils in each of two schools). The majority of respondents (70%, n=40) valued music as (at least) equally important to other subjects in the curriculum and frequently as the most important. The detailed data imply a clear positive shift since the late 1990s, with more musically qualified staffing, a broader range of resources for the music curriculum, more external organisations available to support music, increased use of music technology and improved music therapy provision. Nevertheless, there is always more than can be done and survey respondents would welcome increased opportunities for staff development, curriculum enrichment and funding for resources, in order that many more children are able to engage and be successful *in* and *through* music, whatever their needs. The reported success of the *Sounds of Intent* framework, for example, provides an ideal opportunity for increased numbers of schools to ensure a more systematic assessment of pupils' musical attainment and progress. This, in turn, could support a (national) music accreditation structure that is more sensitive to the needs of the special school population, a topic that is under active discussion with Trinity College London.

References

Cheng, E., Ockelford, A., & Welch, G.F. (2009). Researching and developing music provision in Special Schools in England for children and young people with complex needs. *Australian Journal of Music Education*. [Special edition on music and SEN] 2, 27-48.

Department for Education [DFE] (2014a). *Special Educational Needs in England: January 2014. Statistical First Release*. London: Department for Education.

---

[35] The proportion of pupils receiving music therapy in 1999-2000 was estimated at 5% in respondent schools and 2% of the total special school learning difficulties population. The comparable proportions for 2015 were 11% of respondents and 4% of population.

Department for Education [DFE] (2014b). *Performance – P Scale – attainment targets for pupils with special educational needs.* London: Department for Education.

Ockelford, A., Welch, G., Zimmermann, S.-A. and Himonides, E. (2005), "'Sounds of Intent' – mapping, assessing and promoting the musical development of children with profound and multiple learning difficulties", Proceedings of 'VISION 2005' Conference, 4-7 April, Elsevier: International Congress Series, Vol. 1282, pp. 898-902.

Ockelford, A., & Zapata Restrepo, G. (2012), Sonidos de la intención (SoI): un proyecto para valorar y promover el desarrollo musical en niños con dificultades múltiples y severas de aprendizaje, *Revista Acontratiempo, 18*, available at www.territoriosonoro.org/CDM/acontratiempo/?ediciones/revista-18/traducciones/sonidos_ intencion.html (accessed 1 June 2015).

Office for Standards in Education [Ofsted] (1999). *Special Education 1994-1998.* London: The Stationery Office.

Office for Standards in Education, Children's Services and Skills [Ofsted] (1999). (2012). *Music in schools: wider still, and wider.* Manchester: Ofsted. [see good practice case study report http://webarchive.nationalarchives.gov.uk/20141124154759/http://www.ofsted.gov.uk/resources/music-schools-wider-still-and-wider-good-practice-case-study-whitefield-schools-and-centre]

Vogiatzoglou, A., Ockelford, A., Himonides, E., & Welch, G.F. (2011). *Sounds of Intent*: Interactive software to assess the musical development of children and young people with complex needs. *Music and Medicine, 3*(3), 189-195.

Welch, G.F., & Ockelford, A. (2015). The importance of music in supporting the development of children with learning disabilities. *International Journal of Birth and Parent Education, 2*(3), 21–23.

Welch, G.F., Ockelford, A., Carter, F-C., Zimmermann, S-A., & Himonides, E. (2009). 'Sounds of Intent': Mapping musical behaviour and development in children and young people with complex needs. *Psychology of Music, 37*(3), 348-370.

Welch, G.F., Ockelford, A. & Zimmermann, S-A. (2001). *Provision of Music in Special Education PROMISE.* Royal National Institute for the Blind/University of London Institute of Education.

Zeserson, K., with Welch, G.F., Burn, S., Saunders, J., & Himonides, E. (2014). *Inspiring Music for All. Paul Hamlyn Foundation Review of Music in Schools.* London/Gateshead: Paul Hamlyn Foundation/Sage Gateshead.

The Effect of Selected Parameters on Perceptions of a Music Education Video Posted on YouTube

Jennifer A. Whitaker
The University of North Carolina at Charlotte, USA

jwhitaker@uncc.edu

Evelyn K. Orman
The University of North Carolina at Charlotte, USA

Cornelia Yarbrough
Louisiana State University, USA

Abstract

The purpose of this quasi-experimental study was to determine how selected parameters affect viewers' perceptions of a music education video posted on YouTube. Participants assigned to one of seven groups (control, positive comments, negative comments, high view count, low view count, high likes, and high dislikes) viewed a guitar tutorial video posted on YouTube and completed a questionnaire. Results indicated viewer perceptions were significantly more positive when screen information was positive and significantly more negative when screen information was negative. The type of screen information that was the most influencing was comments. While positive comments significantly influenced viewer perceptions positively and negative comments significantly influenced viewer perceptions negatively, positive comments had a wider range of influence among the various questions.

Keywords: YouTube, online music teaching, viewer perceptions

Review of Literature

Over the past decade, the number of YouTube users increased to more than one billion. Hundreds of millions of hours of YouTube videos are viewed daily with approximately 300 hours of video uploaded every minute. YouTube use spans the globe with navigation of the site available in 76 different languages and 80% of views occurring outside the United States (YouTube, 2015). It is the third most visited site in the world, with only Google and Facebook receiving more web traffic (Alexa Internet,

Inc., 2015). Given the popularity of YouTube, it is not surprising musicians use it for music dissemination, listening, and learning.

Recently, music researchers documented both formally and informally trained musicians' use of YouTube. Lai (2013) found 85% of formally trained undergraduate music students indicated they access YouTube for educational purposes and 81% reported searching YouTube specifically when preparing for lessons or rehearsals. In an examination of undergraduate and graduate music students' information seeking behaviors, Dougan (2012) found that 73% of students used YouTube to identify and access sound recordings, and that more students searched YouTube for scores and recordings than other search engines and websites. Another study that focused on university students' use of technology found 97% of respondents search the Internet, including YouTube, to learn how to sing or play a musical instrument for fun (Hu, Lee, & Wong, 2014).

Several studies have documented the use of YouTube for informal music teaching and learning of folk music in the context of online music communities and noted the participatory culture that occurs when using YouTube (Veblen & Waldron, 2012; Waldron, 2011, 2012, 2013; Waldron & Veblen, 2008). Salavuo (2006) found members of online music communities participate to listen to others' music, disseminate their own music, receive feedback, and learn more about music. Some use posted comments to make more informed musical decisions (Suhr, 2010), while YouTube is also used for promotional means and to develop a fan base (Cayari, 2011).

Other researchers examined specific characteristics of music related videos posted on YouTube. Kruse and Veblen (2012) studied 40 instructional folk music videos for instructor characteristics, musical content, and teaching methods. Whitaker, Orman, and Yarbrough (2014b) categorized 1,761 videos from a "music education" keyword search. Results indicated most videos categorized as teaching videos (n = 381) were tutorials (65%). A follow-up study examined 7,332 comments posted to these videos (Whitaker, Orman, & Yarbrough, 2014a). The largest number of comments was personal experiences related to video content (33%); followed by comments containing negative feedback (29%); and expressing positive sentiments (26%). These studies provide a general picture of the types of music education videos available and how viewers respond to them in terms of written comments.

Recently, researchers in communications investigated how viewers are influenced by comments posted by others on YouTube. Walther, DeAndrea, Kim, and Anthony (2010) examined viewer perceptions of an antimarijuana video accompanied by either positive or negative comments. Results indicated that participants (N = 152) perceived the public service announcement more favorably when viewed with positive comments than with negative comments (*p* < .001). It is unclear if viewer perceptions of music education videos are influenced by comments similarly. Furthermore, other parameters (i.e., view count, number likes and dislikes) found on each video's webpage may also influence viewer perceptions. Therefore, the purpose of this study was to determine how selected parameters affect viewers' perceptions of a music tutorial posted on YouTube.

Method

Undergraduate (*n* = 132) and graduate students (*n* = 8) from three different universities in the United States voluntarily participated in this study. Forty-nine percent were freshmen, 29% sophomores, 11% juniors, 6% seniors, and 6% were graduate students. Ages ranged from 18 to 53 (M = 20.53, SD = 4.05) and the sample included 66 males and 74 females. Participants were non-music majors (*n* = 114) and music majors (*n* = 26). Seventy-three percent reported having musical training and 27% indicated they played guitar.

Participants, randomly divided into one of seven possible groups, watched the most viewed music tutorial posted to YouTube (previously identified by Whitaker, et al., 2014b) on a 15" laptop computer. The guitarist who posted the tutorial had no formal pedagogical or guitar performance training and stated that he made the video to help people interested in learning to play guitar. The tutorial contains information on how to play basic chords and was recorded with a close-up view of the left hand on the fretboard. Pedagogically, the guitarist gave incorrect information, cursed when he confused himself, and modeled incorrectly during part of the tutorial.

The control group (*n* = 20) viewed the video exactly as it appeared on YouTube without having selected the full screen option; however, no information or placeholders for likes/dislikes, view count, or comments were displayed. All others viewed the video exactly as it appeared on YouTube but the likes/dislikes, view count, or comments that normally appear on the screen were purposefully manipulated. The high likes group (*n* = 19) saw 8,466,344 likes and 42,332 dislikes. The number of likes (8,466,344) was selected from the most liked video on YouTube at the time, *Gangnam Style* by Psy, and we decided the number of dislikes would be half of 1% of the likes posted. The high dislikes group (*n* = 23) saw the reverse count (42,332 likes and 8,466,344 dislikes). Two more groups of participants viewed manipulated view counts. The high views group (*n* = 19) saw 10,154,570 listed as the view count while the low views group (*n* = 20) saw

15 as the number of previous views. The final two groups saw comments while watching the video. The positive comments group (n = 19) saw two comments that stated, "Thanx its really helpful." and "Thank you very much! This helped me soooooooo much. Subscribe." Members of the Negative Comments group (n = 20) viewed the comments "This was confusing and you even got confused :/ you should delete your messing up beginnings and as one person said not applying any theory." and "I must say this helps me as much as a piece of paper helps itself."

All screen information was purposely manipulated such that the screen appeared as much like a typical YouTube video screen as possible. We did not want participants to notice anything had been changed. We wanted them to believe what they were seeing was a real posting with correct information while, in reality, the only item that was the same from group to group was the video itself. The fabricated numerical information (likes, dislikes, and view counts) was extremely exaggerated. In fact, no music education videos have even approached the large number of likes or views as represented in this study (Whitaker, et al., 2014a/b). The comments however, were not fictitious. We selected 2 positive and 2 negative comments from the list of posted comments for the stimulus video.

Prior to viewing, all participants signed an Institutional Review Board consent form and received the following instructions:

You will watch a 10-minute YouTube video. The video is not presented in full screen. Please do not attempt to change this. At the end of the video, you will be asked a few questions about your general impressions of the video. You will not be asked any specific content questions. Are you ready to begin?

Subsequent to viewing, all participants answered questions about their perceptions of the video including yes/no, Likert-type and open-ended responses, followed by questions that collected demographic information (see Table 1). All Likert-type responses included a neutral choice so participants did not have to provide a positive or negative response. All data are categorical at the nominal level of measurement. Therefore, descriptive statistics are reported throughout with Chi-square analyses used to determine statistical significance.

Open-ended question responses were analyzed for topic(s) and in the case of the comment viewers would post, whether the comment was positive or negative. A response containing a comment related to two or more topics was counted in multiple categories. We used an inductive approach to determine topic categories. Each comment was labeled until topic saturation occurred, resulting in six categories (i.e., teaching, performance, audiovisual quality, close-up picture framing, nothing, and other). Reliability for topic categorization equaled 92%, which we calculated using the formula: agreements divided by agreements plus disagreements multiplied by 100.

Table 1: Viewer Perceptions Questionnaire

To what degree do you "Dislike" or "Like" the video?	Extremely Dislike	Somewhat Dislike	Neither	Somewhat Like	Extremely Like
If you were to rate this on YouTube, which would you select?	Dislike	Like			
What did you like BEST about the video? Why?					
What did you like LEAST about the video? Why?					
How likely would you be to post a comment?	Extremely Unlikely	Unlikely	Neutral	Likely	Extremely Likely
If you posted a comment, would it be positive, negative, or neutral?	Positive	Neutral	Negative		
If you are willing to share the comment you would post, please type it here:					
How often do you visit YouTube?	Never	Rarely	Occasionally	Frequently	Very Frequently
Have you had any musical training?	Yes	No			
Do you play guitar?	Yes	No			
If you do not currently play guitar, to what degree are you interested in learning to play?	Not at all	Slightly	Somewhat	Moderately	Extremely

Participants (N = 140) viewed a guitar tutorial posted to YouTube under one of seven conditions and then completed a questionnaire. Most participants reported visiting YouTube very frequently (50%), followed by frequently (31%), occasionally (16%), and rarely (2%). One participant (< 1%) did not respond. Twenty four percent stated they played guitar. Participants without previous guitar playing experience indicated they were slightly interested (21%), somewhat interested (17%), moderately interested (19%) and extremely interested (12%) in learning to play.

To obtain a holistic view of the data, positive and negative responses for treatment groups viewing positive manipulations (i.e., high views, high likes, and positive comments) and negative manipulations (i.e., low views, high dislikes, and negative comments) were summed for each of the three value judgment questions (i.e., If you were to rate this on YouTube . . . ?; To what degree do you Dislike or Like the video?; and If you posted a comment, would it be . . .?). Results indicated that participants who viewed positive manipulations were significantly more positive than negative in their responses to the questions, χ^2 (1, N = 123) = 8.85, p < .01. There was no significant difference in the amount of positive or negative responses for those viewing the video with negative manipulations. Of the three value judgment questions, those viewing positive manipulations provided significantly more positive than negative responses for the question "If you posted a comment, would it be positive, negative, or neutral?", χ^2 (1, N = 26) = 7.54, p < .01.

Responses for each treatment group were analyzed separately. Those viewing positive comments provided significantly more positive than negative responses, χ^2 (1, N = 39) = 18.69, p < .001; while participants who viewed negative comments responded significantly more negatively than positively, χ^2 (1, N = 49) = 10.8, p < .001. No other significant differences by treatment group were found.

Responses to individual questions for each of the seven groups were also examined. When asked "To what degree do you Dislike or Like the video?", participants who viewed positive comments responded significantly more positively than negatively, χ^2 (1, N = 12) = 5.33, p < .05; those viewing negative comments responded significantly more negatively than positively, χ^2 (1, N = 17) = 4.76, p < .05. In response to "If you were to rate this on YouTube, which would you select: Dislike or Like?" participants in the positive comments group indicated they would select Like significantly more frequently than Dislike, χ^2 (1, N = 18) = 8.00, p < .01. This same group responded significantly more positively than negatively [χ^2 (1, N = 9) = 4.00, p < .05, with Yates' correction] when asked "If you would post a comment, would it be positive, negative, or neutral?" There were no significant differences to responses for these two questions for those who viewed negative comments and significant differences were not found for those who viewed manipulated view counts or likes and dislikes.

We categorized open-ended responses by group. When asked what they liked best and least, comments related to teaching were the most frequently observed category for all groups, followed by close-up picture framing and audiovisual quality. When present, comments that contained references to performance, other (i.e., not related to the video), or "nothing" occurred far less frequently. Teaching related responses occurred in 55%-79% of comments for most liked and 50%-89% for least liked aspects. For example, one participant liked the "Repetition of chords and step by step teaching" best, while another "…didn't like that the guy confused himself sometimes and forgot how to put into words what he was showing people to do." A participant in the high dislikes group stated "His instructions seemed unorganized, and there were over 8.6 million dislikes which made it hard to determine if his instructions were at all valid." This was the only response that included a comment related to any of the manipulated parameters.

Results for the close-up picture framing category were mixed within groups (e.g., high likes: best = 21%, least = 39%), although responses varied somewhat among groups (e.g., best: control = 37%, positive comments = 17%; least: control = 10%, low views = 25%). Participants within every group stated they either liked or disliked the close-up view of the left hand. Responses such as "… It focused the most important part of the guitar where the chords were being played." were common within the best aspect question, while comments such as "I did not like that it did not show the full guitar…" occurred frequently within the least liked aspect question.

Only one participant, from the low views group, wrote a positive comment regarding audiovisual quality. However, audiovisual quality responses for the least liked aspect occurred in every group, ranging from 6% to 39%. One participant cited "The almost comically low production value and overall quality; it sounded like someone got somewhat drunk and decided to make a guitar tutorial." This sentiment was common throughout the responses for this question.

The final open-ended question asked participants, if willing, to share the comment they would post in response to this video on YouTube. The number of participants who shared their comments ranged from six to fourteen among groups. With the exception of the negative comments group, positive responses (range = 67%-91%) far outnumbered negative responses (range = 33%-50%). Participants (n = 14) in the negative comments group wrote comments that included 86% negative and 21% positive statements, while comments for the positive comments group (n = 8) contained 75% positive statements. All groups commented on teaching (range = 58%-100%), four groups included comments regarding close-up picture framing (range = 7%-17%) and other (range = 8%-25%), and three groups included audiovisual quality comments (range = 7%-14%). Participants in the control and high likes groups commented on performance aspects (range = 11%-17%).

Discussion

What affects viewers' perceptions of YouTube music tutorial videos? This study examined that question in relation to various sources of information provided on screen when one views a YouTube video. The stimulus video was the most watched YouTube music tutorial, although it was not the most pedagogically sound. Our findings showed that regardless of video content, viewer perceptions are significantly more positive when other screen information is positive and significantly more negative when other screen information is negative. Written comments were the most influencing type of screen information. While positive comments significantly influenced viewer perceptions positively and negative comments significantly influenced viewer perceptions negatively, the positive comments had a wider range of influence among the Likert-type scale responses.

Open-ended comments showed the same trend. Eighty-six percent of comments shared by willing participants in the negative comments group contained negative statements, and 75% of comments shared by the positive comments group contained positive statements. These findings support Walther, et al. (2010) in that participants viewing their tutorial with positive comments responded more favorably than those viewing the tutorial with negative comments.

Participants were mostly freshmen and sophomores (77%) and 20.5 years of age on average. Eighty-one percent reported frequently or very frequently visiting YouTube, with more than half of those visiting very frequently. Given their youth and that YouTube began in 2005, it is likely these participants grew accustomed to frequently accessing information on the site during their formative years, which may not be typical for all YouTube users. Watching YouTube videos was a common behavior for most participants, which bolsters the validity of these findings since they likely make value judgments for YouTube videos on a regular basis.

Findings indicated the video topic was of interest to the majority of study participants. Twenty-four percent indicated they played guitar and 91% of those who did not play guitar reported having some interest in learning to play. Given these participants were not from a single geographic area, it seems there is widespread interest in learning to play guitar. Music educators may want to consider this finding when making decisions regarding program offerings.

For music educators creating and posting videos to YouTube, findings indicate audiovisual quality and picture framing is a concern. Participants commented on the lack of audiovisual quality and while the close-up of the left hand throughout the video allowed for clarity in fingering the chords, it also limited viewers understanding of how to strum the guitar. Considering a combination of close-up and distant views might be best when creating music tutorial videos.

While we know nonmusical factors affect viewer perceptions of musical performance, conducting, and teaching, this study shows nonmusical factors also affect viewer perceptions of music tutorials posted on YouTube. In this case, comments included onscreen affected viewer perceptions more than any other aspect. In light of this, music educators who post YouTube videos should strongly consider disabling comments. Otherwise, they can control video content but have limited control over posted comments.

References

Alexa Internet, Inc. (2015, October 12). YouTube.com Site Overview. Retrieved from http://www.alexa.com/siteinfo/youtube.com

Cayari, C. (2011). The YouTube effect: How YouTube has provided new ways to consume, create, and share music. *International Journal of Education & the Arts, 12*(6). Retrieved June 27, 2012 from http://www.ijea.org/v12n6

Dougan, K. (2012). Information seeking behaviors of music students. *Reference Services Review, 40,* 558-573. doi:10.1108/00907321211277369

Hu, X., Lee, J. H., & Wong, L. K. Y. (2014). Music information behaviors and system preferences of university students in Hong Kong. *Proceedings from the 15th International Society for Music Information Retrieval Conference.* 579-584.

Kruse, N. B., & Veblen, K. K. (2012). Music teaching and learning online: Considering YouTube instructional videos. *Journal of Music, Technology and Education, 5*(1), 77-87. doi:10.1386/jmte.5.1.77_1

Lai, K. (2013). How are our undergraduates using YouTube? A survey on music students' use of YouTube and the library's multimedia collection. *Music Reference Services Quarterly, 16,* 199-217. doi:10.1080/10588167.2013.843361

Salavuo, M. (2006). Open and informal online communities as forums of collaborative musical activities and learning. *British Journal of Music Education, 23*(3), 253-271.

Suhr, H. C. (2010). *The mutation of cultural values, popularity, and aesthetic tastes in the age of convergence culture: Social networking practices of musicians* (Doctoral dissertation). Available from ProQuest Dissertations and Theses database. (UMI No. 3397518)

Veblen, K. K., & Waldron, J. L. (2012). Fast forward: Emerging trends in community music. In G. McPherson & G. Welch (Eds.), *The oxford handbook of music education, vol. 2* (pp. 203-219). New York: Oxford University Press.

Waldron, J. (2011). Conceptual frameworks, theoretical models and the role of YouTube: Investigating informal music learning and teaching in online music community. *Journal of Music, Technology and Education, 4*(2 & 3), 189-200. doi:10.1386/jmte.4.2-3.189_1

Waldron, J. (2012). YouTube, fanvids, forums, vlogs and blogs: Informal music learning in a convergent on- and offline music community. *International Journal of Music Education, 31*(1), 91-105. doi:10.1177/0255761411434861

Waldron, J. (2013). User-generated content, YouTube and participatory culture on the Web: Music learning and teaching in two contrasting online communities. *Music Education Research, 15*(3), 257-274. doi:10.1080/14613808.2013.772131

Waldron, J. L., & Veblen, K. K. (2008). The medium is the message: Cyberspace, community, and music learning in the Irish traditional music virtual community. *Journal of Music, Technology and Education, 1*(2 & 3), 99-111. doi:10.1386/jmte.1.2 and 3.99/1

Walther, J. B., DeAndrea, D., Kim, J., & Anthony, J. C. (2010). The influence of online comments on perceptions of antimarijuana public service announcements on YouTube. *Human Communication Research, 36*, 469-492. doi:10.1111/j.1468-2958.2010.01384.x

Whitaker, J. A., Orman, E. K., & Yarbrough, C. (2014a). A content analysis of responses to music teaching videos on YouTube. *Proceedings of the 25th International Seminar on Research in Music Education* (pp. 327-343). International Society of Music Education (ISME).

Whitaker, J. A., Orman, E. K., & Yarbrough, C. (2014b). Characteristics of "music education" Videos posted on YouTube. *Update: Applications of Research in Music Education, 33(1)*, 49-56. doi:10.1177/8755123314540662

YouTube. (2015, October 12). Statistics. Retrieved from http://www.youtube.com/yt/press/statistics.html

Characteristics of Pitch-matching and Rhythm-matching Accuracy for Kindergarten Boys and Girls from Argentina

Debbie Lynn Wolf
Cairn University, Langhorne, PA, USA

dwolf@cairn.edu

Ana Lucia Frega
Academia Nacional de Educación, Argentina

Ramiro Limongi
Music Department, National University for the Arts, Argentina

Luis Melicchio
Escuela de Música Juan Pedro Esnaola, Buenos Aires, Argentina

Abstract

Impetus for this study was to expand the perspective of children's tonal and rhythm development beyond the preponderant studies of Europe and North America that dominate the literature by examining the pitch-matching and rhythm-matching performances of children from another cultural background. The focus of this study was to examine tonal and rhythm performances of kindergarten children from Argentina with the specific aims of identifying the tonal pattern and rhythm pattern characteristics contributing to accuracy and determining how gender differences might impact pitch matching and rhythm-matching accuracy. Tonal pattern characteristics investigated were: mode (major vs. minor), harmonic function (tonic vs. dominant), melodic contour (ascending vs. descending), pattern length (two-notes vs. three-notes), and range (high vs. low). Rhythm pattern characteristics investigated were meter (duple vs. triple), number of rhythm notes in the pattern (few: 4-5 notes vs. many: 9-12 notes), position of rhythmic variation (beginning vs. end), number of different duration values (2 vs. 3 or 4), and rhythmic function (simple vs. complex). Kindergarten children (N=50) were males (n=24) and females (n=26), ages 5-6 years of age, from four elementary schools in Argentina. In pitch-matching, all children favoured two-note over three-note patterns and low-range over high-range patterns. No significant differences were found between major and minor patterns, tonic and dominant patterns, or ascending and descending patterns. These results align with previous studies of pitch-matching performances of children from Europe and North America. In rhythm-matching, all children favoured duple over triple meter patterns and variation at the beginning of a pattern over variation at the end. No significant differences were found for the number of notes in the pattern, the number of different duration values or rhythm function. Except for the characteristic of meter, in which the results of this study align with previous studies, the present results contrast with previous studies of rhythm-matching performances of children from Europe and North America. No significant gender differences in accuracy were found in either pitch-matching or rhythm-matching accuracy. These results align with previous studies comparing gender differences in children from Europe and North America.

Keywords: tonal patterns, rhythm patterns, kindergarten music, tonal development, rhythm development, gender differences

Introduction

Foundational skills for successful elementary music development include the skills of pitch-matching and rhythm-matching. Teachers have been effective in developing students' performance in pitch and rhythm tasks through the isolation of the tonal and rhythm dimensions of learning by singing pitches without rhythmic variance or by chanting rhythms without tonal variance (Gordon, 1985; Walker, 1981). The echo response format is preferred for young children for pitch-matching (Sinor, 1985) and rhythm-matching (Rainbow, 1981).

Tonal pattern characteristics affecting pitch-matching accuracy are not necessarily universal (Wolf, 2012). Characteristics of modality, harmonic function, and melodic contour have been found to be significant in tonal pattern performance for children from some countries but not others (Wolf, 2010). Major patterns were easier than minor for children from Asia (Lai, 1999; Wolf, 2010), while minor patterns were as easy as major for children from North America (Wolf, 2005; 2010); and minor thirds were easier than major for children from Argentina, Poland, Spain, and the USA (Moore, Fyk, Frega & Brotons, 1996). Descending patterns were easier than ascending for children from Europe (Moog, 1976; Moore et al, 1996), Asia (Wolf, 2012) and North America (e.g., Madsen, Wolfe, & Madsen, 1975; Wolf, 2012), although ascending patterns were as easy as descending patterns in some studies of USA children (Sinor, 1985; Wolf, 2003). Hong Kong, Dominican Republic, and USA children performed two-note patterns easier than three-note (Wolf, 2012), but three-notes were easier than two-notes for Taiwanese children (Lai, 1999). Low-range patterns are preferred by children from Europe (i.e., Welch, Sergeant, &

White, 1996; 1997), Asia (Wolf, 2012), and North America (Sinor, 1985; Wolf, 2012).

Researchers investigating characteristics of successful rhythm pattern performances have focused primarily on children from the USA and Europe, resulting in a limited perspective on rhythmic development. For these children, researchers have found accuracy to improve with the following rhythm pattern characteristics: symmetrical construction (Drake & Gérard, 1989; Gérard & Drake, 1990; Drake, 1993); regular subdivisions (Drake & Gérard, 1989); metrical accents rather than arrhythmic or syncopated rhythms (e.g., Drake, 1993; Smith, Cuddy, & Upitis, 1994; Wolf, 2003); fewer durations and variations (Gardner, 1971; Wolf, 2003), and variation occurring later rather than earlier in the pattern (Gardner, 1971; Wolf, 2003). Children perform longer patterns more accurately as they mature, but improvement may be attributed to an increase in either the number of durations recalled (Gardner, 1971) or to the number of beats recalled (Drake & Gérard, 1989). Patterns with subdivisions in two parts (binary patterns) are easier to perform than patterns with three parts (ternary patterns) (Drake, 1993), but in simple rhythm performances, binary is not superior over ternary (Gérard & Drake, 1990; Wolf, 2003). Duple meter is easier than triple meter (Drake, 1993; Smith, Cuddy, & Upitis, 1994; Wolf, 2003; 2005).

No gender differences have been found in simple pitch-matching accuracy (e.g., Welch, 1997; Welch et al 2009). Singing tonal patterns appears to avoid some of the gender biases associated with singing songs (e.g., Cooper, 1995; Hall, 2005; Welch et al, 2009). Most researchers have found rhythm abilities to be equivalent for girls and boys (i.e., Petzold, 1963; Smith, Cuddy, & Upitis, 1994; Volman & Geuze, 2000), although a few (Rose, Fisher, & Shewmaker, 2012; Schleuter & Schleuter, 1989) found girls superior in some rhythm tasks. While some researchers have investigated gender differences in pattern performance, few have focused on identifying gender differences in the characteristics of tonal patterns or rhythm patterns that may contribute to accuracy.

More research is needed to determine if the characteristics of tonal patterns and rhythm patterns related to accurate performance in studies with USA and European children hold true for children from other cultures, and if any of these characteristics provide a gender advantage. The focus of this study was to examine the tonal and rhythm performances of children from Argentina with the specific aims of identifying the tonal pattern and rhythm pattern characteristics contributing to accuracy and to determine how gender differences impact pitch-matching and rhythm-matching accuracy of children in Argentina.

Method

Kindergarten children (N=50) participating in the present study were males (n=24) and females (n=26) from two schools in Buenos Aires, Argentina. All children in this study received weekly music classes taught by a music specialist throughout the kindergarten year.

Research assistants individually administered an investigator-designed achievement test, *Tonal Pattern and Rhythm Pattern Performance Test (TPRPT)*, to all the children during the last quarter of their kindergarten year. The TPRPT consists of two subtests, tonal and rhythm, in which children attempt to imitate patterns presented on a recording. The order of the subtests was varied to control for fatigue due to test length and improvement due to practice.

The tonal subtest consists of 40 tonal patterns, without rhythmic variation, recorded by a soprano, singing with a non-vibrato voice, as recommended by Yarbrough, Bowers, and Benson (1992), using a neutral syllable, as recommended by Flowers & Dunne-Sousa (1990), in D major and d minor to accommodate the average range of the child voice (e.g., Welch et al, 2009). The 40 tonal patterns were arranged in two matching sections of 20 major and 20 minor patterns, with each section featuring tonic and dominant patterns in ascending or descending arpeggios of two or three notes. Patterns were considered high if pitches extended above A4; low if pitches extended below E4. Thus five tonal pattern characteristics produced ten tonal subscores: modality (major vs. minor), harmonic function (tonic vs. dominant), melodic contour (ascending vs. descending), pattern length (two-notes vs. three-notes), and range (high vs. low).

The rhythm subtest consists of 30 tonal patterns, without tonal variation, recorded by the same soprano, chanting a neutral syllable as recommended by Rainbow (1981) at a moderate tempo as recommended by Gérard & Drake (1990). The 30 rhythm patterns were arranged in two similar sections of 15 duple meter patterns and 15 triple meter patterns with each section featuring variety in the number of rhythm notes comprising each pattern (as few as 4 and as many as 12), the position of rhythmic variation (either in the beginning or at the end), the number of different duration values in each pattern (from 2 to 4), and rhythmic function (simple rhythms consisting of only the beat and its division into two or three part or complex rhythms consisting of extensions or subdivisions of the beat including dotted rhythms and syncopation.

Thus five rhythm pattern characteristics produced ten rhythm subscores: meter (duple vs. triple), number of rhythm notes in the pattern (few: 4-5 notes vs. many: 9-12 notes), position of rhythmic variation (beginning vs. end), number of different duration values (2 vs. 3 or 4), and rhythmic function (simple vs. complex).

Children were recorded as they attempted to imitate the recorded patterns of the TPRPT. The primary investigator evaluated all the recorded performances. A pattern was considered accurate only if all pitches or durations were performed correctly. Another experienced music educator evaluated 50% of the performances (n=25) to examine interjudge reliability. Twenty percent of the performances (n = 10) were judged twice by both evaluators to examine intrajudge reliability. Scores for each child were obtained by tabulating the number of correctly performed TPRPT patterns. Scores for each pattern were obtained by tabulating the number of correct performances of that pattern: the greater the number of children who correctly performed a pattern, the higher the score, and the easier the pattern.

Results

Agreement of total TPRPT scores between judges was 92%. Intrajudge agreement was 95% and 93%, respectively. The mean score of the total TPRPT performances (N = 50) was 19.9 (SD =15.1) of a total possible TPRPT score of 70. Scores ranged from 0% to 81% out of 70 patterns. The mean score of the tonal subtest was 10 correct (25%) (SD = 10.4) of a total possible score of 40. The mean score of the rhythm subtest performances was 10 correct (33%) (SD =7.4) of a total possible score of 30. No significant differences in accuracy were found between children who received the rhythm subtest first and children who received the tonal subtest first. A Pearson correlation revealed a significant linear relationship between accuracy of tonal patterns and accuracy of rhythm patterns (r = .435; p = .002), indicating that children who were more accurate in imitating tonal patterns tended to be more accurate in imitating rhythm patterns.

To identify tonal pattern characteristics contributing to accuracy, independent *t*-tests were performed on the five selected tonal characteristics: modality (major vs. minor), harmonic function (tonic vs. dominant), melodic contour (ascending vs. descending), pattern length (two- vs. three-notes), and range (high vs. low). Significant differences were revealed in only two of the five tonal pattern characteristics: pattern length and range. Results are presented in Table 1.

Table 1: Tonal pattern characteristics

Item Characteristic		Percent of items sung correctly	p-value of difference in means
Length:	2 notes	31%	0.009
	3 notes	17%	
Range:	Low	31%	0.01
	High	17%	
Modality:	Major	25%	NSD
	Minor	26%	
Harmonic Function:	Tonic	22%	NSD
	Dominant	30%	
Melodic Contour:	Ascending	25%	NSD
	Descending	26%	

Two-note patterns were significantly easier than three-note patterns (p =.009); children correctly sang 31% of the two-note patterns and only 17% of the three-note patterns. Low-range patterns were significantly easier than high-range patterns (p= .01); children correctly sang 31% of the low-range patterns and only 17% of the high-range patterns.

No significant differences were found between tonic and dominant patterns, ascending and descending patterns, or major and minor patterns. Tonality, harmonic function, and melodic contour did not contribute to performance accuracy.

To identify rhythm pattern characteristics contributing to accuracy, independent t-tests were performed on the five selected rhythm characteristics: meter (duple vs. triple), number of rhythm notes (4-5 notes vs. 9-12 notes), position of rhythmic variation (beginning vs. end), number of different duration values (2 vs. 3-4) and rhythm function (simple vs. complex). Significant differences were revealed in two of the five rhythm pattern characteristics: meter and position of rhythmic variation. Results are presented in Table 2.

Table 2: Rhythm pattern characteristics

Item Characteristic		Percent of items chant-ed correctly	p-value of difference in means
Meter	Duple	38%	.028
	Triple	22%	
Position of Rhythmic Variation	At Beginning	37%	.035
	At End	26%	
Number of notes in the pattern	Few: 4-5 notes	34%	NSD
	Many: 9-12 notes	34%	
Number of different Duration Values	2	34%	NSD
	3 or more	32%	
Rhythm Function	Simple	36%	NSD
	Complex	30%	

Duple meter patterns were significantly easier than triple meter patterns (*p* =.028); children correctly chanted 38% of the duple meter patterns and only 22% of the triple meter patterns. Patterns with rhythmic variation at the beginning were significantly easier than patterns with rhythmic varia-tion at the end (*p*= .035); children correctly chanted 37% of the patterns with variation at the beginning and only 26% of the patterns with varia-tion at the end.

No significant differences were found in the remaining three rhythm pat-tern characteristics: number of rhythm notes, number of duration values, and rhythm function. The patterns with only 4 or 5 rhythm notes were not significantly easier than patterns with 9-12 rhythm notes. The patterns with only 2 different durations were not significantly easier than patterns with 3 or 4 durations. The patterns with simple rhythms of only mac-ro/micro beats were not significantly easier than patterns with complex rhythms. The number of rhythm notes, the number of different durations, and the complexity of rhythm function did not contribute to performance accuracy.

An ANOVA was performed to determine gender differences in total scores and the tonal and rhythm subtest scores. No significant differences were found. Boys performed tonal patterns and rhythm patterns as accu-rately as girls. An ANOVA was performed to determine gender differ-ences in the performance of any of the ten tonal pattern and ten rhythm pattern characteristics. No significant differences were found.

Discussion

The results of this study of children from Argentina align with much of the extensive research on tonal and rhythmic development of children from Europe and North America. The tonal pattern characteristics that influence accuracy for children in Argentina are similar to those reported in previous studies. The two tonal pattern characteristics, two-note and low-range, identified to contribute to accurate pitch-matching performances for children of Argentina, were found to contribute to successful pitch-matching in previous studies of children from different ethnic groups (Wolf, 2010) and cultures (Wolf, 2012). These previous studies included the identification of a third characteristic contributing to accuracy: descending patterns. That melodic contour was not a factor for successful pitch-matching in this study is not surprising: the advantage of descending patterns reported in some studies (Madsen et al, 1975) has not been found to be significant in other studies (e.g., Sinor, 1985) and only slightly advantageous in others (Wolf, 2010; 2012). Results of this study also support previous findings that shorter pattern lengths (e.g., Sims, Moore, & Kuhn, 1982) and pitch ranges lower than B4 (e.g., Welch et al, 2009) contribute to successful pitch-matching. The consideration of pattern length and range should be paramount in structuring successful pitch-matching experiences. As in previous studies (Wolf, 2010; 2012), tonal pattern characteristics of tonality and harmonic function did not affect pitch-matching accuracy of children who spoke non-tonal languages. The equally successful performances of major and minor modes and tonic and dominant harmonic functions demonstrated in this study indicate that the common practice of restricting kindergarten musical experiences to major tonality or pentatonic harmony is unnecessary, and not compatible with children's musical capabilities.

The two rhythm pattern characteristics, meter and position of rhythmic variation, identified to contribute to accurate rhythm-matching performances for children of Argentina, were also found to contribute to successful rhythm-matching in similar studies of children in the USA (Wolf, 2003; 2005). Like the present study, previous studies also reported patterns in duple meter to be easier to perform than other meters (Smith, Cuddy, & Upitis, 1994; Wolf, 2003). But unlike the present study, previous studies revealed variation occurring at the end of a pattern to be easier than earlier in the pattern (Gardner, 1971; Wolf, 2003). This could be a cultural difference for the children in this study, as could be the non-significant results of the other three rhythmic pattern characteristics. Surprisingly, patterns with the fewest notes were as difficult to perform as patterns with the most notes, and patterns with simple beat functions were as difficult as patterns with complex beat functions. These results conflict with previous findings that fewer durations and variations in patterns are easier (Gardner, 1971). Although previous studies report patterns with only two durational values to be easier to perform than patterns with three or more durational values (Drake, 1993; Smith, Cuddy, & Upitis, 1994), the present study revealed no significant differences. The findings of Drake & Gérard (1989) may provide a rationale for these conflicting results: they found that the number of beats in a pattern influences accuracy more than does the number of durational values in the pattern. The four underlying beats of every pattern in the rhythm subtest of this study may be the source of difficulty rather than the number of durations, the number of durational values, or rhythm function. Perhaps an overall limited ability to perform patterns with four beats contributed to the nonsignificant results in this study. Of course, cultural differences could also account for these conflicting results.

The consideration of meter and the position of rhythmic variation seem necessary in structuring successful rhythm-matching experiences. Differences in the characteristics associated with successful rhythm pattern performances may be expected of children from different cultural backgrounds.

The lack of significant differences in scores between boys and girls from Argentina is not surprising: results of the present study align with results of previous studies from Europe and North America (i.e., Welch et al, 1997). Tonal pattern performances have been reported to be similar for kindergarten boys and girls from different ethnicities (Wolf, 2010). The majority of the research shows no gender differences in rhythmic abilities in young children (i.e., Petzold, 1963; Smith, Cuddy, & Upitis, 1994; Volman & Geuze, 2000). While gender differences in some musical tasks have been reported to emerge after age seven years (i.e., Welch et al, 1997), during the kindergarten year, teachers can expect boys and girls to perform similarly. Because the characteristics of accurate tonal patterns and rhythm patterns are equally advantageous to both kindergarten boys and girls, teachers are able to plan successful pitch-matching and rhythm-matching activities using these patterns without concern for gender differences.

References

Cooper, N. (1995). Children's singing accuracy as a function of grade level, gender, and individual versus unison singing. *Journal of Research in Music Education, 43*(3), 222-231.

Drake, C. (1993). Reproduction of musical rhythm by children, adult musicians, and adult nonmusicians. *Perception & Psychophysics, 53*(1), 25-33.

Drake, C., & Gérard, C. (1989). A psychological pulse train: How young children use this   cognitive framework to structure simple rhythms. *Psychological Research,* 16-22.

Flowers, P., & Dunne-Sousa, D. (1990). Pitch-pattern accuracy, tonality and vocal range in pre-school children's singing. *Journal of Research in Music Education, 38*(2), 102-114.

Gérard, C., & Drake, C. (1990). The inability of young children to reproduce intensity differences in musical rhythms. *Perception & Psychophysics, 48*(1), 91-101.

Gardner, H. (1971). Children's duplication of rhythmic patterns. *Journal of Research in Music Education, 19*(3), 355-360.

Gordon, E. (1985). Research studies in audiation: I. *Bulletin of the Council for Research in Music, 84*(fall), 34-50.

Hall, C. (2005). Gender and boys' singing in early childhood. *British Journal of Music Education, 22,* 5-20.

Lai, C. (1999). *An investigation of developmental music aptitude and music achievement in children from Taiwan.* Unpublished master thesis, Temple University, Philadelphia.

Madsen, C. K., Wolfe, D., & Madsen, C. H. (1975). The effect of reinforcement and directional scalar methodology on intonational improvement. In C. K. Madsen, & C. H. Madsen (Eds.), *Research in music behavior* (pp. 68-78). New York: Teachers College Press.

Moog, H. (1976). *The musical experience of the pre-school child* (T. C. Clark, Trans., original work published in 1968 ed.). London: Schott & Co., Ltd.

Moore, R., Fyk, J., Frega, A., & Brotons, M. (1996). Influences of culture, age, gender, and two-note patterns on interval matching skills of children from Argentina, Poland, Spain, and the United States. *Bulletin of the Council for Research in Music Education, 127,* 127-135.

Petzold, R. G. (1963). The development of auditory perception of musical sounds by children in the first six grades. *Journal of Research in Music Education, 11*(1), 21-43.

Rainbow, E. (1981). A final report on a three-year investigation of the rhythmic abilities of preschool-aged children. *Bulletin of the Council for Research in Music Education, 66-67* (spring), 69-73.

Rose, P., Fisher, R., & Shewmaker, S. (2012). Effects of manual/pedal movement, tempo, and gender on accuracy of steady beat in kindergarten students. *Bulletin of the Council for Research in Music Education, 192,* 29-38.

Schleuter, S., & Schleuter, L. (1989) Relationship of rhythm response tasks and PMMA scores with music training grade level, and sex among k-3 students. *Bulletin of the Council for Research in Music Education, 100*(spring), 1-3.

Sims, W. L., Moore, R. S., & Kuhn, T. L. (1982). Effects of female and male vocal stimuli, tonal pattern length, and age on vocal pitch-matching abilities of young children from England and the United States. *Psychology of Music, Special Issue,* 104-108.

Sinor, E. (1985). The singing of selected tonal patterns by preschool children. (Doctoral dissertation, Indiana University, 1984). *Dissertation Abstracts International, 45,* 3299A. (UMI No. AAT8501456).

Smith, K. C., Cuddy, L.L., & Upitis, R. (1994). Figural and metric understanding of rhythm. *Psychology of Music, 22(2),* 117-135.

Volman, M. J. M. & Geuze, R. H. (2000). Temporal stability of rhythmic tapping "on" and "off the beat": A developmental study. *Psychological Research 63,* 62-69.

Walker, R. (1981). Teaching basic musical concepts and their staff notations through cross-modal matching symbols. *Psychology of Music, 9,* 31-38.

Welch, G., Sergeant, D., & White, P. (1996). The singing competencies of five-year-old developing singers. *Bulletin of the Council for Research in Music Education, 127,* 155-160.

Welch, G. F., Sergeant, D. C., & White, P. J. (1997). Age, sex, and vocal task as factors in singing "in tune" during the first years of schooling. *Bulletin for the Council for Research in Music Education, 133,* 153-160.

Welch, G. F., Himonides, E., Papageorgi, I., Saunders, J., Rinta, T., Stewart, C., Preti, C., Lani, J., Vraka, M., & Hill, J. (2009). The national singing programme for primary schools in England: An initial baseline study. *Music Education Research, 11*(1), 1-22.

Wolf, D. L. (2003). Tonal pattern and rhythm pattern hierarchies and the long-term importance of kindergarten music instruction. (Doctoral dissertation, Temple University, 2003) *Dissertation Abstracts International.*

Wolf, D. L. (2005). A Hierarchy of tonal performance patterns for children ages five to eight years in kindergarten and primary grades. *Bulletin of the Council for Research in Music Education, 163,* 61-68.

Wolf, D. L. (2010). Pitch-matching accuracy in children: an examination of tonal pattern characteristics and demographic factors. *Proceedings of the 23rd International Seminar on Research in Music Education.* July, 2010. Changchun, China: International Society for Music Education.

Wolf, D. L. (2012). A Cross-cultural examination of pitch-matching accuracy in kindergarten children from Hong Kong, the Dominican Republic, and the USA. *Proceedings of the 24th International Seminar on Research in Music Education.* July, 2012. Thessaloniki, Greece: International Society for Music Education.

Yarbrough, C., Bowers, J., & Benson, W. (1992). The effect of vibrato on the pitch matching accuracy of certain and uncertain singers. *Journal of Research in Music Education, 40*(1), 30-38.